SOMETHING WAS
TERRIBLY WRONG . . .

Melanie's eyes caught something unexpected, and not quite right. The right side door of the garage was open, and so was the door from the garage into her sister Elizabeth's house. She ran back to the car and told her friend Mike, "I'm going in."

She went through the garage and laundry room, and hurried into the kitchen. The concern and apprehension had not begun to prepare her for what she would see as she turned past the kitchen counter.

Melanie's piercing screams rattled Mike to his bones. He dashed into the house to see what had brought Melanie's screams—screams that would haunt his sleep forever and bring nightmares he never imagined. . . .

. . . WHO KILLED
ELIZABETH DeCARO?

A KILLER AMONG US

*A True Story of a Family's
Triumph over Tragedy*

Charles Bosworth, Jr.

AN ONYX BOOK

ONYX
Published by the Penguin Group
Penguin Putnam Inc., 375 Hudson Street,
New York, New York 10014, U.S.A.
Penguin Books Ltd, 27 Wrights Lane,
London W8 5TZ, England
Penguin Books Australia Ltd, Ringwood,
Victoria, Australia
Penguin Books Canada Ltd, 10 Alcorn Avenue,
Toronto, Ontario, Canada M4V 3B2
Penguin Books (N.Z.) Ltd, 182–190 Wairau Road,
Auckland 10, New Zealand

Penguin Books Ltd, Registered Offices:
Harmondsworth, Middlesex, England

First published by Onyx, an imprint of Dutton NAL,
a member of Penguin Putnam Inc.

First Printing, August, 1998
10 9 8 7 6 5 4 3 2 1

To my sister Mary and her husband, Phil, for having the courage to take Elizabeth's children and raise them as their own. Elizabeth couldn't have chosen better parents.

To my parents, Jim and Georgianna, for finding the strength to go on, and not let Rick win.

To Mike Miller and Tom Dittmeier, who were so dedicated and committed and never asked for anything in return. What an inspiration you are to our system.

To Elizabeth's children, so that you never forget your mother and how much she loved you.

Finally, to my precious sister Elizabeth. Thank you for giving me the strength to get through this, and for the bond between us that no words could ever describe. Your memory is enshrined in my heart—until the day we finally meet again.

—*Melanie Enkelmann*

FOREWORD

This is the true story of a family tempered by the fire of tragedy more painful than most people can imagine. The incidents portrayed in this book have been reconstructed using a variety of contemporary notes, police reports, and court transcripts. The author also has drawn on the memories of many participants and observers, who recounted conversations and events in an attempt to make this book as accurate as humanly possible. In some cases, dialogue has been recreated from reports, recollections, and other sources.

The names of certain people portrayed in the book have been changed to pseudonyms chosen randomly by the author. These pseudonyms bear absolutely no connection to real people who may have similar names. An asterisk marks the first reference to each fictitious name.

The number of important characters has made it appropriate to include an index to provide quick and easy reference—a sort of "who's who" in this complex story. The index is located at the end of the book.

This book would not have been possible without the gracious and courageous cooperation of many members of the Van Iseghem family. They opened their hearts and their homes to me and shared with me their memories of Elizabeth Van Iseghem DeCaro—a woman I wish I had been privileged to know in life as well as I came to know her after she was gone. As those she left behind shared their stories with me, they won my respect, my admiration, and my affection. I wish to thank all of them, especially Georgianna and Jim Van Iseghem, Melanie and John Enkelmann, Mary and Phil Cordes, Theresa Van Iseghem, Margie Ugalde, Jimmy and Joy Van Iseghem, and Randy and Maureen Van Iseghem. My debt of gratitude also extends to Elizabeth's special friend, Pam Hanley.

I also wish to extend my sincerest thanks to my technical adviser and research director, Lieutenant Patrick McCarrick of the St. Charles, Missouri, Police Department. Sifting through the thousands of pages of documents generated by this investigation would have been a more difficult task without his expertise and assistance. And best of all, he coupled his knowledge of this case with an impressive ability to tell a gripping, spellbinding story. For the sake of everyone who loves a good story well told, I hope he follows through on his interest in becoming an author.

There were others whose assistance was just as essential to the writing of this book. I extend special thanks to Colonel Robert J. Lowery, chief of police in Florissant and director of the St. Louis Metropolitan Major Case Squad; Major Tom O'Connor of Maryland Heights, commander of the Major Case Squad; Chief David King of the St. Charles Police; and Detectives Mike Miller and Mike Powell of St. Charles. I also owe thanks to Prosecuting Attorney Timothy Braun of St. Charles County and Assistant U.S. Attorney Thomas Dittmeier of St. Louis.

I want to extend my gratitude again to the special people who have been instrumental in putting this book in your hands: my editor, Michaela Hamilton, and her staff at Penguin Putnam, who continue to guide and direct my efforts; and my agents, Arthur and Richard Pine, who provide constant expert counsel and assistance.

PART ONE

ONE

Friday, March 6, 1992

The light rain that had begun to fall that evening soon would have a name. Such an odd notion would have made no sense to Melanie Enkelmann as she pulled into her sister's driveway, of course. But sense and reality for Melanie Enkelmann were about to be altered drastically and finally. Bent into new and ugly shapes and angles. Reflected through dark and deadly prisms into ghostly shadows that she never dreamed possible, not in her worst nightmare. Life for her and the entire Van Iseghem family—their very concept of life—was about to be exploded through a painful, disorienting rip in the world where they had lived happily for decades. Their old life was all about to end, and a new reality was about to begin. In this new reality, betrayal came as easily as an early spring rain. In this new world, betrayal would have a familiar face. And naming the rain would make perfect sense.

But on this Friday evening, as she sat in the driveway at 12 Hidden Meadow Court in St. Charles, Missouri, Melanie Enkelmann had only the vaguest sense—just a slight nagging in her heart and soul—that something of that magnitude was about to happen. She really just wanted to find her little sister, Elizabeth DeCaro. That was all that counted right then.

Everything about Elizabeth DeCaro's life had been growing stranger and stranger for months. Melanie and their older sister, Mary Cordes, had tried to figure out what the increasingly peculiar events meant for their precious Elizabeth. Everything pointed toward something ominous. Melanie and Mary had talked about it almost endlessly, but they could never get a firm grip on all of the slippery evidence that something was lurking in the dark, waiting for the absolutely worst moment to swoop down and end the suspense—and to alter their little sister's life forever.

But now all that Melanie had on her mind was the mystery of Elizabeth's failure to keep their date for a five o'clock after-work drink with friends. That wasn't like Elizabeth, even these days; it wasn't like her at all. Between margaritas at the popular Casa Gallardo restaurant, Melanie had made several calls to Elizabeth's home. There was no answer. This uncharacteristic absence had gnawed at Melanie until she knew she would have to take action. So with their mutual friend Mike Carroll,* Melanie had traced back the steps on Elizabeth's path through this foreboding Friday. As Mike drove the route, Melanie learned that, no, Elizabeth had never arrived for her afternoon workout at Vic Tanny's and, no, she hadn't been in contact with Mary "Boo" Pohlman, another friend and confidante, at the restaurant where Boo worked. Melanie soon was out of ideas—save one.

So now, at eight o'clock, she and Mike sat in his car in the rain at 12 Hidden Meadow Court, the perfect house, where twenty-eight-year-old Elizabeth—the perfect wife and mother—had lived a perfect life with her perfect husband, Rick DeCaro, and their four perfect kids, and their perfect yappy little dog, Ozzie. The lovely blue-and-white story-and-a-half in one of the newer neighborhoods in this all-American suburb of St. Louis now was Melanie's last resort. Even though the phone calls to the house had still gone unanswered, Melanie was compelled to check it out. She couldn't think of anything else to do, and she had to do something.

She jumped out of Mike's car and sprinted through the rain to the garage, which extended slightly forward on the right side of the house. A peek through the window confirmed her suspicions. There was the empty parking space for that jazzy black-and-silver Chevy Blazer with the red snowplow on the front bumper and the personalized RIK-LIZ license plate. If the Blazer was gone, Elizabeth had to be gone too.

But Melanie's eye caught something unexpected—and not quite right. The side door into the garage was open, and so was the door from the garage into the house. Melanie could see into the laundry room, where the light was burning. Another unusual and discomforting situation on this most unusual, discomforting day. She ran back to the car and told Mike, "Something's wrong. I'm going in." And then she turned back toward the house.

Mike decided to back her up. But before he went into the missing Elizabeth's unlocked house, he looked for a weapon. He headed toward a trash can that had several baseball bats stored in it.

Melanie hurried through the garage and laundry room and into the kitchen. The months of constant uneasiness, of worry and concern and apprehension, had not begun to prepare her for what she saw as she turned past the kitchen counter. There, sprawled on the floor in front of the sink, was Elizabeth—facedown and motionless.

Melanie's piercing scream rattled Mike Carroll to the core and stopped him short of the Louisville Slugger he was about to grab. Still unarmed, he dashed into the house to see what had caused such a scream—a scream that would haunt his sleep forever, bringing nightmares that he could never have imagined.

In a panic, Melanie rushed to her sister's side and felt for a pulse. Nothing was beating in Elizabeth's cold wrist. But that meant Elizabeth was dead, and that couldn't be. Elizabeth could not be dead; Melanie would not let that be true. This did not happen to the loving, happy Van Iseghems. Jim and Georgianna Van Iseghem had not raised their daughters and sons for this kind of horrible end. This could not be a chapter in the storybook lives of the Van Iseghems of St. Ann.

Mike burst into the kitchen and was crushed to see Elizabeth's body on the floor between the sink and the center island. She was dressed just as he had seen her at work earlier that day—blue jeans, red T-shirt-style blouse, and brown ankle boots. But now the side of her head was matted with blood that also had pooled on the floor. The bluish color of her skin told Mike there was no hope for survival—his special friend was indeed gone. He didn't know any first aid, so he grabbed the phone and dialed 911, only to realize that he didn't even know the address of Elizabeth's house. He handed the phone to Melanie and told her to just stay on the line while he ran for help.

The next minutes passed like scenes from a horror movie as Melanie watched, a passive observer. Neighbors summoned by Mike rolled Elizabeth onto her back and began CPR. Melanie could see a little blood on Elizabeth's face. What did that mean? The team of paramedics arrived before long and took over, pulling Elizabeth into the middle of the floor amid more frenetic activity. They cut away her blouse and bra so they could get to her chest and try to restore life. When Melanie moved to the living room on the orders of the brutally efficient paramedics, her new perspective granted her the first view of the small puddle of blood where Elizabeth had lain. And as the team members worked, Elizabeth's shoulder-length blond hair parted and Melanie caught sight of the back of her neck. It was fire-red—blood-red. For the first time, Melanie realized that this was not some natural event, some medical problem that had stricken her sister. Melanie now knew the source of the blood she had just seen. There had been some kind of violence done to Elizabeth, right here in her own home. Melanie's spirit began to falter. She tried to keep a flicker of hope in her heart, but she was so frightened now. As the paramedics lifted Elizabeth onto a stretcher for the trip to the hospital, Melanie realized that all the months of worry and confusion had come down to this moment.

The new reality had begun. This was, indeed, a new and unhappy world.

Melanie's request to accompany her sister's body to the hospital was denied by the police officer who had just arrived; she was needed to stay behind at the house and help them open an investigation. In the squad car, parked in the rain at 12 Hidden Meadow Court, the officers began their interrogation of Melanie Enkelmann. Was there anyone, they asked, who could have wanted this wonderful young woman dead? Who could have such a murderous hate for this wife and mother, this dream-come-true daughter, this loving sister, to come into her beautiful home and kill her in her own kitchen?

Melanie did not hesitate to give them the name of the one person she was certain had to be Elizabeth's killer. Melanie had no doubt she was right about who had taken her sister's young life so cruelly. The darkness in one soul had now eclipsed the light in all their lives. The Devil Incarnate had been found hiding in plain sight in the midst of this living Norman Rockwell painting that had been, until now, the world for the Van Iseghem family.

Not long after this night, singer Eric Clapton would release a new hit song, "Tears in Heaven"—dedicated to his young son, dead as the result of a tragic accident. Melanie Enkelmann and Mary Cordes decided the raindrops that had fallen on March 6, 1992, had indeed come from heaven. They had been Tears for Elizabeth.

In this new world, the rain had a name.

TWO

Murder was indeed a stranger to this family. Jim and Georgianna Van Iseghem had raised seven children in a home protected by an umbrella of unconditional love, devoutly Catholic convictions, humble awe of the goodness and mercy of God, and an air of happiness that engendered envy in everyone who knew them. Certainly, behind the appearance of a perfect life, the Van Iseghems had their share of problems. But their faith and their love had guided and protected them. They had always emerged victorious from every challenge. Crime and hate—and most certainly violent death—were not familiar visitors to this family that had sprung from the purity of young love. That passion fueled an endless enthusiasm for the life that followed, and there was no room for the ugly things that others allowed to destroy them. That just could not happen here, not in this family.

*   *   *

Jim Van Iseghem was a twenty-year-old clerk for the A & P supermarket in Overland, Missouri, in December 1951, when he met a fifteen-year-old customer, Georgianna Hood. Exactly a year later, they married and began their family. Georgianna knew she and Jim were quite young to be taking on such responsibilities in the days even before the TV families of Robert Young and Ward Cleaver defined American society. But she never regretted their early start. Being a wife and mother was all she had ever wanted, and now she had both. She was young, yes, but she could handle this because there was so much love in her heart.

Jim and Georgianna had grown up in Overland, a suburb on the western edge of the increasing sprawl of St. Louis. Now a struggling young couple, they settled in St. Ann, a community just to the north between Overland and Lambert Field, the regional airport that would be at the center of dramatic commercial growth and a population boom in St. Louis County.

The firstborn of the Van Iseghem brood—James Allen Jr.—arrived in June 1953. In October 1955 they welcomed daughter Mary Kathryn. A second daughter, named Margaret Jean but destined to be called Margie, joined the cast just thirteen months after that. They waited all of twenty-two months before delivering daughter number three, Melanie Lynn, in September 1958. Their second son, Randy John, was delayed even longer, not arriving until February 1961. And Elizabeth Ann Van Iseghem seemed to complete the family when she was born in May 1963. Four girls and two boys.

By then, the Van Iseghems were well into their careers, both of them focusing on another of the family's joys—food. Jim had started his own business, Van's Food and Liquor Store, and they still were running Wilson's market, the first store he had taken over. They had bought their first home, on St. Francis Lane, in 1956. But Elizabeth's arrival stretched the limits of the space there, and they moved in 1964 to a larger, two-story house just a few blocks down the same street. Sitting atop the long rise of the front lawn, the warm house would become the Van Iseghem home place, waiting to welcome generations of happy children and loving adults.

St. Francis Lane in St. Ann seemed the center of the universe as the Van Iseghems grew strong and straight. While Jim worked hard to carry his burden as the provider, Georgianna divided her time between her work and the kids. Her seemingly endless energy and love made her the perfect mother, and she reveled in it all. She was never too tired to shuttle this kid to one activity and that kid to another. She encouraged their busy approach to life and school and church—all supported by the strong Catholic faith that was their moral and social center. They flourished in tight-knit St. Kevin's Parish—an amazing, almost anachronistic societal cocoon that provided direction, safety, security, and comfort. As the years passed and the area grew—one of the largest shopping centers in the country, Northwest Plaza, sprang up only blocks from the Van Iseghem home—St. Ann and the insular St. Kevin's seemed immune to urban decay. Most of the areas around the parish fell victim to the familiar predators—crime, drugs, falling property values, ineffective local governments. But that didn't happen in St. Kevin's.

The families in the parish all knew each other and grew up together. The parents socialized and the kids became close as they progressed through the grades at St. Kevin's Elementary School. The girls attended Incarnate Word Academy, a girls' high school in adjacent Normandy, or the coed Mercy High School. The boys went to one of several Catholic or public high schools in the area. When the time came, many of those kids married each other and stayed in the parish, living near their parents and siblings and sending the next generation to St. Kevin's.

Ozzie and Harriet in suburban St. Louis.

As the Van Iseghem children grew, they all soon realized there was something special about little Elizabeth. It wasn't just that she was the youngest and the smallest. There was much more to it than that. Everyone agreed she was as close to perfect as imaginable. As an infant and toddler, she rarely fussed or cried. She never had to be spanked, not even needing the occasional harmless swat on the fanny to get her attention. As she grew older, her special qualities emerged like butterflies from cocoons. She was so sensitive, so kind, so giving, so thoughtful, so infectiously cheerful; she developed a special way of saying "Hi!" with an extra "eeee" on the end that seemed so endearing to her mother. Elizabeth never had an angry word for anyone. Her heart was perilously close to the surface, and she could stand for no soul to be injured or abused or neglected. The older she got, the more pronounced that characteristic became. In school, she always befriended the children whom the others held at arm's length or, worse yet, ridiculed so cruelly. She's so sweet, everyone always said.

Jimmy, the oldest brother, recognized the uniqueness of his littlest sister. From his aged throne—he was, after all, ten years older than Elizabeth—he became her protector. No one was allowed to give her a hard time. Jimmy and Randy, another normally merciless brother, never teased or tortured or antagonized her the way they did the others, especially the effervescent Mary and Melanie.

Margie always thought of Elizabeth—more than seven years younger—as the "little princess." The nickname came not from envy or sarcasm but from love and genuine recognition of Elizabeth's nature. Margie thought she saw much of herself in her little sister's personality, and that made her feel closer to Elizabeth than two sisters that far apart in age would usually have been.

Like all of the Van Iseghem kids, Elizabeth was a good student. Liz, as she was called by most of her friends, excelled in writing poetry and giving speeches. And like her blond sisters, the blond Elizabeth was athletic. She was a cheerleader in junior high school, but forsook that to follow her sisters' path in high school—she played on Incarnate Word's renowned, and often state champion, volleyball team. She was a Girl Scout, and Georgianna, of course, was the troop leader. Mother and daughter enjoyed the campouts and all of the other activities that were such an important part of the Van Iseghems' life.

In eighth grade, Elizabeth even surpassed her sisters' records. Although Mary, Margie, and Melanie had been candidates for the coveted title of Penny Queen, Elizabeth was the first from the clan to win. Everyone knew she would; it just had to be, as if preordained. Each classroom chose a candidate to compete for the school title by raising money for the missions in Pakistan that were led by the same order of nuns—the Dominican Sisters—who taught at St. Kevin's. The candidate who raised the most money was the winner—the Penny Queen. The annual event was something special at the school, and winning was a noted honor. Margie, already in college, was thrilled to attend the coronation and watch in delight as Elizabeth ascended the stage to be crowned queen.

Taking pride in Elizabeth's accomplishments was easy, and not just for her parents, brothers, and sisters. Everyone liked Elizabeth. They genuinely liked her because she genuinely liked them and really cared about them. Years later, one classmate would write movingly to Georgianna and Jim about how kind she had been to him, describing how she had befriended the bookish boy so many others mocked with the nickname of "the professor." Elizabeth had always offered him the wonder of her concern and the dignity of addressing him as Greg.

The young woman whose body now lay on her kitchen floor had, indeed, been a rare and wonderful person.

THREE

The radio broadcast for officers to respond to "a woman in trouble" at 12 Hidden Meadow Court caught Lieutenant Patrick McCarrick's attention as he sat in his squad car and talked to Sergeant Mike Powell in an adjacent car. Not many weeks ago, a woman in that general neighborhood had been raped in her home—an unsolved crime that still bothered McCarrick. There had been very few other problems in that upscale area, and McCarrick wondered if this new call could be connected to the rape. Two women, attacked in their homes, close proximity. Could be a coincidence, or it could be . . .

His curiosity led him and Powell to the Hidden Meadow Court address. They arrived at precisely 8:29 P.M. and parked in a cul-de-sac already filling up with police cars, ambulances, paramedic trucks, and fire equipment. McCarrick—a big, burly man of forty-two with thick, graying hair and a heavy mustache—hurried through the rain toward the open front door of the house. He was met by Officer Ted Holland, who had been the first cop on the scene and who now had an unpleasant report for his afternoon shift commander.

"This looks like a homicide, Lieutenant," Holland said as he motioned backward over his shoulder. McCarrick glanced past him and started to enter the house, only to be stopped in his tracks by the incredible amount of activity inside. Milling about in the midst of what he assumed was a crime scene were at least a dozen people. Just great, he thought—what a way to preserve evidence. He stepped into the living room and could see the paramedics still performing CPR on a woman's body on a stretcher in the kitchen, which was crowded with six or eight emergency personnel. Off to the right, in a parlor or sitting room of some sort, McCarrick saw five people who he assumed were neighbors or relatives anxiously watching the activity in the kitchen through a fashionable cutout in the wall between the rooms. McCarrick immediately ordered that group outside to await formal interviews by the police.

He headed back into the living room, where a young woman in a chair was speaking emotionally into the telephone, apparently notifying someone about what had happened. "She's gone," the woman was moaning into the phone as she wept. McCarrick moved quickly to her and asked her politely but firmly to hang up immediately and join the others outside. She nodded sadly and put down the phone. He escorted her outside, where she identified herself as Melanie Enkelmann, the sister of the victim, Elizabeth DeCaro. Melanie explained about Elizabeth's unusual disappearance that afternoon and the search that had ended here about eight o'clock. McCarrick told Sergeant Powell to take Mrs. Enkelmann's statement.

By then, the paramedics were ready to move Elizabeth DeCaro's body to the ambulance and head for the hospital. Although they were still performing CPR, McCarrick knew the victim was dead. He hadn't seen the body up close and had no idea what had happened. But he knew this: CPR is necessary only when there is no respiration and no heartbeat. The neighbors had started CPR before the paramedics arrived, and they were obligated by policy to continue the procedure until a doctor delivered an official pronouncement of death. In McCarrick's mind, there would be no other outcome upon Elizabeth DeCaro's arrival at the hospital. He sent two officers along to report back the moment a doctor rendered the inevitable verdict.

As the wail of the ambulance's siren began to fade, McCarrick concentrated on the business at hand. He ordered Powell to secure the house to preserve the evidence. He radioed the station for two more cars to control the crowd, and then took it upon himself to shoo the onlookers off the DeCaro lawn. He used his cell phone to call Jim Turpiano, his chief of detectives, and inform him of the murder. He dispatched other officers on the first step of standard procedure—the neighborhood canvass. What could the people who lived near the victim tell the police about her and about what had happened?

McCarrick started to return to his car, but one question had already begun to nag him. He went to Powell's squad car to see if Melanie could give him an answer.

Where was the rest of the family that lived with the victim in this big house?

FOUR

Among the boys drawn to the slender, attractive, blond Van Iseghem girls was Richard DeCaro. Even in the fifth grade, he had shown a marked interest in Elizabeth, then only a fourth grader and even more innocent than her age would imply. By 1976, when she was in the seventh grade and just twelve years old, Rick DeCaro had started spending a lot of time at the comfortable house on St. Francis Lane. He and Elizabeth were "just friends," they both insisted. But Georgianna and Jim still were concerned about Rick's reputation as one of the loud, rowdy "bad boys" at St. Kevin's School. He was so antisocial, such a habitual troublemaker, that he had even been expelled from the sixth grade. That was not the kind of suitor—at any age— that they had in mind for their daughters.

Georgianna—she of the soft heart—couldn't help but feel sorry for the painfully thin, gangling boy with the raven-black hair and the long, angular face. Rick DeCaro had all the darkness of Georgianna's Italian friends, but none of the charm or confidence. Still, she was touched by Rick, perhaps because he was so quiet and uncertain around the Van Iseghems; at times he even seemed a little slow mentally.

The Van Iseghems knew the DeCaro family; they lived only a few blocks apart and attended all of the same functions in the parish. Rick's father, Angelo, had run the family's office-cleaning business for a while and then had gone into banking. He once had succeeded Georgianna as president of the PTA at St. Kevin's. Rick's mother, Grace, was a housewife, and Georgianna was quite fond of her. Georgianna knew the family well enough to understand why Rick might lack self-confidence and find release in rebellion. He was the youngest of four children, growing up in the shadow of two brothers and a sister whose academic brilliance had won them scholarships to the finest private high schools in the St. Louis area. Rick could never hope to match their scholastic accomplishments.

Elizabeth's brother Randy knew that Rick had almost no interest in school anyway. Rick often gave Randy rides to school, and they sometimes palled around together at night, cruising the area in Rick's cool Chevy and sneaking a few beers. Rick wanted no career but auto mechanics, Randy knew, so the classes other than shop seemed pointless to him.

Rick eventually became a familiar fixture on the Van Iseghems' sofa, sprawling there to watch TV almost every day after school. Georgianna spent a lot of time talking to the boy she felt so sorry for—Elizabeth came naturally to her open heart and empathetic soul. Although Rick wasn't very friendly at first, he began to respond to Georgianna's warmth and conversation, and soon she came to know him well. He confided that he had always felt like the black sheep of his family, failing in the things at which his sister and brothers excelled. He preferred the company of girls, partly because he had difficulty forming friendships with the other boys at school. They warmed up to him only when they needed to call on his amazing mechanical aptitude; he did have a way with cars, especially, but could do wonders with anything subject to a wrench, hammer, or saw. The other guys didn't like to talk about things the way the girls did; Rick was more comfortable with girls.

Georgianna had heard that hardly anyone at school liked this boy; they thought he was arrogant and antisocial. Rick finally dropped out of Pattonville High School after his sophomore year and went to work full-time at an Amoco station owned by a family friend. Georgianna could understand how Rick could turn all of that pain into rebellion and misconduct. Dealing with misbehavior and punishment still might be easier than facing disillusionment.

But her compassionate attempts to understand Rick didn't make it any easier when she and Jim learned in 1978 that Elizabeth had begun dating him. She was just fifteen—an especially innocent, naive fifteen—and Rick seemed so much older. Even though he was only sixteen, he had acquired a reputation that would have made him less than welcome at the door of any girl he courted. And, aside from the general concerns about Rick's behavior and personality, Georgianna was terrified by the prospect of sending off her little Elizabeth in whatever latest loud, souped-up hot rod Rick was currently driving, and in which he had so often outrun the cops who were intent on rewarding his driving skills with speeding tickets. She couldn't do much about some of her distress about Rick, but she could address his driving. In a conversation marked by the candor and plainspoken approach that she could summon when necessary, she explained simply that Elizabeth would not be getting into Rick's car unless he drastically altered his habits behind the wheel. No more wild speeding. No more drag racing or tire-smoking blastoffs from stoplights. No more reckless careening around corners and tearing up the straightaways. If Elizabeth Van Iseghem was going to get into his car, he would have to begin driving like a cautious, responsible adult who was carrying a most precious cargo—because to Georgianna and Jim, the girl who would be sitting beside Rick was exactly that.

Much to everyone's surprise, Rick not only agreed to Georgianna's conditions but immediately put them into practice and began driving like there was a trooper on his tail. His mother was so shocked that she told Georgianna she should have laid down the driving law before.

With Rick's behavior toned down a bit and the young romance in full bloom, the Van Iseghems turned their attention toward two important milestones in their personal and professional lives. The first was the latest family wedding. Young Jimmy had married in 1975, and Margie two years later. And now Mary was to become the wife of Phil Cordes in a ceremony planned for September 1978.

The second big event was the opening of a new delicatessen, in nearby Clayton, to be run by Georgianna. But the best-laid plans . . . The week that Georgianna and Jim signed a $100,000 loan for the new shop, they learned there was about to be another addition to the Van Iseghem roster. Georgianna, now forty-two, was pregnant with their seventh child and was due to deliver this late-in-life surprise in July. After adjusting to this new curveball, Georgianna and Mary decided to move her wedding to June. Georgianna preferred to attend as the eight-months-pregnant mother of the bride, rather than coping with a newborn while planning the wedding for September. So for once, a wedding date was changed not because the bride was pregnant but because her mother was.

On July 24, 1978, the fifth Van Iseghem daughter was born. Theresa Marie had arrived, and Elizabeth was no longer the baby of the family.

Hardworking Rick had been using a goodly portion of his income to court Elizabeth with gifts and flowers. He showered her with constant affection and attention. He did everything he could to charm the object of his desire, this lovely blonde that many surely thought was so far beyond his grasp. And although Margie and some of the others in the family thought Elizabeth was captivated by the air of danger surrounding Rick DeCaro, the road to true love was not smooth; by the spring of 1979, Elizabeth and Rick had broken up. Margie had learned how difficult it was sometimes to favor the underdog, and perhaps that had become clearer to Elizabeth. Margie suspected the "underdog" thing had played a big role in Elizabeth's decision to date Rick in the first place.

His response to the end of their romance was to begin dating the girl who lived next door on St. Francis Lane. Watching Rick roar up the street in his new "monster truck" to pick up his date broke Elizabeth's heart, her mother knew; Elizabeth still was crazy about him. She began dating another boy, but the Van Iseghems weren't thrilled with him either. He didn't seem that much different from Rick. But they still took some comfort in knowing that the teenage infatuation between the Penny Queen and the Bad Boy was over.

Or was it? Elizabeth chose the week of the family's vacation to the Ozark Mountains in southern Missouri in July 1979 to drop a bombshell. Now just a few months past her sixteenth birthday, she was pregnant. And almost as shocking as that development in the life of such a naive and innocent girl was the identity of the baby's father: Rick

DeCaro. She had been pregnant when they broke up but hadn't known it yet.

The Van Iseghems were crushed. Yes, Georgianna had been pregnant when she married Jim. And yes, there were some things about Rick that put her in mind of Jim—mostly Rick's willingness to work around the clock. But starting life from this place could be difficult, Georgianna knew that oh so well. And she had wanted so much more for Elizabeth.

Margie was astounded. How could this have happened to such an innocent—someone who seemed so sheltered from that part of life? The thought that Elizabeth—of all people, of all the Van Iseghem girls—would become sexually active at sixteen was almost too shocking to be believed. In fact, some time after Margie got married in 1977, her husband once had said that he thought Elizabeth might wind up pregnant. Margie had been outraged and insulted that he could think something like that about her little sister, let alone express it aloud. "You don't know what you're talking about. How dare you!" she had responded in indignation. But now she had to admit he had been right. He must have seen something. Or perhaps he knew Rick DeCaro too well.

Big brother Jimmy was in shock, too. He was living in Chicago, working for the Venture chain stores, when Georgianna called with the news. Elizabeth couldn't summon the courage to tell him herself, so her mother rode to the rescue again. Mother—the matron and director of the family, Jimmy thought. He didn't know Rick very well, but he had gone to St. Kevin's with his older brother, Tom DeCaro. Tom worked for Venture stores too, so they had yet another link. Jimmy still thought of Rick as the ungainly kid with long hair who drove the souped-up hot rods. Jimmy was not bashful about expressing his opinion of the situation; he was definitely and completely against a marriage between Elizabeth and this kid. Yes, he knew his mother had been pregnant and sixteen when she married. But he also knew that few of those forced unions lasted, and he didn't want Elizabeth going through a mandatory wedding and then motherhood at such an early age, only to end it all with a painful divorce. What a mess, he thought.

The news of the baby changed everything for Rick, too. To his credit, he immediately asked her to marry him. He wanted with all his heart to provide for her and their baby, to love them and give them the best life he could. But Georgianna and Jim decided Elizabeth was too young for that leap. They offered a counterproposal to Elizabeth, Rick, and his family. Elizabeth would stay home and study with a tutor until she delivered the baby. Then she would return to high school as a senior and get her diploma. After that, as a high school graduate and at eighteen years old, she could marry Rick in May or June 1981. Everyone agreed; by waiting, Elizabeth and Rick would start their new lives on a more solid foundation, giving their baby the best chance for a good life.

Again to his credit, Rick paid all of the expenses for the pregnancy. As planned, Elizabeth stayed home and worked with a tutor. On February 16, 1980, Patrick* DeCaro was born. A beautiful, healthy boy had arrived as the product of the unlikely and worrisome union of Elizabeth Van Iseghem and Rick DeCaro. Georgianna's grand plan resumed, and Elizabeth continued with the tutor. Everything seemed in order for her to return to school as a senior in the fall of 1980.

But that was when a new round of challenges began. Incarnate Word Academy informed Georgianna that it would not accept an unmarried teenage mother as a student. Undaunted, Georgianna met with the school's principal and told her tactfully that the policy was well behind the times for 1980. With teen pregnancy increasing nationally, surely Catholic schools did not want to add to these young mothers' problems by depriving them of their education. Wouldn't that just perpetuate the problem? Wouldn't educating these girls better serve them, their children, and society? Georgianna's point of view prevailed, and the school agreed to enroll Elizabeth Van Iseghem as the first teen mother to attend Incarnate Word.

But Georgianna's victory was short-lived. Elizabeth met the news with an announcement of her own. Rick would not "let" her return to school. She wanted to go back, she said, but she had decided to abide by his wishes for now. After all, Rick had said, he didn't have a high school diploma, and he was doing pretty well for himself by just working hard. Despite protests from Georgianna and Jim, Elizabeth stuck to her decision. Besides, she explained, she already had begun to feel out of place among the other girls her own age. "I can't just be a teenager again," she said as she held Patrick. She swore that later, when the baby was older and things had settled down, she would go back and get her degree.

Georgianna and Jim were disappointed, convinced that the decision was a mistake. But they relented. There was a modicum of sense in what Elizabeth said, even if much of it was based on Rick's growing influence over her. Even Margie was sure that Elizabeth would go back to school. Margie had interrupted college for two years to have her baby and stay home for a while, but had returned to school and now was within reach of her degree as a registered nurse. She knew an interrupted education could be completed, even if it was a little more difficult that way. Margie was confident that education was important to Elizabeth, too.

The wedding, on January 16, 1981, was even more pleasant than might be have been expected under the circumstances. Everyone had accepted the situation and decided to make the best of it, and it was more than apparent that Rick's family loved Elizabeth dearly. She had spent a lot of time at the DeCaro home already, and Grace DeCaro had happily taken her new daughter-in-law into the family. Rick's sister, Patty Fiehler, had claimed Elizabeth as the sister she'd never had, and they got along wonderfully.

Rick had already bought a cute little house in St. Charles, the growing community just a few miles to the west across the Missouri River. Although in St. Charles County, the town was still a suburb that drew heavily on St. Louis for its identity. Interstate 70 cut east and west through the center of the town, and a charming section of the original historic French settlement was preserved along the riverfront as a quaint shopping and dining district of small brick buildings and cobblestone streets. The frontage roads along the interstate looked like any other busy commercial district in America, with chain hotels and restaurants popping up to take advantage of one of the city's defining characteristics—heavy traffic that became hellish during rush hour. Just out of sight of the crowded commercial district, subdivisions filled with new homes sprang up all over the landscape. A town that had been considered the country not long ago was now becoming an upscale community and filling in with houses and businesses and bustling families.

And, despite the traffic, the Van Iseghems knew Elizabeth was really only minutes west of the home parish in St. Ann. As soon as Elizabeth and Patrick were officially joined to Rick DeCaro in the beautiful wedding, they moved into their first house and Rick's almost workaholic nature took over. In no time, he had completely remodeled the place.

Elizabeth developed into a fabulous young mother, caring not only for her son but often for her toddler sister, Theresa, while Georgianna worked. Elizabeth was maturing wonderfully and happily, just as Georgianna could have predicted. Elizabeth's generous and giving nature melded perfectly with her role as mother, and she was rapidly becoming another member of the cast of prosperous young Van Iseghems.

FIVE

David King had been the chief of police in St. Charles for only a few weeks on Friday, March 6, 1992. He wasn't even settled in yet, at the station or at his new house. His pregnant wife was still back in Perkasie, Pennsylvania, trying to sell their house in the town that was halfway between Philadelphia and Allentown. On this Friday evening, King busied himself alone at the new place, working away in the basement, staining woodwork. He heard the sirens rolling

down some not-too-distant streets sometime after eight
o'clock and thought briefly about turning on the police
radio to see what had caused all the activity. Nah, he decided, if it's anything important, they'll call.

Only a few minutes passed before the phone rang.

"Chief," the dispatcher said, "it looks like we've got a
homicide at 12 Hidden Meadow Court. Lieutenant McCarrick said you probably should check it out."

"Okay, thanks." King paused. "Uh, how do I get there?"

The new chief learned that he actually lived quite close
to the crime scene—barely three-quarters of a mile away.
He quickly changed clothes and sped toward the unfamiliar address.

The scene in the circle outside the house should have
warned King that he was about to be drawn into the most
trying, emotional case in his twenty-two years as a police
officer. The only time he had seen anything like what
awaited him on Hidden Meadow Court was in cop movies.
The cul-de-sac was full of flashing red lights atop every kind
of emergency vehicle, the glare reflecting off the crowd of
neck-craning onlookers.

Lieutenant Pat McCarrick met the chief as he got out of
his car and gave him the basics—they were facing what
appeared to be the murder of a young woman in her own
home, perhaps during a burglary she had interrupted. And,
McCarrick explained ruefully, he had been forced to order
a crowd of people out of the house when he arrived.

Terrific, Dave King thought. A crime scene contaminated
by neighbors, relatives, and who knows who else. What
have I gotten myself into? he wondered. He was brand-
new in this busy, growing town of fifty thousand, and he
was already facing what had all the earmarks of a sensational murder case.

For the first time in his career, he felt what he could
identify only as fear. Was there a homicidal maniac out
there, preying on innocent, defenseless housewives whom
he targeted and slaughtered for some bizarre, unfathomable
reason that would confound the police? Was there a slick
career criminal willing to summarily execute anyone who
interrupted him while he looted the homes in this upscale

subdivision? This was the kind of place where things like that weren't supposed to happen. If they happened here, could they happen where King lived, where he was bringing his pregnant wife? And if the chief of police was scared, what was the average citizen in St. Charles feeling on this rainy Friday night?

Lieutenant McCarrick had other news for the chief, news that added to the intrigue already swirling around this murder. McCarrick related some shocking suspicions from the dead woman's sister. Learning everything possible about the victim often led to the killer and, if this Melanie Enkelmann was right, this case could be even more complicated and worrisome than it had appeared at first glance. King was eager to begin checking into these surprising allegations.

McCarrick explained to King that officers were already fanning out through the neighborhood for a canvass, leaving the chief confident that his lieutenant had started the investigation off on the right foot. King would have expected no less. After all, not only had McCarrick been a St. Charles police officer for nineteen years but he had served four years as chief himself, from 1987 until just seven months ago. McCarrick had enjoyed the run at the top, but had tired of the political baggage that came along with the job. When a lieutenant's spot came open, he decided he would rather return to the streets. That broad range of experience and knowledge made him a valuable asset to the department and to King.

McCarrick now had another opportunity to apply his experience to assist the new boss whom he already liked and respected. Standing in the cul-de-sac on Hidden Meadow Court, McCarrick told King about a special regional resource available to police departments—the St. Louis Metropolitan Major Case Squad. As a member of the elite group himself, McCarrick knew how important it was for King to understand its purpose and operations—and how necessary it was for him to understand that as soon as possible. The squad was made up of the best detectives from departments all across the St. Louis area, drawing on the most expert officers serving more than two million people.

The squad was administered by a board of directors and its chief executive officer, the Florissant police chief, Colonel Robert Lowery—a respected officer in his own right. On the streets, the Major Case Squad worked under a group of commanders experienced in the most demanding murder investigations. This group could spring into action and deliver a crushing response of manpower and expertise in an amazingly short time—all focused on solving a case that might be beyond the means of an individual department. The squad had a stellar record of success in big cases. Activating the squad required only a request from the local chief—but that step had to be taken within four hours of the discovery of the murder.

This was a new and intriguing concept for King. At forty-one, a handsome, distinguished-looking man with a full shock of prematurely graying hair, he already had an impressive résumé. He held a master's degree from the Michigan State University School of Criminal Justice and was a graduate of the FBI Academy and the Penn State Police Executive Institute. A member of the International Association of Chiefs of Police. A lecturer, published on the topic of police administration. He already had served as chief for the departments in Coldwater and Eaton Rapids, Michigan. He was well rounded and experienced in police work. But he had never run into a murder quite like this, and he had not run into this concept before, this Major Case Squad. He remembered hearing it mentioned during the orientation process in St. Charles, but it was an unknown entity. He hadn't heard any details before McCarrick explained it and vouched for its value and effectiveness. And, the lieutenant had stressed, the request for the squad's assistance had to made within four hours.

It sounded like a hell of a good idea to King. After all, he was still assessing his new department's capabilities. Could it handle a case like this, a case that could be a damned difficult whodunit? Although he liked what he had seen in his officers so far, he still couldn't know the answer to that. And that uncertainty seemed to answer the question about the Major Case Squad.

"I'll make the call," he told McCarrick.

SIX

Tom O'Connor and his wife were standing in line for popcorn at the nine o'clock showing of a cop movie when his pager went off. The number that flashed across the screen was the Major Case Squad's command post—and he knew what that meant. The movie and the popcorn would have to wait. As one of the squad's top commanders, Tom O'Connor was being called out.

The command post told him only that a woman had been murdered in her home in St. Charles. Using his car phone as he hurried toward the scene, O'Connor began making his initial contacts. From a detective in St. Charles he got the basics and a brief account of Melanie Enkelmann's statement to the police. He reacted to that just as McCarrick and King had: it was an intriguing, and dangerous, place to start an investigation.

Still in the car, he sent a squad supervisor to the St. Charles Police Department to set up a command center; from there, O'Connor would supervise the investigators already on their way from their home jurisdictions across the St. Louis area. Although some commanders preferred to set up the centers themselves, O'Connor left that to others; he always started a case the only way that made sense to him—with a visit to the crime scene. Years of experience had taught this Irish cop that he could gain insight into the killer's personality by what was left behind.

Not only was O'Connor a Major Case commander but he carried the ranks of major and assistant chief in Maryland Heights, another growing town in St. Louis County just across the Missouri River from St. Charles. He had one of the most varied backgrounds of any cop in the area. Twelve years in the St. Louis Police Department's Homicide and Arson Squad, followed by a six-year tour as a murder investigator for the Illinois State Police, working an amazing series of cases in the suburban area just across the Mississippi River from St. Louis. Then he crossed back into Missouri and had been in Maryland Heights for ten years. He had served with the Major Case Squad for twelve. During his career, he had become an expert at interrogation, even teaching his techniques at police academies in several states and serving as an adjunct professor of criminal justice at St. Louis Community College.

He was a well-muscled, intense, passionate, and brutally direct man. Behind his quick smile and ready laugh was a policeman who countenanced no bull from anyone. The flash in his eyes when he talked about a case made that clear. He was the cop everyone except the killer would want on a major investigation. Despite what some detectives say about keeping an emotional distance from cases and victims, O'Connor intentionally personalized every single case. Each one became a contest between himself and the killer. But it was not just about O'Connor's sense of justice or his professional pride. Above everything else, he considered his role to be that of an ordained avenger for the victims. He didn't know much yet about Elizabeth DeCaro. But he knew she hadn't deserved to die like this, cut down in her own kitchen, in her own lovely home. Like other murder victims before her, Elizabeth DeCaro now counted on Tom O'Connor for justice. And that was saying something.

By the time O'Connor arrived at 12 Hidden Meadow Court after ten o'clock, the crowd of onlookers had dispersed and the first wave of cops was gone. Only the crime scene technician remained inside, combing the kitchen and the rest of the house for anything that might point toward the killer's identity. The tech took O'Connor on a tour of the beautiful, impeccably decorated house. His heart ached as he saw the toys and all of the other evidence that proved that this house was built around children. He could always tell when the kids were a family's focus, and evidence of that was abundant here. The photographs on the walls. The well-furnished kids' rooms. These children had lost a mother who loved them very much, and that intensified O'Connor's resolve.

A few obvious items were missing—TVs, VCRs, and stereos mostly—and a couple of drawers had been disturbed. But the rest of the house had not been ransacked in a search for valuables and money. Very little was out of place. O'Connor's eye was caught, however, by a purse on the table in the living room, its contents spilled out and scattered across the polished wood. Among the portable clues to a woman's life—those possessions so mysterious to men—lay a set of wedding and engagement rings. What did that mean?

The tech told O'Connor about the victim's head wounds and then showed him the kitchen where she had suffered them. O'Connor noticed immediately how little blood there was at the spot where Elizabeth DeCaro's body had lain on the shiny linoleum floor. Was the kitchen chosen because it was the one place in the house where trace evidence would be minimal? No telltale remnants of carpeting, no transfer of fibers. Intentional or coincidence? If the site had been chosen intentionally, O'Connor could be up against someone who knew what he was doing—a pro, wise in the ways of physical evidence and smart enough to try to eliminate it.

Tom studied the spot where the body was found and compared it to what he already knew about Elizabeth De-Caro's death. That gave him some valuable insight. Had she struggled or had she gone to her death in terrified resignation? Had she died in a blitz attack or had she been executed on her knees? Had she had been ambushed, never suspecting the fatal shots that were about to end her life? Or had she been with someone she trusted, assuming she was safe and secure in her own home? Much of that could be inferred from what O'Connor could learn at the death scene.

He had concluded over the years that people were murdered for three basic reasons: sexual misconduct, revenge, and money. This victim had not been sexually molested. Revenge? Not likely in the murder of a suburban housewife and mother, unless something dark were to be discovered about this woman, some secret life that would lead her to this violent end. She wasn't a prostitute, prowling the streets and selling herself for cocaine. She didn't seem the type for life in the fast lane, cruising along the sharp edges where death could come so easily. No, Elizabeth DeCaro was a low-risk victim.

That left O'Connor with one possibility: money. He saw no genuine evidence of a burglary or a robbery, and he found no suggestion of a struggle. That made it unlikely that she had interrupted a burglar cold-blooded enough to gun her down just to eliminate a witness. This whole crime scene suggested someone smooth and cunning—not a small-time, smash-and-grab punk willing to risk a murder rap to avoid a couple of years in the joint.

To O'Connor, it was looking increasingly like the purpose of this crime was only one thing—the kill. Money—the last option—may have played a role, perhaps with a dash of revenge mixed in. She had been executed, and her killer had been comfortable in the house after accomplishing his purpose with chilling proficiency. The small amount of blood meant she had died quickly. The two shots had been well placed. A contact wound behind the left ear seemed the classic, military coup de grace. Was this a "hit," an efficient job by a professional? An assassin—for this petite housewife? If she had died at the hands of a pro, this could be a damned tough case. Those guys knew what the cops needed, and they seldom provided it; they didn't often make mistakes.

And how did Melanie Enkelmann's allegations fit in with all of that?

O'Connor could already feel the pressure mounting. This was going to be one tough son of a bitch to solve.

SEVEN

By July 1984, the young DeCaros were growing and prospering—the kind of family that attracted attention and envy. Rick worked endlessly to give his family everything he possibly could. He wanted them to have the best, and he gave it to them in abundance. The more and the better he could buy, the happier he seemed. Clothes, cars, appliances. Whatever was latest and hottest, the DeCaros had it, and they had it before anyone else did.

Amid that abundance, they had just delivered a third child. Joining Patrick, now four, and his sister, Rachel,* just fourteen months old, was another son, William,* to be called Bill. Elizabeth and Rick were thrilled with their second boy, but Bill's arrival meant the already tight quarters in their house would be pushed past tolerance. It was time to move up. They listed their lovely little house for sale and found a buyer so quickly that they were left with nowhere to live while they shopped.

Georgianna and Jim Van Iseghem came to the rescue with the kind of offer that came directly from this family's heart, a proposition made in love because it was the right thing to do. They asked Elizabeth and Rick, and their three children, to move back home to St. Francis Lane. Sure, it meant overcrowding for a while, with Theresa and Randy still living at home. But they could handle it in the short term, because it was the kind of thing the Van Iseghems did for each other. But that was not all there was to the offer. Georgianna and Jim refused to accept a penny in rent from Elizabeth and Rick. That money was better applied toward their new house. Rick was overwhelmed, and deeply touched. He had not seen sharing and love carried to this level in his own family.

The months of extended family crowded together under one roof actually were fun. Elizabeth learned more about cooking, adopting her mother's fabled recipes and adding another generation to the Van Iseghems' kitchen mastery. The children grew even closer to their grandparents, seeing daily the manifestations of the love and concern so common in this family, but so noticeable even to those of young ages. Georgianna delighted in these days. She loved having her precious Elizabeth home again; she had departed too soon anyway. And Georgianna was thrilled to bestow her special love on another generation of children; oh, how she loved being a grandmother.

But these months seemed to bring the most profound change in Rick DeCaro. As quickly and completely as he had changed his driving habits years ago, he became a new man now. Almost with the snap of his fingers, he became a real part of the Van Iseghem family, growing closer to each and every member. To Mary Cordes, who had gone to school with him, he now became like another brother. He was more like a third son to Jim and Georgianna— the only reward they ever sought for sharing their love with him.

Only once was there a problem. On Christmas Eve 1984 a shopping trip by Rick and Elizabeth lasted so long that they were terribly late in joining the twenty other relatives already gathered for the traditional family dinner at the house on St. Francis Lane. Georgianna, a gracious hostess, was unable to restrain her anger at such thoughtless conduct from Elizabeth and Rick. When she told them exactly that, Rick responded in anger too. After a brief exchange of words, Rick stormed out of the house. Now Georgianna was hurt and sorry; she called Rick at his mother's and apologized. When he returned later, he greeted everyone warmly and offered no hint that there had ever been a problem. The holiday was saved.

The DeCaros stayed with the Van Iseghems for nine months, moving out when the new house on Eagle Ridge in St. Charles was completed in May 1985. But they never liked the new house; they lived there barely a year before they bought a lot in the new Woodfield Meadows subdivision and built yet another house—at 12 Hidden Meadow Court—in June 1986. By the time they moved into the blue house with the white trim and the white stone front, four bedrooms, and two and a half bathrooms, there seemed to be nothing they couldn't achieve and little they hadn't accumulated.

Elizabeth was blooming as a mother and wife, following in her own dear mother's footsteps as a frequent hostess renowned for wonderful entertaining. Guests actually wanted to attend her Tupperware, jewelry, and home-furnishings parties. She served fabulous food, and at least forty people always showed up. Her older sisters were in awe. Rick bought her the most lovely furniture to complement the interior decorating talents that seemed to come so naturally to her. She had a real flair for it, and friends often encouraged her to take it up professionally. She thought she just might do that someday, after the kids were raised.

Rick's fortunes continued to improve, too. He was now managing the profitable Amoco service station owned by his brother Dan in the upscale community of Webster Groves. The Old Orchard Amoco Station and attached repair garage attracted terrific business, and Rick worked long, hard hours. In return, he was pulling down a salary topping $70,000—not bad for a high school dropout. He used his money to help make his home a showplace to complement his beautiful family. He installed a swimming pool in the backyard and built an elaborate wooden deck around it. He made sure his family had all the latest and best appliances inside. His love of anything mechanical also manifested itself in his vehicles. The DeCaros were among the first to have a conversion van, complete with a television, VCR, and Nintendo.

Rick thrilled his in-laws by building a wonderful sunroom across the back of their home on St. Francis Lane. The expansive room—with walls made almost entirely of glass—quickly became Georgianna's special place, and she spent hours meditating there. The Van Iseghems paid Rick handsomely for the work, but the results could not be measured in dollars and cents, and they had Rick to thank for it.

In June 1987, the DeCaros added a second daughter, Erin,* to the family, bringing the grand total to four DeCaro kids. As had the generations before them, the children attended Catholic schools. Rick coached their athletic teams, and Elizabeth was an energetic room mother. In keeping with the rest of their possessions, the DeCaros all wore the best of clothes, and all seemed perfectly color-coordinated when they went out together. One manifestation of Rick's doting affection for Elizabeth was that—to the amazement of her sisters and girlfriends—he gladly accompanied her on shopping trips for her clothes. He helped her select the conservative dresses with the long skirts and high necklines that defined her wardrobe and her style. During those years, Rick began to take great pride in his own appearance too. He had become obsessed with working out, making almost daily visits to Gold's Gym to add some muscle to his skinny frame. His favorite movie now— watched over and over and over—was Sylvester Stallone's *Rocky*.

What a great-looking family the DeCaros were!

By then, Elizabeth had become best friends with her next-door neighbor, Pam Hanley. Pam and her husband, Larry, had moved from the adjacent town of St. Peters to Hidden Meadow Court shortly after the DeCaros moved there. Pam and Elizabeth first met while walking through their subdivision—Elizabeth had just recently learned she was pregnant with Erin—and they soon saw each other again at one of the many product parties that popped up regularly among the neighbors. While playing some kind of Q & A game at the party, Elizabeth mentioned the dates of Patrick's birth and her marriage. The always straightforward Pam high-kicked her foot into her mouth by casually remarking, "Oh, so you guys had Patrick before you were married." The women all swallowed hard and quickly moved past the awkward moment, but Pam felt just awful for calling everyone's attention to the obvious and perhaps hurting Elizabeth's feelings. Pam phoned her the next day, invited her over for coffee, and apologized. The sensitive and gracious Elizabeth shrugged off the incident as harmless, and the two women found that they really clicked. Before long, they were equal halves of a wonderful friendship that extended to their broods of four children each, who, at similar ages, hit it off as well as their mothers had. Rick DeCaro and Larry Hanley also became friends—not as close as their wives, but they got along well and their social visits were enjoyable for everyone. Rick helped the Hanleys enclose their back porch, and the couples spent many happy nights there or on the DeCaros' deck.

Pam and Elizabeth were inseparable—petite blondes forming a dynamic duo. They felt as if they had known each other all their lives. Neither worked outside the home, and they soon were spending long days together and taking evening shopping trips that could last until two in the morning by the time they finished their late visits to Victoria's in St. Charles for ice cream. They fed and bathed each other's kids. They shared their most intimate secrets about husbands, sex, money, and anything else that came up for discussion. They even talked about death, and Pam would remember later how Elizabeth said she could not understand people who visited cemeteries. They should get past the grief and get on with their lives, she insisted; if anyone ever spent time weeping at her grave, she would be spinning in it. Their different-but-so-similar personalities—they both understood that a date at two o'clock really meant fifteen or twenty after—complemented each other, drawing out the best in each one. Elizabeth's naturally empathetic nature softened Pam's way of looking at things, while Pam provided guidance and support for Elizabeth when she hesitated to make her needs known to Rick and others. When too practical Pam complained that Larry planned to get her a thousand-dollar diamond ring for Christmas when what she really needed was a new sofa, Elizabeth reminded her that this was something Larry wanted to do out of love for his wife. On Elizabeth's advice, Pam explained her dilemma to Larry and they compromised—she accepted a less expensive garnet ring and got a sofa later. She never dreamed then what she would do with that ring one day.

Pam was always struck by Rick DeCaro's possessiveness about everything in his life, from his wife to his children to his house to his car to his smallest belongings. He would erupt in anger if rocks from the landscaping around the house somehow got scattered onto the driveway or sidewalk. He obviously didn't like it when Pam dared to sit on his car one day. He was very jealous about Elizabeth; he wouldn't allow her to wear a bikini outside the backyard, and he sometimes complained when he thought her friendly nature had crossed over into flirting with other men.

On the other hand, his focus on Elizabeth meant he showered her with flowers and gifts, called her at least twice a day from work, and kissed her the moment he walked in the door at the end of the day. In return, she doted on him, rising early every morning to prepare a full breakfast, pack his lunch, and iron his shirts. Pam thought it was neat that Liz and Rick still had that kind of intensity in their relationship after years of marriage. But she also thought it odd that Elizabeth, who was independent about most things, seemed so dependent on Rick emotionally.

A lot of Rick DeCaro's behavior struck Pam as typical "macho man" stuff. Elizabeth mentioned that he never cried, not even when his children were born. In fact, he had such difficulty expressing his emotions that he usually got angry and left if the couples started playing the game Scruples, which posed moral and ethical questions that the players had to answer. Pam noticed that the only time Rick's eyes seemed to soften was when he talked about his favorite grandfather and the farm he had owned; Rick had truly loved the old man and that farm. But that affection contrasted with his angry feelings toward his own father and brothers, Pam thought. Rick seemed unable to forgive his father for leaving his mother; they were divorced now. In his immediate family, Rick seemed to really love only his sister, Patty.

Rick's in-laws had been noticing some of those same peculiarities for years. Jim and Georgianna Van Iseghem were happy for Elizabeth and Rick and their full, active, prosperous life. But Georgianna knew that Rick's spending habits concerned Elizabeth. The Van Iseghems and the DeCaros traded visits to each other's homes regularly, and they enjoyed each other's company. But Georgianna thought the philosophy "I am what I own" seemed a DeCaro trademark. The whole family had always struck her as quite materialistic, and she sensed that that had hatched a special need in Rick—he always had to own more and more, better and better. That attitude really bothered the more frugal Elizabeth.

Georgianna was quite willing to overlook that one worry because Rick was so good to Elizabeth and the children. His concern was genuine and intense—so much so that some thought it bordered on obsessive. Once, after Elizabeth's car broke down, Rick spared no expense to assure her safety; he became one of the first to acquire a cellular phone, for her car. He used it regularly to stay in touch with her when she was away from home.

The blossoming of the DeCaros seemed to be just part of the bounty now enjoyed by the Van Iseghems. Their efforts to raise loving, happy, well-adjusted children were paying dividends. The older children were making their own ways in the world, building marriages and careers. Only Margie had moved any distance from the home parish; her second marriage, this time to Dr. Sergio Ugalde, had taken her to Long Beach, California. She lived there with her daughter, Jamie, and her husband's five children from his first marriage. Theresa remained at home—just entering her teens. The children were growing up, but not growing away. They loved to come back to the house on St. Francis. The rooms often echoed again with the sounds of happy children—a new generation of beautiful kids calling out to "Grandma and Grandpa."

Life seemed so good. Only later would they learn how sheltered and naive they all had been.

EIGHT

Melanie Enkelmann began to notice the changes in Elizabeth and Rick DeCaro in late 1991.

Melanie hired Elizabeth to replace their sister Mary at the family-operated concession stand for St. Ann bingo games, and the new arrangement gave "Mel" and "Liz" a lot of enjoyable time together. It soon became clear to the older sister that the younger sister wasn't happy. She and Rick had begun clashing regularly over his extravagant spending. He bought what he wanted, when he wanted, without a thought to the cost or the impact on the family budget. She nearly exploded when he came home with a hot, high-powered, fire-engine red, and expensive '91 Chevy Camaro RS—without even discussing it with her first. For his new wheels, he got vanity license plates that read, RIK-LIZ. And beyond the cost, his precious car continued to generate conflict because he complained endlessly about the kids messing it up inside. That drove Rick nuts, and it just added to Elizabeth's resentment of the damned machine and Rick's recklessness with their money. Pam Hanley urged Elizabeth to stick to her guns on the spending issue. "Liz, that's your money too," Pam insisted.

Elizabeth needed that kind of support, but it wasn't long before fate separated the previously inseparable women. In March 1991 Larry Hanley was transferred to Kansas City by his pharmaceutical company. The good-bye was devastating to both families.

The women compensated for this painful move with family trips back and forth across the 230 miles of rolling Missouri countryside at least every other week. They vowed that nothing could separate them for very long.

Meanwhile, Georgianna tried valiantly to smooth the troubled waters for her daughter. She urged Elizabeth to give Rick some room; he worked hard and he deserved some rewards, some toys, some diversions for the little free time he had. She reminded Elizabeth that Rick was a lot like the father she loved so much. Jim and Rick both worked hard and rated a little extra latitude.

Georgianna was surprised when Elizabeth recounted how she had told Rick in January 1991 to give her more breathing room, to back off a little with the gifts and flowers and constant attention, to quit smothering her. That had been a mistake, Georgianna thought; most men would probably see that as rejection of their love. Indeed, Rick had proved it so; on that Valentine's Day, the normally extravagant and thoughtful husband had given his wife nothing, not a single token of his love.

But Rick never changed when it came to his desire for bigger and better toys. Next on his avaricious agenda was a zippy twenty-one-foot ski boat. They could keep it docked and ready for weekends at Lake of the Ozarks, the popular resort area about 140 miles southwest of St. Charles where he hoped to buy a condo for those weekend getaways. Elizabeth couldn't believe this latest financial frolic. She reminded him of all of their activities, that the kids were busy in sports and even joining the special "select teams" formed for only the best players. They both spent most of their time off ferrying kids to and from this game and that tournament or some other event. Where would they get the time to make enough trips to the lake to justify an expensive boat they couldn't really afford at a dream condo they could never support or use? But Rick was resolute; he wanted the boat. So Elizabeth screwed up her courage and set her conditions: he had to sell the Camaro to pay for the boat. He agreed, but he was angry and resentful about it; she had intruded on his prerogatives and his pleasures.

Once again, Georgianna weighed in on the side of understanding and compromise. Rick needed the boat so he could get out of town, get away from all the hours of work, and relax; let him have this release. Georgianna hoped Elizabeth could get over what seemed to be the first big disagreement in her married life.

Before long, it became clear to Melanie that something deeper than financial differences was going on in her sister's marriage. Melanie understood Rick very well, perhaps better than anyone else in the family. They were both workaholics; she could appreciate that drive to excel, to achieve, to accomplish. They had always gotten along quite well, too; in fact, Melanie was the only person Rick would let Elizabeth accompany on shopping trips to the Ozarks without him. But now Melanie began to notice that Rick was changing. It wasn't the usual growth and development of young adulthood. No—his personality was changing in very basic and alarming ways.

That became apparent while he was remodeling Georgianna and Jim's delicatessen in August 1991. They had always paid him for his work. But this time, in gratitude for all they had done for him and Elizabeth and the kids, Rick remodeled the deli "gratis." He even brought along one of his employees from the service station to help him— Craig Wells, who had once worked at Jim Van Iseghem's store. The Van Iseghems appreciated Rick's gesture, but it soon became clear that he wasn't doing it with a joyful heart; he seemed angry all the time and didn't show the pride in his work that had always marked his efforts before. They realized that he really didn't want to be doing this at all.

Melanie and the rest of the family also were worried by

the dramatic weight loss they had seen in Elizabeth. She had dropped twenty pounds at first, and then another twenty until her five-foot-four frame now carried only 102 pounds. She had always wanted to be thinner, and now she was even slimmer than her sisters. They wondered if she was anorexic, and she was genuinely irritated when they asked. She said she simply couldn't eat, wasn't hungry. And she had started working out a lot in an effort to feel better about herself.

But at a lunch at the fashionable Galleria mall in October 1991, Elizabeth began telling her mother and sisters about the increasing tension in her "perfect" household. She described all the conflicts and then shocked everyone by revealing her suspicion that Rick had a girlfriend. Mary Cordes assured Elizabeth that such a thing was completely impossible: Rick was too crazy about her to even consider cheating. Georgianna agreed; she found the concept of an adulterous Rick absolutely ridiculous, and told Elizabeth so. But Elizabeth said things had changed. Rick had even allowed her and the kids to go without him to visit Pam Hanley in Kansas City. Before, he had always insisted on going along, but this time he stayed home alone. Surely that, along with everything else bubbling in this pot, meant something.

When sister Margie made her yearly trip home in October, she was distressed by how anorexic Elizabeth looked. With her nurse's training and her understanding of the mind-set of the Van Iseghem women, she recognized immediately that something was seriously bothering Elizabeth. When the women all took a day trip to visit the wineries in the quaint town of Augusta, Elizabeth shared more of her concerns with them. Sitting at an open-air cafe on a beautiful day, surrounded by the changing palette of fall foliage, Elizabeth wept as she revealed her fear that she was losing Rick. He was playing mind games with her, turning everything she said into a weapon he then used against her. If she were slimmer and worked out more—if she looked better—perhaps he would notice her more, want her more. If he did have a girlfriend, perhaps Elizabeth could use a better figure to convince him to stay with her.

She had even thought of leaving him but had decided she couldn't. She wanted to save the marriage, despite everything that had happened. Sometimes, Elizabeth confided, she wondered if she was going crazy.

Margie had always felt close to Elizabeth, now even more so. Margie had been through all of those emotions. She told Elizabeth she could do anything she decided to, even leaving Rick, despite his efforts to convince her she was incapable of living on her own. That course wouldn't be easy, but she could survive it. Margie had. Rick would be forced by law to help Elizabeth and the children financially, and that might give her a new start. Elizabeth even talked about going back to school and getting her G.E.D. That would allow her to get more training, perhaps even to go into interior decorating, as Margie had suggested.

Margie ached for her sister. She herself watched what she ate closely and worked out too. But she could tell Elizabeth's worries were pushing a normal concern toward an obsession, perhaps toward an illness. Margie knew all too well the need to present the facade of a perfect life; all of the Van Iseghem women wrestled with that. Whether it was in the genes, or just in the way they were raised, they knew that everyone had seen their family as perfect, and they labored under the daily pressure of making that perception a reality. As they grew up, they realized that nothing was perfect. But that didn't keep them from seeking perfection in every aspect of their lives—motherhood, marriage, work, religious faith, their bodies.

Margie was living that life at that very moment. She was married to a doctor, living in Southern California in a nice house with nice furniture, nice jewelry, nice cars—but nothing seemed really fulfilling. Margie and Elizabeth had talked about all of that in the past. But now Elizabeth was experiencing a deeper, darker problem in her marriage. She said she could feel Rick pulling away, and she didn't know what to do.

When Elizabeth visited Pam Hanley that November, she told her old friend about her suspicions that Rick was seeing another woman. Pam, remembering Rick's devotion to Elizabeth for so many years, rejected the idea completely, but told Liz that a mere suspicion meant there was a problem in the marriage. Pam suggested counseling, even if Elizabeth had to go alone. Elizabeth was hurt that weekend when Rick never called to see if she had arrived safely—as he always had done before—and was never home when she called him—all evening.

Back at home, the strain between Elizabeth and Rick was more than obvious at Thanksgiving 1991, when they arrived at Georgianna's quite late. Elizabeth's puffy eyes provided unmistakable evidence that she had been crying. Rick—his face still red with anger—went directly to the sofa and sat quietly and stiffly. In hushed conversations later, Elizabeth told her mother and sisters that she had found Rick lying on their bed crying. He said at first that he couldn't explain the tears. But then he shook her world by adding that he wasn't sure he loved her anymore. Elizabeth was devastated. She had felt his withdrawal, been hurt when he stopped calling her in the middle of the day to chat, and worried when he had refused to discuss their growing problems. But this was beyond all of that. This threatened everything her life was built upon. And it was just that much more evidence that he had found someone else and was, indeed, having an affair.

Mary Cordes was dumbfounded by her little sister's account of Rick's comments. Mary couldn't have been any more surprised if her own loving husband, Phil, had made such an announcement to her. Everything pointed to Rick's involvement with another woman, but Mary couldn't bring herself to admit that he could do such a thing.

Melanie was so upset that she even called Rick at work one day and offered to meet him anytime he felt like talking. They had always seemed to understand each other, and perhaps Melanie could help sort through all of this. Rick wasn't very responsive then, and he never called.

But he delivered an unusually angry and profane blast Thanksgiving night at Georgianna and Jim's house; his target was Maureen, Randy Van Iseghem's estranged wife. While she was enjoying her first visit with the family in some time, Rick unexpectedly exploded and demanded that she move her "fucking car" that was blocking his in the driveway. Maureen and the others were flabbergasted, and a stunned Elizabeth apologized for her husband. The outburst was just one more indication that Rick was changing in more ways than anyone could understand.

Elizabeth continued to confide in Melanie and Mary over the next days. With the facade of the "perfect family" shattered, Elizabeth was looking to her sisters for guidance. And when Margie returned home to be there when their father underwent hip-replacement surgery on December 2, she was shocked to see Elizabeth even thinner than before. Her size nine figure had shrunk to a size three; her cheeks were hollow and she looked exhausted. Margie urged her mother and sisters to get Elizabeth to a doctor. After all, anorexia was a serious disease, and the Van Iseghems didn't want Elizabeth to fall victim to it. Elizabeth finally visited a doctor, who—unfortunately—found no reason for concern. Elizabeth's response to her family's worries was to comment only that for the first time, she was buying smaller clothes and giving her hand-me-downs to Melanie—instead of the reverse.

But there were more serious revelations to come. On December 3, the day after Jim's surgery, Elizabeth called her mother with a tearful account of Rick's confession that he was having an affair with Cathy Dillon,* his married secretary at the service station. Georgianna could not believe Rick would do such a thing and demanded a meeting to confront him. She had to hear it from the mouth of the man she thought she knew so well. Even though she was attending to her ill husband, she knew she had to take the time to help Elizabeth. Georgianna and Margie went to the DeCaros' house, and Margie took Elizabeth and the kids out for ice cream. Facing his mother-in-law in the living room, Rick surprised her by not only confirming that he was having an affair but insisting that he was really in love with this Cathy Dillon. Rick explained that Elizabeth had wounded him deeply when she told him to stop smothering her with affection and gifts and attention; her rejection of his way of showing love had left him confused and devastated. Something inside him had snapped. Eventually, he had turned for comfort to this friend at work, who appreciated his attention and compliments. He had not meant for the affair to happen, but it had.

And then he really rocked Georgianna. "I'm not sure I ever loved Elizabeth," he said.

Georgianna began to cry. "Oh, Rick, surely this thing with this other woman is just an infatuation."

"No," he said, "now that I've been with Cathy, I know what love really is."

Georgianna warned him that he risked losing everything—Elizabeth, the kids, his house, all of the comforts and possessions he had worked so hard to accumulate.

"I know," he said stiffly. "I'm trapped."

Georgianna hardly recognized the cold, emotionless expression on her son-in-law's face, but she never would forget the way Rick DeCaro looked that night. When the others returned, Elizabeth could see in her mother's eyes that Rick had confirmed the worst news of all.

As Christmas neared, the Van Iseghems hoped things might be improving for Elizabeth and Rick. He swore he had ended the affair; she hoped they could repair the damage and save the marriage. Georgianna happened to run into the DeCaros on a Christmas shopping trip, and they seemed happier, more relaxed, almost like old times. Later, they asked Georgianna to watch their kids so they could spend a weekend at Lake of the Ozarks to try to rekindle their love and save their marriage. But when they returned, Elizabeth described the trip as miserable—the same old tensions frustrating any effort to improve their rocky relationship.

Christmas Eve was terrible. A sullen Rick sat quietly, and obviously unhappily, on the sofa. Elizabeth said he was embarrassed because everyone in the family knew about his affair. The tension between them threw a wet blanket over the whole evening. But New Year's Eve was worse. Elizabeth had rejected Rick's request that they go to a party hosted by Cathy Dillon—the very woman with whom he had had an affair. After an ugly quarrel, Rick agreed to Elizabeth's demand to go to the annual party at St. Elizabeth's Church. But once there, he acted like a fool, argued with her loudly and publicly, and then stormed out. Elizabeth was left behind in tears and had to prevail on friends for a ride home.

Rick's behavior became worse yet with the arrival of the new year. While Elizabeth was starting classes to get her G.E.D. at St. Charles Community College, Rick was busily confiscating her checkbook and credit cards and avoiding her physically, as if she had leprosy. Elizabeth complained that he had begun staying out later and later, going to hockey games or drinking with friends from the station and Gold's Gym. He usually didn't come home before ten o'clock, claiming he had been working late. And he never called Elizabeth during the days or evenings to check in with her, as he always had before.

Georgianna and Elizabeth naively wondered what all of that could mean, but Mary and Melanie were more suspicious. Melanie remembered what one of her friends had said when he divorced his wife: "You've got to have a plan." He had spied on her, caught her being unfaithful, and won custody of his kids. Melanie and Mary equated that to Rick's conduct. "He's up to something no good. He's planning something," they insisted. They even wondered if drugs—cocaine, perhaps?—could be responsible for Rick's Jekyll-and-Hyde personality changes. They urged Elizabeth to pay attention to his emotional abuse because it did not seem logical in light of his recent transgressions. Melanie offered her characteristically blunt assessment of the situation: "He just admitted having an affair. Shouldn't he be kissing your ass?"

Melanie was so concerned that she decided to speak to their father. In early January she sat down with Jim, told him of her worries, and asked him to hire a private detective to try to figure out what Rick had up his sleeve. "We need to find out what's going on. I don't want to find Elizabeth dead and read about it in the newspapers," she told her father. The words sent a shiver, a vibration of some kind through her body, from head to toe. She couldn't believe what she had just heard from her own mouth. Where had that grotesque thought come from?

Jim Van Iseghem was astounded. Like Georgianna, he

thought Melanie and Mary were making too much of their sister's marital difficulties. Every marriage had problems, and some survived horribly rocky times when they seemed all but lost. And now, even faced with this startling suspicion from his daughter, Jim could not justify that kind of fear about Elizabeth's well-being. He told Melanie that he really didn't think it was necessary to have a detective chasing specters of marital discord.

Later that month, in another of the unending conversations between mother and daughter, Georgianna told Elizabeth to pack up the kids and move home if conditions became intolerable in St. Charles. Elizabeth threatened to do just that, she reported to her mother later, and Rick hadn't even flinched as he coolly called her bluff. "If you leave me," he had warned, "I'll get custody of the kids and you'll never see them again." He had even asked how much it would cost him for Elizabeth to leave. When she shot back, "Two thousand dollars a month," Rick had become enraged, and an argument had erupted.

Despite all of that, Georgianna still planned to carry on a Van Iseghem family tradition. At a party she scheduled for Friday, January 24, she planned to celebrate her fifty-sixth birthday and Rick's thirtieth—both falling on January 28. This would be one of her fabled soirees, complete with a professional disc jockey and an elaborate buffet for fifty guests. But a call from Rick's mother, Grace DeCaro, revealed just how strained the family ties had become—she urged Georgianna to cancel the party. Grace, who with the rest of the DeCaros was furious at Rick over his affair, reluctantly explained that she was sure he would not attend. The Van Iseghems were willing to host the party to thank Rick for the things he had done for them and to say that the family could forgive what had happened and move on. But Grace was absolutely adamant that her son could not be convinced to show up.

All of the Van Iseghems waffled about what to do. Georgianna even thought about canceling the whole affair. Margie had bought six round-trip air tickets for her, Sergio, her daughter, and three of his children. But Margie knew all about the events on Christmas Eve and New Year's Eve, and she decided she was not going to spend that much money to be a hypocrite and celebrate the thirtieth birthday of the son of a bitch who was making her sister so miserable. Margie decided to come home alone. She told Elizabeth she would use the other tickets to bring the entire West Coast contingent home to celebrate when Elizabeth got her G.E.D. Little did Margie imagine how she would use those tickets in March.

In the end, Grace DeCaro's prediction was accurate. Her son boycotted the party where Georgianna's kids presented her with a heart-shaped pendant that Elizabeth had designed. The touching inscription read, "First Our Mom—Now Our Friend." Although Rick's absence cast a pall over the evening, Georgianna made sure plenty of family photographs were taken. She had no idea how precious those pictures would become in the very near future. They recorded Elizabeth's last attendance at a Van Iseghem family event.

Two incidents on January 26—Super Bowl XXVI Sunday—left the entire family even more perplexed about Rick DeCaro. The first was odd, but not particularly disturbing. While most of the family assembled at Georgianna and Jim's for their annual Super Bowl party, Rick and Elizabeth went out with friends. In the middle of the evening, Rick called and asked Jim for the name of the man he used to place bets—his bookie. That shocked everyone; Rick had never been known to gamble. Once again, his personality was taking a new twist.

If that was surprising, the second event was frightening. When Rick and Elizabeth returned home that night and pulled into the garage, they found one of the kids' bicycles blocking the parking place for their van. Elizabeth got out to move the bike, and as she rolled it toward the rear of the garage, the white van suddenly surged forward, smashed into her, and drove her through the wall, almost into the kitchen behind it. Amazingly—and fortunately—the little bike absorbed some of the impact, and Elizabeth broke through the drywall directly in the space between the wooden studs. She was saved from serious injury, perhaps death, by those two lucky flukes.

But without a word to the wife he had just pounded into the wall as if she were a nail under his four-thousand-pound GMC hammer, Rick got out of the van and hurried out of the front of the garage. He never said a word to Elizabeth, and he didn't even use the side door from the garage into the house. He walked across the front of the house and went through the front door. When he encountered eleven-year-old Patrick inside, he calmly ordered him to go to his room.

Elizabeth painfully pried herself out of the crushed wall-board, and climbed over the bike and past the van. She limped through the door into the kitchen, where she was greeted with an odd look from Rick. He turned and picked up the phone, as if to call 911. He still seemed stunned to see her.

"What are you trying to do, kill me?" she demanded. He hung up the phone, broke into tears, and asked how she could think that. It was an accident! When he had turned to reach for his coat in the backseat, his foot had slipped off the brake and slammed onto the accelerator. Surely she knew it had been a horrible accident!

Elizabeth was fortunate. She spent an uncomfortable night, while a concerned Rick never left her side. The next day she went to the hospital, where X-rays confirmed that her injuries were limited to a badly bruised left leg and hip; nothing was broken. Elizabeth's mother and sisters were struck dumb when she called and told them what had happened. Georgianna could say only that it surely had been an accident. Elizabeth said it had almost been worth the pain to see Rick so upset, to see him showing that he still cared about her.

Later, Mary cracked to her mother, "Well, it's not like he has taken out life insurance on her recently." But Georgianna offered a surprising and hesitant reply: "Well, yes, he has." She told Melanie and Mary how Elizabeth had recounted a visit from their Allstate insurance agent earlier that month. Rick had increased his coverage to $250,000 and had taken out their first policy on Elizabeth—for

$100,000. Although Georgianna still preferred to look at that as simply a prudent fiscal move by the husband and father of a young family, the suspiciously timed insurance policy changed things drastically for Melanie and Mary. Surely that was proof that Rick was up to something, as they had been suspecting. "He has a plan," Melanie insisted as she recalled her friend's comments. What could Rick's strategy be? A divorce? A legal separation? Was he planning to disappear with the family funds? What the hell was going on?

Their constant suspicions were beginning to irritate Georgianna; she was tired of what seemed to be their concocted, exaggerated stories of devious activities by Rick. She even complained about them trying to "stir up shit," unusual language for the Van Iseghem matron to use. But Melanie and Mary were undeterred; they simply stopped telling their mother about their misgivings and hunches. From that moment on, they vowed, they were the detectives whose job it was to learn the truth about what was happening in the DeCaro household. All of this was especially difficult for Mary. She had put her little sister's marriage—and, indeed, her entire seemingly happy, rewarding life with Rick—on a pedestal. Seeing all of this intrigue and misery inflicted on Elizabeth was like watching the whole world crumble.

Late on the day after the crash, Georgianna drove to St. Charles to visit her injured daughter and found Rick in the garage already repairing the damaged wall. As she approached, she was surprised to find him crying as he worked. Struck by what she interpreted as his obvious remorse over hitting Elizabeth with the van, Georgianna assured her son-in-law that she knew it all had been a terrible accident. He swore it had been exactly that. Inside, Georgianna visited with a sore but cheerful Elizabeth as she rested on the sofa. In a gesture so indicative of her grandmotherly instincts, Georgianna took all four of the DeCaro children out to supper at McDonald's to give their parents a much-needed respite.

All kids should be blessed with grandparents such as the Van Iseghems.

But that night, a terrifying visitor came to Georgianna. She was jolted from a deep sleep and sat straight up in bed. Something invading her dream world—a premonition of some kind—told her that Elizabeth was going to be murdered. Not endangered, not threatened, not injured. Murdered. Specifically and clearly—murdered. This was not the kind of vague fear that awaits unguarded sleep to rush out to deliver a quick blow in the middle of the night. No, this was throat-clutching panic that makes a return to sleep all but impossible and claws at the heart long after daylight has chased away the other shadows.

This nocturnal omen indeed haunted Georgianna's every thought all the next day. Within three days, Georgianna was driven to ask Elizabeth a question that should have seemed, should have *been* ridiculous.

"Honey, do you think Rick would ever hurt you, on purpose? Are you afraid?"

Elizabeth offered her mother that reassuring, warm smile and a sincere, "Oh, no, Mom, no. He would never hurt me. I'm not afraid of that at all."

But the specter that had appeared to Georgianna was never far from her thoughts for the next six weeks.

Elizabeth called Pam Hanley to tell her about the garage fiasco. She assured her stunned friend that it was an accident, stressing how bad Rick felt about it. "He's just so upset. He cried all night. He said, 'I'll always love you,'" Elizabeth explained. Pam found Rick's comments more than odd, remembering that Rick never cried and wondering why he expressed his love in that way. Most people would have said simply, "I love you" or "You know I love you." Saying "I'll always love you" sounded suspiciously like someone saying good-bye, and that left Pam very uncomfortable about what was happening back on Hidden Meadow Court.

The odd events continued.

Rick had been refusing to go to a birthday party on February 7 for Elizabeth's friend Mary Pohlmann. But he suddenly called Elizabeth that day and volunteered to accompany her. Melanie urged Elizabeth to give him some of his own treatment by ignoring his "gracious" offer and going alone. But, as Melanie expected, Elizabeth relented and agreed to go with him. Melanie tried to talk to Rick at the party that night, but he seemed a different person from the man she had known for so long. He was so distant, almost like a stranger. She wondered why he had come at all; he certainly was not enjoying himself. Rick wanted Elizabeth to leave before midnight, even though she wanted to stay and party. "I want to go home and make love to you," he told the woman he had not touched for weeks, perhaps months. Elizabeth, seizing on Rick's passion as a hopeful sign, agreed to leave with him then. When they got home about twelve-thirty, Rick backed the van into the driveway and uncharacteristically left it sitting there, outside of the garage. He never did that and now, just hours after he had cleaned it out—it seemed doubly strange.

They made love, and the next morning Rick slept late—a rarity for a man who was usually an early riser, popping out of bed about four-thirty in the morning. He hadn't been up too long on this morning before the phone rang about ten with a call from one of his employees. The sheriff's department in Cape Girardeau County, Missouri, about 110 miles south of St. Charles, had called the station. The white 1989 GMC van registered to the business had been found burned—completely destroyed in what appeared to be an explosion and fire—in a field in an isolated area off Route 4, about five miles north of the city of Cape Girardeau. Rick seemed stunned and ran to the driveway to confirm that the van was, indeed, missing. He said he had not even noticed its absence from its conspicuously unusual parking space in the driveway.

He later filed an insurance claim for the $23,000 van, which had been leased by the service station and was owned by a bank. Rick's personal losses, according to the claim, were his Sears video camera, a small television set, a VCR, a Nintendo game and four game cartridges, a CB radio, two stereos, ten cassette tapes, a radar detector, his leather jacket, a garage-door opener, and a set of jumper cables.

Within days, Rick replaced the white van with a dark
blue 1992 GMC Vandura.

Elizabeth told her sisters she was bothered by the suspicious van theft and the dubious insurance claim for items
she believed had been removed before it disappeared so
mysteriously. She even remembered how Rick had once
commented that he knew someone who would steal vehicles for owners looking to get out from under mechanical
or financial problems. Elizabeth knew Rick well enough to
offer a blunt assessment of how he handled such problems.
"When Rick gets tired of things, he gets rid of them," she
once told her sisters. That statement would haunt Melanie
and Mary the rest of their lives.

Elizabeth was more direct when she talked to Pam about
this latest escapade; she was sure Rick had arranged the
theft and burning of the van. Pam, who had worked for an
insurance company, gave her friend a serious warning: "If
you think he did that, you need to get out of that house
now. Go to your mom's, to Melanie's, to Mary's, anywhere.
This is illegal and it's wrong, and he's acting really bizarre."

Elizabeth had visited a counselor but did not like him
much. Rick had refused to go, then said he would, but it
had not happened yet. Pam recommended another counselor she knew and urged Elizabeth to keep trying. She
obviously needed help now, during what she called this
"hellish month." She offered Pam a heartbreaking description of her husband's conduct toward her: "It's like living
with ice." If she complained, his answer was, "This is the
new Rick. Get used to it." He often sat at the kitchen table,
poring over paperwork; Elizabeth wondered if he was doing
his planning, preparing to leave her. She told Pam that Rick
was building an emotional wall between them, brick by
brick. He had instructed her to change her habits—he absolutely did not want her making his breakfast or packing his
lunch or ironing his shirts. He was separating himself from
her emotionally, and it was driving her crazy.

"Leave him," Pam advised.

"I can't. He'll claim desertion and take the kids away
from me if I leave him. He told me I'd be sorry if I ever
tried to leave him."

*   *   *

By mid-February, Melanie and Mary decided they had to do something to help their sister; they began looking for someone to follow Rick. They even discussed it one afternoon with the reluctant Elizabeth, who stood at her stove, crying as she cooked her family's supper. Mary's heart broke again. This was all so hard for everyone. But Elizabeth was her little sister and she loved her. Someone had to help her. She wasn't emotionally able to do it herself. No matter how difficult it was, Melanie and Mary would do whatever was necessary for Elizabeth's sake. They couldn't afford a genuine private detective, so they suggested enlisting a police officer Elizabeth had met at the St. Ann bingo games. They had become friends, and surely he would come to her aid. But Elizabeth vetoed that idea; she didn't want him involved.

The sisters finally settled on a candidate for amateur PI— Mike Carroll, one of the workers they had come to know well while catering lunches for Georgianna's business at a large corporation's training center. He was a good friend and would be willing to help. He agreed and, one cold night in mid-February, he set out to tail the suspect. He followed Rick DeCaro from the service station to a parking lot, but was surprised when Rick stopped suddenly at a mailbox and just sat there. Mike couldn't risk calling attention to himself by sitting behind Rick in the middle of this huge lot, so he pulled around him and drove on. He circled the lot, but by the time he got back, Rick was gone. Mike saw no trace of his target after that. The first attempt to get the goods on Rick DeCaro had failed.

At work the next day, the three sisters decided to try again, and an opportunity presented itself sooner than they expected. That evening, Elizabeth called Melanie and suggested they pin a tail on Rick then. He had claimed he needed to run an errand after work, and Elizabeth suspected he was lying. Without much time to prepare, Melanie turned for help to her husband, John. After all, they were driving a rented car while theirs was in the shop, so Rick would be less likely to spot John. He reluctantly agreed to shadow his brother-in-law that night, mostly to prove to Melanie and Mary that they were nuts. Instead, John proved they had been right all along. He followed Rick back to Gold's parking lot and watched as Cathy Dillon pulled up in her red Chevy Camaro. Rick got into her car and they drove off, but John lost them. The sisters finally had evidence that the affair Rick had sworn was over was still in full bloom: parking-lot intrigue, secret assignations—the whole ugly nine yards.

Melanie called Elizabeth that night to file John's detective report and was shocked by her little sister's reaction. Elizabeth burst into nearly hysterical weeping. That was not what Melanie had expected from a wronged wife. "Why are you crying? I thought we hated him," she said. Elizabeth was too heartbroken to respond.

An extremely upset Elizabeth told Melanie the next morning that she had confronted Rick about his continuing affair, explaining only that her intelligence reports had come from a friend who had followed him. She never mentioned the involvement of her sisters. But Melanie wished Elizabeth had not told Rick at all; that ruined the plan to keep him under surveillance. Elizabeth said Rick had been astounded by the news that he had been tailed. How many times? he had asked. Only once, Elizabeth said.

That seemed to be enough to shock Rick into behaving. Informed that his sneaking around had not been sneaky enough, he immediately reverted to his former persona as the perfect husband. He stayed home all the time and resumed his endless repair work around the place. The sisters were convinced he actually was readying the house to be sold, especially after Elizabeth found a realtor's card in his coat pocket and Melanie realized that he was uncharacteristically using poor materials for the repairs. Something was up, the women were now sure, and fixing up the house on the cheap was probably part of the plan. Melanie thought it would be wise if Elizabeth left, but she wouldn't hear of it.

Melanie and Mary had a good chance to observe Rick closely on February 22, at a ninth birthday party for his and Elizabeth's daughter Rachel. Could cocaine be the reason for his weird behavior? Would they be able to detect it if he was using drugs? They watched him intently all evening. He was quiet and withdrawn, and the sisters even thought his eyes looked funny. But what did any of that really mean?

A week later, Elizabeth worked with her sisters and mother at an auction to benefit the apostolic works program for St. Elizabeth's Church, an event that raised twenty-five thousand dollars. Georgianna was surprised at how tiny Elizabeth seemed in her new clothes. She was dressing younger and sexier now, sporting a short skirt and a beautiful blouse. But her waist was so small, and she seemed even thinner than she had been before. Rick was sick, she explained, so he had stayed home. She actually seemed relieved.

The next Tuesday, March 3, Rick told Elizabeth he was ready for the "Daddy's weekend" he had proposed some time earlier. He now planned to take the four kids to the Ozarks on Friday for a weekend with just their dad. Elizabeth was disappointed. They were supposed to spend that weekend with Pam and Larry Hanley in Kansas City; two of the DeCaros' kids—Patrick and Rachel—had birthdays, and so did two of the Hanleys'. They had planned a weekend of partying with their dear friends. But Rick had made up his mind; he was taking the kids to the Ozarks, so the trip to Kansas City was off. Okay, Elizabeth said, she would go with him and the children. Rick said no, this was just for him and the kids. All right, she would go to Kansas City alone and enjoy some time with Pam anyway. Rick vetoed that idea too. He would be taking the new van on the trip, and the Blazer wasn't running well; it would never make the 250-mile trip without breaking down. Georgianna would have offered the use of her car, but it was in the repair shop. Elizabeth, it seemed, was to stay home alone, no matter what she really wanted to do. Melanie consoled her by planning a fun weekend for just the two of them— the first time they could spend days together without children and husbands and do all the shopping, lunching, ice cream eating, and everything else they loved. That seemed to lift Elizabeth's spirits.

Pam was surprised and disappointed when Elizabeth

called on Wednesday to cancel the planned visit. After all, Pam had just received Elizabeth's card on Saturday confirming the trip in her typical fashion. At the end of the card's "Twinkle, Twinkle, Little Star" verse—after "I wish I may, I wish I might, have the wish I wish tonight"—Elizabeth had written, "I wish you were here. Can't wait to see you. I love you. Liz." And, beyond that, Pam had talked to Rick on the phone on Sunday. In the awkward conversation with the man she no longer trusted, he had said that Elizabeth was gone. "She's never home anymore," he complained. When Pam then invited him to come to Kansas City with the rest of his family for the weekend, he had responded that he was too busy at work to get away.

So now, a devastated Elizabeth announced that the much-anticipated weekend in Kansas City was off. Pam was even more shocked when she learned that Rick had forbidden Elizabeth to go to the Ozarks with him and the kids. He had claimed, according to Elizabeth, that the kids only wanted her attention when she was around. For this weekend, he had said, he wanted them to himself. But, Elizabeth added, the kids really hadn't wanted to go with him; they wanted to go to Pam's. Elizabeth had to convince them they would have fun with their dad instead.

And Pam knew that being separated for the night was a rare event for the DeCaros. They had been apart overnight only a few times, and Pam remembered the first—when Rick went to Kansas City for some computer training a few years ago. Before Rick had left then, Elizabeth had asked Pam if she ever worried about Larry's faithfulness when he traveled. "Not a second," Pam had responded; if that kind of thing happened, it meant there was a serious problem in the marriage. Elizabeth wasn't sure she could be that confident. While Rick was gone, however, he had called every afternoon and evening, fitting into the pattern Pam had always thought was so excessive. Even that brief separation had been a really big deal for the DeCaros.

"So, why don't you come here alone?" Pam asked Elizabeth now. "We'll still have a great time."

"Don't you think Rick has already thought of that?" Elizabeth responded. She explained his warning about the

mechanically unreliable Blazer, drawing another response
of disbelief from Pam.

"But he drives it to work every day, and that's got to be
a fifty-mile round trip!"

Elizabeth's response was another surprise. "Pam, you
sound as suspicious as I am."

The conversation ended with Elizabeth explaining her
plans with her mother and sisters, and adding her assurance
that she would be all right. They bid each other a disappointed good-bye. Pam never dreamed it would be their
last conversation.

On Wednesday, March 4, Melanie went to Rick's service
station to pick up her car after it had been repaired. It
seemed that all of the Van Iseghem vehicles were in need
of repairs at the same time. Melanie noticed that Rick was
gone when she arrived, and so was Cathy Dillon. They were
both missing in action, at the same time? Damn that cheating Rick, Melanie thought.

But she was also struck by someone else's conduct that
day. Craig Wells, one of Rick's employees who had worked
for Georgianna and Jim, was unusually and disturbingly
attentive to Melanie. He had always seemed to like her,
but on this day his demeanor was so disconcerting that
Melanie just wanted to get away from him as soon as possible. He even walked her to her car, chatting and asking
how her parents were doing. Melanie decided he really
seemed more nervous than friendly—as if he wanted to tell
her something but just couldn't get it out. His behavior was
strange but didn't seem suspicious—yet.

Wednesday afternoon, Rick surprised Georgianna with a
phone call. In sincere tones, he explained that he really
wanted to make this marriage work, but Elizabeth didn't
believe or trust him anymore. He was staying home all the
time and cleaning the house, but Elizabeth was always
gone. Would Georgianna talk to her for him and tell her
how much he really loved her?

"Of course, I will, Rick. I'll do anything I can to help.
But you really shouldn't be taking the kids to the Ozarks

this weekend. You should be taking Elizabeth. That would be better for your marriage."

"Well, I can't break my promise to the kids now," he responded.

Georgianna delivered Rick's message of love and devotion to his wife at a special meeting that night at the Van Iseghems' favorite spot for ice cream, Victoria's in St. Charles.

"Darling, pray about it. God will help you. Ask Him for the painful memories to be healed and for your marriage to be saved. He'll answer your prayers."

Elizabeth met her mother's advice with deep, wracking sobs and another surprising assessment of the DeCaro marriage. Through her tears, Elizabeth looked into her mother's eyes and said, "Mom, I can't stand to look at him anymore."

She explained that she and Rick couldn't even talk face-to-face now. She had resorted to writing him letters about their problems, and he sometimes would call her on the phone at work to talk about them. But he would never face her. "I can't do it that way, Mom. I want to talk to him face-to-face."

"I understand that, honey. But you can work this out. You just have to keep trying."

When Elizabeth learned from Melanie Thursday morning that Rick and Cathy had been gone from the station at the same time on Wednesday, she was furious. In front of Melanie, a raving Elizabeth called Rick at work and accused him of being with Cathy the previous afternoon. His protestations of innocence made no difference as she mercilessly shredded him for his continuing infidelity. Melanie was shocked at her sister's uncharacteristically venomous attack. Elizabeth was losing it, Melanie decided; Rick had finally driven her little sister crazy.

And later, Melanie learned that the information she had provided—the word about Rick and Cathy that had fueled Elizabeth's rage—had been in error. Mary also had been to Rick's service station while he was gone, but she had seen Cathy there. That meant Elizabeth had to call Rick back and apologize for her manic outburst. Maybe, Elizabeth said to Melanie, she should start trusting him again.

NINE

On the day that Rick DeCaro was to leave for the Ozarks with the children after their half day of school, Elizabeth arrived at work nervous and upset. "Something is going to happen to me," she told Melanie in a frightening echo of the portent that had descended on Georgianna weeks before. Rick had been completely withdrawn Thursday night, Elizabeth said, and had left for work at the crack of dawn without even telling her good-bye, let alone giving her a kiss. He simply rolled out of their bed and disappeared. She was furious. Sometime before noon, she called a neighbor and confirmed that Rick had driven the kids' car pool, dropped off their classmates at their homes, stopped by the house so the kids could change clothes, and then departed for their special weekend in the Ozarks.

Elizabeth called Rick twice on the phone in his van, but Melanie heard only the first conversation, when Elizabeth told Rick how angry she was at the way he had left. But after the second call, an even more worried Elizabeth told Melanie that Rick's voice had sounded nervous, a special sound she had noticed on the day when the van had been stolen and the day when Rick had smashed her into the garage wall. That worried her now—the first day she would be alone in their house.

"He's up to something," Elizabeth said. "I'm scared. I'm afraid to go home."

She startled Melanie with a more detailed account of what Rick had said after he learned he had been followed in February. He wanted to know how long that had been going on because, he explained, he had been involved in a drug deal. Elizabeth's nearly matter-of-fact delivery shocked Melanie as much as the news. It was almost as if

Elizabeth knew there had been other drug deals before. The sisters even wondered aloud if Rick could be taking the kids on this unprecedented, uncharacteristic trip to the Ozarks to use them as a cover for a drug deal down there.

The bizarre day at work ended after the sisters shared lunch and drank the beers Mary had packed for them as a joke to kick off their special weekend. They agreed to meet some friends from work for margaritas at Casa Gallardo at five and then got into their cars to leave for the day. At precisely 2:20 P.M. Elizabeth gave Melanie her trademark little wave from her car, and they went their separate ways.

Melanie could not know she would never see Elizabeth alive again.

Melanie arrived late at the restaurant. She had been held up by the most frustrating traffic she had ever encountered, even on the routinely insane roads of St. Louis County. She had tried several routes—St. Charles Rock Road, Interstate 270—but they were all backed up unlike anything she had ever seen. Just crazy, she thought. She didn't arrive until after six o'clock.

When her sister still hadn't joined them by sometime after seven, Melanie and Mike Carroll began their search by phone and car. Melanie even wondered if Elizabeth had headed for the Ozarks after hearing that Rick's drug deal had blown up in his face and he had been busted. Almost anything seemed possible at this point—*almost* anything.

Elizabeth's misgivings about that day were horribly and fatally justified, as Melanie would learn about eight o'clock in the kitchen at 12 Hidden Meadow Court. She and Mary had known that something ominous was in the offing, but they never dreamed it would be a violent end to their baby sister's life.

Standing in the kitchen over Elizabeth's body, Melanie told Mike Carroll, "The son of a bitch did it. He really did it."

And standing in the rain in the driveway later, Melanie told Lieutenant Patrick McCarrick that she had no doubt about the identity of Elizabeth's killer.

It was Rick DeCaro.

PART TWO

PART TWO

TEN

The first reports from the canvass of the DeCaros' lovely neighborhood amazed Lieutenant Patrick McCarrick. These sweeps sometimes yielded useful bits of information—strange cars cruising the street, shady characters hurrying through a yard, unusual noises. But what struck McCarrick this time was how widely known the DeCaros were throughout the Woodfield Meadows subdivision. People several streets away knew this family well, even the names of the kids. Many of these neighbors were Catholics from the same parish as the DeCaros; they went to church together, their kids went to school together, they played on the same ball teams, they took turns driving the car pools.

Some of the neighbors had seen Rick DeCaro driving the car pool that morning and then loading kids and gear into the van. Others had noticed the two bottles of milk sitting undisturbed on the DeCaros' front porch after Rick and the children left; the deliveries usually were made around three o'clock on that street.

A neighbor two doors away—who knew about the theft of Rick's van in February—thought it rather odd that Rick would leave town this weekend; after all, he was a coach for the school's sixth-grade basketball team, and games were scheduled on Saturdays and Sundays. The neighbor's wife offered an observation about what she thought was Rick's bad temper: she often heard him yelling at the children and the dog.

That couple's ten-year-old daughter contributed to efforts to establish timing for the crime. She had been playing basketball in front of the DeCaro house about five-forty-five that afternoon and had noticed that the side door into the garage was open, providing a view all the way into the lighted kitchen. And the Blazer was missing from the garage.

Another neighbor behind the DeCaro house had noticed that the blinds on the patio doors had been drawn that afternoon. That was an important point; those blinds were never drawn, she said.

Despite all of these minutiae about the DeCaro home, what impressed McCarrick the most from these interviews was that so many of the neighbors had offered the same observation about what was going on inside that house: they knew something was amiss in the DeCaro marriage.

One very close neighbor who attended church with the DeCaros said there had been rumors about marital problems and reports that Elizabeth was actually the one having an affair, with someone from their parish. The appearance of a slimmer Elizabeth—unescorted—at the Leap Year dance at the church on February 29 had fueled those gossipy speculations; Rick had always been with her at such events in the past, and his absence this time was remarkable.

Debbie and Jerry Brennan lived near the DeCaros and were among their best friends in the subdivision. They visited often, went out to eat together, even vacationed together. And the Brennans knew a lot about the discord in their friends' marriage. In fact, they were the ones who had driven Elizabeth home after Rick abandoned her at the church on New Year's Eve. They were aware that Rick's boat had aggravated the financial conflict between him and Elizabeth and that he had opposed her plan to get her G.E.D. to make up for dropping out of high school to have his son. This couple was surprised to hear that Rick had told Elizabeth the Blazer was mechanically untrustworthy; they thought he had recently put a new engine in it and were sure he was as meticulous about maintaining it as he was about all of his other vehicles.

They also described an uncomfortable birthday party for one of the DeCaro children on February 15, when the tension between Elizabeth and Rick was palpable. They weren't even speaking to each other. In fact, Rick eventually lay down on the sofa and went to sleep, completely ignoring their guests. That was out of character for him. Debbie added a tidbit about the accident with the van too:

Elizabeth had told her that Rick had "revved up" the engine before the vehicle lurched toward her. But she said Rick had been terribly remorseful about the incident, repeating over and over in anguish, "I could have killed you!"

All of those reports from the neighborhood would have made husband Richard DeCaro someone to look at closely. But Melanie Enkelmann had given McCarrick a much more direct, solid reason to wonder about Rick. When McCarrick had first asked her the whereabouts of her sister's family, Melanie had explained that Rick and the four children were in the Ozarks for this first-time weekend away from Elizabeth. Rick had intentionally—insistently—kept her home alone.

"Have there been any problems between your sister and her husband?" McCarrick asked.

Melanie eyes flashed. "That son of a bitch tried to run over her with the van a few weeks ago. He smashed her right through the wall."

That was plain enough. It didn't require McCarrick's vast experience and superior instincts as a detective to recognize that as a clue. "Anything else?"

"Yes, Elizabeth's Blazer is missing from the garage, and about two months ago, Rick's van was stolen from the driveway."

Two vehicles stolen from the same house within weeks, and the second theft is accompanied by a murder. More startling leads, as subtle as a tornado.

Her eyes still wet with tears, Melanie drilled McCarrick with an intense stare and told him bluntly, "I know Rick DeCaro did this. He may not have pulled the trigger, but he did this. He's been planning it for months. That son of a bitch killed my sister. I know it."

That kind of direct, angry allegation was rare, and it certainly put Rick DeCaro at the top of the list of people to investigate. But for this wary cop, it did not make Rick a full-fledged suspect. It was too soon for that tag. Every marriage has problems—sometimes even as severe as those Melanie had described—but they rarely end in murder.

No, McCarrick had been through this before and he'd

heard all of this, in one form or another. He never ceased
to be amazed at the deeply personal things that people
would tell a cop in the heat of a murder investigation. They
would never offer such intimate details otherwise, not even
over too many drinks. But when there had been a murder,
people assumed everything would come out under a cop's
investigative microscope. So they held nothing back.

Despite Melanie's allegations—"vehement" was the
word McCarrick would use to describe them in his report—
there were good reasons not to call Rick DeCaro a suspect
yet. For one thing, if Melanie's information was correct, he
was with his children in a resort area more than a hundred
miles away. That meant that, if he was involved in his wife's
murder and the alibi in the Ozarks held up, the guy had to
have arranged it somehow. He probably had been careful
to put layers of insulation between him and the murder,
and between him and the person who actually did the deed.
Could the cops sort through all of that? Was this a professional hit? That could be tough—perhaps impossible—to
prove. McCarrick wasn't ready to put the mark of "suspect" on Rick DeCaro yet—but even at the Lake of the
Ozarks, this absent husband was close enough to the brand-
ing iron to feel the heat.

By the time Chief David King had arrived at 12 Hidden
Meadow Court, McCarrick had already told Detective
Mike Miller and Sergeant Mike Powell to prepare for a
trip to the Ozarks. One of the neighbors said they believed
Rick had mentioned staying at the Inn at Grand Glaize, a
motel just above the Grand Glaize Bridge in Osage Beach.
Miller and Powell would start their search in that busy re-
sort town.

ELEVEN

The Van Iseghems were scattered across the area that night, happily involved with their various interests and hobbies. But the drumbeat of disaster, pounded out by Melanie from the horrifying scene of Elizabeth's murder, spread quickly. While paramedics continued CPR on Elizabeth and then rushed her to the hospital, a frantic Melanie rifled hurriedly through her mental Rolodex of family phone numbers and then made hurried calls. She decided that lacking the final word on Elizabeth's condition that Melanie's heart warned her was inevitable, she would tell the family only that Elizabeth had been hurt. It was better that they should await the final word that Melanie feared so much at the hospital in the way they did everything else—together.

Her first contact was with her brother Randy, at their parents' home, where he was staying. The tearful Melanie told him that Elizabeth had been hurt, but then couldn't keep from giving voice to her fear that their sister was dead. Randy couldn't believe that; surely Melanie was overreacting.

"Mel, she's probably just passed out or something. Maybe she's knocked out."

"No, Randy, I think she's dead," she sobbed.

"Mel, I'm sure she isn't."

Randy knew where their parents were and promised to track down all the family so they could meet at Barnes Hospital in St. Peters, the town just west of St. Charles on Interstate 70. Randy then made a call to Maureen, but the urgency and trauma of the moment left her unsure what had happened; she somehow believed that Randy had said Elizabeth had been stabbed. Maureen would, in fact, not learn her sister-in-law's fate until the next morning.

Jim and Georgianna were attending a political fund-raiser at the St. Ann Community Center when the public address system announced a call for them shortly after eight o'clock. Georgiana was not particularly alarmed; one of the kids was always tracking them down for some reason or another. But this time, she heard Randy's nervous voice telling her that something had happened to Elizabeth, that she had been hurt. Georgianna's heart leapt into her throat and, as she began to shake violently, she relived the premonition that had invaded her sleep six weeks before. She immediately called Elizabeth's house; Melanie answered but would say only that Elizabeth was hurt and that they should all meet at the hospital.

Some friends offered to drive, realizing the Van Iseghems were in no emotional condition to be behind the wheel in what was now a full-fledged thunderstorm. But in the confusion they went to St. Joseph's Hospital in St. Charles. After realizing that they had missed the mark, they began a hurried trip to Barnes as Georgianna prayed without stopping, "Lord, please let her be okay. Please, Lord, please." But deep in her heart Georgianna knew the warning she had received on that night weeks ago had come to pass.

Mary and Phil Cordes were enjoying themselves at a show of recreational vehicles at the convention center in downtown St. Louis when they were paged. Mary feared first that her father's uncertain health had taken a terrible turn; perhaps he was already gone, she worried. Phil took the call and then, with deep shock in his eyes, told Mary, "It's Elizabeth. She's been shot. They're taking her to the hospital." Only after they were in the car did Phil break the news that Melanie had not been able to hide from him: "Mary, she's dead."

Mary was not surprised; something in her heart had already told her that truth. But her reaction to the unimaginable was immediate and certain. "The son of a bitch did it. He really did it." Her mind kept repeating that over and over as they drove through the rain toward a moment Mary feared as she had never feared anything else.

Theresa, the youngest of the Van Iseghem children, had played on her school's eighth-grade basketball team that night and was surprised to return home to find her parents' car missing and several family friends awaiting her. Like Mary, thirteen-year-old Theresa thought first of her father. As her parents' friends hurried her toward the hospital some fifteen minutes west on Interstate 70, she had to drag the news that Elizabeth had been hurt out of them.

Jimmy Van Iseghem had just returned from a shift at the concession stand during one of his kids' basketball games when Melanie called. She couldn't hold back the full, unvarnished truth from her big brother. "Elizabeth's been shot, Jimmy. She's dead."

All during the panicked drive to the hospital, he prayed, "It can't be true. God, don't let it be true." Through the shock, he managed to cling to a flicker of hope; there could have been some mistake at the scene, or some medical miracle at the hospital. Maybe, just maybe, his little sister—that special, precious little girl he remembered so lovingly—was still alive.

At Barnes Hospital, the first family members to arrive were ushered into a private room by an ER doctor. As Melanie, Randy, Georgianna, and Jim held their breath, the doctor delivered the news that no one wanted to hear: "I'm sorry. She didn't make it. She's dead."

Georgianna Van Iseghem's world crashed around her in a way she had never known was possible. "Oh, God, no, no," she screamed as she collapsed to the floor. Jim could not believe that his little "Betsy" was gone. Randy—so sure that Elizabeth would be okay that he had hardly even hurried his drive to the hospital—erupted in anger and smashed his fist through a wall.

Melanie had tried to believe that she might hear something else, but a voice deep inside had warned her to be prepared. Still, the words rocked her, tearing a hole in her heart that she knew even then would never heal.

Over the next minutes, the other units of the Van Iseghem family arrived one by one. The family's priest joined them, and even some of their old friends and neighbors showed up. As each anxious, frightened group burst through the doors and found Melanie waiting at the end of the long, long hallway with the devastating news, a new course of sobbing and hugging erupted. Wives and husbands melted into each other's arms, and the tears flowed unchecked. For Melanie, everything seemed to be moving in agonizing slow motion. She hated grieving in front of the strangers sitting there, but there was no way to stop each new wave of tears.

Little Theresa was among the last to arrive and was greeted by Mary. "It's Elizabeth."

Theresa could feel the knot in her throat as she looked into her sister's red, wet eyes. "Is she dead?"

"She didn't make it."

Theresa fainted into Mary's arms.

Some eighteen hundred miles west in California, Margie Ugalde was attending a school play with her daughter, Jamie, and Jamie's boyfriend. Margie's husband, Sergio, was out of town. Her pager went off, and a call home was answered by her stepdaughter with a message that an upset Melanie had called but left no specific message. Margie got a busy signal on Melanie's home phone, and no one answered at their parents', Mary's, or Jimmy's. Margie even called her father's store, but a clerk had no information. She finally asked an operator to make an emergency interruption on Melanie's line, but her eleven-year-old son, Michael, didn't know what was happening either. Margie called the store again, and now the clerk had learned that something had happened to Elizabeth. For some reason, Margie's mind decided that her sister must have been beaten and raped; that seemed to be the most likely injury to befall a woman in today's world, and that must have been what had happened to Elizabeth.

Margie returned to her seat, but was so worried she decided to go home and continue her long-distance efforts. There, a message from Phil Cordes was waiting. Margie called, learned she had reached the emergency room at Barnes Hospital, and was passed through a number of extensions until she reached a doctor who delivered the news: "Elizabeth was the victim of a gunshot wound. She died."

As her sisters in Missouri already had, Margie screamed immediately, "My God! That son of a bitch! He did it!"

Accompanied now by some friends, Margie decided to catch the midnight flight out of Long Beach. She hurried to the airport, only to learn the plane was full. The group of mourners spent a long, grief-stricken night in the airport awaiting the next flight out, at seven-thirty in the morning.

Some 230 miles west, in the Kansas City suburb of Overland Park, Pam Hanley was zoned out in front of the television, but still planning to call her pal Elizabeth later when she surely would have arrived home from whatever fun event Melanie had planned. A phone call from an old neighbor from St. Charles shattered the evening's calm, and the rest of Pam's life. Something must have happened to Elizabeth, the neighbor reported, because the cul-de-sac was filled with ambulances and emergency crews and police cars and curious onlookers. Pam tried to assume the best; Liz was hurt, but she would be okay. By phone instead of by car, Pam traveled the same mistaken route Georgianna and Jim had taken, calling St. Joseph's Hospital first. Somehow, a nurse there knew that Elizabeth had been taken to Barnes. The operator there connected Pam to the emergency room, and she talked to yet another former neighbor and friend, Jackie Balunek.

"Jackie, is Liz okay?"

"Pam, get Larry there with you."

"No, Jackie, tell me now. Is Liz okay?"

"Pam, she's dead. She's been shot. She's gone."

Pam dropped the telephone and dissolved in unrestrained grief. But even through that, she knew Rick had done it.

As Elizabeth's family wept and held each other in the little room at the hospital, some of them were beginning a painful process of blaming themselves. Melanie and Mary wondered why their suspicions hadn't led them to this obvious, horrifying conclusion. Why hadn't they seen this coming? How could they have been so blind? What else could Rick have been planning? It had been right there in front of them!

Jim Van Iseghem asked himself why he hadn't hired a

private detective, as Melanie had proposed. Why hadn't he taken her fears seriously? And why hadn't Elizabeth come to him and her mother with the truth about her crumbling marriage? Georgianna was asking herself why she hadn't done more to protect her daughter. How could she have let this happen to her darling Elizabeth?

When the news came on the television in the corner of the hospital waiting room, Jim Van Iseghem heard a reference to the murder of an unidentified woman in St. Charles and the cops' urgent request for help from the public as they searched for a missing Chevy Blazer. Oh, my God, Jim found himself thinking, they're talking about my daughter. Elizabeth is that murdered woman who has already become just another anonymous crime victim getting her two minutes of posthumous fame on the ten o'clock news.

Across the little room, Jimmy Van Iseghem struggled to hold his emotions in check. He would not cry in front of everyone—not here, not now; that would wait for private moments later. But he kept wondering about Rick. Where were he and the kids? Someone explained that they were out of town on this so-called Daddy's weekend. That didn't sound suspicious to Jimmy, who knew little of the recent dark events in Elizabeth's life. He began asking repeatedly why someone hadn't called Rick to break the horrible news; that was not like the members of this close family. Finally, sitting down next to Melanie, he heard her repeating over and over, "The son of a bitch did it. The son of a bitch did it."

"What are you talking about?" the perplexed big brother asked. And, for the first time, his sisters started to tell him about their suspicions and the series of menacing incidents behind them.

"You're crazy" was his first response. But the accusations from the sisters who were closest to Elizabeth began to grow from molehills to mountains, and his heart began to sink. He didn't want any of the events on this night to be true, but something in his heart told him life could be no truer than this. God, why hadn't he been close enough to her to know about all of this? Had his role as the wiser older brother—the substitute father useful for financial advice and employment counseling—gotten in the way? He had last seen Elizabeth the Sunday before, when he stopped by her house to pick up some of the equipment for the girls' basketball team he coached; Rick, the athletic coordinator, kept the supplies. Jimmy had been struck by how thin Liz was. He even went to her and put his arms around her. "Are you okay?" he had asked. She flashed him that familiar and reassuring smile. "Oh, yeah, I'm fine." Why hadn't she told him then, when he could have done something? Now, it was too late. And as he sat in this room not far from her lifeless body, the allegations about life in the DeCaro house began to pile up around him.

And none of it sounded like the Rick DeCaro he knew.

TWELVE

Tom O'Connor and Dave King connected with each other immediately, from the moment they were introduced at the Major Case Squad's command center on that Friday night. The new chief was still shocked by this murder, and it was comforting for him to meet this commander who seemed so at ease as he took charge of the steadily increasing number of detectives assembling in the station. O'Connor's demeanor and strong presence instilled a new confidence in King that this case would be handled well, and for the first time since he had arrived at 12 Hidden Meadow Court, he didn't feel alone.

King watched the growing activity in the squad room as the detectives greeted each other, exchanged information, and peppered their conversation with the sardonic cop humor that King enjoyed. The hubbub and chatter melded into a scene that struck him as a combination of *Hill Street Blues* and *Barney Miller*. Each cop in this unusual cast—this unique blend of personalities—brought a different perspective and varied experience. He was amazed that they had all dropped what they were doing on this rainy Friday evening to trek to St. Charles to help him solve his new case in his new town. He was damned glad they were there. It was fascinating to watch them jell into what was destined to be an effective organization of professional officers, all working toward one simple goal—finding the killer of Elizabeth DeCaro.

Lieutenant Pat McCarrick was even happier than his chief to see O'Connor show up. McCarrick had worked eight or ten Major Case Squad homicides, some of them under Commander O'Connor. McCarrick had learned that 75 percent of the squad's effectiveness came from the leader, and he knew O'Connor was as good as they got.

As soon as everyone had assembled—about midnight—McCarrick delivered the first of many twice-a-day briefings. He described the young, attractive housewife with four kids and a lovely house, and what the killer had left behind. He explained Melanie's allegations about the vacationing husband. He ran through the evidence that could suggest a burglary. Everyone agreed by now, however, that the scene had been staged to offer a false motive and a wrong direction. There was no evidence of forced entry or a struggle. A television, VCRs, and stereos were missing, leaving only outlines in the dust on the shelves. But knickknacks and beer steins next to the electronics were undisturbed. Burglars aren't that careful; they flash in and out and they don't take the time for discriminating selection of loot. They knock the little things out of their way and grab what they want, fast. A thief this careful knew that he had all the time he needed. A few drawers had been pulled out in a lame attempt to give the scene the look of the proverbial ransacking. But none of it felt right.

Then the videotape of the crime scene was played. Dave King watched the detectives' faces as they concentrated on the video, and he was struck by the eerie silence in the room. These eighteen cops were focusing only on what flickered across the TV screen, and not one said a word to distract his partners. The scene took on a surreal feel. When the tape ended, Tom O'Connor stepped to the front of the room and took charge. "Okay. We've got our work cut out for us, and here's how we're going to get started."

In a flurry of activity, he began handing out assignments to two-person teams. King watched in awe as a new stage of the investigation began—from eerie silence to organized pandemonium in an instant. What an operation, he marveled. All the Major Case Squad asked from its host department was gasoline and food, and in return it handled the rest. Just damned amazing.

O'Connor set immediate goals and targets. The first was already under way; two detectives were looking for Rick DeCaro in Osage Beach. The commander dispatched most of the crews to learn everything they could about the two focal points in this case—the dead wife and the absent husband. He put about half of his detectives on Elizabeth DeCaro's trail. Good detectives knew that the key to a murder was usually in the life of the victim and those closest to that person. Look at the in-laws before you look for outlaws, the old saying went. The victim's last forty-eight hours often could lead directly to the killer. How was her marriage? Other family problems? Any serious enemies or odd incidents lately? Who saw her last? What about her job? Drugs? Affairs?

What was already known made Rick DeCaro a real VIP in this drama. O'Connor knew about the changes and problems in the marriage, about the talk of divorce, about the van incident in the garage, about the theft of the van later. Those chapters of this story had to be examined for more clues, and the cops had to know everything about Rick and his life away from Elizabeth. The same questions they would ask about her had to be asked about him. O'Connor assigned three or four teams to Rick.

Next, O'Connor wanted an all-out blitz to locate the missing Blazer. Find the Blazer, find the killer. He sent a detective in search of a photo of an identical Blazer to distribute to the TV stations and newspapers. He already had broadcast a plea for anyone who had seen the Blazer with the RIK-LIZ license plates to call in.

He put three more crews on the February theft of the

van; that could lead to the killer. He wanted to build an insurance-fraud case separate from the murder investigation. Since the van had been torched, part of the investigation would involve an arson case—right up O'Connor's alley from his days on the Homicide and Arson Squad for St. Louis city. Proving murder often was very difficult. Proving arson or insurance fraud might be easier. Mistakes avoided in a murder might be made in another crime.

O'Connor wanted no stone unturned. He was now the avenging angel for Elizabeth DeCaro.

THIRTEEN

The detective teams went to work, and shortly after midnight the grief-stricken Van Iseghems began arriving at the St. Charles Police Station for the first round of interviews. The hungry media pack in front of the station forced the police to slip the family members through the back door. Chief King and Commander O'Connor met with the family briefly and impressed the grieving relatives with their sincerity and professionalism. Rest assured, these officers promised, that the Major Case Squad would do everything possible to find the killer and deliver justice for Elizabeth.

The detectives assigned to the interviews kept them as brief as possible for these hurting survivors, looking only for something bombastic that would point them toward the killer. From Melanie, Mary, and Georgianna, the police drew brief accounts of the growing tension in the DeCaro marriage that had led up to Rick's silent departure that morning. They described the odd occurrences, from Rick's crashing the van into Elizabeth to the women's clumsy attempts to shadow him. The sisters offered their direct and unrestrained accusations that Rick was responsible for Elizabeth's murder.

Melanie laid out in some detail for the police how Elizabeth had described Rick as being paranoid since he learned she had arranged for him to be followed. He had been setting up a drug deal, he claimed, and was afraid Elizabeth's amateur detectives might have accidentally seen him making a contact. Pretty curious stuff for this man at this point in his life, the cops thought.

Mary described the DeCaros as "mortgaged to the hilt" and said she knew they had recently been rejected for a home refinancing loan. She called Rick "a creature of habit" and said the trip to the Ozarks with the kids was "just not right." She had heard that Rick's aberrant behavior was so noticeable that his boss and brother, Dan DeCaro, had made an appointment for a counselor to see Rick, but he had refused to go.

Georgianna explained that Elizabeth had been insisting for the last two weeks that Rick had to fire Cathy Dillon. If they were going to save their marriage, he couldn't be working with the former lover who had threatened it. And Georgianna added that in their last-ever conversation the night before, Elizabeth had told her mother she had decided to confront Cathy face-to-face and to tell her in no uncertain terms to stay away from Elizabeth's husband. Georgianna had offered to go along for moral support, but no date for the showdown had been set.

The men in the family had little substantive to add, mostly just what they had heard from their wives. Jim Van Iseghem knew the DeCaros were having financial and marital problems, and he had heard they had three mortgages. He could only speculate that drugs were the cause of Rick's transformation from the "good, hardworking son-in-law" Jim had known into this stranger.

Mary's husband, Phil Cordes, thought Elizabeth had seemed a little more at ease, not so strained, when he had seen her the previous Saturday night. He knew little about the DeCaros' problems firsthand but was aware enough to describe Rick indelicately as "up to his ass" in debt.

By far the most intriguing interview came from Michael Carroll—the slim, brown-haired, thirty-one-year-old corporate training planner who had once followed Rick DeCaro and who had chauffeured Melanie on the ill-fated search for Elizabeth. Mike had begun suffering from the worst headache of his life that night as he waited so long to be interviewed. Sitting down finally with the police at 12:40 A.M., he recounted how he had heard Melanie's anguished shriek and how he had tried to grab a weapon before he charged in and found Elizabeth lying there, her face almost purple.

Mike had met Elizabeth—"Liz" to him—about three months earlier, when she helped her mother cater lunches at the corporate training center. They had become very good friends. He had recently gone through a painful divorce and had become something of an adviser to Liz; she had told him the whole sad story of her deteriorating marriage. He had never met Rick, although he had followed him that one night. Liz had told him that Rick had threatened her, although she never suggested physical abuse. She complained that he was distancing himself from her emotionally and physically. Mike knew about the new insurance policy, the van crash in the garage, and the big argument after Liz announced that it would cost Rick two thousand dollars a month for her to leave. Liz had repeated Rick's bizarre yarn about setting up a ten-thousand-dollar drug deal, and she had added that the story had made her afraid of him for the first time in their lives together. She had never known him to use or be involved in drugs, and this story was one more peculiar twist to Rick's new personality.

Liz obviously was upset by the trip-to-the-Ozarks scenario. She couldn't figure out why it was so important that he take the kids that weekend, when they had planned the trip to Pam Hanley's for weeks. Liz knew something was up; this was the first time Rick and the kids had left her alone in eleven years. And then Mike Carroll's emotions came to the fore, and he ended the interview by telling the police he was absolutely certain that Rick DeCaro was involved in Liz's death.

Mike had put his hand on the doorknob to leave when one of the detectives called to him.

"You know, I don't think you had anything to do with this. I don't think you're involved in Liz's death. But I've been doing this for twenty years, and I know you're holding back. You're not telling us something. You want to tell us what it is?"

Mike Carroll sat back down and shocked the officers by explaining that a weeping Liz had arrived at his house at 8:20 that morning. She had been upset by Rick's departure—no kiss, no good-bye. She stopped by Mike's to talk about it over some tea. She was scared and knew that something was wrong, that something was going to happen; she just didn't know what. She feared for her life, a worry that had increased since the crash in the garage. She often remarked how odd it was that Rick went into the house without even checking on her as she lay crunched between the wall and the van. Mike and Liz had talked for a while that morning, and he had seen her again at lunch. She seemed much happier and more relaxed then, and they made plans to meet the others for drinks that evening.

And then Mike Carroll really stunned the cops. He and Liz, he now confessed, had engaged in a brief sexual fling the month before. They had made love three times at his house after being out together for the evening. She had stayed at his place until two in the morning at least twice. Their last rendezvous had been about two or three weeks earlier, when they mutually agreed to end their romance and just remain friends.

"We put a stop to it," Mike explained. "It just wasn't right. I didn't want to be the third party in a divorce. She said she still loved Rick and wanted to try to save their marriage. So we just decided to stay friends."

Mike said Liz had told Melanie about it, but he didn't think many other people knew—especially Rick.

When Mike left the police station, he realized he was terrified. Was he a target for revenge by Rick DeCaro? Had Rick learned of Mike's fling with Liz? Mike drove to a friend's apartment and spent the night there, mostly thinking about Liz. She had been such an attractive, bright, cheerful, wonderful woman. She was so easy to talk to, to like. They had developed a warm friendship as they shared their common unhappy marital experiences. She was so kind, so sensitive, so caring. This sad, lonely woman deserved so much more from life than she was getting from Rick DeCaro—especially what had happened this day.

Mike had always been attracted to Liz and, one night after drinks, the sex had just happened by default; she got none of the affection she needed from her husband, and Mike was able to give it to her. He was not proud of himself for making love to a married woman, and the irony in being unfaithful to an unfaithful husband had been difficult for Liz, too.

Mike had worried during the interview with police, especially when one of the officers seemed to imply that Mike could be a suspect. He realized then that he really couldn't account for all of his time that day. He had been off work and had run a lot of errands. How could he prove where he was when Liz was killed? In the middle of Mike's awful night, the police called and asked if he would submit to a chemical test to see if there was gunshot residue on his hands. He readily agreed, since he hadn't fired a weapon in a long time. He met the police at 3:45 A.M. in the parking lot at his friend's apartment complex so they could collect the samples from his hands. He knew the police still harbored suspicions—they asked him to take a lie detector test Sunday afternoon. He agreed again; he had no reason to lie, even if the police wondered if he were a spurned lover with a motive to murder.

Faced with getting through the rest of this horrible night, most of the Van Iseghems and their friends headed back to Jim and Georgianna's. About twenty of them—family, friends, their priest—sat up all night, paging through photo albums in a desperate attempt to find a connection to Elizabeth, to relive the happier moments when she blessed them all with her special light. As they slowly turned the pages, they shared stories about how wonderful she had been, slipping often into tears as they realized anew that she was gone. Much of the time was spent fretting about how her children would get along without the mother who was so loving and good to them. How could four-year-old Erin possibly understand what had happened, that her mommy was gone forever? How could the others go on without the special presence that had shone so brightly for them?

Melanie Enkelmann had not been able to go to her parents' that morning to join the others. She had to go home, to grieve with her husband, John, in her own private way. But first she had to feel safe. Had Rick marked her for murder too? Did she know too much about the DeCaros' problems? Would he target her next, to rid himself of another problematic Van Iseghem woman? She called the police in Chesterfield and asked them to meet her at her house. The officers were gracious and understanding as she explained her fears and asked them to search her home. They obliged, checking each room.

She spent the next several hours thinking of her little sister and the events of the past few months. How could she go on without Elizabeth? How could she rest until the killer was found and justice assured? As the realization that Elizabeth was dead and gone forever stung Melanie, she vowed that Rick DeCaro would pay for what he had done.

Amazingly, Melanie eventually drifted into sleep, and she did not dream about the living nightmare that had just taken over her life.

The Major Case Squad had no time—and no desire—for rest on this first night of the Elizabeth DeCaro murder case.

After the Van Iseghem family had been interviewed, Lieutenant Pat McCarrick wrote an affidavit explaining to a judge why a search warrant was needed to collect evidence at the DeCaro residence. Although the police had been called to the house to respond to an emergency—and that was one of the general categories of searches allowed by the law—everyone wanted the procedures in this case to be letter-perfect. Getting a search warrant was always a good idea, but it was especially prudent in a case in which the other spouse might become a suspect and could claim a privacy right. The last thing the squad wanted was good evidence made useless by a bad search. So McCarrick wrote that there had been a murder and the house appeared to have been ransacked, indicating a burglary. In addition, a 1985 Chevy Blazer was missing from the garage.

Another indication of the seriousness of this crime to this community was that a judge took the unusual step of going to the police station to sign the search warrant at 3:20 A.M. on a Saturday.

Some 230 miles to the west, Pam Hanley was having a night similar to Melanie Enkelmann's. When Pam had battled back to coherence after the soul-rattling news of Liz's murder, she called the police department in her own town and told the officers what had happened. She wondered if Rick—surely on the run now—would show up at her door to drop off the children and lighten his load. She wasn't the least bit afraid for herself, but she was sick with worry about Elizabeth's precious children. She didn't know what that kind of cold-blooded murderer would do in such a situation. But she thought the police ought to be aware that a wife-killer might show up in their town. The police responded as she had hoped, sending two cars to watch her home and the neighborhood.

As she struggled to find a way to deal with all of this until she could begin the trip to St. Charles the next morning, she sought the advice of her brother, Steve, a psychologist in California. She called and told him of her fears for the kids.

"Does this guy have nice cars, nice clothes, jewelry, things like that?" he asked.

"Yeah, he's a real car fanatic. He loves cars and takes good care of them."

"Does he have a cabin or something like that?"

"He wants to buy a vacation condo, and he has a nice boat."

"Okay. Pam, these kids are like his other possessions. He'll take care of them. They're perfectly safe. It sounds like Elizabeth had to be dispensed with, but the kids will be okay. I deal with guys like this all the time."

"The police said they sent someone to find him down in the Ozarks."

"Oh, they'll find him. He'll be exactly where he is supposed to be."

FOURTEEN

The simple, direct, eloquently angry accusation kept echoing through Sergeant Mike Powell's head.

"That son of a bitch did this."

The petite blond woman who had sat in his car barely two hours earlier had looked hard into his eyes without blinking and delivered a declaration as basic and certain and true as anything she had ever known, a truth that had sprung from her soul in the most horrible moment in her life. Melanie Enkelmann had not offered this to Mike Powell as an opinion or a suspicion or a possibility, or even a probability. She had uttered it as the uncomplicated, painful truth that she knew as certainly as she now knew her beloved sister was dead.

"That son of a bitch did this."

The echo reverberated in Powell's ears as he and Detective Mike Miller—two tall, rangy, dark-haired young men—rocketed west through the darkness on Interstate 70 to Kingdom City and then roared south on old U.S. Route 54 toward Osage Beach. Miller's eagerness to track down Rick DeCaro and find out what he would tell them about his wife's death was manifesting itself in a heavy foot on the accelerator; he set the hood ornament on the center line of the highway and let it rip. The dark-blue, unmarked Ford Crown Victoria chewed up the pavement through Jefferson City, within sight of the Missouri state capitol, and then careened on through the night toward the Lake of the Ozarks, where the object of Melanie's boiling hatred waited. They would be delivering devastating information to a man who might be totally unsuspecting of how his life was about to change or who might be awaiting their arrival to begin his act. Powell and Miller had to wonder just what they would see when they looked at Rick DeCaro in the almost blinding glare of Melanie Enkelmann's truth.

The midnight search would not be as easy as the officers had hoped. They drove directly to the Inn at Grand Glaize. Nope, the desk clerk said, there was no one by that name registered. Great. In a resort city packed with motels, the needle they were after had just fallen deep into the haystack. The perplexed officers cruised through the parking lots of several nearby motels, hoping they might blunder upon that blue GMC Vandura with the DEK-308 license number. No such luck. Faced with growing frustration and impatience, they turned for help to the local police station. The officers at Osage Beach helped them call down the list of motels until Miller hit pay dirt—Richard DeCaro was registered in room 410 at the Holiday Inn on Business Route 54 in adjacent Lake Ozark. The desk clerk automatically connected Miller to the room, but he hung up before anyone answered.

But now there was a new complication. The search had crossed jurisdictional lines into Lake Ozark. A call to the police there arranged for an official rendezvous at a gas station near the motel. Powell and Miller soon connected with this new batch of officers, finding two detectives and two women dispatchers ready to assist. The squad drove immediately to the Holiday Inn.

They knocked on the door of room 410 about 1:15 A.M., and Miller was shocked when a voice behind the door immediately asked who was there. It was as if the man had been standing on the other side, just waiting for their arrival. And then Milller heard another important voice from inside. Ozzie the dog barked; he had accompanied the DeCaros on this weekender.

"It's the police," Miller announced.

A tall, slender, muscular man, wearing a T-shirt and jeans, opened the door. His tousled black hair and the squint in his eyes suggested he had been asleep, but the speed of his response made it difficult for Miller and Powell to believe that.

"Are you Richard DeCaro?"

"Yes."

"Mr. DeCaro, I'm Detective Mike Powell from the St.

Charles Police Department. Would you step into the hall-way, please?"

Rick stepped out and closed the door behind him.

"Mr. DeCaro, I have some bad news to give you. A friend of your wife's found her dead at home tonight."

Hearing the worst news a loving husband could imagine, Rick leaned slowly back against the wall, paused, and then asked calmly, "What happened?"

Oh, the question certainly was reasonable, even de-manded under these circumstances. But Mike Powell and Mike Miller were shocked at the flat, totally emotionless voice and the expressionless face that had just delivered it. There was almost no response—nothing that they would ever be able to describe when asked about Rick's reaction to this life-shattering news. And even more remarkable, they detected absolutely no surprise—not a hint of shock that his vital, vibrant wife had been found dead. The man standing in front of the cops was as cold as anyone they had ever seen.

Everyone handles shock and grief differently, and the detectives tried not to judge people on the basis of what came naturally. They had delivered the news of loved ones' deaths to other people before, and they had seen many different reactions, from pure shock and disbelief to howl-ing hysterics. But in this hallway, from this man, there was not even a suggestion of simple surprise. To Powell, Rick DeCaro's reaction implied that Elizabeth's death was really no big deal—no more important than the news that some-one had inflicted a little scratch on his van in the parking lot would have been. It was, Powell thought, as if Rick DeCaro had known this was coming.

Detective Miller held back for now as he responded to Rick's almost casual inquiry. "We don't really know what happened, Mr. DeCaro. We're just starting the investi-gation."

"Where'd they find her?" Rick asked softly.

"In the kitchen."

Rick nodded and said no more.

Powell wanted to shake his head in disbelief. There were a hundred good, sane questions that should be born out of

hurt and confusion and pain and sorrow. But for some reason those questions did not come from this man.

Miller asked Rick to accompany them to the Lake Ozark
Police Station for an interview; they had brought two
women to stay with his sleeping children. Rick nodded in
agreement, and the detectives escorted him to the car for
the silent drive.

While Powell met with the desk clerk from the Holiday
Inn to get more information about the DeCaros' arrival,
Miller took Rick into an interview room about 1:45 A.M.
and had him recite his activities that day. He had arisen as
usual at 4:30, gone to Gold's Gym in Webster Groves for
a workout, spent a few hours at work, and then had taken
off at 10:50 to start the weekend with the kids. He didn't
get to spend a lot of quality time with them, and he thought
a few days in the Ozarks without their mother would be
good for them and him.

He described how he had picked the kids up at school—
"That is the only time I have driven the car pool in my
life"—dropped off the neighbor children, gone to the house
so his kids could change clothes, packed up the van, and
departed at noon for Osage Beach. He was some miles
down the road about twelve-thirty, between St. Peters and
Wentzville on I-70, when Elizabeth called on his cell phone
to tell him to have fun. That evening, Rick called Elizabeth
from the phone in the van about ten o'clock, but she didn't
answer and the machine didn't pick up. That wasn't unusual, he explained; the kids sometimes turned off the answering machine.

On the trip down, they drove through a McDonald's in
Kingdom City for lunch on the run and checked into the
Holiday Inn just after three o'clock. By four, Rick had
driven to a real estate agent's office to confirm an appointment for one o'clock the next day to shop for a getaway
condo. After that, he and the kids hit a video arcade,
played miniature golf, ate dinner at an Italian spot, made
quick visits to a grocery store and the local Wal-Mart, and
were back in the motel room by seven-thirty. They watched
a movie on TV and then turned in for the night.

What could be more normal for a dad and his kids enjoying some quality time together?

But in another interview room, the motel desk clerk was bluntly telling Sergeant Powell that guest Rick DeCaro had been "a pain the ass." Well, not Rick exactly, but the number of phone calls that had come in for his room. While the clerk tried to deal with too many demands on her time, some six to eight calls for Mr. DeCaro had arrived between seven-thirty and ten. She thought all the calls had come from the same man.

Powell knew Miller would want to hear about this, so he interrupted the interview with Rick and asked his partner to step into the hallway. When Miller returned, he found Rick sitting with his face in his hands. When Rick looked up, Miller could detect what he believed were a couple of tears in Rick's red eyes. But Miller wasn't buying; to him, Rick appeared to have been rubbing his eyes in a transparent attempt to work up some dramatic and necessary tears. After all, those tiny drops of moisture were as close to emotion as Miller had seen from this man.

Rick denied the desk clerk's allegations about phone calls, insisting that he had received only two, and only after he had gone to sleep. One of them had been a hang-up call, which Miller confessed had been him. The other, Rick said, had been a wrong number—a man asking for "Joe." How imaginative, Miller thought.

But the detective was intrigued again. There was a vast chasm between the desk clerk's account and Rick's, and there had to be an explanation for that. If the desk clerk was right, she may have been fielding calls from a "contractor" trying to let his employer know the deal had been "executed"—in his kitchen with two shots to the head. If Rick was right, the desk clerk either was incapable of counting phone calls or was a liar with some unimaginable reason to complicate the life of a grieving widower she didn't even know.

Miller pushed on with the interview. Rick could offer no motive and no suspect, no reason and no one who would want to harm his wife. He was certain *she* was not having an affair, nor—even more ludicrous—was she involved in drugs, gambling, or any other criminal activity.

Miller asked about life insurance, and Rick confirmed that he had taken out a new policy on Elizabeth for $100,000 in January when he increased his coverage to $250,000. But he added that he was unsure whether the policy on Elizabeth was even in effect yet; the premiums were to be automatically deducted from his bank account, and he wasn't certain that the process had started.

"Will anyone say they ever saw any bruises on your wife?" Miller asked.

That question drew a pause, and then Rick explained the accident with the van in January. As he reached back to get his jacket behind his seat, his foot slipped off the brake pedal and hit the accelerator. The van lurched out of control, smashing into Elizabeth and the wall before he could hit the brakes. Her leg and hip had been bruised, but fortunately she had not been badly hurt. It had been, Rick said, "no big deal."

Although he was sure Elizabeth had not been having an affair, he now admitted that he had. He and Cathy Dillon had been just friends at work, but that had evolved into a secret romance in late November 1991 after some lunches and a hockey game. They had sex twice, he said, before he ended the affair in December because he loved his wife and wanted to save his marriage. He had told his wife about his indiscretion, and that had been it. He didn't think Cathy's husband, Jeff, knew about it. And he was confident that the affair had nothing to do with Elizabeth's death in any way.

Miller thought it odd that Rick would dismiss his unfaithfulness so lightly at this moment, and without showing any more remorse for that transgression than grief for his wife.

By 2:45 A.M., Miller had gotten about as much as he could from Rick, so he asked him to sign forms giving the Major Case Squad permission to search his home and his car. Rick not only agreed to that but consented to a test for gunshot residue as well. Mike Powell swabbed Rick's hands with a solution that would detect the presence of nitrates from gunpowder if he had fired a weapon recently.

The detectives didn't expect a positive reaction, but they wanted to cover the bases. As Powell collected the samples for analysis, he thought again that Rick seemed almost unconcerned about this whole affair. Powell kept thinking of the word "businesslike." None of this seemed to be a big deal to him. But then the new widower really rocked the detective.

"Do you think I should go back to St. Charles now?"

Powell couldn't believe his ears, and he realized the look on his face must have betrayed his amazement. Once again, this man was showing an incredible lack of concern and sensitivity for his murdered wife, her motherless children, and her grieving family. The question had come so matter-of-factly, so . . . businesslike.

"Well, yes, I do," Powell stuttered. "They'll need you for funeral arrangements and things. You probably should go on back right away."

"Well, I think we might stay an extra day before we go back." Rick hesitated again. "But the kids might not want to stay and continue the vacation, after they find out what happened. I'll tell them when they wake up in the morning."

The kids might not want to continue the vacation after they find out their mother has been murdered? Really? No kidding? Rick's demeanor was so strange that Powell couldn't believe it. To the echo of Melanie's eloquent accusation, Powell now added his own appraisal: either this is the strangest man I have ever met, or he's involved in his wife's murder.

The officers delivered Rick back to the motel about four o'clock, and Mike Miller decided he had to speak to the DeCaros' oldest child immediately. Miller asked Rick to wake Patrick up for a brief interview. Rick obliged, lamenting aloud that he would have to break the news to Patrick sooner than he had planned. Miller stayed with the father and son; he couldn't leave them alone before the boy could be interviewed. Rick brought his sleepy son into the hallway and told him bluntly that his mother was dead.

The twelve-year-old boy began to cry, sobbing deeply. Finally, Miller thought, some genuine grief for this woman.

"What happened?" Patrick asked in a tone remarkably more distressed than his father's. Rick answered that all the police could say was that someone had shot her at the house.

Miller watched the boy's face closely. Despite all the tears and confusion, Miller could see that Patrick's mind was going a thousand miles a minute as he tried to assess what had to be an inconceivable event for someone so young. The boy was in shock, but his mind was racing. Miller sensed Patrick was dealing not only with the murder of his mother but with suspicions about his father.

Miller asked Rick to step into the room for a minute and leave him alone with Patrick in the hallway. Patrick then told Miller that there had been several calls to the room that evening, and someone had hung up when his dad answered one of them.

"Did your mom and dad fight a lot? Did they argue a lot?"

"They argued, but no more than any other parents."

"Did your dad ever hit your mom?"

"No, I never saw him do anything like that."

Patrick gave a quick description of the day, confirming his father's account. That was enough for Patrick to endure, Miller decided; he ended the interview.

Miller suggested to Rick that one of the detectives drive the family's van back to St. Charles so he and the kids could sleep or grieve. Rick said he preferred to get some sleep at the motel and tell the other kids when they awoke. He would decide then whether to go home or stay another day and do some more fun things first. Just unbelievable, the cops thought again.

Before ending their visit, Miller took as evidence the black polo shirt and jeans Rick DeCaro had worn that day. And then the cops made a much slower drive home. Mike Miller kept thinking he had never seen anyone as cold as Rick DeCaro when they talked in that little interrogation room.

And when Mike Powell told his wife about the events in Osage Beach, he added to Melanie's eloquence his own blunt cop's appraisal of the husband in this case.

"He's good for it."

FIFTEEN

As the hours of mourning dragged by at the Van Iseghem house, Georgianna kept wondering why she had not heard from Rick. Why hadn't he called to share in the grief and tell them when he would be getting home with the kids? She placed no blame on Rick for the ghastly new reality of Elizabeth's death, but she wondered where he was.

These hours were agonizing. Georgianna's only comfort was, once again, a house full of loving family and friends. Despite the violence that had just destroyed her life, she somehow felt safe with everyone there on this dreadful night, carrying her through. Like her, none of these wonderful people could figure out how someone could just walk into Elizabeth's house and shoot her down in cold blood. How could such a thing happen to this family?

By four in the morning, Georgianna was sparked to life by another question, one that seemed so odd on its face but struck so deeply that she had to call Melanie. She awakened her daughter with this startling new query.

"Melanie, where's Ozzie? Where's Elizabeth's dog?"

"My God, Mom, I don't know. I never saw him. He never showed up the whole time we were there. I hadn't even thought about that. No one has mentioned him."

Melanie was provoked by the question and the lack of a reasonable answer. Ozzie, the lovable mutt of indecipherable breed, hated strangers. He would have gone absolutely crazy when Elizabeth's killer arrived. He even barked insanely at some people he knew well, including Pam Hanley. That made Ozzie an integral part of the scenario. How had he been silenced? Where was he now? He wouldn't have just run away; the DeCaros had installed an electric fence to contain him within the yard. Obviously, if the killer had eliminated Ozzie too, the police would have found his body. So, just where the hell was Ozzie?

Georgianna had learned in a call from Grace DeCaro, that Rick was staying at the Holiday Inn in Osage Beach. As five o'clock neared, Georgianna couldn't stand the waiting any longer, and she called him there.

"Rick, why haven't we heard from you? What's going on? Why haven't you come back yet?" she cried.

"Well, the kids are still asleep. I haven't told them yet," he said in an amazingly flat tone.

"And Rick, where's Ozzie?"

"He's here."

Georgianna was stunned. Rick loved Ozzie, but he had never taken him anywhere before. He always complained that the dog would get hair in the car.

"You've got him with you there?"

"Yeah. Erin wanted to bring him."

"When are you coming home?"

"I don't know yet. I'm going to ask the kids if they want to stay and do some fun things before we come home."

Georgianna couldn't believe her ears. "What? What do you mean 'do some fun things'? You need to be here, Rick! You need to be here with us! Those kids need to be here with us!"

"Well, I'll see when the kids get up."

Georgianna was too shocked to say anything more. What could be going through his mind? He had just found out that his wife had been murdered, that his children were motherless, that the family he loved had lost their daughter and sister—and he was considering miniature golf and go-carts with the kids before coming home to plan the funeral?

My God, Georgianna wondered, what has happened to our world?

SIXTEEN

New widower Rick DeCaro finally arrived at St. Francis Lane sometime around eleven o'clock Saturday morning, but the callous look in his eyes did not suggest he was consumed by grief. And the four children who followed him walked into their grandparents' house almost as if nothing happened, almost the way they had come through that front door so many times with their mother. None of the five DeCaros showed any sign that they had been crying—no puffy eyes, no rubbed-red noses, no looks of confusion, loss, or sorrow. None ran to their grandparents or aunts or uncles for comfort and reassurance. They seemed to be arriving for a family barbecue.

Melanie Enkelmann and Mary Cordes looked at each other in astonishment. Did these children not know their mother was dead? Had Rick not told them? When the sisters quietly asked him, he said he had broken the news after they awoke that morning. After Patrick talked to the police, Rick sent him back to bed with instructions to be careful not to wake his brother and sisters. When Rick told the kids their mother had been killed, he gave them the option of staying in the Ozarks for another day. But they had wanted to go home immediately. They had left at 5:45 A.M., driven the two hours back, stopped at Rick's sister's first, and then come to the Van Iseghems'.

No wonder the kids showed no emotion, Melanie and Mary thought; they were taking their lead from their father, and he was like ice. His instructions to Patrick just minutes after telling him the horrible news had set the tone: go back to sleep, hold back your emotions, don't make any noise. Mary contrasted that with the grief of her own children. They had learned of their aunt's murder on television before Mary could reach them to break the news more gently. The kids were devastated, overwhelmed by a torrent of tears and confusion and childlike disbelief. Her youngest daughter, Nichole, just eight, later would write an essay for school calling that moment the worst of her life.

But Elizabeth's own children spoke not at all of their mother's murder, of her absence, of their loss of her forever, of their confusion about how this could happen to her and to them, of their fears about their lives without her—and neither did their father. He asked nothing about the police investigation, how the Van Iseghems had learned of his wife's death, how they were coping with this awful reality. He offered no words of comfort to the parents who had lost a child or to the siblings who had lost a sister.

Rick soon left for an appointment at the funeral home, and within an hour Grace DeCaro gathered the children and left too, leaving another void in Georgianna's heart on this day.

Again, the Van Iseghems were learning, things were different in this new world.

SEVENTEEN

Major Tom O'Connor and Chief David King had the investigation in full swing by Saturday morning. The St. Charles Police Station bustled with the comings and goings of detectives as they chased down leads and returned to report their findings. An extra bank of telephone lines was already being installed to provide plenty of power and to receive, O'Connor prayed, a steady stream of tips from the public once his call for help was broadcast across this metropolitan region of more than 2,500,000 people. He had put out the word on the missing Blazer with its distinctive license plates and was pleased that the *St. Louis Post-Dispatch* and the TV stations were focusing on that.

The coverage had already drawn one report by nine-thirty Saturday morning. Kathy Ortinau told police that she and her family had seen the Blazer as they were driving home to south St. Louis County from Lambert International Airport about seven-thirty Friday evening. Kathy's twelve-year-old son, Thomas, noticed the RIK-LIZ license plate on the bulky vehicle next to them on southbound Interstate 270 at Ladue Road. As usual, Thomas announced his discovery to the rest of the passengers and they all checked it out. Kathy even wondered aloud if Rick and Liz were in their vehicle. But alas, no one had paid attention to anyone in the vehicle. Unhappily for the cops, there could be no description of who was behind the wheel, no look at the driver, who probably had killed Elizabeth DeCaro not long before taking to the highway in her Blazer. But at least the police now knew the vehicle had been on the busy roads at the height of Friday evening rush hour. Surely someone else had seen the snazzy Blazer and would remember the all-important face behind the wheel.

Within a few hours, O'Connor had two detectives high above the interstate in a police helicopter, looking intently for black-and-silver vehicles. They conducted an aerial survey around the spot of the Ortinau sighting and then swept across all of the collar counties—St. Charles, St. Louis, Jefferson, Washington, and St. Francois. No luck.

Although the media campaign was important to O'Connor, he was not about to rely on it to solve this case. He already had spread his men across the area, with varied assignments to bring in every bit of information they could about the DeCaros and their lives.

From the family's insurance agent, the police officers learned that the claim for Rick's stolen and torched van had led to a payout of $17,976—but it went to the bank that leased the van to the Old Orchard Amoco Station, owned by Dan DeCaro.

A contact with Southwestern Bell rounded up the past month's record of calls made on Rick DeCaro's cell phone. Most were to relatives or to work, but two were very interesting. One on February 3 went to the number for Jeff Dillon, the husband of Rick's lover, Cathy. And another on January 31 went to Mike Carroll, Elizabeth's lover. Ob-

viously, both DeCaros had been using the phone for their
own separate purposes. By the next afternoon, the police
had put a tap on the phone in the Blazer. Unfortunately,
there had been no calls on it the day of the murder. It was
too much to hope that the killer had been stupid enough
to make calls after he drove away from Hidden Meadow
Court.

Checking the source of the milk bottles on the DeCaros'
front porch also failed to turn up anything useful. The milk-
man had dropped off the standard order of two gallons at
his standard time, between two and two-thirty Friday. As
was his standard procedure, he rang the doorbell before he
walked away. No one came to the door before he left, but
that was pretty standard too.

Other detectives had the grisly job of observing the autopsy on Saturday morning. Dr. Mary Case, the expert
medical examiner for St. Charles County, conducted the
"post" on Elizabeth's body. There was no doubt about the
cause of death—two bullet wounds, point-blank into the back
of the neck at the hairline. The first bullet passed between
the second and third vertebrae and ended its path in muscle
on the right side of the neck, where it was recovered. The
second bullet entered on the left side of the midline of the
neck. An upward path blasted a destructive route just
under the victim's brain and ended in the sinus cavity behind the upper left cheek.

While some detectives handled the mechanical and medical details, others were delving again into the DeCaros'
personal lives. Stories of a deteriorating marriage were
abundant.

According to Elizabeth's good friend and neighbor
Jackie Balunek, the marriage had been sliding toward disaster. Elizabeth wanted to save it, but she was determined to
leave Rick if they did not solve their problems soon. Jackie
and her husband, Charlie, had seen the conflict firsthand;
they witnessed the fight between the DeCaros on New
Year's Eve. And Jackie said they weren't the only ones in
the DeCaros' circle of friends with suspicions about Rick.
When Jackie took Pam Hanley's phone call at the hospital
the night before, Pam's husband immediately said he

thought Rick had something to do with Liz's death. Larry Hanley had then told Jackie about the circumstances Rick had engineered to keep Elizabeth home alone while he and the kids were away.

Another pair of neighbors, Jenny and Jerry McKay, said Elizabeth had spoken in general terms about her marital problems and had complained that Rick had refused to join her for counseling, but then he reversed that decision in early February. Jenny had baby-sat for Erin DeCaro on Friday and had dropped her off while Rick was loading the van about eleven o'clock. Later, about twelve-fifteen, Elizabeth had called to see if Rick and the kids had departed. Jenny had peeked out the window; yep, the van was gone and the garage door was closed.

Boo Pohlman told the police that Rick was very jealous but not violent. Even so, Elizabeth—Boo's best friend since grade school—had gradually grown afraid of him. She hadn't disclosed many details but had said her marriage was in trouble. Boo knew about Elizabeth being smashed by Rick's van and how it had been suspiciously stolen. Elizabeth didn't think Rick was taking drugs, but Boo thought that was a possibility. And, Boo said, she didn't think Elizabeth was having an affair, but she had been friends with a local police officer, Cliff Dugan.*

Elizabeth's brother Randy met the police for his first interview at 11:20 that morning. Like his older brother, he hadn't known much about his sister's troubles. Their mother had told him a little about a month ago, but Elizabeth had never said anything. Since the murder, Melanie had told him about Rick's claim of a drug deal. Randy thought Elizabeth's murder looked professional and, perhaps, drug-related. He also suggested that the police check with the two men he thought were closest to Rick—his brother Dan and one of his employees, Craig Wells.

And then Randy offered his opinion on the theft of Rick's van in January. Randy had sold insurance for a while, and he definitely thought the theft was an "insurance job." When someone wanted to get rid of a vehicle permanently, it was common to arrange to have it stolen and burned. That was a profitable solution to car troubles.

But he still was unaware of his sisters' suspicions about Rick. Randy would not hear for two more days that they and so many others were convinced that Rick was behind it. And even when his sisters shared their suspicions with him, he found it hard to believe that the Rick he knew was capable of such a thing. Rick's conduct since the murder seemed natural enough to Randy; he would withhold judgment until he had more evidence.

Mary Cordes found herself the subject of a second interview that morning. The police especially wanted to pursue their discovery that Elizabeth had been involved sexually with Mike Carroll. Without showing their hand, the detectives asked Mary if Elizabeth had been having an affair. Not that Mary knew about.

She would not learn about her sister's affair until later that day, when Melanie decided that the family should know the facts before they leaked out through some other source. Mary was shocked to hear about Elizabeth and Mike Carroll—just as shocked as she had been about Rick and Cathy Dillon. She had just never expected that from Rick or Elizabeth—even though she now could understand why Elizabeth had turned to someone else.

Back at the police station, a second interview with Dan DeCaro drew two revelations. Not only had he known about his brother's financial problems, but he also had been aware that Rick was dallying with the service station's secretary. Dan then added a new, even more convoluted twist to this romantic scenario. Cathy Dillon was married to the brother of Dan's wife; that meant Dan's brother had been having an affair with Dan's sister-in-law.

All in the family, so to speak.

Dan DeCaro said he had been unaware that Elizabeth was not accompanying the rest of her family to the Ozarks, even though he had talked to Rick as late as ten-thirty that morning.

Saturday afternoon, O'Connor sent Detective Mike Miller back to the man he had interviewed in the Ozarks. All of the detectives had been fascinated by Rick DeCaro's exceedingly odd reaction to his wife's murder and his icy behavior in the hours after that. Even these cops who thought they had seen and heard just about everything were shocked by Rick's suggestion that he might stay in the Ozarks for a day of fun—after hearing that his wife had been blown away in his own kitchen. What kind of man entertains such a thought, even if he's not involved in the murder—or especially if he is?

McCarrick tried to rein in his suspicions, even though some of the others jumped to the conclusion that Rick's conduct was absolute proof that he had killed Elizabeth. McCarrick was suspicious, certainly, but there were other things to consider. For one, if Rick was guilty, wouldn't he have been more likely to offer the detectives an Oscar-winning display of grief? His reaction had been so under-stated that it had made him even more of a suspect than a bad acting job would have. Sure, McCarrick thought, Rick's reaction stank, but it was too soon to jump all the way to the ultimate conclusion.

Amid all of that, O'Connor now wanted Miller to take Rick to the place where his wife had died. Miller tracked him down at his sister's house and asked him to accompany the cops on a walk through his home to identify what had been stolen. Rick obliged and met the officers at 12 Hidden Meadow Court about 12:45 P.M. McCarrick was there to get his first look at Rick DeCaro. They did not speak, and McCarrick felt no real reaction to the man. But he did note that Rick lacked the physique of someone supposedly dedicated to a daily regime of weight lifting—and perhaps addicted to the muscle-pumping, behavior-altering steroids popular with some guys who pursued that lifestyle. Rick just was not the big, beefy specimen McCarrick had expected. *This guy's using the wrong steroids,* he thought.

Mike Miller led Rick through the house, to his first view of the murder scene in his otherwise immaculate kitchen. As he looked at his wife's blood smeared across the linoleum—at the precise spot where she had bled, breathed her last, and died—he asked in a casual but pointed tone, "When can I get this mess cleaned up?"

For Miller—already deeply suspicious of Rick DeCaro—this second encounter, illustrating such inappropriate reactions to a wife's murder, was just more evidence of this man's cold-blooded nature. Once again, there had no emotional collapse, as would be expected from a man seeing the place in his own home where his wife had been brutally executed, "assassination style," as the media already were calling it. What kind of man wouldn't give in to the grief, to the realization that his heart would be tortured forever by those haunting images?

Mike Miller thought he knew exactly what kind of man wouldn't react that way.

The rest of the visit was fairly routine. Rick strolled from room to room, pointing out what had been taken by the killer. The VCRs from the family room and living room. The color TV and boom box from Patrick's room. The CD player, stereo, and speakers from the shelves in the family room, and the AM-FM receiver from the basement.

And then Rick walked out of the house, without even a backward glance.

EIGHTEEN

The first tactical move by the Major Case Squad awaited Rick DeCaro when Detective Miller brought him back to the police station after the house tour—but Rick wouldn't even know about it. Tom O'Connor and Dave King had hatched an idea, an interesting angle on finding out what was going on in this man's mind. They were about to employ Melanie Enkelmann's drive to know what had happened to her sister. The police wanted her to sit down for a face-to-face confrontation with the brother-in-law she had been accusing of murder ever since the first cop arrived at 12 Hidden Meadow Court. This conversation was not solely for Melanie's satisfaction, of course—it wasn't just a chance for her to expand the detective role she had been playing for months already. This was more serious than that for the Major Case Squad. Melanie had agreed without hesitation to a suggestion by O'Connor and King that they tape the conversation with a recorder secretly installed in the chief's office. The authorities wanted to know what Rick would say when confronted by Melanie's angry suspicions, by questions from one of the strong-willed women so similar to the wife he was so reluctant to mourn.

Miller escorted Rick and Melanie into King's office, where the chief met the widowed husband for the first time. King was still keeping his suspicions in check, refusing to allow himself to consider Rick DeCaro the prime suspect just yet. But as the two men shook hands, King stared directly into the most expressionless dark eyes he had ever seen. King felt as if Rick's eyes were boring right through him.

Shark's eyes, the chief thought, the eyes of a merciless predator.

The chief ushered Rick and Melanie to the conference table and seated them just above the microphone that had been secreted under it. He spoke to them briefly in what actually was just a maneuver to set up the conversation to follow. He reassured them that his department and the Major Case Squad were doing everything that could be done to find the killer. And then he left them alone for what the cops hoped would be a productive session. King slipped into the room next door to join O'Connor and the other officers as they monitored this unusual conversation.

In the chief's office, Melanie stared intently across the table. Rick wouldn't return her gaze; he wouldn't look into her eyes. Surprisingly, he spoke first, asking softly, "How are you?"

She took it right to him. "I'm not feeling very well at all. I'm mad. I'm real mad, Rick. I want to talk to you. I've been wanting to talk to you for months. I don't understand what's going on. I don't understand what happened. What happened?"

Her voice carried an edge of urgency, wrapped in a soft plea. His response was flat, devoid of any emotion.

"I don't have any idea what happened."

She pushed for details. Why was he so intent on leaving Elizabeth home alone on this particular weekend? Rick said he had been planning the getaway with the kids for some time; this weekend was chosen for no special reason. The conflict between his plans and the trip to the Hanleys' in Kansas City had been a simple lack of communication between him and Elizabeth—they hadn't been talking much lately.

Melanie was just warming up. "Something is going on. I mean, something has been going on with you for months. I know there has been. You're not the same person, Rick. You don't act the same. You don't treat Liz the same. You don't treat me the same. We used to be good friends. We used to talk about everything."

He kept his eyes locked on the table, still offering no reaction as she jumped to the suspicious circumstances of her sister's death.

"I'm going to be honest with you. I'm really upset with you. This isn't right. It's the first time she's ever been home all by herself. She was only going to be home two hours. She's never been home by herself. To me—I'm sorry—it looks like it was set up."

"So you blame me?" Still flat—he couldn't even pose that question with indignation or resentment.

"I'm asking you. I don't want to blame you, but I've got to tell you my feelings."

Melanie's emotions began to take over, and the tears and hurt rushed out of control. "She was my sister. I loved her dearly. We did everything together, and she's gone now." She fought to keep it all from choking off her voice as she remembered what she had seen in that kitchen. "I had to find her. I had to go in there and find her on the floor. Do you know how hard that was? I can't believe that someone just went in that house—for what?—and shot her in the back of the head, for no reason. They didn't take anything. What's going on?" She drilled him with her stare again, but softened it to plead for help and understanding. "Are there drugs involved?"

"No, no. There's no drugs involved. There's nothing going on."

"There has to be something going on, Rick."

He went to the heart of it all. He had ended the affair

with Cathy Dillon in December and had been trying to repair his marriage for weeks. But Elizabeth was always gone now. "She wouldn't open up to me."

Melanie shot back that Rick had failed to show Elizabeth any attention, even refusing to kiss her good-bye before he left on Friday. How could he do that? "Make me understand, please."

Her insistence began to irritate him. "I don't understand, myself. How can I make you understand? I don't know what the fuck happened."

She was undeterred. Was something going on at that gym? Something with drugs? Rick shook his head and shot back indignantly, "I've never done anything like that in my entire life and I never will."

What about the stolen van? It looked like a set-up job to Melanie.

Now he was getting more defensive. "I had nothing to do with any of it. I can't even believe you're thinking that. I mean, no matter how bad it was, I always loved her and I always will. I wouldn't have been around if I didn't love her."

Why had he taken Ozzie, the dog?

"Erin was crying about wanting to take him, and we decided to go ahead and take him." Pretty simple.

Why was he looking at vacation condos at the same time he had been talking about getting out of debt?

"When I want something I always . . ." he began.

She was so anxious to get at the truth that she couldn't keep from interrupting to make her point. "I know you do. That's what worries me, that maybe you were getting some money on the side somewhere, so you could get what you want, because you are that type of person. You get a job done. When you start a job, you finish it. That's what I've always admired about you."

He said he was doing a little mechanical work on the side, but that was all. No drugs. Then he offered what almost seemed like remorse for the deterioration of the relationships in the family.

"I couldn't face your family because I felt so guilty for what I had done."

"The affair? The affair is not even a big deal. Okay?"

"Well, maybe to you. I couldn't face you guys, though. I just couldn't do it."

What about his claim of a drug deal?

"That was a gimmick. I lied about that."

"Now why would you lie about that?"

"Because I had met Cathy a couple of times, just to talk, and I knew Elizabeth would freak out if she knew that."

"Do you think she wouldn't freak out over you meeting somebody over a drug deal?"

"I don't know. It just came to mind."

"Why won't you even look at me? You won't even look me in the face."

His irritation was increasing, and now there was resentment in his voice. "Don't you know I feel just as damned bad as you do? Why are you putting the blame on me? I had nothing to do with it."

"Because the circumstantial evidence does go to you. I wish it didn't. I wish she got hit by a car, but she didn't. The first time that girl is in the house by herself in her entire life, and somebody comes in and shoots her? I'm sorry, but it has to be something you know. It has to be."

"I do not know anything about it."

When Melanie charged again at Rick's lack of affection and attention to Elizabeth, he shot back, pointing to his wife's own request that he back off. "I was trying to show it. She wouldn't accept anything. For two years I was told to quit doing something. For two years, I've been pulling away from her because she wanted her space, she wanted her room, she wanted to be able to go out. . . . She told me to quit buying things for her. She told me I did too much for her—everything that I loved doing. . . . What am I supposed to do? I'm totally fucking confused here. I was damned if did and damned if I didn't. So, then I let her go and let her do what she wanted to do, without bitching every minute she came home and everything, and that didn't work."

"I want you to convince me that I'm wrong," Melanie shot back.

"I don't know how to convince you of that."

"You still can't look me in the eye, though. Why can't you look me in the eyes? I want to believe . . ."

"I'm having a really hard time with this myself. I've been crying all goddamned night. I'm drained . . . I don't know anything at all. I've been thinking and thinking and thinking, and I have nothing at all."

What about the kids? Melanie asked. "They didn't look like they were crying. I don't understand."

"We cried for an hour straight last night."

Melanie offered her concerns about the children. "It's going to be hard on them. There are already rumors."

"Rumors about what?"

"Why she died? Who did this? Who did what? You know how your neighborhood is. It's nothing but a big Peyton Place. I'm really concerned for them."

"It's all I've been thinking about."

Melanie returned to her suggestion that it was a "setup." Elizabeth's killer knew so much—when she would be home alone, even when "the dumb dog" would be gone. Rick had an answer for that; someone must have been casing the house.

What was the motive? Melanie wondered. Why was there no forced entry? Rick explained that the sliding door didn't lock tightly; even his son Bill could jimmy his way past that.

After forty-five minutes, Melanie had run out of lines of attack and Rick had run out of answers. He said softly, "I can't think of anything else to say. I really can't." But it was clear he had been giving his new world some thought. "I've got my sister looking for a psychologist for the kids, you know. And I'm trying to figure out how in the hell I'm gonna live my life, raising four kids. And to ask me the 'why' questions . . ."

His voice trailed off. There was nothing more to say, and he stood up to leave. He and Melanie locked in a tight embrace, and Melanie wondered if this was their last farewell. For forty-five minutes, she had listened to the man she knew in her heart had murdered her sister, and he had never strayed from the role of wounded, grieving husband. But he never once made the vow that had become Melanie's oath; he never once expressed any interest in finding the man who had murdered his wife. And, even more important to Melanie that day, he couldn't look into her eyes. That said more than his lips could ever tell.

In the room next door the police were disappointed. Rick DeCaro hadn't come close to an admission of guilty knowledge, let alone a confession. But Melanie and the cops had come to the same realization about what he hadn't said. He had never once mourned his wife or wondered how he would live without her. He just bemoaned how inconvenient this was for him. "How in the hell am I gonna live my life, raising four kids?"

Melanie was wondering how she could live without bringing her sister's killer to justice. She decided then to put her grief on hold, replacing it with a vow that she would not rest until Elizabeth's murderer was caught and punished. Elizabeth would have done no less for her.

Despite a performance that had strengthened everyone's suspicions about Rick, O'Connor and King were wondering how the hell they were going to build a murder case against him. If he was involved, how could they prove it? He would never confess; he had no reason to, so far. Faced with this cool character, they would need a miracle to break this case.

NINETEEN

The Major Case Squad got its first look at the other woman in this unromantic triangle—Catherine Ann Dillon—while Melanie Enkelmann was trying to drag information out of Rick for the tape recorder. In an interrogation room on the other side of the station, two detectives sat down with the petite, attractive, twenty-five-year-old blonde who had come between the DeCaros.

She told a simple story of two struggling, stumbling marriages. She and Rick had become friends at work and had enjoyed a few lunches together. She had mentioned that she had never been to a hockey game, and he invited her to a St. Louis Blues game one night in November. They met for drinks first, went to the arena for the game, and then stopped for a few more drinks. They ended the night the way both of them had secretly expected—before they went to their separate, unhappy homes, they made love in her red Camaro.

The image of that was difficult for the detectives to shake. And thereafter Cathy Dillon came to be known as "Cathy Camaro"—just another example of the dark cop humor needed to cope with the unpleasant realities of such investigations.

The sexual relationship between Rick and Cathy had lasted for several weeks, she explained. Rick came to her house a couple of mornings while her husband was off exploring caves in New Mexico. Rick even spent a few hours there one evening. They had each talked of a deteriorating marriage, but never had she heard Rick say anything even vaguely menacing about Elizabeth. Finally, a few days before Christmas, Rick had broken off the affair. He wanted to try to work things out with his wife, to save the marriage for the sake of his children. Elizabeth knew about Rick and Cathy, but she had never confronted her competitor. Cathy was confident her husband had known nothing about what was going on between her and Rick. And she was absolutely certain that Rick had nothing to do with his wife's murder.

The detectives ended the interview by getting Cathy's promise to return the next day for a polygraph. The session on Sunday morning would add only a couple of new details to the story of Rick and Cathy. She told officers that, two weeks earlier, Rick had asked her to quit the job she had held for more than two years. Elizabeth, it seemed, had become insistent that Rick fire his ex-lover. Elizabeth probably would have been even more upset if she had known that Cathy and Rick still were having an occasional lunch together or meeting in her Camaro to commiserate about the problems on their home fronts. Cathy had agreed to leave her job, and Rick had brought her some newspaper want ads to assist her job search.

The questions on the polygraph were simple and direct. Did she know who killed Liz DeCaro? Was she deliberately withholding information from the police about who killed Liz? She said no to every question, and Detective Richard Plummer—an expert polygrapher and one of the very few people whom Lieutenant McCarrick would trust for an accurate reading—determined that there was no evidence of deception in her answers.

Continuing the pace from Friday night and Saturday, this Sunday was not a day of rest for the Major Case Squad. Not only did they administer a polygraph to Rick's partner in adultery, but they gave one to her counterpart on Elizabeth's side, Mike Carroll. Did you shoot Liz? Were you physically present when Liz was shot? Do you suspect anyone in particular of shooting Liz? Do you know for sure who shot Liz? Like Cathy, Mike offered solid "no's" and drew the same conclusion from Plummer: no evidence of deception.

Pam and Larry Hanley also paid a visit to the St. Charles Police Department that cold Sunday. They had made a solemn trip back to town on Saturday, a journey so different from the joyful trips to see the DeCaros and their other friends. Pam had never lost someone she loved so much before, and she floundered as she tried to cope with the unwelcome emptiness. When McCarrick walked into the interview room, Pam expected him to say there had been some dreadful mistake, some inexplicable miscommunication, Elizabeth was not really dead at all. But instead, the reality of this new world without Elizabeth fell heavily on them, and Pam and Larry spent four hours telling McCarrick everything they knew about Elizabeth and Rick. The Hanleys had little to offer that the detectives had not heard before, but there were a few new nuggets.

When Rick told Elizabeth that he had ended the affair with Cathy, he had added, "It was the hardest thing I've ever done in my life." Not exactly what a wife hopes to hear from her apologetic sinner. The Hanleys had been so disturbed by Rick's affair that they had written him a letter, urging him to stay in the marriage. And even after the end of his fling, the DeCaros' romance had faltered; Elizabeth admitted that they had not made love for months before Rick's unexpected passion the night the van was stolen, nor in the weeks after that. The temperature between this husband and wife had been "like ice," she had said.

Elizabeth recently had reported that Rick was staying out late, hanging out and drinking with his friends from work and Gold's Gym. The Hanleys were under the impression, from Elizabeth's attitude about those places, that Rick might have met people there who would be capable of murder. Long ago, he had offered Elizabeth and the Hanleys some disparaging comments about some of those guys' conduct. But now he suddenly was spending more time with some of them than he was with his family. Most nights, however, he simply explained his absence with the transparent claim that he was working late.

After Rick and the van hurtled into Elizabeth, she cracked to Pam, "If I didn't know better, I'd think he was trying to get rid of me." Even the insurance agent had been suspicious. He called not long after the "accident," referred to the new policy on Elizabeth, and wondered sarcastically, "Do you think I'm stupid?"

Larry had been surprised to learn that Rick had bought the insurance policy at all. He had always spent all of his money on possessions and comforts; he never did any financial planning. He had even discussed pulling the kids out of the Catholic schools and sending them to public schools to save the tuition. That had been another source of arguments between him and Elizabeth, the Hanleys said.

The whole "Daddy's weekend" scenario also disturbed Pam and Larry. Rick had never proposed anything like that with the kids before. And then there were Rick's explicit orders to Elizabeth that "under no circumstances" was she to go to Pam's. Elizabeth had been as nonplussed as the Hanleys; as Rick prepared to leave her alone that weekend, she asked Pam facetiously, "This is the way he's trying to work on our marriage?"

And finally, Elizabeth had reported that in recent days Rick had twice told her, "I will always love you." She said his tone and those words made her wonder if he was planning to leave. That certainly sounded like a good-bye to Elizabeth.

McCarrick asked if Elizabeth was a strong, independent person. Certainly, Pam said; in fact, it made no sense that she had allowed Rick's warning about the Blazer to keep her from going to Kansas City. The old Elizabeth would have risen to that challenge and made the drive specifically because Rick had said she couldn't.

Okay, McCarrick said, but why was there no evidence of a struggle? Would she have fought an attacker who surprised her in her home? Pam couldn't answer that without asking a question of her own. Where was Ozzie? Pam snapped, "Ozzie would have chewed this guy's fucking head off!"

"Rick took Ozzie to the Ozarks with them," McCarrick explained. He wasn't prepared for Pam's response. She literally leaped out of her chair and shouted angrily, "That's pretty goddamned funny! He would never do that! He always had one of the neighbors watch the dog when they left town! He'd never take the dog with him!"

Pam realized she was ranting at poor McCarrick, but she couldn't help it. She wanted to scream, "How can you guys solve this crime if you don't even understand the importance of this dog?"

They did—now. To McCarrick and the other detectives, Ozzie had just become a major player in this investigation.

To Pam and Larry Hanley, Ozzie's Ozark adventure confirmed that his suddenly benevolent master was a cold-blooded wife-killer.

TWENTY

The tension at Collier's Funeral Home on Sunday was as oppressive as the grief. The latter, a natural consequence of Elizabeth DeCaro's murder. The former, a grotesquely unnatural burden resulting from the growing suspicion that her husband was her killer.

A seemingly unbridgeable chasm now separated Rick from the Van Iseghems, and the distance across that funeral parlor could not have been more noticeable to everyone who arrived to say their good-byes to Elizabeth. Rick stood apart and separate from his wife's family, and many of the mourners thought he seemed reluctant even to look toward her casket, let alone approach it. To Georgianna and so many others, he seemed incapable of returning the perfectly normal hugs from those who offered that touch of comfort; he looked so awkward, so ill at ease as he leaned down and stiffly put his arms around them. Not even these hours of mourning, it seemed, could bring Rick and his wounded, confused in-laws together.

He had already set a tone of confrontation, late Saturday. He had angered and injured them by suggesting a closed casket without consulting them or seeing Elizabeth's body. When his mother called Georgianna to see if Rick's decision was acceptable, Georgianna sputtered, "What? Oh, my God, no! Who suggested that?" Grace DeCaro was almost as dismayed. "Rick did, but I didn't think so, either," she said.

Georgianna was outraged that Rick would even consider denying the Van Iseghems their chance to say good-bye to the lovely face that soon would remain only in their memories. But Melanie had no trouble interpreting Rick's wish for a closed casket. He hadn't even been able to look into Melanie's eyes. How could he look into the face of the wife whose murder he had arranged? Wouldn't it be so much easier for him if he didn't have to look at the cold consequences of his conspiracy?

In those same hours—less than a day after Elizabeth died—Rick had already planned to move the children to public schools as soon as possible. And, in a stroke of emotionally detached and obsessive behavior that shocked the Van Iseghems, he had scheduled haircuts for the children on Saturday afternoon. After all, the DeCaro kids would have to look fresh and sharp for the funeral home on Sunday and the final service on Monday. While all of that was under way, he already had his sister and others looking for a counselor to provide therapy for the children. A wise and sensitive decision, indeed, but the Van Iseghems thought getting through his wife's funeral might have been his first priority. The rest of the family had spent the last twenty-four hours in a fog of unimaginable pain and distress, barely able to function. But he had managed to organize his activities and make his plans as if he were preparing for a wedding, not a funeral. Margie Ugalde's trip to Dillard's department store at Northwest Plaza to select her sister's burial ensemble—a blouse and matching sweater that was a typical Elizabeth outfit—had been almost more than Margie could bear. But Rick was accomplishing his thorough plans without any noticeable anguish. He had even found time Sunday to stop at a car wash and get the van a good cleaning inside and out. His calm sailing through the weekend aggravated the family even more in light of what the Van Iseghems thought was an intentional slight—Rick didn't let them see the children between the brief visit Saturday morning and the wake Sunday evening. Just another thoughtless, unemotional act by this stranger they had thought they knew so well.

The streak of bizarre behavior continued Sunday night. As Rick tried to distance himself from the Van Iseghems, he also shocked some of the mourners with curious, almost scandalous comments. Boo Pohlman was taking advantage of her first opportunity to press him for answers to her questions when Melanie joined the conversation. As the women discussed the multitude of intriguing and perplexing angles to this violent assault on their loved one, Rick set them back again.

"Elizabeth is dead," he snapped. "I need to get on with my life."

Melanie and Boo were stunned. A period of mourning lasting somewhat longer than forty-eight hours seemed reasonable for a husband who had just lost his wife to murder. But at least his callous comment gave Melanie an opportunity to send a barely veiled warning to the brother-in-law who was fleeing the family so quickly.

"Well," she growled, "I won't rest until the person who did this is on death row."

Rick's dark eyes stared at her but betrayed no reaction.

An equally surprising exchange took place after Pam and Larry Hanley arrived. Melanie escorted Pam to the coffin for the unbearable sight of her dear friend in death. The reality really set in then: Liz was indeed gone forever. After those first awful moments, Pam handed Melanie a garnet ring and asked her to put it on Elizabeth's finger to stay with her forever; the ring was the one Elizabeth had advised Pam to accept for Christmas from Larry instead of the extravagant diamond he had planned to give her. That special memory for Pam now would be enshrined with Elizabeth, a symbol of a friendship that not even death could end.

And then Pam greeted Rick, who leaned down and put his arms around her. That was a difficult moment for her, but she returned his embrace and then asked to speak with him alone in a side room. She sat next to him on a sofa, leaned in very closely and took his hands in hers as she spoke the words she had to say in order to be able to live with herself, and Elizabeth's memory.

"Rick, you know everybody thinks you did this. Tell me you didn't do it."

Did Rick explode in anger at being accused so directly of murdering the wonderful wife whose body lay in the next room? Did he rage against such false and hurtful allegations from someone so close? No, he offered a cool response more shocking to Pam than a confession would have been.

"You know, she hurt me really bad when she told me to stop bringing her flowers and buying her gifts," he said softly. Then he looked almost angrily into Pam's face and snapped, "And you've been listening to all of that Melanie shit."

Pam rocked back in her seat. My God, what amazing things to say at such a moment! Aside from the outlandishness of the second comment, it wasn't even true; Pam had not discussed any of this with Melanie or any other Van Iseghem. Like so many before her, Pam had reached her own conclusions, based on what she knew about the events in the DeCaro household.

As Pam reeled from Rick's blast, he finally offered what

she had expected to hear. "I didn't have anything to do with it," he said.

But now his disclaimer was absolutely unconvincing.

One of those who was similarly unconvinced, and damned angry in his grief, was Jim Van Iseghem. He was losing a wrestling match with his heart as he tried to come to grips with this new world that no longer included one of his precious daughters. Fleeing the parlor where her body lay, Jim and his brother sought sanctuary in the men's room. As they railed against Rick DeCaro and his heartless performance that evening, Jim's furious suspicions led him to a vow of revenge.

"I'll get that son of a bitch," he swore.

He had no idea that one of the Major Case Squad detectives, sent by Tom O'Connor to watch for clues at the wake, had heard the oath from his hiding place in a toilet stall. That moment of rage would give the cops something else to worry about, and they would keep a close eye on this frustrated father—even though every one of them knew he himself would have felt exactly the same way. Later, one of them would call daughter Mary to ask if she thought there was reason to worry about her father's comment. She thought for only a second before answering, "Yes, I do."

After the funeral, Jim would hand over his guns to a friend and ask him to keep them in his safe. Jim knew it was unlikely he could ever use them in the way that some feared, but having them safely out of reach was still the most reasonable course.

Mary had been shocked when the detectives arrived at the funeral home Sunday night. A brassy move, she thought. Melanie was less surprised and more pragmatic; she assumed the police were there just in case the conflict between the Van Iseghems and the DeCaros exploded into something more bombastic than discomfort.

The family would never have believed what was really happening. Tom O'Connor had decided to take advantage of that special place and time to make his first move on Rick DeCaro. Rick had spurned several efforts by the police to reach him since Saturday afternoon. He had played his hand well, using the kids and the relatives and the funeral plans and all of the other supremely convenient excuses for not meeting with the detectives again. One of the reasons O'Connor wanted to sit down with Rick as soon as possible was to get him to sign release forms giving the police access to all of his personal and business records, his telephone records, and every other document in his name that might be valuable to the investigation. St. Charles County did not have a sitting grand jury, so O'Connor lacked the power of a subpoena to compel Rick to hand over the records. He needed Rick's signature to get the papers for the detectives to work with.

So, the commander—never bashful and certainly not hesitant to play hardball with a suspect or to make a tactical chess move against a reluctant witness—sent his detectives to the funeral home Sunday night with explicit instructions. They were to wait until Rick DeCaro was at his wife's casket with his children and the Van Iseghems—at his most publicly vulnerable time—and only then were the detectives to move in, with their apologies and their request for him to sign the documents. Detectives Vince Cowdry and Ellen Ritchter did exactly that, and Rick was shocked as they handed him the forms and explained their purpose. He restrained his reaction and listened as the detectives told him how much they needed his assistance and how confident they were that he wanted to help them find his wife's killer. Under the watchful eyes of his family, Rick was powerless. He looked at everyone standing nearby, scanned the documents briefly, and then signed them.

Score one for O'Connor and the squad.

The hours of receiving mourners were excruciating for Georgianna and the rest of the family as they stood at the coffin shaking hands, hugging friends, accepting condolences, sharing tears and memories. In the first of what would be many such experiences, Georgianna felt as if Elizabeth's spirit were standing just behind her, whispering in her ear the name of each mourner who passed through the line. Georgianna hadn't seen some of these people since

Elizabeth was in grade school, but somehow she remembered each name. There could be only one way for these names to be so readily recalled. Oh, Lord, Georgianna began to pray, please keep Elizabeth's spirit close to me.

TWENTY-ONE

The secret affair between Rick DeCaro and Cathy Dillon had been anything but, the police were learning. In fourteen interviews Sunday and Monday with some of the surprisingly large number of employees at the busy and profitable Old Orchard Amoco Station, it became more than clear that the trysts between the manager and the secretary had been grist for the rumor mill all along. One called the rumors simply the "Rick and Cathy thing," adding that he had paid no attention to whether they were true; he didn't want to jeopardize his job by spreading them. There was good reason for that concern, the cops would learn.

Most had heard the gossip. Some didn't believe it for a minute; Rick and Elizabeth were a happy couple who loved each other and their kids and were dedicated to their marriage. Some insisted that the boss and the blonde were just good friends. Others were just as sure that the affair was a fact. One worker was absolutely convinced that Rick and Cathy had been seeing each other; they ate lunch together and they left work at the same time. He heard that another employee had once noticed the telltale sign of Rick's shirt-tail hanging uncharacteristically outside his pants when he came back from lunch with Cathy. And the worker himself had twice watched them carefully coordinate their departures, with Cathy's Camaro exiting the driveway—in the wrong way from the direction of her home—followed within a few minutes by Rick in his Blazer, going the same direction as the Camaro.

One worker had, indeed, been fired for wisecracks about

the lunchtime liaisons. He had noticed that Cathy was seldom using Dan DeCaro's office anymore, even though that had been her assigned work station. She had begun using Rick's office, and the two had been seen sitting much closer than the job required.

Two days before Elizabeth's murder, the observant worker had been talking to a customer when he made a vague reference to the considerable demands on Rick's time by this back-office romance. "I wish Rick would do his job so I don't have to do it," he grumbled. Unfortunately, Rick overheard the behind-his-back banter on the security monitor and fired the employee on the spot. The worker appealed to the ultimate boss, Dan DeCaro, who hired him back on Friday—the same day as the murder. The ironies abounded in this case, the cops mused.

As had many of the employees, the reinstated worker had heard rumors—as well as comments by Rick—that suggested there were problems and financial worries on the DeCaro home front. The worker once heard Rick talking on the phone to Elizabeth, protesting, "I can't believe you had me followed!"

The cops were beginning to realize that Rick DeCaro had not been as discreet as he had believed.

The firing of the worker with the big mouth was cited as part of the swirling intrigue at Old Orchard by one of the other employees, too. Dan DeCaro's decision to rehire the dismissed complainer had led to a confrontation between the brothers, with Rick getting a dressing-down as Dan explained the facts of life—it was his station and he would have anyone he wanted working for him. Rick couldn't argue with that; it wasn't worth jeopardizing a 70K salary over a guy with a smart mouth. But Rick did take the time to go back to the complainer with another admonition—just keep your mouth shut.

The worker who had seen that exchange also offered a couple of damning opinions that tracked the things being said by so many others. He had always thought something was seriously wrong with the way the van had crashed into Elizabeth and then been stolen on the one night it was left outside. He thought the theft was an insurance job. And why, he wondered now, had Rick suddenly decided to take the kids to the Ozarks and leave his wife at home? "It looks bad for him," the worker concluded. The cops surely agreed with that analysis.

Rick didn't fare very well on questions about the Blazer either. Every worker who knew anything about it offered the same comment—it was in extraordinarily good mechanical condition and could be driven anywhere without concern. Several were aware that Rick had put in a new engine recently, and they said he maintained the vehicle flawlessly. He told one of the guys that he had to be sure it was safe because his wife and kids were in it so much.

One of the employees with very little to say to the police was Craig Wells, who had worked there for six years and lived in Fenton, a small town in neighboring Jefferson County. Wells told the police he was a friend of the Van Iseghems' and had helped Rick remodel his in-laws' home and delicatessen. Wells just couldn't believe anyone would hurt Elizabeth. And, he insisted, he wasn't aware of any problems between her and Rick.

As the detectives had for all of the other Old Orchard employees, they asked Craig Wells to fill out a SCAN test. The form called for handwritten responses to a series of questions. The technique for analyzing the responses had been developed especially for investigations that involved a large number of people, some of whom probably were reluctant to provide truthful or complete answers. Specially trained officers could find hints in those answers that could be useful indications of whether the subjects were offering valid information. The test was not foolproof, but in a case like this it could be helpful.

After Craig Wells completed his test, the examiner gave Lieutenant McCarrick a straightforward, scatological appraisal.

"It's bullshit."

Craig Wells was holding back—a lot.

TWENTY-TWO

If Elizabeth DeCaro was going to have an affair with anyone, Officer Cliff Dugan said, he had hoped it would be with him. He had fallen in love with her.

The police officer was the last of the interviews for the Major Case Squad on Sunday, and he had much to say when he sat down with the detectives at 10 P.M. He lived not far from the Van Iseghems and had come to know them fairly well. He had eaten at their deli and had even visited their home. He had met Elizabeth three years ago. "I fell in love with her," he admitted.

He was, in fact, the "Cliff" whose letter the police had found among Elizabeth's belongings, the one describing the author's "strong emotional feelings" for her. His wife was aware of those feelings for another woman and was trying to deal with them.

Dugan said Elizabeth had told him almost everything about the decline of her marriage, including Rick's affair. She believed their problems could be worked out and she wanted to save the marriage, if Rick would end the affair. Dugan said he may have been responsible for Elizabeth's insistence that Rick fire Cathy. Dugan had asked Elizabeth how she could believe the affair was over if Rick and Cathy still worked together. Dugan had offered to follow Rick, but Elizabeth declined.

The officer knew Elizabeth was afraid of her husband. She had listed her reasons. First, there was the new insurance policy that made her death worth a cool hundred grand. There was the van incident and her conclusion that he had intentionally tried to kill her. She was sure he had arranged the theft of the van, since he had removed the phone and Nintendo just hours before it disappeared from the driveway—where he had never parked it before.

And recently Rick had encouraged her to go to Kansas

City to see Pam Hanley or to California to see Margie—both suggestions that Elizabeth thought were efforts to set her up for an allegation, in the inevitable custody battle, that she had abandoned the kids.

There was nothing in Officer Cliff Dugan's information that reached the level of evidence. All that was really clear was this sad fact: he had loved Elizabeth, but she apparently had not felt the same way about him.

TWENTY-THREE

The missing tears finally arrived on Monday.

After two days with Rick DeCaro looking as if he was coping with a dull toothache instead of mourning a murdered wife, he finally found the tears that should have flowed all weekend. He actually wept during the funeral service on Monday. Still mimicking their father's reactions, the four children cried more openly than they had all weekend. Melanie and Mary—growing ever more critical of this man as the days passed—could not find room in their broken hearts to judge his tears genuine even then.

In the sanctuary of St. Kevin's Church, Rick DeCaro was only one of hundreds of weeping among the standing-room-only crowd. Jim and Georgianna, their children and their children's children, every relative and friend and acquaintance—all were unable to restrain their emotions. Mary was so overcome that she fainted and had to be helped from the church. But Jimmy Van Iseghem may have been the most stricken; he could not stop crying as the reality of his sister's death flooded over him. For the first time, the ugly side of the world had broken through the walls that the Van Iseghems had built so carefully around their lives. And, my God, how it hurt, Jimmy thought. As the service ended and the procession formed for the drive to the cemetery, he still could not stop crying.

Through all of her misery, Melanie offered a special

prayer—not *for* Elizabeth, but *to* her. Please send me a sign, she begged her departed sister. Make it something loud, something I will know was from you. Send me a signal that you want me to pursue my promise to prove Rick was behind your murder, to push and push and push and to never rest until justice is done for you. Please, Elizabeth, send me a sign.

Georgianna was lost in a fog of pain and grief, but she still was able to appreciate the love and affection shown by everyone who took the time to mark the end of her daughter's life. She began to realize that she would survive this nightmare—if she did at all—only through the grace and love of God and the caring and support of her family and friends. She was deeply touched when the seemingly endless line of cars—stretching a mile into the distance—wound its way toward Elizabeth's waiting grave.

The graveside service was the family's last chance to say good-bye to Elizabeth's earthly remains, but Tom O'Connor could not give them any more privacy than he had at the funeral home the night before. He had to send his detectives to the cemetery too, on the off-chance that someone in the crowd would strike a suspicious chord. But all the police witnessed was the Van Iseghems' sad, painful, final farewell.

The cemetery duty was certainly not the detectives' only activity on what would be a key day in the investigation of Elizabeth DeCaro's murder.

Not long after the service at the cemetery, Melanie Enkelmann had her second interview with the police. For more than four hours, she went over the same ground, covering again every detail and anecdote she could pry out of her memory of her sister's last months, down to her last minutes. But the only truly new information came when the detectives bluntly asked Melanie why she had lied to them. Why hadn't she told them about Elizabeth and Mike Carroll? Yes, Melanie admitted, she had known about that. But it had nothing to do with the murder; Mike certainly wasn't a suspect in Melanie's mind. And when it came down to her sister's brief extramarital transgression, Mela-

nie took a liberal view. If Elizabeth had found someone
who gave her comfort and pleasure and tenderness and
care and support in those awful weeks, then by God, good
for her. There would be no condemnation from Melanie;
she knew too much, and loved her sister too much for that.

Melanie's husband finally got to tell the police what he
knew later that day. John Enkelmann hadn't believed that
Rick was having an affair, even though for the last several
months Rick had been treating Elizabeth, in John's words,
"like crap." Skepticism that his brother-in-law was cheating
had led to John's adventure as an amateur detective. Just
to prove to Melanie and Mary how foolish their suspicions
were, he had agreed to follow Rick that Wednesday night
in early February. The self-conscious sleuth tracked Rick
from the service station to the lot at Gold's Gym, where
he parked the Blazer quite far from the other cars. John
assumed that Rick was parking that way to avoid dings
from other people's car doors, protecting his own vehicle
as always. John left his car and walked down the row to
get a better view while Rick sat there. Within minutes,
Cathy Dillon arrived in her red Camaro; Rick hopped in
and they sped off. John ran to his car, but by the time he
swung out of the lot, his target had disappeared into the
winter night.

The intense search for the missing 1985 Chevy Blazer
also got a boost early Monday from Mark Speckert—the
man who had sold it to Rick DeCaro. Speckert had seen
the publicity about the search for the vehicle and decided
he had better talk to the cops. He even furnished a photograph of the black and silver truck. Shortly after the sale,
he remembered, Rick had come to him with a complaint—
the engine had blown up and Rick had been forced to
replace it. Speckert agreed to rebate $500 to cover part of
the costs. He knew that Rick had replaced the transmission
too, and that should have left the vehicle mechanically
perfect.

O'Connor released the photo to the media and got great
play on the story again. The TV stations ran the photo that
night and renewed the squad's call for tips on the Blazer

with the RIK-LIZ license plates. The *St. Louis Post-Dispatch* published the photo the next morning. A number of sightings were reported, but none seemed to have been the right vehicle. The cops were frustrated; somebody had to have seen the vehicle. They just needed that person to get the news.

One team of detectives made the rounds of local pawn-shops Monday—checking to see if any of the DeCaros' missing electronics had shown up and to ask the dealers to watch for them. While that was under way, Lieutenant Pat McCarrick and Detective Rich Plummer were proving just how aggressively the Major Case Squad would pursue a lead. Glenda Moon, the mail carrier for the DeCaros' neighborhood, offered a tip. She remembered seeing two men in a pickup truck on Autumn Wood Drive, one street over from Hidden Meadow Court, on the afternoon of the murder, possibly the day before. The truck was moving slowly, and the occupants—white men in their late teens or early twenties—were scanning the neighborhood. Finally, they stopped and stared intently between two houses. The detectives took Ms. Moon on a drive down Autumn Wood until she found the spot that had attracted the men's atten-tion—the north side of the street between the houses at 2046 and 2050. This time, McCarrick and Plummer were left staring—directly at the back of the DeCaro house. Had Glenda Moon seen the killers scoping out their target's house?

At four o'clock Monday, the detectives delivered Glenda to a Dr. Terry Rohen, a psychologist and hypnotist. With her cooperation, he hypnotized her and directed her mind's eye back to the encounter on Autumn Wood Drive. She now described an older-model, reddish-orange pickup truck, all bright and clean and "fixed up." But she still couldn't get a good look at the two men inside. The next day McCarrick and Plummer took her on a tour of used-car lots, looking for a truck that matched her enhanced memory. Failing to find a look-alike there, they showed her the trucks owned by workers at DeCaro's service station; no luck there, either. The next stop was the St. Louis Police

Department's auto theft bureau, where she pored over the vehicular equivalent of mug books, looking at hundreds of photographs of pickup trucks. She finally settled on a mid-1970s model with round headlights, white running boards, "blocky-looking" front fenders, and a high cab. But after all of that, they still couldn't get enough of a description to be of any assistance. All that work had led to nothing.

Among the hours of tense investigation and interrogation, there was time for little moments of humanity that kept Pat McCarrick from losing his sanity. While he was waiting to deliver the evening briefing in the squad room, he overheard Detective Mike Riley of the Third District in St. Louis taking a phone call. McCarrick was intrigued.

"No, huh-uh, no," Riley was saying with a firm tone in his voice. "No, no, I can't tell you about that."

What is this all about? McCarrick wondered.

"No, I can't tell you. I can't discuss it with you unless you're a member of the Major Case Squad . . ." A nosy reporter, McCarrick guessed. ". . . and you can't be a member of the Major Case Squad because you're only ten years old. Now, put your mother on the phone."

McCarrick felt the grin split across his face. Being a cop and a parent could be difficult sometimes, but these detectives always remained both.

The bare financial facts were pretty grim, convincing the detectives that the DeCaros were in about as deep as they could get—mortgaged to the hilt, indeed. Rick earned about $70,000 a year—an impressive salary for a man of limited education. But he had been spending as if he made much more. The house that cost $145,000 about six years ago was now valued at $160,000, but the first mortgage was for $144,000, with monthly payments of $1,480 and they still owed practically the full cost. Even if he sold it at full market value, he would realize only $16,000 in equity—just 10 percent.

And that was the good news. The bad news was that any equity they had in theory had been wiped out in reality by a second mortgage of $15,000, taken out just eighteen months ago. They had borrowed that money to pay off the bills still outstanding because it had taken so long to sell their house in the Eagle Ridge subdivision. They had just unloaded it two years ago, and the debt had forced them into a second mortgage.

There was even worse news. They were paying a hefty $190 a month for that boat Rick had to have. The twenty-one-foot, open-bow 1982 Celebrity had cost $7,000, and Rick still owed $6,000 on it. He owed even more than that for two more debts—$3,000 to the Beneficial Credit Corporation at $90 a month, and another $4,578 on a Visa card that had been maxed out to $78 over the credit limit.

Their insurance was a fairly standard package—the only remarkable item being that new policy on Elizabeth for $100,000. Rick was insured for $250,000; the two policies cost a combined $501.50 a year. The house and its contents were underinsured at $142,000, with an annual premium of $332. Insurance on the new van was $760 a year, and the boat added another $190 annual premium. The missing Blazer was insured through the service station.

Rick had collected $2,570 from an insurance claim for the damage to the garage wall—a cynic might have suggested the hole had been in the outline of Elizabeth's body. A check for the claim on the stolen van—$17,497—had gone to the bank that held the title for the lease. Another check from that suspicious theft had been issued to Rick— $405 to cover the difference between the value of the van and the amount still owed the bank. A third check for $652.45 was issued to the DeCaros to reimburse their loss of personal items in the van.

The possible open claim? Elizabeth's death benefits. If approved and paid, the check was to be sent to—Rick DeCaro.

TWENTY-FOUR

"He asked me if I knew someone who would 'hit' someone for him."

Magic words. Seventy-two long hours after the murder of Elizabeth DeCaro. Finally, those magic words.

As Tom O'Connor, Dave King, Pat McCarrick, and all the other detectives had learned over the years, the clues to a murder most often could be found in the victim's and suspect's normal lives. O'Connor had his teams prying into every facet of the lives of Elizabeth and Rick DeCaro, and a great deal of hearsay evidence already had piled up. The Van Iseghems, Pam Hanley, Mike Carroll, Cathy Dillon, the employees at Old Orchard Amoco—they all held little pieces of a puzzle that formed a dark picture of Rick De-Caro. But not even all of that together came close to making a murder case against him.

As O'Connor dug deeper Monday afternoon, he sent his men to another of the places that seemed to be so important in these troubled lives. Gold's Gym in nearby Shrewsbury was as much a part of Rick DeCaro's daily routine as work and home; he was almost fanatical about his weightlifting workouts. And beyond that, Elizabeth had told several people that Rick was spending more and more time with his friends from the gym. Detective Ken Wallingsford and Lieutenant Tony Umbertino were assigned to find out what they could about the Rick DeCaro known to the people at Gold's.

One of their first interviews was with James Torregrossa, who not only worked out there but had been employed there part-time. He had known Rick for about a year. They were slightly more than acquaintances, but not quite friends. Torregrossa offered the police his recollection of one of Rick's few comments about his wife: he had complained that she was nagging him to spend more time at home instead of working so much, and she even suspected that he was "messing around" on her.

Torregrossa had taken his truck to Rick's station for service a few times and, late on Friday afternoon, January 10, had taken his girlfriend's Ford Mustang there for a new tire. Torregrossa had forgotten the special key needed to unlock the lug nuts on her wheels, so he had to hang around until she could drop it off about twenty minutes later. While he and Rick sat in the office and shot the bull, a blond secretary came in briefly. When she left, Rick told Torregrossa she was the one his wife suspected he had been "screwing around with."

After Torregrossa's girlfriend dropped off the key and left, Rick asked casually if they were planning to get married. Yeah, Torregrossa replied. Rick snapped, "Well, I wouldn't put marriage on anybody . . . I used to walk around with two hundred dollars in my pocket. And now I don't have anything."

Torregrossa changed the subject, invoking the one topic guys can always talk about—cars. He opened by complaining about his girlfriend's Mustang: the interior was junk, the car was almost falling apart, and he wished she hadn't bought it. Rick raised the bet. He knew what Torregrossa meant; the payments on Rick's van were killing him, the dealer never fixed it right, and he wished he could get rid of it. He looked at his friend.

"Do you know anybody who can get rid of cars, who can do that kind of thing?"

Torregrossa was surprised by this clear inquiry about finding someone to steal a lemon for the owner. Wanting to look like a big shot, he lied and said maybe. Rick nodded and said, "Get ahold of me later." Torregrossa had no intention of following up on that; he didn't really know anyone who did that sort of thing.

Rick had another question. And it was a quantum leap past the first.

"Do you know anyone who could 'hit' someone for me?"

Now Torregrossa was stunned. "What are you talking about?"

"Do you know anyone who would kill someone for me? I need that done too."

Torregrossa couldn't believe this. Had Rick DeCaro really just asked him about a hit man, a professional killer? Torregrossa wanted out of this conversation as fast as possible. He gave Rick a quick "no" and changed the subject.

The unbelievable requests by Rick that day had never come up again. But Torregrossa told the police he had interpreted the questions as a sign of Rick's deep trust in him. You don't ask that kind of question of someone you don't trust completely.

Torregrossa said he had gone to the funeral home to see Rick. He shook Rick's hand and told him how sorry he was. It was a strange experience. The rest of Elizabeth's family was standing far away from Rick, obviously avoiding him. Torregrossa thought Rick seemed as if he was on some kind of medication; he had a "stone-cold look."

And Torregrossa offered the cops one more opinion: he strongly felt that Rick DeCaro had had his wife killed.

After this interview, pegging Rick for a murder conspirator was hardly jumping to conclusions, in the detectives' view. Now, for the first time, they had someone who could put guilty words in Rick's mouth. This was more than whining about an unhappy marriage and more than the fallout from an affair. They had heard Rick DeCaro betray his deepest desire, giving voice to it in a revealing request.

Tom O'Connor decided to try the secret-recording routine again with this incredibly incriminating witness. Torregrossa agreed to give it a shot, and that evening the police wired the telephone at his parents' house to see just what Rick would say when confronted by someone who had such damaging information. They coached Torregrossa briefly: act nervous, complain about worrisome questions from the cops, and seek Rick's advice about how to keep their little secret.

For an amateur, Torregrossa played the role well—in fact, he almost overplayed it. He assumed a character that seemed to have come from a bad gangster movie. As soon as Rick answered the phone, Torregrossa slipped into his new persona and ratcheted his voice into a state of high agitation.

"Hey, what's up, man?" the excited Torregrossa almost shouted. "There's a bunch of fuckin' cops asking me questions and shit."

"Yeah?"

"I mean, what? Just fuckin' ignore them? They said, are you talking about anything? I said, 'Fuck, no.'"

The cops grimaced. That kind of language wouldn't make this tape the most jury-friendly evidence in the event that Rick said anything useful and it had to be played in court later. But that didn't seem too likely. From the sound of it, Rick was taking the same tack he had with Melanie two days earlier.

"Yeah, I know," Rick was saying. "They're taking me as . . . they just said it's normal for me to be the number one suspect."

"You?"

"Yeah. They said that's just normal, as a spouse."

Following the script suggested by the police, Torregrossa told Rick that the Major Case Squad had threatened to put him on the polygraph. Rick assured him they wouldn't do that, but Torregrossa said they had told him twice they would. What should he tell them? he asked anxiously.

"You know," Rick suggested, "we've gone out and had a few drinks and that's it. Right?"

Torregrossa shot back, "Yeah, as far as I'm concerned, that's what I said."

"Yeah, okay, yeah. I appreciate it."

The men ended their conversation on a warm note as Torregrossa assured Rick, "Okay, you got my prayers, brother."

"Okay, Jim, thanks."

The police decided to have Torregrossa rattle Rick's cage again the next afternoon with an even more worried call, placed from the police station. This time Torregrossa reported that the cops had been to Gold's Gym to interview everyone, and they were pushing him hard on whether he knew anything about the theft of the van. He had denied any knowledge about it but was worried about his story "jibing" with Rick's.

Rick told him to stay the course. "I never mentioned that to you. You don't know nothing about that."

"Yeah."

"I mean, it was stolen out of my driveway. That's all I know."

Rick advised him again just to say they had done a little social drinking and that was all there was to their relationship. That's what he was going to tell the police, Rick said.

Another tape clogged with crude language, yielding little evidence. How about a third strike? An hour later, the police had Torregrossa make yet another call, pumping up the tension even farther by claiming the cops had given him fifteen minutes to report to the police station for yet another interrogation. They somehow knew about the conversation about the van, Torregrossa babbled excitedly.

"Uh, what conversation?" Rick asked coolly. "I never had a conversation . . . about anything."

When his gym buddy reiterated the cops' ultimatum, Rick's voice carried a slight air of resignation. "Well, do what you have to do. I don't know. I guess you have to cooperate."

That was not exactly what the police had to hoped to hear from Rick in response to Torregrossa's profanity-packed pleas for guidance. But they still had the magic words from Torregrossa the day before. And those words had come without a single common vulgarity—just the obscenity of Rick's intent.

"He asked me if I knew someone who would 'hit' someone for him."

TWENTY-FIVE

The detectives had a problem with one of the employees at Old Orchard Amoco—Craig Wells. The cops didn't believe the thin story told by this slightly built, light-haired man who claimed to know nothing about anything. He was friends with the Van Iseghems and worked every day for Rick DeCaro, but he had never heard any suggestions of problems in Rick and Elizabeth's marriage. The results of his SCAN test suggested that he was providing a drastically abridged version of his knowledge. In addition, Wells was the overfriendly and equally nervous man who had walked Melanie to her car so disconcertingly two days before the murder. Wells had even visited Jim Van Iseghem's store a couple of times in the days before that. Each time he had been pale and nervous, as if there was something he wanted to say to Jim but just couldn't find the words or the courage to say.

Tom O'Connor didn't like leaving hunches hanging, so the detectives went back to the service station Monday, convinced Wells to talk to them again, and delivered the clearly anxious man to the police station—a slightly different ambience for a second interview. Even at the station Wells didn't have much to say. The detectives pushed him hard about his relationships with all of the players in this case, but his amnesia was persistent. He couldn't remember anything that would help the cops.

Chief Dave King and Tom O'Connor, watching through the two-way mirror from the room next door, decided it was time for some attitude adjustment, time to offer a little cagey encouragement to Craig Wells in hopes that his recollection could be "refreshed," as they say in court. King and O'Connor stepped into the interview room, and King took what he knew was a hell of a gamble. If this worked, it would be worth the risk. If it failed, he might alienate an important, perhaps crucial, witness. He leaned in close to this very uncomfortable young man.

"We have a terrible murder here," the chief began in a low, firm voice, "and I believe you have information about it. I want you to understand something. I am giving you every assurance I can that if you do have information and you do not give it to us, I will do everything in my power to be sure that you are charged with capital murder, just as if you had put the gun to Elizabeth DeCaro's head yourself. Do you understand me?"

Craig Wells sat silently for a long time, his eyes cast down as King drilled him with a stare intended to impress on him just how serious all of this really was. The Major Case Squad was not investigating the theft of a hubcap here; this was the big time, one of the most horrible murders in the St. Louis area in years. King had promised the Van Iseghems that he would find the killer, and no one had better mislead the police or stand in their way.

Finally, Wells looked up. "Can I talk to the detectives again?" With this new incentive, he was ready to offer the police not only an improved memory but some more magic words.

Wells had, indeed, heard the rumors that Rick and Liz were not getting along and that Rick had been seeing Cathy Dillon on the side. Rick had complained about financial problems—a second mortgage, the van, the boat—but Wells assumed the DeCaros' money situation was not that different from that of most families.

About the third week of January, Rick had come to Wells at the station and asked if he knew anyone who would steal the van. Unlike Torregrossa, Wells was fairly sure he knew someone who would be interested in that job. He immediately thought of an ex-con named Danny Basile. Wells and Basile—whose name was pronounced with an Italian flair—"Buh-silly"—were connected by one of those broken-home, multiple-marriage, chain-reaction relationships so common in some parts of society. Wells's stepmother had a foster son named Doug Meyer, and Meyer's half brother was Danny Basile—a short, muscular man with shoulder-length brown hair and a scraggly mustache. Wells considered Doug Meyer his foster brother, an emotional connection that extended to the next link in that chain, Danny Basile. Wells called Basile and Meyer his brothers, even though they shared no blood. It was almost too clumsy to explain in one sentence—Basile was Wells's foster brother's half brother.

The bond was strong enough to draw Danny Basile into this eddy. In fact, Basile had been staying at Wells's house in Fenton for the last month while attending Vatterott College—a vocational school in St. Ann—to learn the heating-

and-cooling trade. He picked up odd jobs to support himself. Wells arranged a meeting between Rick and Basile, the two men who now shared an interest in making a van disappear. Several nights later, Wells picked up Basile and drove to that popular parking lot at Gold's Gym, where they met Rick DeCaro in the white GMC van in question. As Basile climbed into the van, Wells drove away to give the men time to talk. He went to Old Orchard Amoco, picked up his paycheck, and returned a little later to pick up Danny Basile.

"I'm not sure what this guy wants me to do," Basile reported to his deal-arranging friend. "He said he wants me to steal his van . . ." He hesitated for a long moment and then added, ". . . and he asked me to do a 'hit.' "

Wells was surprised by this new wrinkle. "Who?"

"On his wife."

Several days later, Wells drove Basile to another meeting with Rick at the same place. And several days after that, Rick gave Wells an envelope to give to Basile. Wells said it contained keys to the van, two hundred dollars in cash, and a handwritten map illustrating the route to DeCaro's house on Hidden Meadow Court.

That was the last he had heard about any of it, Wells said.

More magic words. The cops now had a name—Danny Basile—and the witness who had made the connection for Rick to put money, keys, and a map in the hands of this ex-con.

The investigation definitely was in high gear now.

TWENTY-SIX

About ten o'clock Monday night, in the quieter hours after Elizabeth's funeral, Melanie was standing alone in her mother's kitchen on St. Francis Lane. The house was almost silent now. The crush of family and friends sharing the hours after Elizabeth was buried had eased, and everyone was beginning to let the grief soak in. Melanie stood in the darkened kitchen where she and Elizabeth, Mary and Margie, Georgianna and Theresa—the whole family— had enjoyed the togetherness of so many wonderful family meals. Melanie could feel another of those moments of realization coming on as she understood that such a scene could never be played again there. The cast would never be complete again.

The almost deafening crash made Melanie jump. The growing storm outside—an early spring rain rumbling through March in St. Louis—had built up a tremendous thunderclap that rattled the windows and shook Melanie deeply. Then she realized that what she had heard was not just thunder. It was the sign she had asked Elizabeth to send, the signal confirming Rick's guilt and cementing Melanie's pledge to follow this crusade, wherever it went and however long it took, until justice was served.

In this new world, not only were the raindrops tears for Elizabeth but the thunder was a demand for justice.

TWENTY-SEVEN

By Tuesday morning, Rick DeCaro had already registered his children in the St. Charles public schools. Their mother was barely in her grave before Rick had implemented the change he had been demanding for some time—no more expensive Catholic schools. He also told the family that he had set up counseling appointments for the kids and had managed to arrange his work schedule so he could be home by three o'clock, when the children arrived from school.

Melanie was outraged. Elizabeth had begged Rick to spend more time at home. All she had ever wanted, she had said repeatedly, was him—not gifts and flowers, just him. No, he had said, the station's demands on his time precluded that. But now that Elizabeth was gone, Rick suddenly had the time. Damn him.

On this Tuesday, Detective Vince Cowdry had a special question about the kids' schools. He tracked down the DeCaros' oldest son, Patrick, at a friend's house that evening for an interview that his father knew nothing about. Yes, Patrick said, he knew his parents had engaged in some verbal fights, and he thought they were having financial troubles. He had heard them talking about the fact that keeping the kids in Catholic schools was costing them four thousand dollars a year. Another source of conflict, the cops thought.

An interview Tuesday afternoon offered more illumination on the strain in the DeCaro marriage. Dan DeCaro's ex-wife, Judy Martin, told the police that she had remained friends with Elizabeth even after the divorce took Judy out of the family ten years ago. Judy had even watched the DeCaros' dog during the funeral on Monday. When Rick picked Ozzie up later, Judy asked how he was holding up. He said the toughest part so far had been the funeral and burial, but he believed the biggest obstacles were yet to come.

The drought of contact with Richard DeCaro seemed about to end for the Major Case Squad. He had finally agreed to an interview at the police station at three o'clock on Tuesday. Armed with the information from James Torregrossa and Craig Wells, Tom O'Connor planned to put his considerable skills to the test. There was a good reason he taught interrogation techniques to other detectives, and now he was about to apply that expertise in a face-to-face confrontation with Rick. How would this untested man hold up under the psychological assault that O'Connor could bring to bear? Would he break under the intense pressure that O'Connor knew so well how to apply? Rick had never experienced that kind of grilling; he had never sat in the suspect's chair and felt the heat; he had never tried to deny incriminating allegations like those delivered by Torregrossa and Wells. O'Connor was eager for this session.

He had sent a detective team to stake out DeCaro's

house about ten o'clock, just to be sure he did not have other plans for the day. Just before noon, the crew called in to report that two men in a car had arrived at DeCaro's house. The police ran the license plate on the car, and it came back registered to Ronald E. Jenkins, a prominent lawyer in Clayton—a busy legal center and the seat of St. Louis County government. Was DeCaro about to lawyer up? O'Connor wasn't surprised, but it did piss him off.

When three o'clock arrived, so did two lawyers—without Richard DeCaro. O'Connor was furious now. When Ron Jenkins and his associate met O'Connor and King, O'Connor was immediately put off by what he interpreted as the lawyers' attitude toward the police—that they were fools. O'Connor could not tolerate that, and the Irishman went on the attack.

"Why are you here?" he demanded impatiently. "Do you want to say something to us? Have you got something in that briefcase to present to us?"

Jenkins handed O'Connor a document signed by De-Caro, declaring that he intended to invoke his Fifth Amendment right to remain silent, to refuse to answer any questions from the police from that moment on. O'Connor nodded. That was it, then. An innocent man whose wife had been murdered would be doing everything he could to help the police, to provide every bit of information he could think of that might help in any way. He probably would be living at the police station, dogging the cops every minute to make sure they weren't backing off for a second. Or he would be phoning every few minutes with some new and probably useless recollection. Instead, Richard DeCaro had dispatched two attorneys to deliver a document guaranteeing just the opposite; he wanted no further contact with the police. O'Connor's Irish temper was flaring as he turned to the lawyers.

"Well, Mr. DeCaro has the right to invoke the Fifth Amendment," he said through clenched teeth. "But we have rights, too. So, gentlemen, just watch how we exercise our First Amendment rights."

After the lawyers departed, O'Connor scheduled a news conference for Wednesday afternoon.

* * *

None of Tuesday's activities had provided much hope for Chief Dave King, and he was beginning to feel despair creeping in. Maybe the best efforts of all of these dedicated, expert cops couldn't crack this one. Things like that happened in police work. Tragic, horrible cases went unsolved. He had never seen a group of harder-working cops than those who had answered the call on this one. They had been living it for five days now, around the clock, with little rest and no complaints. King had become a confirmed member of the Tom O'Connor Fan Club. Tom consulted King at every step and cleared every move he made—even though, as commander, he didn't have to do that. King knew there was nothing more that could or should be done. But still, perhaps all that hard work wouldn't pay off. Would this be one of those cops'-worst-nightmare cases— the unresolved case that would forever haunt every man on the squad?

King knew that some of the detectives were beginning to experience that same gnawing in their bellies. The frustration of setting their sights on a target, yet lacking the ammunition to get the job done, was getting to them all. But then King heard Detective Ken Wallingsford encouraging his partner with a surprising sentiment.

"We've got to solve this for the chief."

Dave King's eyes stung with tears. These guys hardly knew him; they hadn't gone through the years of camaraderie needed to build devotion to an old friend. Yet here they were, hardened professionals investigating a savage murder, and they had the time, and the heart, to care about Dave King, the new guy. Seldom had King felt this kind of emotion rise in his throat on the job, but the moment reached inside and touched him deeply.

And within an hour the outlook for the Elizabeth De-Caro case changed dramatically.

An investigator for the St. Louis County prosecuting attorney's office called the Major Case Squad, explaining that a lawyer had asked him to open the lines of communication for a client, a potential witness. That was certainly taking the long way around, but anything that worked was okay.

An appointment was set for this mystery guest, who signed in at the police station at ten-thirty that night. While some of the detectives were searching for background and information on Daniel Anthony Basile, an old friend of his, Susan Jenkins, arrived to be interviewed in the company of her attorney, Claude Hanks. Hanks and prosecuting attorney Tim Braun worked out a deal: in return for information that she could provide about Basile, Susan Jenkins would not be prosecuted for any crimes, unless she was directly involved in the murder. Although Missouri's laws do not give a prosecutor the authority to grant immunity to a witness, this agreement had the same effect.

So the deal for Susan Jenkins was cut, and she began to tell her story. This slightly heavyset, twenty-five-year-old blonde was frightened of the ex-con she had known since junior high school, a man who smoked marijuana and used cocaine and drank, a man who was in trouble with the cops a lot, a man who was aware that she had very damaging information about his recent activities. That, she explained, was why she had been so careful, and reluctant, about contacting the authorities. But finally her conscience—tortured by what she thought she knew about the murder of Elizabeth DeCaro—had driven her to call.

With that preface, Sue Jenkins delivered a fascinating story to the anxious detectives. On February 7, Danny Basile had told her he was doing a job for a friend; when he told her the details a little later, he called it an "insurance scam." All the arrangements were made. He had the keys to the van he was to steal and handwritten directions to the house. But he needed a driver; he needed her help.

That evening, she picked Basile up in Fenton and drove him the twenty-five miles north to St. Charles, while he read from the special directions he had been provided. As they got close to their destination, Basile pulled his hair back into a tight ponytail, pulled on a pair of latex gloves, and then put on brown work gloves. When they reached the Woodfield Meadows subdivision and found the right street—a "court" of some kind—he told her to stop several houses away from the one where the white conversion van had been backed into the driveway. He got out, walked toward the van, and soon drove it back past her car. She followed him on a return trip the way they had come, except that he passed the turnoff to Fenton and instead took I-55, cruising almost a hundred miles south in a course parallel to the nearby Mississippi River.

In tandem, they took an exit and turned west toward the little town of Jackson. Susan Jenkins explained that their destination was a few miles north of the largest city in that part of the state—Cape Girardeau—a nice town along the Mississippi that neither she nor the police could ever have dreamed would play such an important role in this drama much later. She said she followed Basile off the interstate for several miles until they reached the home of his sister— Sherry Keller*. According to Susan, Sherry seemed frightened and concerned by the whole situation and urged her brother to return the stolen van. "I've already spent the money," Basile shot back. He stripped some parts off the van in Sherry's driveway and loaded them into Sue's car trunk. And then Sherry got into Sue's car and provided the directions for a long drive into the rural countryside, with Danny Basile behind them in the van. Finally, about six o'clock, almost sunrise, they stopped in a deserted, hilly area. While Sue and Sherry waited, Basile drove the van out of sight. Before long, Sue could see the orange glow from a fire on the horizon. Danny obviously had torched the van; when he returned to her car, he reeked of gasoline.

They dropped Sherry at her house and headed back toward I-55. Basile was carrying one of the license plates from the van, but complained that he hadn't been able to get the front plate off. When they reached the interstate, Basile surprisingly turned south again. Several miles down the highway, he folded up the metal plate and threw it out of the window toward the right shoulder of the road. Then he swung the car around at a crossover between the divided lanes and headed north again. When they got to St. Louis, Basile drove to the home of a woman he called Mom but who wasn't really related. He dropped off the parts he had stripped from the stolen van. The only item Sue Jenkins could remember was a small TV set. Then Basile drove to the Old Orchard Amoco Station, bought eight dollars worth of gasoline for the car, and chatted briefly with an employee inside.

And the eventful evening was over.

The cops would have been thrilled even if that was all Sue Jenkins had been able to describe. But, oh, there was one more story she had to tell.

About six-thirty in the early evening of Thursday, March 5—the day before Elizabeth's murder—Basile had called Sue with a request. Could she use her employment at a doctor's office to get him some more latex gloves? He needed them for a "job" the next day. She had been growing frightened of this dangerous man, and the ominous "job" story he offered now was too much. She said she couldn't help him and hung up.

As she watched the accounts of Elizabeth's murder on the news over the next few days, Sue Jenkins began to put together all the pieces of what she feared had been Danny Basile's role in a contract murder. And he had made her a part of it by drawing her into the theft of the van. She was so frightened of Basile that she even changed her phone number. But that did nothing to assuage her conscience. She had knowledge about the murder of an innocent young woman, a murder the police were frantic to solve. Knowing that tormented her for days, until she finally decided she had to tell someone. She talked to her parents, called her attorney, and asked him to contact the police.

And after she had purged her conscience, she had one basic thought for the cops: "If you find Danny Basile, I think you're on the way to solving this murder."

Dave King was thrilled. Sue Jenkins struck him as a credible witness who had provided irrefutable proof of a conspiracy between Rick DeCaro and Danny Basile. Rick had engineered the insurance scam, and Basile had carried it out with Sue's help. Her story, coupled with Craig Wells's account of how he assembled the team of DeCaro and Basile, should lock up the case against the two men on the van theft. But Sue had also offered a damaging clue—the gloves—to Basile's involvement in the "job" on March 6. Now the cops had a real shot at solving a murder so diabol-

ical that it had included an insurance scam and arson a
month earlier.

The mood in the Major Case Squad's command center
had just improved dramatically, to something like a stadium
after a touchdown.

TWENTY-EIGHT

Daniel Anthony Basile. DOB: 12-5-66. Last known addresses: 795 Chancellor, Fenton, and 4320 Fuchs Road, St.
Louis County.

Pleaded guilty to felony burglary and stealing more than
$150 in 1984; sentenced to probation. Violated probation
in November 1987 by failing to follow directives; suspended
sentence of seven years. Probation revoked again in July
1988 for refusal to follow directives; committed to prison
in August 1988, paroled in May 1991. Parole case filed
transferred recently to Jefferson County probation officer
Jackie Alexander. First and last personal visit with Basile,
February 24, 1992.

Among the few relatives listed in the files were a brother,
Douglas Meyer, and a stepbrother, Craig Wells.

Those were the vital statistics on Danny Basile, the suspect in the murder of Elizabeth DeCaro and, in all probability, the man who had pulled the trigger of the gun behind
her head. According to the new evidence, those shots had
been fired at the behest of her husband.

On this Wednesday morning, March 11, Tom O'Connor
and Dave King were hot on Basile's trail. O'Connor also
decided to ratchet up the already intense search for the
Blazer. He sent detectives back into the air in the St. Louis
County Police helicopter for a bird's-eye view of the areas
around the houses where a hot vehicle might be hidden.
They targeted the two addresses listed for Basile, as well
as the home of Douglas Meyer. The search produced noth-

ing, but that was not O'Connor's only play. He was also flooding that same area with detectives to conduct surveillance on Basile—but not to arrest him yet.

Another assignment already was proving fruitful. Two detectives drove south to Cape Girardeau County, talked to colleagues at the sheriff's department, and arranged for the burnt-out shell of Rick's stolen GMC conversion van to be towed back to St. Charles. That was part of a special plan that O'Connor had hatched, and he couldn't wait to spring it.

But the second part of the detectives' trip to Cape Girardeau was the most exciting. They followed the route Sue Jenkins said she and Basile took after the van had been torched, driving south along I-55 from the Jackson exit. When the police found a crossover between the lanes, as Sue had described, they parked and began to search along the road on foot. The sharp eyes of Officer Gary Koeller, a Major Case Squad cop from Chesterfield, spotted something lying in the grass close to the guardrail on the right shoulder at mile post 105. The bent-up piece of metal was indeed a Missouri licence plate and, as Koeller carefully unfolded it, the magic letters and numbers revealed themselves to be B9Z-696. The unremarkable combination may have lacked the vanity and style of RIK-LIZ, but it packed almost as much evidentiary wallop: it was the license number issued to the 1989 white GMC conversion van driven by Rick DeCaro. It was the very plate Sue Jenkins said Basile had folded up and thrown out the car window at precisely that location.

The police had just verified an essential element of her story in a way no one could challenge, and that gave her a new luster of credibility. It also gave Tom O'Connor another candidate for a taped conversation. The attempts to catch Rick DeCaro in a mistake on tape had failed. His conversations with Melanie and Torregrossa had proved him a cold fish, but they had not reeled him in. O'Connor was undeterred, however; now he hoped the same approach might prove useful against Danny Basile.

From her home telephone—now wired to a recorder—Sue Jenkins began tracking down her old friend. She had several numbers for his numerous temporary residences, but each one failed to produce him. Every few minutes, as the detectives watched and the recorder whirred, Sue tried again. After more than two dozens calls between one o'clock that afternoon and nine-thirty that evening, she finally caught up with him at Craig Wells's house. Following the cops' script, Sue told Danny how worried she was about what to say if the police found her. She had seen the news about the murder of the woman at the house where he had stolen the van, and she had to know the answer to the burning question. "Did you do it?" she asked. No, he swore, he hadn't killed anyone. She asked again, and then again, and he denied any involvement. She changed her tactic, and this time he offered the kind of teasing response that drove the cops crazy.

"Do you know who did this?" she asked.

"In a weird way, maybe."

The cops shook their heads. What the hell did that mean?

O'Connor was frustrated again. Danny Basile was no genius, but he was too smart to be drawn into a murder confession by phone.

TWENTY-NINE

The abyss separating the Van Iseghems from Rick DeCaro continued to widen and deepen on Wednesday, even without Elizabeth's family knowing what the police were learning about her husband's suspicious activities. When Rick failed to show up at Georgianna and Jim's that night to sign thank-you cards, Georgianna found her patience wearing thin. When he called later—from his lawyer's office, yet—she couldn't hold her tongue.

"Why aren't you here?"

His voice was cold and distant. "I had the kids with me,

and I wanted to drop them off to spend the night at my brother's before I went to my lawyer's."

"Rick, the kids don't even know your brother or his kids. They've never spent the night there. They should spend the night here. They're Elizabeth's kids, too, and they should be here with us now. You should be here with us."

She couldn't contain her growing anger. "Do you want everyone to think you're guilty? Almost everyone thinks that already. Is that what you want? That's what everyone is going to think if you stay away from us. You should be here!"

Her tone was so provoking that her sister, Toni Byrd, was shocked. Toni whispered, "Georgianna, don't talk to him like that. You're gonna make him mad. He'll never let you see those kids again." That thought seemed absurd, until Georgianna heard Rick's voice, now even colder than she could have imagined.

"If that's the way you feel about me, if that's the way you're going to talk to me, I'll make sure you never see the kids again."

She sucked in her breath. She would never have believed he could threaten her with that, especially now. Her daughter had been ripped from her arms forever, and now Rick dared to threaten withholding Elizabeth's kids from the family who loved them so? Suddenly the veil lifted from her eyes and she saw clearly.

"Oh, Rick, I'm sorry," she pleaded in a quickly softened tone. "You know I don't think that about you, that I don't feel that way about you. Don't you understand that I want to believe you? You know I'm on your side. But you have to be here with us. You have to bring those kids over here with us. I'll do anything I can to help, but you have to be with us."

Georgianna Van Iseghem now realized that she would have to conduct herself differently if she wanted to keep her daughter's children close. The detectives whom Mary Cordes was carefully cultivating as sources through daily phone calls had already warned her that if Rick were arrested, the Missouri Department of Family Services could take temporary custody of the four DeCaro children and place them in foster homes. The Van Iseghems had to make sure that did not happen; they had to prevent such a devastating displacement of the kids, who already seemed adrift in a sea of confusion. Mary had urged her parents to go to their trusted attorney, Frank Vatterott, and have him draw up papers that would give the Van Iseghems temporary custody of Elizabeth's children if their father were arrested.

In this shocking conversation with Rick, Georgianna decided this was the moment to put that bell around his neck.

"Do you want foster care, the state, to come in and take your kids? If you're afraid the police are going to arrest you, what's going to happen with them? We need to get a paper so I can get custody of the kids if you get arrested."

She knew Rick was thinking carefully on the other end of the phone line. "You're right, Mom. I want you to have the kids. But I want you to talk to my attorney about this."

Georgianna spent the next few minutes convincing lawyer Ron Jenkins that her proposal for the kids' care was the only logical course. He finally handed the phone back to Rick with a vote of confidence: "You can trust her, Rick."

At that moment, getting custody of her grandchildren was more important to Georgianna than anything else. No price was too high to pay for that.

THIRTY

The detectives flooding Jefferson County in a search for Danny Basile Wednesday afternoon were striking out. Crews covered the highways and side roads around Basile's home and anywhere they thought he might hang out, but he was nowhere to be found.

Fortunately, though, things were hopping back in St. Charles. Detectives stopped Craig Wells as he left work and took him to headquarters for yet another little talk. This time, he offered a surprising opinion: he doubted that

Danny Basile had done the "insurance job" on the DeCaro van in February. Okay, the cops answered, would you be surprised to learn that we had found the video camera and Nintendo game—the same ones Rick claimed were in the van—in the DeCaro house after the murder? Given that new information, Wells seemed to realize he may have been implicating himself in a crime during each of his interviews with police.

Was he going to be charged? he asked. He could be an accessory, the detectives explained; after all, he had connected Rick DeCaro to Danny Basile, and Rick had given Wells the van keys, the money, and the map to give to Basile.

Wells knew he was now teetering on the edge of serious trouble. Perhaps, he said, he shouldn't say anything else until he had talked to a lawyer. The police asked if he had anything to tell them about the murder. Yes, he had some information.

After a conference with Tim Braun, the police conveyed to Wells the same deal given to Sue Jenkins. "We're not going to pursue you for setting up the van theft. But if you're involved in the murder, then you'd better get a lawyer."

"I'm not involved in the murder."

That was enough for the police to continue the interview, and Wells now offered new details elaborating on his efforts to dissuade Basile from accepting DeCaro's "package deal." In the car after that first meeting, when Basile said DeCaro had proposed a "hit" on his wife, Wells had felt sick. He and his fiancée, Gayle Dorman, knew Elizabeth; surely Rick couldn't really be planning to kill that terrific girl. Wells had tried to steer Basile away from even considering such a monstrous act.

"You can't do that, Danny. Liz is a friend of mine and Gayle's."

Basile had shrugged. "Okay. I won't do it, out of respect for you. But the money is almost too good to pass up."

"How much?"

"About fifteen thousand or so."

Wells shook his head. "You can't do it."

"Well, I think it's a package deal—the theft and the hit."

"Then I guess you're just going to have to let both of them go."

"Okay."

But it had not ended there, Wells explained now. A couple of days later, Basile had announced he had talked to DeCaro again and had decided to do the van job.

"I thought you said it was a package deal," Wells protested.

"I guess he changed his mind. Now he just wants me to do the van."

After Wells ferried Basile to another meeting with Rick at the Gold's Gym parking lot, Rick had given Wells the envelope with the keys, money, and map. And the morning after Basile had stolen and torched the van, he stopped by the service station and told Wells the job was done. The always-broke Basile even paid Wells twenty dollars he owed him. Wells just hoped that it was all over.

He hadn't heard any more until he went to work on Saturday morning, March 7, and his colleagues showed him the newspaper story about an unidentified woman being shot in her home. Her Blazer—the one with the RIK-LIZ plates—was missing, the police had said.

"I knew it was Liz," Wells told the cops, "and I immediately thought Danny had done it."

Basile called later and said Gayle Dorman had told him about the shooting. When Wells asked Basile if he had been involved, he responded, "I had nothing to do with it. I think Rick DeCaro set me up."

When Wells got off work that day, he went home and checked the .22-caliber pistol he kept in a closet at the trailer. He smelled it and concluded it had not been fired recently. He gave the police permission to search his home and test the gun.

Tom O'Connor's news conference began at five o'clock and he quickly explained its purpose. The investigation into the murder of Elizabeth DeCaro was being hindered by her husband's refusal to talk to police. The obstruction was so blatant that, in what O'Connor called "a very significant incident," DeCaro had sent two lawyers to what was supposed to be an interview between him and some of the twenty-one detectives trying desperately to find his wife's murderer. The police had been considerate, waiting until after the funeral to schedule the interview with the husband they hoped could give them vital clues to those he considered to be suspects and to what he thought might be a motive. Instead, they got the cold shoulder and a chilly visit from the barristers.

"It's a little unusual, to say the least," O'Connor cracked in a tone that did nothing to mask his pique as the TV cameras rolled. "It's perplexing, I'll tell you. We'll do our damnedest to work around it."

Was Rick DeCaro a suspect? the reporters asked. "We consider many people suspects," O'Connor replied with the practiced straight face of an experienced homicide detective.

When reporters called classy defense attorney Ron Jenkins for a response, he was ready. Yes, he had told his client to stop talking to the police because they had lost their focus and were making improper innuendos about the crime. Rick DeCaro, a grieving husband, was stonewalling no one, Jenkins insisted; in fact, Rick had spent a total of five or six hours talking to the police since the murder, and that included a tour of the ransacked house to determine what was missing. Everyone in the family had cooperated fully. But now, as the frustrated police floundered, Rick would remain silent, on the advice of counsel.

O'Connor had to grin. DeCaro could exercise his Fifth. The cops would exercise their First. And we'll see who comes out ahead in the ninth.

While Craig Wells was telling his detailed story to detectives at the station Wednesday night, Pat McCarrick was writing reports in the squad room. Sometime around nine o'clock, he heard a detective say someone named Doug Mayer was on the phone, saying, "I think I may know where that Blazer from the murder is."

McCarrick sprang out of his chair. "I'll take that," he volunteered. His offer was not the result of youthful exuberance or a veteran's dedication; he just happened to know that Doug Meyer was Danny Basile's half brother and that Meyer's name had popped up in one of Basile's old arrest reports as someone who had contacted Basile while he was in prison. If Doug Meyer said he knew where the Blazer was, he damn well did.

By ten-thirty, McCarrick and Detective J. B. Fann were sitting in the home of Meyer's foster mother, a woman with the unlikely name of R'Neil Wells, who lived in St. Louis County. With her were Doug Meyer; his girlfriend, Iva Hanson; and, curiously, Craig Wells's girlfriend, Gayle Dorman. McCarrick didn't have to leap far to guess that Doug Meyer's fortuitous call to the police was somehow linked to Craig Wells's location in an interrogation room at headquarters at that very moment. The scramble had begun—everyone who knew anything was trying to cover his or her posterior.

"I have information on the Blazer," Meyer confirmed. McCarrick thought he could hear the dominoes falling. "I think Danny has been chopping a Blazer in a vacant garage at the Green Jade Condo Complex where I work. Danny works there with me sometimes."

Find the Blazer, find the killer, Tom O'Connor had said all along. McCarrick was certain that this Doug Meyer fellow, and probably the others there that night, had interesting stories to tell. But his first concern was getting to that Blazer. He called the command center and asked for more detectives to be dispatched to R'Neil Wells's home. And then he asked Doug Meyer and Iva Hanson to lead him to this tremendously important garage. They hurried outside, only to discover that the squad car driven by a St. Louis County police officer—sent along as an escort—wouldn't start. Just great, McCarrick thought. A dead battery is keeping me from what could be key evidence in a sensational murder case.

The best option was perfectly clear. McCarrick, Fann, and the embarrassed patrolman unceremoniously pushed his crippled squad car out of the way. Then Doug Meyer and Iva Hanson got in their car and led McCarrick and Fann in their car on a convoluted drive to the condo complex. Before long, McCarrick was shaking his head; he was way out of his territory and completely lost. When they finally arrived at their destination, just off Highway 141 in Fenton, McCarrick looked at the closed garage door and asked Meyer about his connection with the property. "I work here; the owner gave me permission for Danny to use it." Not good enough for a search. The cautious McCarrick sent Fann to the owner's house to get her signature on a consent-to-search form. Fann was gone for what seemed like an eternity while McCarrick and the others guarded the garage. When Fann returned with the essential document—in what really was only thirty or forty-five minutes—the eager cops popped open the overhead door for a first look at what McCarrick had been thinking about for a couple of hours.

On the concrete floor lay an assortment of disjointed parts—a frame, an engine, a transmission housing, a hood, fenders, doors, seats, miscellaneous mechanical parts. This scattered collection of components could have been the remnants of almost any vehicle—from a Volkswagen Beetle to a Rolls-Royce Silver Cloud. McCarrick and Fann began pawing through the junk, looking for something bearing a serial number. When they finally turned up a number, they made an anxious call to the command center so someone there could compare it to the Blazer's records.

1G8EK18H4FF163587—on both ends of the call.

Bingo! They had found what was left of the shiny black-and-silver 1985 Chevy Blazer that had been the most talked-about vehicle in the St. Louis area for the last six days.

That was good enough for now. McCarrick ordered everyone out of what had just become a crime scene associated with a murder investigation. He told the command center to call out the evidence technicians to process everything in the garage for clues. McCarrick decided he would continue to guard the treasures until the technicians arrived. Fann would take Doug Meyer and Iva Hanson back to Meyer's foster mother's house to begin taking down their detailed statements.

As the others drove away, McCarrick decided to close

the garage door, just on the off-chance that Danny Basile might show up to continue his chop shop operation. As the door rolled down, it jammed about two and a half feet from the floor. McCarrick started to try to force it but feared doing even more damage to the crime scene. So he just left it, with the light on inside and the door raised slightly. Damn, it's always something, he thought.

The evidence against Danny Basile continued to pile up. Just before McCarrick and Fann struck gold with Doug Meyer, Detective Mike Miller conducted an interview with an old friend of Basile's, Eddie Bonds.* Basile had contacted Bonds on a Thursday night in February, looking for a spot to stash a conversion van he was about to steal on an "insurance scam"; the owner had already given him the keys. But later in the conversation, Basile said he would just drive the van to southeast Missouri, where his sister lived; he would just "dispose" of it there. Basile's cut, he had explained, was whatever he could strip off the van. He called it a "double job," suggesting there was another part to the deal. But Basile had said he wasn't going to do the second act.

In another call later, Basile had mentioned a need for a "throwaway," a term that Bonds explained meant, in their circles, a handgun that could be disposed of after the job. Bonds replied that he had no idea how to get one but would let Basile know if something came up. Actually, Bonds said, he had no intention of getting involved with the guy he had known since Hazelwood High School as "Dago" Basile.

A couple of weeks later, Basile called again to talk about an identical scam with the same owner, this time involving what Bonds remembered as a GMC Jimmy (a cousin to a Chevy Blazer) with "real nice wheels." Basile was looking at bigger bucks this time; he said he was getting close to "double digits," another bit of streetwise slang that clearly meant this deal was worth ten thousand dollars. Again, Basile was looking for a garage, and he offered to split the profits with Bonds if he helped; Bonds turned him down flat.

But about six-thirty or seven on Friday evening, March 6, a very "upset, scared, stressed-out" Basile called back, looking for a ride out of town. "I was doing this job, and something really went wrong," he said. "Something went bad, and I need some help. I really screwed up this time. I'm scared. It was supposed to be a fairly simple job—in and out. It wasn't supposed to happen this way."

Bonds turned down his old buddy again. With that kind of money involved, Bonds knew that more than a van theft was going down. "You don't get that kind of money for doing something like that," he told the cops.

Just a day or two before the police talked to Bonds, a more relaxed Basile had called again. "Hey, man, have you watched the news lately? Why don't you watch the news tonight?" he asked. Bonds usually skipped the news in favor of sleep, but he watched that night and was particularly struck by a report about some woman shot to death in her house and the mention of her missing Blazer. What was his reaction to that news report? the police wondered.

"I have no doubt in my mind that he did it," Dago Basile's old buddy said.

Back at R'Neil Wells's home in the very early hours of Thursday, March 12, Detective Fann was drawing an intriguing story out of Doug Meyer—a clean-cut, bespectacled man of thirty with an average build on a five-foot-ten frame. He had become the third witness in this case to receive Braun's equivalent of immunity in exchange for information.

In a soft voice, Meyer opened with an event at about three o'clock on Monday, March 2. He and Basile were installing some electrical wiring in a dilapidated house on a horse farm on Fuchs Road, called South County Stables. Basile had been working there, feeding the horses mostly, and the owner had agreed to let him live in the house in exchange for his labor. Basile and Meyer had been rehabilitating the place when they got the time. That day, their work was interrupted by a visit from a man driving a sharp black and silver Blazer with a red snowplow on the front and the license plates RIK-LIZ. When the Blazer rumbled up, Basile went outside and talked to the driver, a man

Meyer remembered as tall and slender with short black hair and a mustache. He wore blue work pants and a white shirt.

After fifteen minutes, the Blazer drove off and Basile got into his car and drove away too. He soon returned with a sack of hamburgers—a simple enough thing in some circles but a shocking development in the hands of Danny Basile. He never bought anything because he never had a dime to his name; Meyer was always lending money to this ne-er-do-well half brother. But Danny explained that he had just been paid for a job he had done for the Blazer driver. The suddenly flush Danny flashed a half-inch stack of twenty-dollar bills that added to Meyer's surprise. But he didn't ask any more questions; knowing Danny, Meyer assumed the money was the ill-gotten gain from some illegal activity. Danny was feeling so generous, in fact, that he even repaid Meyer thirty-five dollars for the electrical parts he had brought.

Two or three days later, Basile had shown Meyer a .22-caliber pistol—dark finish, white grips, and a barrel three or four inches long. Basile claimed he bought it from his father, Jack Basile, for $100. Meyer knew that a gun in Danny's hands was nothing but bad news.

"Danny, do you realize that you could get in big trouble just for having that gun? You're a felon in possession of a firearm."

"Yeah, I know. But I'm going on a deal, and I need the gun for protection."

Ominous words.

On Friday, March 6, Basile had not gone to work at the condo complex with Meyer. At five o'clock that morning, he came to Meyer's house and said he had something else to do that day, adding only that "Rick" was going to pick him up at the horse farm.

At six o'clock that evening, Basile called Meyer and asked him to arrange for the use of the vacant garage at the complex so Basile could work on his battered 1977 Pontiac Sunbird. Meyer called the owner and got her permission. About nine o'clock, Basile picked up Meyer and Iva Hanson for an evening at a tavern called the Family Affair. Basile was in good spirits, and the trio ran up a forty-dollar bar tab; miraculously, Basile paid again.

Danny had been busy over that weekend. On Sunday, he asked Iva Hanson to go with him to the Fenton Rental Center to pick up an engine hoist and cutting-torch outfit. They rented the equipment in Doug Meyer's name, paid with one of Iva's checks, and then Basile reimbursed her in cash. On Wednesday afternoon, Meyer's boss asked him to check on a complaint from a tenant whose garage was adjacent to the one Basile was using; the tenant had reported that antifreeze was leaking into his garage from next door. When Meyer went to the garage, Basile showed him a set of black-and-silver doors that Meyer now believed had come from the Blazer. Meyer also helped Basile haul off some trash bags and return the cutting torch to the rental store. In the garage once more, he saw the frame, roof, and assorted parts of what had been the Blazer.

After all of the publicity about the missing vehicle from the DeCaro murder, it had not been difficult for Meyer to make the connection. When he confronted his brother, Basile denied any involvement in the killing. Yes, he had taken the Blazer; the dead woman's husband had given him the keys and some money to do that. But someone else had shot the guy's wife.

Meyer's decision that day to tell his mother what he knew and then to call the police had been spurred by the helicopter flying repeatedly over the condos as he was picking up trash at the complex. And he had been positive earlier that he saw police cars conducting surveillance at the stables on Fuchs Road.

When the police administered the polygraph to a nervous Douglas Lee Meyer later, the examiner was unable to deliver a definite opinion on his subject's truthfulness. Meyer denied being present when Elizabeth was murdered, and he denied driving Basile to her house that Friday. But all of the polygraph charts showed inconsistent psychological responses, perhaps the result of several factors. Meyer said he had just had an argument with his father and his lawyer; he was nervous about his girlfriend's medical examination, under way at that moment; and he was upset about his own possible involvement in his brother's criminal activities.

When Doug Meyer completed his tale that night, Fann drew what he could from Gayle Dorman. As Craig Wells's fiancée, she was aware of Danny Basile's connection to the DeCaros—and she had her own links to the parties in this case. She had worked for Rick at the Old Orchard station for two years, until 1990, and she had worked for the Van Iseghems at the deli too.

Gayle recalled that on a Friday night about a month ago, a woman had come to Craig's mobile home and picked Danny up for what he said was a visit to his sister's house. Ah, Fann thought, another witness to the theft of the van. Gayle said Basile returned about ten o'clock the next morning, smelling of gasoline and covered with grease. When Gayle asked him a little later if he had change for a five-dollar bill, he sent her to his wallet on the table. She was shocked to see it chock-full of cash—at least one hundred-dollar bill and a number of fifties.

"What did you do?" she asked the unusually cash-rich Basile.

"I've been working all weekend," was his feeble explanation.

She knew better. "Bullshit! It's only Saturday morning."

He had no response.

Gayle's memory then jumped to Friday, March 6. Basile had left the trailer about eight-thirty in the morning and wasn't home yet when she went to bed that night. No alibi for the time of the murder there, Fann thought. When Gayle got up at six-thirty Saturday morning, Basile was asleep in the recliner chair, wearing the same white painter's pants and blue work shirt he had on when he left the morning before.

Now Fann was sure he knew what Elizabeth's killer had worn. What a night this was turning out to be, and it had really just begun.

The lone car driving down Highway 141 in the darkness slowed as it neared the Green Jade Condo Complex. The turn signal flashed on and the car seemed just about to swing into the driveway when it hesitated, the turn signal went off, and it sped away.

McCarrick watched in anticipation from his car parked nearby in the shadows. He shook his head. Could that have been the elusive Danny Basile? McCarrick looked at the half-open garage with its now unprotected and essential contents, and decided against giving chase. He had too much to lose there.

Another car rolled up before long, and this one—an unmarked detective's car—pulled into the complex. Detective Richard Harris had spotted McCarrick and stopped to see what was going on. McCarrick filled him in, and Harris exploded.

"Why didn't someone let me know? I've spent all damned day looking for Basile and this damned Blazer, and you've been sitting on it for three hours?"

Harris sped off, not knowing what awaited him less than an hour down the road.

The crime scene technicians soon arrived and began their laborious analysis of the dismembered Blazer. McCarrick hurried off to join the interviews of Doug Meyer, Iva Hanson, and Gayle Dorman. Doug Meyer told the reunited detective team that he had already thrown away some of the smaller parts from the Balzer—things like wiring, floor mats, and decals. Basile had bagged them up and asked Meyer to get rid of them on Wednesday. Meyer had tossed them in his pickup truck, stopped by the horse farm on Fuchs Road to pick up some more trash, and then dumped it all at a hauling company in nearby Kimmswick. McCarrick nodded; he knew that two of the detectives staking out the horse farm to watch for Basile had seen Meyer come and go earlier that day—apparently on this trash run. McCarrick and Fann hopped back into the car. Time for a drive to Kimmswick.

THIRTY-ONE

Sometime around midnight Wednesday, Tom O'Connor and Dave King changed the marching orders for the troops still combing Jefferson County for Danny Basile. "Locate and conduct surveillance" now became "arrest on sight." Doug Meyer's report on Basile and the chopped Blazer provided probable cause for an arrest.

To implement that new order O'Connor sent three two-man teams of detectives to search Craig Wells's trailer at 795 Chancellor, where Basile had lived for the last month or two. When that was completed uneventfully, the detectives decided to try to interview the girl they believed Basile had been dating—she lived just six trailers down the street. While some of the detectives went into her home, Vince Cowdry and Rich Harris stayed in the front yard and discussed their next moves. While they were talking, something in the dark not far away attracted Cowdry's attention; he looked past Harris and asked, "Who's that?" Harris turned and saw the shadowy figure of a man walking behind a mobile home and toward the one where Basile had been staying. When Harris looked again, he thought he recognized the man from the photograph circulating among the detectives that day.

The man obeyed Cowdry's order to stop, and Harris—his gun drawn and ready—told him to hit the dirt facedown. Cowdry asked the man his name, and the answer was the one they had awaited all day.

"Daniel Basile," he said.

The cops had their man—the ex-con sent by his stepbrother to answer Rick DeCaro's search for a car thief, the man who said the money on the package deal was too good to pass up; the man who turned his former girlfriend into his driver; the suddenly affluent man who had his brother find the garage to chop up the Blazer.

Was he the man who would lead the Major Case Squad right back to Rick DeCaro?

While Vince Cowdry read Basile his rights, Rich Harris frisked him, confiscated a silver pocketknife from his jeans, and cuffed his hands behind his back.

On the drive back to St. Charles, the only words from Daniel Basile's mouth were, "How'd you get on to me?"

THIRTY-TWO

The crew operating the hauling company in Kimmswick couldn't have been any more accommodating to the cops who were waiting when the gates opened on Thursday morning. One of the workers even offered breakfast to the official visitors. Detective Fann passed, but Lieutenant Pat McCarrick dug into the eggs with grateful enthusiasm. And when McCarrick called headquarters to request more manpower for what was probably going to be a messy search through the trash, he got the good news about the arrest of Danny Basile. McCarrick's only regret was that the little bastard hadn't shown up at the condo garage again. McCarrick would have loved to arrest him within sight of the Blazer's remains.

Detective Rich Plummer joined Fann and McCarrick for what was a fruitless search of the hauling company's trash compactor. But, the workers explained, that didn't mean all was lost; if the trash from the condo complex wasn't in the compactor, it already had been taken to the landfill in Valley Park, another nearby town. This time the trail led the detectives to a mountain of garbage. Thank God it was too cold for all of this to really stink, McCarrick thought.

So there were the cops—in suits and topcoats—wading knee-deep through dirty diapers, eggshells, coffee grounds, and assorted other evidence of society's abundance. Some of the landfill workers joined the search for buried treasure, and soon the effort paid off. Several bags containing Blazer parts were located and, much to Rich Plummer's displeasure, loaded into his car trunk. McCarrick's decision to stuff more bags into the backseat drew some really inspired bitching from Plummer, but McCarrick had the rank to dump on Plummer—or at least into his car.

THIRTY-THREE

Tom O'Connor had waited anxiously for what was about to occur as the detectives hauled Daniel Anthony Basile out of the squad car and escorted him through the back door of the St. Charles Police Station. O'Connor had carefully constructed the surprise for the suspect, and the cop positioned himself so he wouldn't miss a moment of the unfolding drama.

Basile, ever the banty rooster, was still practicing the cocky-suspect strut and wearing the tough-guy smirk as the officers ushered him through the garage—just as O'Connor had instructed them to do. O'Connor stood off to the side and watched Basile as he recognized what had been placed there especially for his benefit. He stopped dead in his tracks and stared, as the "You ain't got shit on me" sneer faded from his face and the steel in his backbone wilted. O'Connor couldn't hear it, but Basile had muttered something. And O'Connor could see what he knew to be fear in Basile's eyes.

The effort and expense had all been worth it. Basile was staring at the burned-out frame of a GMC conversion van, towed in for $500 from Cape Girardeau, and the piles of parts that had been a Chevy Blazer, hauled on a flatbed truck from the condo garage in Fenton. Basile's eyes now betrayed his realization that the cops had put the whole ugly picture together before they ever found him. And O'Connor was there to see the light dawn on the man the cops had needed almost a week to reel in. O'Connor now prayed that his trusted instincts had been right.

They had found the Blazer. They had found Danny Basile. Now there was one more step to take.

THIRTY-FOUR

Georgianna Van Iseghem's interview with one of the most recognizable news anchors on St. Louis television had been scheduled for Thursday morning even before the telephone conversation with Rick had set off so many sparks the night before. She had never dreamed that she would be surrounded by such a crowd by nine o'clock, when broadcaster Mary Phelan arrived at the house from KMOV-TV, Channel 4, the CBS affiliate. Not only had Rick shown up—newly confident of Georgianna's faith in him—but he had brought the children and his mother, Grace, as well. When Grace learned that *the* Mary Phelan was on the way, she began to sputter with such concern about her appearance that Georgianna sent her to the bedroom and supplied her with tons of makeup.

Georgianna had planned to use the interview to appeal to the public for a halt to the rumors and innuendo and idle gossip and baseless accusations; all of that could only hurt the four children whose well-being had become her top priority. Her family needed support from the community now, not suspicion and insinuation, she had planned to say. But now she was joined in front of the camera by Grace, and then Rick, and then three of the DeCaro children. Only Patrick would not participate; he steadfastly refused to go in front of the camera, despite his father's pathetically desperate pleas—"Come on, son. This will help Dad." Patrick looked directly into his father's eyes and said sternly, "No!"

With the sympathetic Mary Phelan holding the microphone, Georgianna explained for the viewing audience that her daughter and Rick had, indeed, suffered some problems in the marriage in the last six months, but that did not make Rick a suspect. "What married couple that you know of doesn't have problems at times in their lives? But I don't care about that. That's just circumstances, and you can't convict a person on circumstances," Georgianna preached.

Grace DeCaro defended her son like a mother lion. "We know he's totally innocent. It's impossible that he's involved. All of the Van Iseghems feel that way and all of us, and anybody we know and who knows him, feel that way."

How has Rick been affected by his wife's death, Grace was asked. "He's devastated because of Liz. He's devastated because of what his family's being put through. He's such a good father, and I don't know of anyone that will disagree with that."

And then the two sorrowful mothers swore their undying love for each other, as the videotape rolled. Grace explained, "We've been friends for twenty-five years. It'll never happen that we'll be anything but family with each other."

Georgianna nodded convincingly.

THIRTY-FIVE

The RIK-LIZ license plates on the slow-moving vehicle blocking her way on the interstate had caught her eye last Friday, and now she had a story to tell the police on this Thursday morning. The vanity plate had been a natural attention-getter for this driver. After all, her name was Elizabeth and her ex-husband's name was Richard. That her trip was now slowed by the vehicle with this license plate seemed so ironic.

Elizabeth Burrows—a petite, attractive woman with short brown hair and dark eyes—came to the police with her memory of the Blazer she had roared up behind sometime between 4:15 and 4:25 P.M. on Friday, March 6. She had left a beauty shop appointment and was hurrying eastbound on I-70, just past the Cave Springs exit in St. Charles. She was trying to make good time because she was running a little late for an appointment to sign the refinancing papers on her mortgage. The Blazer was going too slow—forty-eight miles per hour, she remembered precisely—forcing her to brake and lose precious moments as she waited for an opening to pass in the maddening rush-hour traffic. She couldn't help but notice the license plate and its odd, unintended reference to her former marriage. When she finally zipped around the slowpoke, she shot the driver an aggravated glare meant to express her disapproval of his dawdling on the highway. The man—in his thirties with long black hair, dark eyes, and a muscular build under a white T-shirt—returned her gaze and then brushed his hair back from his face in a sweeping motion with his right hand.

When Elizabeth Burrows had read the newspaper Thursday morning, poring over the detailed description of the missing Blazer, she knew she had seen something important.

At last, O'Connor thought, we've got the witness who just might be able to put Basile behind the wheel of the murder victim's vehicle not long after it pulled away from 12 Hidden Meadow Court and left the body of Elizabeth DeCaro behind. And Ms. Burrows had contributed more than that—with her memory of the time of the highway encounter, she had given the police a reasonable approximation of when Elizabeth was shot. O'Connor asked Ms. Burrows to return later to view a lineup, and she readily agreed.

By the time she got back to the station at five o'clock that afternoon, Pat McCarrick had returned from his tour of the refuse storage facilities. When O'Connor had McCarrick drive the witness to the county jail in St. Charles for the lineup, she described how Basile's eyes had seemed to widen as she passed and glared at him. McCarrick came to a conclusion that brought a wry smile to his lips. He would have bet good money that Danny Basile had been making eyes at this attractive woman. He was the kind of guy who fancied himself a ladies' man, despite considerable evidence to the contrary. And here this bum was—driving away from the house where he had gunned down an innocent woman in her own kitchen—and he didn't hesitate to flirt with another woman on the highway. McCarrick shook his head; these guys never ceased to amaze him.

This time, however, it was Elizabeth Burrows who would be "making eyes." As she watched through the two-way mirror, six men were brought into the room. Although they bore a striking resemblance to each other, she immediately turned to the police and asked, "Do you want me to tell you now which one he is?" McCarrick told her to take her time and watch carefully as each man was instructed to step forward and turn around to give her a full view. At Elizabeth Burrows' request, the police had each man brush his hair back with his right hand—the motion she remembered so well.

And then she pointed to number three and said with an air of incredible confidence, "That's him. I recognized him as soon as he walked in."

Number three was Daniel Anthony Basile.

THIRTY-SIX

Craig Wells would be the next witness set up for a mike job, Tom O'Connor had decided. Wells was the logical choice for this fourth application of one of O'Connor's favorite techniques, especially after he had revealed himself to be so deeply involved in connecting Rick and Basile. The detectives put Wells on a phone that they had attached to a recorder. The first call to Rick's home at 11:50 A.M. Thursday morning went unanswered. Wells placed another one ten minutes later to the Van Iseghem residence. This time Rick came to the phone.

With an intentionally nervous edge to his voice, Wells complained that the police had kept him at the station all night Wednesday grilling him about Basile. Although this might have been a familiar story to Rick by now, Wells upped the ante dramatically with a potentially catastrophic announcement.

"Man, they got Danny in here. They found the fuckin' Blazer in my brother's garage."

But Rick's voice was flat, incredibly unconcerned. "Oh, so they did find it, huh?"

Wells took the murder right to Rick, mentioning his meeting with Basile. "Which meeting?" Rick asked. Wells added for clarification, "By Gold's Gym, when you asked him to hit Elizabeth."

Rick was still unshaken and his voice was rock-solid. "I never met him."

Wells injected an even edgier panicked tone as he remarked that all of his friends were being asked a lot of questions by the police.

Rick seemed absolutely sure of his advice. "The only thing I can say is, answer them."

As he had been instructed by the police, Wells suggested a meeting between him and Rick. But Rick was having none of that. "Well, I can't talk to anybody about anything." And then Rick said he had to go and hung up.

A fourth strikeout on tape.

But the session was not entirely wasted. Wells told the police that since his last interview he had remembered serving as Basile's chauffeur to two more meetings with Rick. One was at a popular burger place called Fuddruckers in Sunset Hills, and there had been another one at Gold's. After those meetings, Basile had not needed more rides from Wells; Rick had driven Basile to his classes at the technical school.

Thursday would become the day for picking up an odd assortment of new tidbits about Basile.

Dennis Wayne Williams, an old friend of Basile's, was a little reluctant to talk to the police about his buddy Dago at first. But he finally said he had seen him a couple of times in the twenty-four hours before his arrest. Their last meeting began sometime after ten-thirty Wednesday night when Williams went to the home of his teenage girlfriend. Shortly after Williams arrived, Basile showed up. They watched part of a movie called *Warlock,* and then Basile suggested they go for a beer. Williams drove him to the Queen of Hearts bar in Fenton, and they stayed until sometime after closing time at one o'clock. Basile then asked for a ride to yet another friend's trailer in Hillsboro, even farther south into Jefferson County. As they tooled down Highway 141, Basile asked Williams to turn in at the Green Jade Condo Complex, where Basile's brother, Doug Meyer, lived. Williams had flipped on his turn signal and was slowing down when Basile abruptly snapped, "Never mind." Williams drove on past and then asked his passenger for an explanation.

"I saw some people who are trying to pin a murder on me," Basile answered.

Williams assumed Basile was talking about the cops, but curiosity led him to ask, "How are they doing that?"

"They're trying to connect the murder to a van—an insurance job I did." Basile explained that he had been paid to take a van and burn it at the owner's request and that the owner had left the keys and a can of gas in the fully fueled van. Basile was allowed to take anything he wanted off the van, and he had scored a radar detector, a TV, and a VCR. He then took the van "way out and torched it."

Then he asked, "Have you heard about that murder of that woman who was Craig's friend?"

"Yeah."

"Well, that's the murder they're trying to pin on me."

When Williams dropped him off at the trailer, Basile said they might not see each other for a while.

"If you didn't commit the murder, why are you going to hide?" Williams asked.

"Because I don't like to be harassed."

Another witness described meeting Basile through Doug Meyer just a few days earlier and then spending a very odd day with Meyer on Wednesday. Jerry Gromer had known Meyer for five years and had called him on March 1 to ask about getting some work at the condo complex. When Meyer invited Gromer over to talk about it, Basile was there and the men were introduced. Gromer had called Meyer on Monday, March 9, to ask about a salary advance, and Meyer had mentioned offhandedly, "I could have used your pickup truck to move a Blazer shell." Meyer said the Blazer belonged to Basile.

While Gromer was painting a condo for Meyer on Wednesday morning, Meyer borrowed his truck. When Meyer finally returned at two-thirty that afternoon, he still had two bags of trash in the back. Gromer then left with Meyer for what turned out to be an amazingly convoluted series of stops. The first was at Meyer's apartment, where he left Gromer to wait alone for ten minutes while he made a secret trip. Then they drove to South County Stables, the horse farm on Fuchs Road, to pick up some more trash bags, which they tossed at the Imperial Dump in Kimms-wick. Gromer assumed that the intrigue surrounding the trash hauling probably meant drugs were involved, especially since he had heard that Basile had done time on a drug rap. Meyer drove Gromer back to the apartment for another ten-minute wait while he was gone. This time he returned with Basile and an engine hoist in the truck bed. They took the hoist back to the Fenton Rental Center, dropped Basile off along the way, and then drove to a house in Arnold to drop Meyer off.

Gromer described Meyer as jumpy, constantly looking around to see if they were being followed. When Gromer finally demanded to know if his truck had been used for something that would get him into trouble, Meyer told him not to worry about it.

"If anybody asks what I did today, you say I was working on my truck," Meyer cautioned. And then he added, "I'm trying to cover up something for my brother, and I'm gonna end up losing my ass."

"Cover up what?" Gromer asked.

"Leave it alone," was Meyer's response. Gromer did just that.

The cops knew Meyer had been throwing out parts from the Blazer that his brother was stripping in the condo garage. Gromer had been sucked into it because they needed his truck—the one the cops had seen Meyer driving in and out of the horse farm all day.

The police got one insight into Danny Basile's private life from a special witness. Dawn Colby,* a sixteen-year-old girl who lived not far down from Craig Wells, told the police she was ten weeks pregnant—with Basile's baby.

Dawn offered an odd assortment of recollections. The week before the murder, Basile had shown her a small pistol he was packing in his jacket pocket. He had called her the night of the murder and they had talked for a few minutes. He stopped by about ten-thirty the next night; they talked about getting married and where they would live. She had tried to find him on Sunday but couldn't. And her last comment was among the most interesting: her sister had seen Basile on Friday or Saturday—and he was driving a Blazer.

THIRTY-SEVEN

Armed with a ton of new evidence from witnesses flushed out in the last few days and hours, the police met late Thursday with the prosecuting attorney for St. Charles County, Tim Braun, and his assistant, Charles Teshner, to discuss charges in the murder of Elizabeth DeCaro. Tom O'Connor, Dave King, and Pat McCarrick were confident that Braun would realize what a masterful case the police had assembled.

Tim Brawn—a forty-five-year-old brown-haired, bespectacled, pleasant-looking man—was fourteen months into his first term as prosecutor after eighteen years as a public defender and a top trial attorney. He had served for twenty years as a judge advocate in the Air Force Reserves. He had run the public defender's office from 1976 to 1988 and then had spent about eighteen months in the state's death-penalty unit, defending those facing execution across Missouri. Over the years, he had stopped twenty-three attempts to send his clients to a date with an executioner—never losing one of them. Well, one had been sentenced to death, but Braun appealed, won a new trial, and beat the executioner again.

Braun had been at the police station the night of the murder and had kept close tabs on the case since then. Now, in Chief King's office, Braun was looking at another case that could lead to death row. Only this time, Braun might be the one unlocking the door and reserving a double date in the death chamber for Daniel Basile and Rick DeCaro.

The police ran through their evidence for Braun:

Rick DeCaro's bizarre behavior, his extramarital affair, his smashing into his wife with the van, his new $100,000 life insurance policy on her, his unprecedented trip to the Ozarks with the kids and the dog, his insistence that his wife stay home alone that weekend, and his inexplicable conduct after her death.

James Torregrossa's account of Rick's stunning, out-of-the-blue solicitation for a hit man.

Craig Wells's getting the request for a thief and then serving as the conduit between Rick and Basile. The parking-lot conferences between them—the keys, the cash, and the map. The package deal and the $15,000 that was "almost too good to pass up."

Sue Jenkins's extraordinary narrative of accompanying Basile as he stole the van, torched it, and ditched the license plate that the police had later recovered. Her memory of his search for latex gloves for the "job" he needed to do the day of the murder.

Doug Meyer's story of his brother's meeting with the guy in the sharp Blazer and the sudden influx of cash for the always bankrupt Basile. His risky possession of the pistol he needed for protection on the "deal" he was doing. And the chop shop in the condo garage, where the Blazer's scattered remains were found.

Elizabeth Burrows's identification of Basile driving the eye-catching RIK-LIZ Blazer down I-70 just miles from Hidden Meadow Court and just moments after Elizabeth DeCaro had been gunned down.

And even Eddie Bonds's memories of Basile's search for an accomplice and a "throwaway" gun, and his frightened description of how "something really went wrong" on the double-digit job.

With that evidence laid out before him, Braun agreed to charge Daniel Basile with first-degree murder and theft of the van. Braun would decide later on additional charges, including arson on the van, theft of the Blazer, armed criminal action, and burglary. He also reserved a decision on the ultimate question—whether to seek the death penalty for this heinous murder. Bond would be set at $1 million—surely enough to hold this small-time hood in jail.

But, Braun cautioned, he was not ready to charge Richard DeCaro. The cops were furious, and soon O'Connor and King found themselves almost screaming at the reluctant prosecutor. How could he fail to see the overwhelming evidence linking DeCaro to the man Braun had just charged with Elizabeth's murder? If there was probable cause to charge Basile with shooting Elizabeth, did it not have to follow that the man who had all those meetings with Basile was responsible for setting this murder conspiracy into motion? Was DeCaro not guilty of murder just as surely as Basile? Wasn't Rick DeCaro, in a perverse twist, now "married" to Danny Basile? "We can't just let this guy off now!" the cops protested loudly. "He's obviously good for this murder!"

Braun held his ground, amid what he viewed as strutting and posturing by the police. They had, indeed, developed significant physical and circumstantial evidence linking Danny Basile to the theft of the van and the Blazer, and therefore the murder. Charging him was not a difficult decision. But the case against Rick DeCaro was entirely circumstantial. Before Braun would charge this man with the monstrous, premeditated murder of his own wife, he wanted more evidence. Lacking a direct eyewitness, a gun bearing DeCaro's fingerprints, or some other devastatingly incriminating proof, Braun wanted a confession. Maybe the police could get that, now that so much other evidence had been collected.

As the police tried frantically to change the prosecutor's mind, a frustrated Dave King picked up an aluminum baseball bat that rested in a corner and began pacing his office. And when he finally swung the bat, whiffing it through the air just to release his building tension, it seemed clear that

Braun interpreted the forceful action as a physical threat, or at least a gesture intended to be coercive.

"I'm not going to be intimidated or bullied," Braun announced.

McCarrick thought it should have been obvious that King's swing was not menacing. And King was immediately sorry he has used the bat to vent his frustration. But within seconds the damage was done, and Braun had left the office. The meeting was over, and there were no charges against Rick DeCaro.

This was not a victory yet.

THIRTY-EIGHT

Melanie Enkelmann and Mary Cordes had taken all they could of their mother's increasingly sugary, syrupy, gratingly naive confidence in Rick's innocence. While the sisters were counting the seconds until they would hear that the cops had enough evidence to arrest Rick, Georgianna had begun chastising anyone who dared suggest there was anything sinister about him, let alone anything linking him to Elizabeth's murder. She had even gone on TV, for God's sake, to practically nominate her son-in-law for sainthood. She was spreading that optimistic goo around the house in such a thick layer that Melanie and Mary couldn't stand it. They began to fear their mother had lost her mind. Mary wanted to slap her and scream, "Wake up and smell the coffee, Mom!"

To make matters worse, Georgianna's gullible attitude was supplemented Thursday morning by Rick's return to the house where he had courted Elizabeth and won over her family as well. For everyone—except Georgianna, it seemed—just looking at his face or even sensing his presence in the room was almost unbearable. Despite her defense of Rick, Georgianna was worried about what she feared could be a dangerous, perhaps fatal, combination in the Van Iseghem household now—her husband's simmering anger and the constant proximity of the man he held responsible for his daughter's death.

The Van Iseghems were walking softly around Rick, hoping to calm the surface while they tried to stay informed about everything swirling unseen below—especially at the police station. That made for some odd moments, even though Rick remained distant and spent most of those hours pacing the floors or sequestered in whatever room was unoccupied by the others at the moment.

Margie had been astonished from the very first time she had seen Rick after the murder; there was a hard, cold stare in his eyes that she had never seen before. She had touched his cheek softly and lied that she knew he didn't have anything to do with her sister's death. His answer was a flat "Thank you, Margie." But later that week, when she once offered him a cup of coffee, she was startled when he rebuffed her with a gruff and unexpected response. "I hate coffee," he snarled. "I only drank it for Elizabeth."

Margie was speechless. He had seemed to love the flavored coffees so popular among the Van Iseghems. And now he announced venomously that he hated it. How weird, she thought. This man had been able to take on whatever characteristics he thought would ingratiate him to those around him, would help him gain the confidence of others. Had this chameleon been only an artificial reflection of the Van Iseghem love all these years? Had he never really been part of it, never really shown his true colors, until now?

The Van Iseghem sisters were in close and constant contact with the police, and by late Wednesday they had picked up on the vibes that something good was happening. Mary almost exploded with anger, however, when the police called that afternoon to ask if she knew where Rick was. "Do I know where he is? I thought you guys were watching him!" she screamed. She was irate that the police didn't have twenty-four-hour surveillance on their prime suspect.

Melanie had gone back to work on Wednesday, partly

just to get out of the house and away from her mother—
Rick's cheerleader. On Thursday, Melanie and Mary went
to work, promising their mother they would keep her informed and would return Thursday night to fill her in. At
last, the women thought, we're free from the tension in
that house. They couldn't believe it when Georgianna
brought Rick to the deli for lunch and then came back to
the kitchen and urged everyone to go out and make an
extra effort to be nice to him. The sisters held their ground
in the kitchen, and their husbands retreated out the back
door. Jim Van Iseghem slipped back to his office; he was
caught in the middle between his wife and his daughters,
and that was a tight spot to be in.

When Melanie and Mary finished their day about two
o'clock, they hid in their father's empty office to check in
with the Major Case Squad. But before long, sister Margie
joined them, only to be put off when someone whispered,
"Shhh," as she entered. The room suddenly fell silent.

"What's going on?"

"Nothing," her sisters responded.

Margie almost exploded. "All right, that's enough of this
shit! What is going on?"

"We can't say anything in front of you. You're on
Mom's side."

"Are you crazy?" Margie shot back. "I'm not on Mom's
side. I can't take her anymore either. I think Rick is guilty
as hell.'"

Ahh, thought Melanie and Mary, finally another ally.

The trio began to work the phones, calling their police
sources to confirm their suspicions that something was happening. Margie even called a family friend, Ron Saschel,
the chief of security at the St. Louis County Courthouse in
Clayton. He already knew the police had made some head-
way in their search for the Blazer, and he suggested they
all meet at an out-of-the-way place so he could fill them
in. Saschel, who was black, led them to an all-black bar
with the amazing name of the Jamaican Jerk Pit, where he
was certain the Van Iseghem sisters would not be found.
Saschel escorted the three blond women into the almost

empty bar about five o'clock for what would be an incredibly long and eventful evening.

After commandeering the Jerk Pit's phone from the accommodating owner, the women began calling the police again. Before long, they learned that two of the three events they had prayed for had, indeed, happened earlier that day. A detective told them about the discovery of the chopped-up Blazer. The sisters were thrilled; they had been warned repeatedly by the police that it would be almost impossible to connect the murder to Rick if the Blazer were not found. And then the women learned of the second big development: the arrest of a man named Daniel Basile as the trigger man Rick had hired to kill Elizabeth. Melanie and Mary celebrated with a fist-pumping "YES!" and a high five. Melanie knew Rick's arrest was the next domino. One cop suggested that Basile was "singing like a bird," which the sisters hoped meant that he was serving Rick to the police on a silver platter.

Melanie turned on the TV in the bar, and by the time the stations broke for the eight o'clock news briefs, Basile's mug shot was being flashed on the screen. The women were awestruck; he looked exactly the way they would have expected some low-rent, bargain-basement, scumbag, half-assed hit man to look. Beyond that, Margie felt sick at the sight of his face, a face like the Devil himself. He was not, she thought, the kind of person the Van Iseghems would ever have encountered in their lives.

Even as customers began arriving at the bar, the three blondes remained in control. These boisterous, hard-drinking white women became something of a floor show as the crowd realized who they were and why they were celebrating with such vigor. They controlled the telephone so completely that when someone called and asked to speak to the owner, Melanie brazenly snapped that he should call back later and then hung up. After all, she was waiting for an important call from the cops.

Melanie's husband, John, eventually joined her at the bar. But poor Phil Cordes had no idea what had happened to his Mary. She simply had not come home from work at three o'clock, as she always did. He was frantic by the time she finally called him. But she told him only that she was in a bar on Olive Street Road, and then she hung up. Phil ran through the Yellow Pages, calling every place he could find, up and down Olive, until he found the women. Then he and some of their neighbors drove down and joined the bizarre revelry at the Jamaican Jerk Pit.

The three Van Iseghem sisters were ashamed of themselves, but they had no intention of ending their gala night to return to St. Francis Lane and face their mother.

The news bulletins were not cause for such celebration back at the home place, where Georgianna and Rick watched together. Georgianna had felt some relief earlier that evening when Rick returned from his lawyer's office and announced he had signed the custody papers drawn up by her attorney. Rick gave his lawyer's business card to Georgianna with instructions to call him if Rick were arrested. The lawyer would then give her the papers so she could retain custody of the kids. Finally, she thought, we have the kids and they are protected.

The first broadcasts of Georgianna's interview with Mary Phelan drew an angry call from Tom O'Connor. How could she do that? he demanded. While his detectives were trying to find Elizabeth's killer—busting their butts, going without sleep, missing their families, working long hours, many of them without pay—her mother was undermining their efforts, questioning their motives, and stealing their enthusiasm with a goody-goody defense of the prime suspect. Had she given no thought to what damage she might do to this investigation with such an interview? Georgianna did not offer much of a defense, except to say that she was just trying to protect her family and Elizabeth's children. Just the same, O'Connor blustered, the Major Case Squad did not appreciate having her misguided sentiments broadcast on TV for everyone to see.

Despite his raw anger, O'Connor withheld what he was really thinking: what a hardheaded, stupid woman she was to believe Rick was innocent. O'Connor's only concession was that she may have been too deeply in shock to understand the facts or appreciate how much she could have weakened the police with her ill-conceived comments.

There would be more about this in the not-too-distant future, and everyone would be surprised.

The TV news continued to generate conversation among the players in this case. At five o'clock, Rick was watching the news in the Van Iseghem sunroom with Christina Byrd, Georgianna's twenty-one-year-old niece. She had baby-sat for the DeCaro children for almost ten years and had considered Rick a father figure. But now she was compelled to ask him the hard questions.

"Did you have anything to do with this?"

"No, I couldn't have done this," he said flatly.

She asked about the insurance policy. Nothing unusual there, he insisted; they finally could afford the coverage on Elizabeth, and they had both agreed to take it.

And then Rick snapped, "This is all Melanie's fucking fault because she talked to the police and told them about our problems."

"Well, you had problems, right?"

"Yeah, but just like everyone else does."

Christina watched the ten o'clock news in Theresa's bedroom, where she had just helped Elizabeth's younger children into their pajamas. Rick joined her for the news again, and they sat transfixed by the face of Danny Basile. Did Rick know this Basile guy? she asked. "I've never seen him before," Rick replied in that familiar emotionless tone. He would, in fact, deny knowing Basile three times during that one newscast.

And how could he react like that? the cops would wonder later. If Rick was innocent, why had he not offered some genuinely profound reaction to the first sight of the face of his wife's killer? What manner of man could sit like stone when his wife's executioner had just been arrested?

After the news, Rick went out to his van and used his cellular phone to make a call. Christina's curiosity compelled her to follow him, and she knocked on the driver's window. He was startled by her unexpected appearance, and he quickly jerked the phone aside, as if to make sure she did not see the number he had dialed. A minute later, he returned to the house and asked if anyone had a quarter he could borrow to use a pay phone. Although it was pointed out that the house held several phones he could use, he persisted until he had bummed a quarter.

Georgianna was deeply hurt. None of her daughters had come home that night, as they had promised. She had been left to watch the developments on television essentially alone—at least *without* the girls who meant the most to her and, even worse, *with* her sullen son-in-law. As she sat in her favorite chair, in the sunroom Rick had built when he and Elizabeth lived with them, Georgianna cried bitterly. Elizabeth was gone, and now her other daughters had excluded her from their lives. They had never done that before, and it hurt.

She went to bed about midnight. Her daughters had not come home yet.

THIRTY-NINE

Danny Basile was not exactly singing like a bird.

He was, however, wisecracking plenty. When he was placed in a holdover cell at the St. Charles Police Station early Thursday morning, a detective asked if he wanted his free phone call. "Yeah," he snapped, "I want to order some beer and a pizza." Real cute. Not long after that snappy retort, Detective Mike Miller made the squad's first run at this street-smart suspect. But in the private session, Basile's bravado disappeared and his cold, dark eyes just stared at Miller.

"I want to talk to you about the Elizabeth DeCaro murder. We have significant information implicating you."

Basile shrugged, and Miller proceeded to the next step; he read the mandatory Miranda rights statement. Basile refused to sign the standard form acknowledging that he had been advised of his rights, and then he asked for a lawyer. That was a setback. Miller had hoped Basile was cool and confident enough to go it alone, to try to deal with the police face-to-face. Basile explained that he had no money for a lawyer but wouldn't even consider accepting a public defender. "They always end up losing and they never listen to you," was the assessment from the man who had been through the system, and to prison, before. Basile asked Miller to call a lawyer named Greg Lubber, but there was no answer. Miller returned Basile to the cell until he could work the phones again.

Miller reached Lubber at nine o'clock. Lubber had represented Basile in a personal-injury lawsuit some time ago, but he didn't handle criminal cases; he sent a colleague named Tom Burke, who arrived at the jail at 11:22 A.M. Before the lawyer met with Basile, Miller delivered his blunt appraisal that the cops had a good case and a witness who was to come back for a lineup later that afternoon. But they would be willing to work out a deal with Basile— if he could provide incriminating information against De-Caro. Burke met briefly with his potential client, and when he came out, he explained that Basile would have to produce five thousand dollars up front to retain him. Burke was going to call some people suggested by Basile to see if they would put up the money. And then the lawyer offered his assessment of the case against Basile: maybe enough to get past a preliminary hearing but far short of a conviction. But then he surprised Miller with an unusually frank, and generous, observation—for a defense attorney: "I think you're on the right track."

Burke's search for a retainer would take until Friday morning, and turn up unsuccessful. He begged off the case about nine o'clock, leaving Basile alone with the cops again. When Miller faced him then to break the news, Basile's grave situation obviously was taking its toll. Miller thought Basile looked like a whipped puppy—not a tough ex-con, and certainly not like a hardened hit man. Basile was ready to deal; he offered incriminating details about Rick DeCaro's involvement in the murder, but only if that got him—Basile—a good break.

It was clear to Miller that Basile was looking for an exit

from death row. Cut him some slack—reduce the sentence to life—and he just might roll over on the guy who had sucked him into this mess. Miller took the proposal into the reopened command meeting between the police and prosecutors in Chief King's office. To Miller's surprise, prosecuting attorney Tim Braun showed no interest in this vague offer from Basile. Braun was convinced there was enough evidence against him to take a hard line.

"No deal. We're not dealing with this guy. See what he'll tell us, but we're not dealing with him."

Miller went back to Basile and explained that they needed some show of good faith, some examples of what he had to offer.

"Okay, but you can't use it unless I get a deal."

"Agreed."

"I can give you a witness to conversations between me and DeCaro. This witness can also testify that DeCaro paid me money."

Miller shook his head at the apparent reference to Craig Wells or Doug Meyer. "We've already got that. We need physical evidence that directly links DeCaro to the murder."

"I can tell you about a call he made from the phone in his van that morning, while I was in the van with him on the way to his house. I can tell you who he called, and that there was no answer. And I can tell you how the call had something to do with a detour we had to take on the way to the house."

Miller waved his hand and shook his head again. He didn't know what the "detour" was, but Basile still wasn't coming across with the goods. "DeCaro could explain away a call somehow. We need more of a link to the murder."

"Okay. If you found the Blazer, you should have found a set of keys in it."

Miller didn't react, but Basile was right. There was, indeed, a set of keys in a pocket on the door. He waited for more.

"I can give you the location of an extra key that DeCaro gave me. I hid it under some rocks. I didn't need it, and it's still there."

Miller nodded. "I'll talk to the prosecutor."

The detective went back to Braun with the new details, but he was unbending. No deal. For one thing, Braun didn't think the public in St. Charles would want him to give an inch to this cold-blooded killer, someone who was willing to violate the sanctity of a private home in this normally secure town and gun down its innocent inhabitant. No, the people here would demand the ultimate penalty for that kind of terrifying transgression.

Braun sent Miller back with the final word: no deal for Basile. And Braun also stuck to his earlier decision that had angered the cops: there would be no charges against DeCaro.

Miller delivered the news to Basile, and the diminutive suspect clammed up. The detective returned him to the cell and wondered unhappily about this lost opportunity.

McCarrick was disturbed too. He thought Braun had made the wrong decision, but it was his to make. McCarrick could understand Braun's reluctance to charge DeCaro. That was not unusual; cops always wanted charges now and prosecutors always wanted more evidence. But Braun's refusal to negotiate with Basile could have frittered away the only chance to get him to flip on Rick, to get him to come across with information that could put DeCaro on death row. McCarrick, O'Connor, and most of the cops would have given Basile the deal in exchange for testimony against Rick. Put away the hit man for life and save the death penalty for the mastermind who had started the clock ticking on his own wife's premature death. That seemed right to the squad.

To O'Connor, Rick DeCaro was guilty not only of his wife's murder but of killing her family and, in a sick way, his own family too—even his children. He had taken away their mother, someone they could never replace, someone whose loss would haunt them forever. Only a cold, cruel, emotionless, heartless bastard could do that to his own children. To O'Connor, Basile was a killer and a career thug, but his crime was mindless. He would have been willing to kill anyone for the right price. DeCaro had carefully and intentionally chosen his own wife as the victim, and that deserved the death penalty.

Sparing Basile's life to put DeCaro on death row seemed a good deal. But it was Braun's decision to make—his opportunity and his case to lose. And he would have to live with it.

FORTY

Away from the emotion-charged atmosphere at the police station, Tim Braun took some time to ponder the evidence in this horrible murder case. He had not been pleased or impressed by the tactics he had encountered at the police station when he refused to charge DeCaro. Granted, Braun was fairly new as a prosecutor, but he was hardly a rookie when it came to criminal law. He knew that decisions made in the heat of the moment were seldom wise. In a calmer environment, he reconsidered, met with his staff, and took another look. He returned to the police station Friday morning with the words that Tom O'Connor, Dave King, Pat McCarrick, and the rest of the squad so wanted to hear.

"I'm going to issue murder and stealing-by-deceit charges against Richard DeCaro. You'll have the warrant by this afternoon and you can pick him up then. He'll be held without bond."

O'Connor was thrilled. Rick DeCaro was about to take the fall, and that meant that all the hard work by all those dedicated detectives was about to pay off.

Melanie Enkelmann made two calls early Friday morning. The first was to one of her mother's neighbors, asking her assistance in a vital activity. Melanie wanted her to watch the Van Iseghem house, partly to keep track of Rick's activities and partly to make sure the police didn't show up without Melanie's knowledge. Then Melanie called her cousin Lisa Byrd and asked her to take her shift that day at work. Rick might be arrested, Melanie explained, and she had made a solemn vow to Elizabeth that she would be there to see it. Lisa agreed to cover for Melanie. But Lisa believed Rick to be innocent, and she immediately called him and told him about Melanie's comments.

At nine o'clock Rick stormed into Georgianna's bedroom, informed her of the conversation between Melanie and Lisa, and demanded to know what was going on. "I'll find out," she promised. As an indignant Rick stood there, she called Melanie but got no answer. So she called Mary and angrily chewed her out. How could she and her sister spread such rumors so soon after their mother had appeared on TV to ask everyone else to show some restraint? Mary offered no response, but she was convinced her mother had now lost it completely. Mary tried to suppress her fury at being subjected to such castigation in Rick's presence and at his behest. Her only refuge was in the old saying about "the last laugh."

Melanie and Mary returned to their father's empty office at the deli and hit the phones again. Now the cops were promising that Rick would be arrested that afternoon. The sisters' hearts soared; finally, a glimmer of justice.

When Margie arrived at the office to join her sisters, she had another amazing news bulletin. At six o'clock that morning, an angry Georgianna had awakened Margie and ordered her to report to the sunroom. There—while Rick still slept upstairs—the girls' mother had quietly but firmly demanded to know why her daughters had deserted her the night before, leaving her alone to wonder about the important developments. Why had they not come home, as they had promised? Margie decided to beard the lion in her den. Honesty was another Van Iseghem trademark.

"Mom, everyone knows you think Rick is innocent, and we can't stand it anymore. We're all mad at you."

Georgianna's eyes widened and her mouth fell open. "What? Do you really think I believe him?"

"Everyone thinks that, Mom."

"Don't any of you understand what I've been doing? I've only been trying to stay on Rick's good side until I got him to sign the custody papers, and until I get those kids safe

in this house. You all don't really think I believe he's innocent, do you?"

Margie was truly stunned. "Yeah, Mom, we do. Why
didn't you tell us what you were doing?"

"Because I knew the only way I could pull this off was
to make everyone think I believed Rick was innocent. If
anyone knew I was lying, I was afraid I wouldn't be able
to do it. I've never been a good liar, so I decided I'd better
not tell anyone."

Georgianna had known she could make her charade
work; everyone thought she was so naive and gullible that
they could readily believe she saw Rick as innocent. "The
poor thing," they had all thought. But that was so far from
the truth. She had known with all certainty that Rick had
killed her daughter from the moment that she heard that
icy-hard anger in his voice on Wednesday night. Never—
she now could warn the world—never, ever underestimate
the love of a mother for her children or the love of a grandmother for her grandchildren. When the power of that love
was channeled, miracles could be accomplished and mur-
derers could be fooled.

The sisters were amazed. As well as they knew their
mother, she had conned them completely.

Margie added, "But Mom's still mad at us about last
night."

Melanie shrugged. "That's the least of our worries right
now. We're trying to get Rick arrested for Elizabeth's murder, and we're supposed to worry because Mom's mad at
us? We'll worry about that later."

There was more to learn about Daniel Basile this Friday
morning. One detail would come from a visit to his father,
Jacob "Jack" Basile. The fifty-four-year-old laborer at a
refrigeration company had his own history—prison time for
a manslaughter rap from the fatal shooting of one man and
the stabbing of another, all some twenty-one years ago.

Interviewed at his job, Jack Basile told the police that
he had last seen his son when he showed up for two hours
on March 7. The younger Basile had asked for help ob-
taining a pistol. Although that request on that date didn't

fit with the rest of the evidence the police had assembled—
it was after the murder—that was Jack Basile's recollection.
He insisted he had turned his son down and warned that
they both could get in trouble for such a transaction between ex-cons with felony records. That had been the end
of that conversation, Jack insisted, and he had no idea if
Danny was involved in the DeCaro case.

The youngest Van Iseghem sister had been shut out of
the intrigue swirling around her older siblings. Theresa was
just thirteen, and the others did not want to add to her
grief with the burden of dealing with suspicions about Rick,
the brother-in-law who had been like a second father for
her entire life. He had helped her with soccer, carved a
Halloween jack-o'-lantern for her, and taken her trick-or-
treating. She had even presented him with a card on Thursday, promising to baby-sit for the kids or help him in any
way he needed as he cared for her sister's children.

But by Friday, Theresa was angry; it was clear that she
was being kept in the dark. She had spent a lot of time
helping with the children, and that day she was instructed
to accompany them to the deli for lunch and then to a
movie. That was fine. And when she realized they were
being followed—by the police, she was sure—she assumed
it was out of concern for their safety; the police were just
protecting the kids.

But when the young group returned to the tense house
on St. Francis Lane later and Mary asked her about four
o'clock to take the kids to the park, Theresa dug in her
heels and refused. Once again, she was being ordered
around while being shut out. Mary couldn't explain that
the latest information suggested the police could be arriving
almost any minute to arrest Rick. She didn't want the kids
there to see their father arrested. A week ago at that time,
the kids were having a blast in the Ozarks with their dad,
and everything seemed right in their world. Now their
mother was dead, and their father was about to charged
with her murder. His arrest was a memory they had to
be spared.

When Theresa balked at the walk to Tiemeyer Park a few

blocks away, Mary decided to escort her sister and the kids. In fact, Mary did not really want to witness this arrest either. But she was shocked when the nervous Rick announced, "I'll go, too." He had spent the day pacing the house, peering out of the windows, and generally reflecting his concern over Melanie's prediction of the cops' agenda for the day. At one point he noticed a squad car cruising slowly by, and he remarked to Margie, "Man, there seem to be cops all over this place today." And now he had volunteered for a walk to the park. Mary assumed Rick knew the inevitable visit from the police couldn't be far away. My God, she wondered, what happens if they come and he's not here?

By five o'clock, Melanie's patience was exhausted; she couldn't wait any longer for word from the police. When the Van Iseghems' neighbor Jeff Rehagen visited the store, Melanie and John proposed a strange plan. Jeff agreed to hide the Enkelmanns in his car and drive to his home, two doors down and across the street from the Van Iseghem house. They slipped into the Rehagen house, and Melanie conducted her own surveillance from the living room window.

Rick and Mary and the kids had already returned from their long walk in the park. Rick and Mary had made small talk—and not much of that—but Rick seemed more relaxed than he had all day. Mary and Theresa were sure they were being watched by the police again while they took their little field trip.

Finally, at 5:45 P.M., Melanie saw the first police car swing into the Van Iseghem driveway. She bolted across the street, but stayed back from the house to watch as police cars seemed to move in from every direction. In a scene straight out of the movies, the cars screeched up, and what seemed like dozens of officers surrounded the house. Detectives Ron Livingston—one of Melanie's best sources—and Tim Brennan knocked on the front door, and Melanie could feel her adrenaline start to pump. But still she hung back. She did not have to be inside to see the arrest. Her purpose remained outside.

At the house, the detectives' arrival sent a shock wave through every room. Margie and Theresa answered their knock, and Theresa was confused when they asked to see Rick DeCaro. She couldn't believe this was happening. She went to the sunroom, where Rick sat as his mother wrote thank-you cards, and told him someone was there to see him. Rick took the news calmly, but Grace DeCaro began to tremble and say, "Oh, my God."

From upstairs, Mary realized what was happening and ran down the steps, past the waiting detectives, and into the living room, where the kids were playing in front of the television. She gathered them around her on the sofa and began talking to them in a deliberately calm voice. They weren't even aware yet that the police had arrived.

When Rick met the officers at the front door, they informed him that they had a warrant for his arrest for the murder of Elizabeth DeCaro. His face offered no reaction as they slipped his hands behind his back and snapped the cuffs on his wrists. He looked at Georgianna and said the words that made her week of hellish ruse worth it: "Mom, call the lawyer."

Despite Rick's calm, his mother became nearly hysterical, shrieking repeatedly, "Oh, my God! Oh, my God!" A terrible chaos seemed to descend on the house, and Mary knew she had to explain to the children that their father was being arrested on charges that he had been involved in their mother's death. The kids began to cry, and Mary tried to hold all of them securely and lovingly in her arms. That was something she would never stop trying to do.

As accused murderer Rick DeCaro stepped out the front door of the house on St. Francis on this Friday the thirteenth, the first face he saw was that of Melanie Enkelmann, the sister-in-law who had vowed she would be there when he was taken to jail. She wanted to be the first person that he saw, hoping he would know it was she who had brought the police there that day to arrest him. She pushed as close as she could to his face—literally within inches—and locked her eyes on his. He kept his gaze down, but he knew she was there. She walked with him all the way down the long driveway toward the waiting police car, silent but speaking volumes through her angry eyes. From behind her, she heard her husband's voice deliver the words that all of Elizabeth's survivors were feeling: "I hope you burn in hell, Rick."

Melanie even gave fleeting thought to slapping him hard across the face—confident that Detective Livingston would probably give her the chance to do it before he moved to protect his suspect. But she decided against it. The walk was too short, and soon Rick was folded into the backseat of the police car for the ride to jail and the waiting TV cameras.

Back in the house, nearly everyone was crying and hugging each other. Margie couldn't help but wonder how her family had come to this; Elizabeth was dead and now they were torn between mourning her loss and celebrating the arrest of her husband. Margie was thinking, Yes, they finally got him, but her heart ached, too.

Grace DeCaro was still wailing, so genuinely convinced of Rick's innocence that she had not seen this coming. Another neighbor—a woman who had been friends with Georgianna and Grace for years—arrived in the nick of time to see what was happening, and Georgianna asked her to take Grace home. Georgianna's sister, Toni Byrd, was trying to hurry Georgianna so they could go to the police station, but Georgianna explained that she now had to await a return call from her attorney. She had to tell him to pick up the custody agreement from Rick's lawyer—the whole purpose of Georgianna's grand performance that week. Toni, who had believed Rick was guilty all along, was stunned that her own sweet sister had pulled off such a masterful ruse and hooked everyone.

The crying Theresa, still in shock over the arrest, wanted desperately to go with everyone to the police station. But Georgianna and Theresa's older sisters vetoed that idea. She was sent to a friend's to catch a ride to the school basketball game that night, where her distress was made worse by the stares of people who had seen the TV coverage of Rick's arrest on the six o'clock news. People pointed at Theresa; even strangers knew she was the sister of that DeCaro woman whose husband had just been arrested for her murder. Theresa couldn't believe her family was in such ruin and she was at a basketball game, pretending everything was normal.

After Theresa left, Melanie and Mary gathered the weeping kids together and prepared to take them to Mary's. As they stepped outside—it was now about six-fifteen and just dusk—they stood off to the side for a moment in the front yard. A light snow began to fall—just on them. The sisters looked toward the gray sky, at the soft flakes, and then at each other; they knew instantly that this, too, was a sign from Elizabeth. She had sent her blessing, and her message of purity.

In this new world, the snow also had a name. It was Justice for Elizabeth.

FORTY-ONE

The arrest of Rick DeCaro sent a wave of satisfaction through the Major Case Squad. After the handcuffed Rick—somber and sullen in his red knit shirt, blue jeans, and white tennis shoes—was paraded past the waiting TV cameras and into the police station, the detectives could not keep from congratulating each other. The film crews captured the cops' hugs and handshakes and grins. Tom O'Connor was tremendously proud of the two dozen detectives, who had worked like dogs for a week and had assembled a solid case, and he told the reporters exactly that with a typically direct comment. "It's not very often you can lock up a contract killer," he said.

O'Connor knew this investigation was one of the best things the squad had done in a long time. He later would do something he had never done before or since—he framed the arrest warrant for Rick DeCaro and hung it on his office wall.

Dave King had found significant satisfaction in the irony of timing—Rick DeCaro's arrest had come almost exactly a week, damned near to the hour, after King had first heard the sirens screaming down St. Charles streets on their way to 12 Hidden Meadow Court. And now he was facing the TV crews as the new chief who had just helped bring in the mastermind in one of the city's ugliest murders. In this

short period of time, King had learned an amazing amount
of information about the Van Iseghems and the DeCaros—
two families he had never heard of a week ago. But he
had learned even more about his new town and his new
department, and he liked everything he had discovered.
This was a good town and this was a good department. He
was overwhelmed with gratitude for the colleagues in the
Major Case Squad who had supported him so vigorously
and professionally. This weeklong blur of activity had been
one of the most incredible periods of his life.

As the investigation had put together the pieces of the
puzzle, O'Connor, King, and the others thought a familiar
picture was forming: this man was willing to kill to keep
what he had and get what he wanted. Rick DeCaro was
an uneducated man who had married too young and had
relentlessly chased a life he probably never could afford to
live. He wanted nothing but the best and was drowning in
debt in his struggle to get it. By the time he factored in his
mortgages and loans, he barely owned the doorknob to his
$160,000 home. He drove vehicles he couldn't afford. He
had trouble molding his wife and children into exactly the
family he wanted. His wife had even turned away his gifts
and doting affection, and his children always pursued their
mother's attention over his. He had sought solace in another woman's bed, but that hadn't made him happy either,
and it had ultimately wreaked havoc in his marriage. When
his wife held him at a distance, she became the symbol for
all that was wrong in his life. He grew desperate to fix it
all, any way he could, and he found in his heart a malig-
nancy that allowed him to trade his wife's life for his desires. In the end, he had decided that an insurance check
for $100,000 and a fresh start with a new woman were his
tickets to happiness.

The police still had some business to finish on this night.
First, they wanted to make one strategic move with the two
men who were the beginning and the end of this murder
scheme. When the officers brought Rick DeCaro into the
jail, they placed him in a holdover cell right beside Danny
Basile's. The cells were under audio and video surveillance,

and any noise or action would be taped—sight and sound. The jailers even walked out of the area to give the men some time alone.

If Rick DeCaro was innocent, surely he would have some choice words for the SOB who had murdered his wife. In fact, most husbands would find a way to rip through mere steel bars separating them from their wife's killer. But these two men sat silent and motionless, never even looking at each other, let alone speaking. To the detectives, those were not the actions of innocent men thrown together unjustly.

That silence contrasted completely with what was happening in another part of the police station as the leaders of the investigation met for a briefing with Elizabeth DeCaro's survivors. The police introduced the Van Iseghems to prosecuting attorney Tim Braun and then laid out most of the evidence that connected Rick to Basile and the murder. The officers' hearts ached as they watched the family come to the realization of how easily Rick had chosen to exchange Elizabeth's life for his new one.

When Dave King explained that Rick had offered Basile fifteen thousand dollars for the hit, Melanie and Mary stared at each other in disbelief. Basile had killed Elizabeth just for the money, just for a lousy fifteen thousand dollars? That's all it had cost? That was nothing! How could that be the value these monsters had placed on Elizabeth's life? Margie was floored by the word that her sister's life had been bartered away as one item in a "package deal." That pierced her heart as no other bit of news had that week. As she left the station later, Margie would nearly collapse as she began to scream, "Oh, my God, this is real."

Georgianna was so shocked by the detective's discoveries that her mind tried to apply a rational approach to such irrational acts. My God, she thought, if it was the money, why hadn't they just asked her for it? She would have given them the money. She would have given them anything!

And then King explained how the killer had come to Hidden Meadow Court. "Rick drove Basile to the house and hid him there to wait for Elizabeth," he said.

The roof caved in on Georgianna then. As the weight of

reality in this new world overpowered her, she dissolved into sobs and tears in perhaps the most heart-wrenching moment Dave King had ever witnessed. "No, it can't be," she cried to the police. "You're wrong. It can't be."

When she began to recover, O'Connor's uncompromising candor kicked in and he told her again how disappointed he had been about her interview on TV, about the fact that information the police were sending back to the family had not convinced her that they knew what they were doing and were onto the right suspect.

But now it was Georgianna's turn to lay out the facts and explain the situation. She shoved the custody papers Rick had signed, which she had just retrieved from her lawyer, toward Tom O'Connor. And then she slammed her hand on the table and shook her finger in the commander's face. "Don't you dare think for a minute that I don't know who killed my daughter!" she almost screamed. "I was just doing what I had to do to get those children! And I knew exactly what I was doing!"

O'Connor had never been so shocked—or so pleased. This Irish cop made a living—and prided himself deeply—on his ability to detect deception. This had been the best he had ever seen. She had fooled everyone, especially him. Georgianna Van Iseghem was a much stronger woman than he had imagined and a much more clever plotter than he could have dreamed. She had played her role convincingly. He had to admire someone who loved her grandchildren enough to go through all of that amid everything else swirling around her. An iron butterfly, he thought, and God bless her.

There was some relief—or something approaching it—after the family had heard the painful facts. Still, they battered themselves with guilt. Why hadn't they seen what was coming? the sisters asked themselves. Why hadn't she saved her daughter somehow? the mother sobbed. Why didn't I hire that private detective? the father asked.

But Melanie thought that now that Rick had been arrested, everything eventually would be fine. The justice system worked, and it would work for them and for Elizabeth, and for Rick.

Mary thought this was the end. He was arrested, and that was the end.

It was the end of nothing. No one there that night could have predicted how far from the end—and how far from justice—they all were at that moment. No one could know what nightmares still lay ahead in this new world.

PART THREE

PART THREE

FORTY-TWO

The essence of the DeCaro murder plot was revealed to the public when the police filed a petition for a search warrant late Saturday. To support this request for the authority to examine Rick's van, the detectives laid out the basics, supported by the evidence they had collected so far. The *St. Louis Post-Dispatch* seized on those details to produce a front-page story for its Sunday editions that quoted the cops' allegations that Rick DeCaro had offered Dan Basile $15,000 to kill Elizabeth while Rick was in the Ozarks with his children. The police wanted to search the van he had driven to see if they could find the murder weapon, fingerprints, signs of blood, or any of the items missing from the house after the murder. And, the documents revealed, the police believed Basile had been in the van and that it "could have been used in connection with the murder"—a tantalizing tidbit for the media. Chief David King was quoted as saying that his speculation on a motive centered on the $100,000 life insurance policy Rick had recently taken out on his wife.

The *Post-Dispatch* had also tracked Elizabeth's family to St. Francis Lane, and a reporter's call to the house reached Margie Ugalde. She decided to be as candid as possible, explaining that Rick had been a loved member of the family, but they had come to believe he had hired the trigger man to kill Elizabeth amid their marital difficulties. "It breaks my heart to say that, but, yes, I think he set it up," she said. "The family feels pretty sure the police have the right guy. It was our worst fear." Margie even disclosed that Elizabeth had told her sisters of her worries for her own safety the morning of her death, after Rick had left on his uncharacteristic trip with the kids.

At the end of the newspaper story, Georgianna also mused on Rick's transformation from cherished son-in-law to suspected killer. "Even now," she said, "I think something happened to this man, something snapped." And then she revealed that she and Jim would raise their daughter's children at their home in St. Ann. "I cannot bring my daughter back, so I want to make her children's lives as normal as possible," she said.

An unnamed member of Rick DeCaro's family had no comment for the reporter.

The press could not know, of course, that the Van Iseghem and DeCaro families had already met to share their grief Saturday morning. Georgianna felt so guilty about the family's animus toward Rick that she had son Jimmy take her to the home of Rick's sister, Patty Fiehler, to see her and Grace. In a meeting that Georgianna found to be thankfully warm, she enumerated the troubling events that had transpired in the DeCaro household in St. Charles and why the Van Iseghems believed Rick to be guilty. His mother and sister had been aware of parts of the story; Grace had talked with Elizabeth about Rick's affair with Cathy Dillon and the resulting marital problems, and even Rick's brother Dan had tried to get him to seek counseling. But the women were shocked to hear so many other disturbing details for the first time. There were no angry or bitter words, just two heartbroken mothers trying to find a way to comfort each other. When Georgianna left, she was convinced that her in-laws had come to accept their son's culpability in her daughter's murder.

Georgianna and Jim had decided the night of Rick's arrest that they would raise Elizabeth's children now that they would have custody of them. Georgianna loved them as her own already, and it was clear to her and Jim that they were the best choice for the kids. Elizabeth's sisters and brothers had children of their own and could not afford the financial burden that four more young ones would impose. Georgianna and Jim might have trouble with the finances as well, but they still were the best situated for this major life change, they were sure. Theresa and Patrick were close anyway—more like sister and younger brother than aunt and nephew. And the kids had lived with their grandparents before, while Rick and Elizabeth built their second house. The plan made such perfect sense that Georgianna even began telling the children about it over that first difficult weekend after their father's arrest. They would all live at the house on St. Francis Lane in St. Ann, but Georgianna would drive them to their schools in St. Charles every day. They had lost enough, and Grandma would see to it that nothing else changed in their lives. The children seemed happy with that plan.

But all of the others in the family were just as willing to take the children, and each of them volunteered as they talked about the choices—without their parents' knowledge. Jimmy thought his position as the eldest sibling and family problem solver made him and his wife, Joy, good candidates. Melanie would gladly take them, but she recognized in her heart that she was not the best choice. And Rick would never allow his kids to live with the sister-in-law he now hated—the one he knew hated him, too. Margie really wanted to take the kids; she could better afford it than anyone else. Her daughter, Jamie, was going to be a high school freshman, and her husband's children were older now too. The Ugalde household was much better prepared for a new brood of children than the others. She called Sergio in California to propose moving back to St. Louis to raise her sister's family. But he was not receptive to the idea. According to Margie, he was calling within two days and asking her to return home, alone. Margie had given up her home in St. Louis to go to California and help him raise his kids, but now he seemed unwilling to make the same sacrifice for her. She knew then that her marriage was doomed.

Mary Cordes felt strongly that she was the only choice for this mixed blessing. Something deep inside told her this was her destiny, that she had been preparing quietly and without knowing it all of her life. She couldn't help but think back to her frivolous visit a year ago to a psychic, who had told her she would have two sons. Mary had laughed; Phil had had a vasectomy and she wasn't about to

marry anyone else, so that was one prediction that would
never come true. But now—it could happen. Adding four
children to her own three daughters would be difficult, to be
sure, and their three-bedroom, fourteen-hundred-square-foot
ranch house would bulge at the seams with nine people
living in it. But Mary had no doubt that it was the only
choice. She certainly knew her mother could not fulfill her
promise of keeping things the way they always had been
by shuttling the children back and forth across the Missouri
River between a house in St. Ann and their schools, friends,
and activities in St. Charles. Nothing would ever be the
same, and pretending the past could be preserved was
pointless. Mary understood Georgianna's goodhearted motivation; she was the mom who took care of everyone, so
this task naturally fell to her. But Mary knew this decision
had to be absolutely right, the first time; the children's emotional stability and security could not withstand being
traded back and forth among their relatives like a favorite
silver chafing dish. Her husband, Phil, was in complete
agreement. In fact, he was the one who raised the issue
Saturday by simply announcing, "If you want those kids,
you'd better speak up and say something." That was the
only discussion needed in the Cordes home before their
decision was made.

Melanie and Margie agreed with Mary; in fact, Melanie
had an additional reason for seeing the wisdom in that decision. Mary had been silent so far about her judgment on
Rick's guilt. While Melanie had led the charge, Mary had
held back; Rick would not assume that Mary believed him
guilty, and that would give her an edge when it came to
keeping the children.

So the three sisters went to their parents on Sunday to
deliver their surprising announcement. Georgianna and Jim
were shocked, and then angered, by their daughters' usur-
pation of their parental rights. In the midst of this tremendous grief over Elizabeth's death, Georgianna did not need
the rest of her children adding another emotional jolt by
telling her she was not the best one to raise the kids she
loved so completely. Everyone around the Van Iseghem

table that afternoon sensed that the discussion could take a painful turn if they were not careful. But the young women explained their reasoning with all the love they carried in their hearts for their parents. Not only was Jim's health worrisome enough already on this day after his sixty-first birthday, but he and Georgianna had already raised their children. Before long, Theresa would be gone too, and it seemed unfair to make Jim and Georgianna start over with four children between the ages of four and twelve. Mary had children almost the same ages as Elizabeth's, and they could all grow up together. If Georgianna and Jim took over as their parents, the children would lose their grandparents. They had lost too much already. They needed Jim and Georgianna to be the perfect, loving grandparents they had always been. Becoming parents was up to the generation in between, and Mary and Phil were ready and able to assume that role.

Faced with those facts, presented with love and honesty, Georgianna and Jim realized their daughters were right. They had no choice but to relent—and they promised to do everything they could to help Mary and Phil make it work, for everyone's sake.

When they all sat the children down later on Sunday to announce the new plan, the kids were not happy. They didn't want to relocate to Mary's house in Florissant—another suburb in St. Louis County—and leave behind their friends, their schools, and the rest of their lives in St. Charles. Georgianna assured the children this was the best plan for them, for everyone.

Mary and her mother also decided to tell the children what the police had revealed about the evidence. The information was presented in a honest and direct way. The adults took pains to be sure the kids realized this was not the family's speculation or opinion—but the facts as determined by the police.

In her perfectly innocent and childlike way, Rachel asked why her father hadn't simply gotten a divorce if he didn't want to live with Mom anymore. That, Mary and Georgianna said, was the question that was so hard for any of them to answer.

This new life for the children would be difficult and sometimes painful, but with the legendary Van Iseghem love, and a little help from their friends, it could be made to work.

FORTY-THREE

The laurels provided by the arrests in the DeCaro murder offered no respite for the detectives of the St. Charles Police Department. Chief David King kept his officers hustling on the follow-up investigation, and Detective Mike Miller became the case leader. He would spend hundreds of hours—many of them on his own time—scrambling for months and months to find every useful shred of evidence against the two men he was convinced had killed Elizabeth. What he and his colleagues found seemed to lock in the case so tightly that the police were thrilled.

One nice surprise came when Detective Rick Plummer interviewed Roberta Paulus, a woman who kept her horses at South County Stables and knew Danny Basile. One afternoon in late February, about five-thirty or six o'clock, she had just arrived to feed her horses when a "nice-looking guy," about six feet, medium build, with dark hair and a mustache, approached her. He had been parked nearby and met her as she got out of her pickup truck. "Is Danny here?" asked the clean-cut man in his thirties. She directed him across the creek, where she thought Basile might be feeding the horses. The man got into his vehicle and drove away. When she saw a photograph of Rick DeCaro in the newspaper, she thought he looked like the man she had seen. She had wondered then why such a nice-looking, clean-cut man would be looking for Danny Basile.

On March 18, Ms. Paulus arrived at the county jail to view a lineup. As the men filed into the room on the other side of the window, she immediately picked Rick. Lieutenant Pat McCarrick asked, "Are you sure?" The forty-six-year-old woman put her hand to her chest and replied, "So sure my heart's pounding."

Doug Meyer was then ushered into the room to see if he could identify the man he had seen talking to Basile outside the house at the stables that day. Without a moment's hesitation, Meyer pointed out Rick and said, "Yes, that's him."

Two for two.

Among the dozens more witnesses who would be interviewed were those who knew Dan Basile as a student of the heating-and-cooling trade at Vatterott College. An instructor, Murphy Giegerich, had become well acquainted with Basile, often giving him rides home after classes. Basile's excellent work had fallen off seriously in recent weeks, probably around the time he had made some curious remarks to Giegerich. He often bragged about doing drugs, doing time in prison, doing some car thefts, and doing the girlfriend who was now pregnant. But he once added that some man had asked him to kill his wife, a surprising part of a conversation in which Basile mentioned doing an "insurance job." About two weeks before the murder, Basile had been asking other students if they were interested in buying two captain's chairs from a vehicle. When Giegerich once asked what Basile did with the cars he stole, Basile offered nonchalantly, "Cut them up." Where? "Down south."

Three days after the murder, Giegerich remembered, he had encountered a "bummed-out" Basile sitting by himself in a corner at the college. He explained his mood by saying he was worried about his relationship with his girlfriend.

Several students remembered Basile's attempt to sell the captain's chairs, and some had heard him explaining that he had "a job to do." He had disclosed to some that he had been approached to steal someone's van, and once he even bragged that he had done exactly that the night before. He had taken it somewhere and "torched it," he added. One student remembered the location of this misdeed as being somewhere near Cape Girardeau; Jackson sounded familiar. Basile had even displayed some trophies from his arson safari—keys to a General Motors vehicle

and the curled-up, pried-loose plate bearing a vehicle identification number.

Detective Mike Miller knew several of the new witnesses
would be valuable at trial, and prosecuting attorney Tim
Braun was glad to see the police turn them up. But one
left an especially deep impression on Pat McCarrick.

A woman who knew Danny Basile had tipped off the
cops that she had seen a Sony "boom box" stereo that he
had given to a mutual friend after the murder. She knew
nothing about the case itself, but she had visited Basile in
jail and he had denied any connection to the DeCaro killing. The police were most interested in the name she provided for this friend with the stereo—Carl Swanson.*

He had been expecting a visit from the police when they
stopped by on March 19; after all, he said, he was a friend
of Basile's. He denied at first that he had any property that
might have come from the DeCaro house, but he relented
when Mike Miller emphasized how important it was to tell
the truth to the police. Swanson escorted the officers to his
back porch and handed them a black plastic trash bag that
he said contained the almost-new boom box. The police
decided to take his word on the contents for the time being;
they would rather preserve this package unopened and let
the evidence technicians investigate it later.

Swanson struck McCarrick as a fairly typical example of
someone on the fringe of society, someone with a drug
conviction in his past and a question mark for his future.
He and Dago Basile had known each other for some time;
they both liked to hang out with the local rock bands, even
working sometimes helping them set up for performances
and tear down afterward. Short-haul roadies.

In a tape-recorded interview back at the police station
that afternoon, a nervous Swanson told a fascinating story
about Basile's arrival at his home about six-thirty on the
evening of the murder. Basile was driving a beautiful Chevy
Blazer that he claimed belonged to his brother-in-law. Basile not only paid Swanson ten bucks on the forty-five he
owed him, but he had an extra surprise. Swanson would
turn thirty-three the next day—Saturday, March 7—and

Basile opened the back of the Blazer to present his friend with a dandy boom box as a birthday present. It was so new that the edges still bore the adhesive bumpers applied to protect it during shipping. Swanson was overwhelmed, and gave his pal a hug in gratitude. The stereo featured a compact-disc player—something Swanson had wanted but couldn't afford—as well as dual cassette decks with high-speed dubbing. All the bells and whistles. Really cool, Swanson said. He had invited Basile to a birthday celebration planned for that evening at Swanson's favorite watering hole. He could get free drinks after midnight, he explained, because that would be his actual birthday. But Basile had declined; he had something to do.

Sometime before all of that, Swanson remembered, Basile had complained about the transmission on his old car not working well. He had said he was going to take it to someone Swanson remembered as "Rich" to get it repaired.

But Swanson didn't think Basile had anything to do with Elizabeth DeCaro's murder. Since he was paroled, Basile had been trying to get his life back on the right track. Swanson claimed to have been the one who talked him into taking classes at Vatterott College. And he had tried to steer Basile away from the crooked path. When they got out of Swanson's wreck-damaged Pontiac Trans-Am in a theater parking lot and saw a similar one parked nearby, Basile had nodded toward it with a glint in his eye. "Parts," he had suggested. Swanson had discouraged even the idea. "Evil thoughts, man," he warned. Swanson had a clouded past, to be sure. But now, he insisted, he was "Mister Joe Legal."

Swanson also provided a uniquely personal observation that he thought cut in Danny Basile's favor when it came to this shooting.

"Dago carries knives. Dago ain't got nothing to do with guns. Dago's a knife guy," Swanson explained. He could imagine Dago slitting some dude's throat, but he could not see him shooting a woman. "He's too much of a womanizer," Swanson added.

But what struck Pat McCarrick about this witness was his reflection on the boom box. With a wistful tone in his voice, Carl Swanson seemed to be summing up his existence as he explained, "It was one of the best birthday presents I've ever got in my life. Now I wish I had never gotten it, because now it's got me sucked up in all of this. I don't want nothing to do with it."

That struck McCarrick as unbelievably sad. One of the best presents this guy had ever received in his life had come from an ex-con-thief-turned-murderer, and even then it had all gone sour. Swanson even had to depend on free drinks at a bar to celebrate his birthday. And beyond that, he counted among his best friends Danny Basile, the man who had murdered Elizabeth DeCaro for pennies, stolen her Blazer, and then found time within hours of this brutal killing to stop by a friend's house and gift him with a boom box stolen from the murder scene. My God, McCarrick mused, what did all of that say about the lives of Danny Basile and Carl Swanson?

FORTY-FOUR

Rick DeCaro was taking no chances. By the time of his initial appearance in court on Tuesday, March 17—just four days after his arrest—he had made a surprisingly strong move. His attorney, Ron Jenkins, had given him some good advice, and he took it. Jenkins never took capital murder cases, and so he sent Rick to one of the top defense attorneys in the St. Louis area, if not the Midwest. Donald L. Wolff had spent years representing some of the most noted, if not notorious, defendants to walk through courtroom doors, and he had done it with impressive class, style, integrity, and success. Not only did he lecture on criminal law but the courts sometimes called on him as an independent counsel or "special master" to review thorny questions such as attorneys' conflicts of interest. He was a brilliant lawyer, an articulate advocate, and an imposing presence—a tall, dark man with sharp features and closely cropped graying hair. He cut an elegant figure in expensive suits that accentuated his straight carriage. His personal and professional sophistication was supplemented by such love and knowledge of jazz that he had his own popular radio show in St. Louis featuring his favorite music. Truly a Renaissance man.

And now he would bring all of that to the table as Rick DeCaro's defense attorney. The Van Iseghems were less than pleased to see Rick acquire such a formidable champion. Prosecutor Tim Braun had met Wolff and knew of his reputation. He had never faced off against him in court, but he wasn't particularly intimidated. After all, few lawyers had tried as many cases as Braun.

At the initial appearance on March 17—the first formal reading of the charges—Rick's family and friends lined the benches as Wolff asked circuit court judge Jon A. Cunningham to set bond. Rick was, after all, a lifelong resident of the area, a father of four, a gainfully employed citizen, a property owner, and a man with no criminal record at all. There was absolutely no evidence that he would flee, and holding him without bond was excessive.

But Braun was having none of that. Rick DeCaro was a dangerous man who not only was charged with soliciting at least two men to help him find a hired gun to murder his wife but had made a substantial assault on her life himself. Braun explained the van crash that came not long after Rick had bought a $100,000 life insurance policy on Elizabeth. Judge Cunningham did not take that incident lightly; he rejected Wolff's request for bond.

Outside the courtroom, Wolff told reporters that Rick and his family believed he had been framed. And Wolff charged that Braun and the police had leaked information to the media to bolster their case in the eyes of the public and gain political favor for Braun.

The battle had been joined.

Later in the day, Braun would win another skirmish, this time against Daniel Basile and his court-appointed lawyer, Kristine Grady, an assistant public defender. The prosecutor sought the revocation of the $1 million bond set for Basile. In a memo to circuit court judge Norman C. Steimel III, Braun alleged that one of his witnesses already had been threatened by the Aryan Brotherhood, a white supremacist organization formed by inmates of Missouri prisons. Braun left the reference at that; he didn't explain that Gayle Dorman—Craig Wells's girlfriend—had received a call March 13 from a man who called himself Randy and said Dan Basile had supplied her phone number. Randy invoked the name of the Aryan Brotherhood and explained he was upset because his "brother" was in jail; whoever was responsible for that would have to pay. "The snitch will go down," he warned. Nothing would come of it, but it was still cause for concern.

Braun was successful again; the judge revoked Basile's bond. Now both of the men charged with bringing such a cruel death to Elizabeth DeCaro would sit in jail cells until it was time for them to face a court of justice. Or so Braun assumed.

But Don Wolff was not the type to surrender after just one adverse ruling. He came back quickly with a formal motion for bond, and Judge Cunningham set it for a quick hearing on Monday, March 23. Braun called Lieutenant Pat McCarrick as his only witness, guiding him through the evidence to try to sink this renewed effort to put Rick DeCaro back on the streets. McCarrick offered the essence of each witness's story, marrying Rick and Basile to each other and to the murder. Don Wolff countered with an interesting approach on cross-examination, asking McCarrick about Rick's affair and the duration of the DeCaros' marital problems.

"My information was that they were still having difficulties at the same time she was killed," the lieutenant answered.

"So, she wouldn't have written him a love letter?"

The question puzzled McCarrick; he knew nothing about a love letter, but he was not about to let his surprise show in court. He shrugged and responded, "She was very much interested in reconciling and saving the marriage, so I would say she very well may have written a love letter."

The Van Iseghems were bewildered by the reference to a "love letter" that none of them knew anything about. Don Wolff had something up his sleeve, but it would be some time before it would be revealed.

Wolff called Dan DeCaro to the stand to recount his conversation with Elizabeth about a week before she was killed. "She was excited. She told me Rick had told her that he loved her," Dan explained. He was aware of the sexual activities between Rick and an unnamed woman at the station. But Dan said that Rick's lover and his wife had told Dan the affair "was terminated shortly after it began."

Wolff clearly was trying to show that the prosecution and police were making too much of the problems between Rick and Elizabeth, and to diminish them as a motive for murder. Braun assumed Wolff had just tipped his hand on his trial strategy.

The defender argued to the judge that bond had been set for defendants in similar cases in St. Charles County. Rick DeCaro deserved the same break. "He is presumed innocent," Wolff argued. "He has never been in trouble before in his life. He is no threat to the community."

But Wolff's tactics failed to sway Judge Cunningham, and he reaffirmed his order holding Rick without bond. The Van Iseghems were pleased. So far, the courts seemed to be taking the correct view of this case and seemed to be dedicated to keeping Rick where he belonged.

Meanwhile, the Van Iseghems were just beginning to deal with the daily facts of life without Elizabeth. Ten days after the murder, Georgianna had to keep her commitment to cater a huge St. Patrick's Day party for a bank. Georgianna, Melanie and Mary were all on the job, but they were just going through the motions. None of them found any pleasure in the work now. The first Saturday in April brought even more of a challenge—catering four weddings in one day. Georgianna's worried clients called, wondering if the emotionally battered mother would still be able to meet her commitments. Of course, she said. That was the way the Van Iseghems did things; work was always first.

But these days were bringing something the family had never really expected—an amazing, heartwarming show of support from family, friends, the entire community—support that would overwhelm and then sustain them. A flood of cards and letters arrived at St. Francis Lane. Hundreds of them, all expressing sympathy and concern and love. One that touched the family deeply was signed simply, "Greg." He recounted how the other kids at school shunned and teased him because he didn't quite fit in, giving him the derisive nickname "Professor." But one girl had always given him friendship and respect and dignity. Elizabeth had always called him Greg.

Another friend, Lori Kliethermes, sent a four-page letter remembering how Elizabeth had been there for her through good times and bad. "She taught me the meaning of friendship. She taught me to appreciate every day and not to waste time. I will desperately miss her, but I feel that the time with her was such a gift."

And now the kindness Elizabeth had shown to others was about to be returned to her family. Many of Jim Van Iseghem's friends arrived at Mary Cordes's house in Florissant, armed with hammers and saws, lumber and drywall. They descended on her basement and in record time had finished off two new bedrooms, a bathroom, and a family room—a project Phil had started a long time ago but seldom was able to find time for. And now, it was complete, free of cost for the children.

Over the next few weeks and months, the community would pour out its heart and tap its wallet at a fund-raiser dance, golf tournament, and auction; such a huge crowd attended that some had to be turned away from the hall, though it held six hundred. A special collection taken by St. Elizabeth Ann Seton Parish brought in an incredible amount of cash, raising the grand total in a special trust fund for the DeCaro children to more than $43,000. The church's apostolic works program even hauled in an oversized refrigerator so Mary could store the food for her huge brood.

The St. Charles Crime Stoppers weighed in with a reward fund of a thousand dollars for information leading to discovery of the murder weapon or any of the items stolen from the home during the murder.

Jim Van Iseghem asked family lawyer Frank Vatterott to handle the legal arrangements for Mary to retain custody of the kids through state foster care. Vatterott set up an appointment for Mary and Phil to meet with the Division of Family Services. When Jim promised to make payments on the legal fees, Vatterott waved his hand and smiled. "There'll be no charges, Jim."

Mary was astounded at how many free services were offered to help her and Phil deal with their new responsibilities. The food piled up in enormous amounts, providing dinner for the newly constituted Cordes-DeCaro clan every night for two months. Soap powder and canned goods arrived by the case. Contributions to the kids' trust fund—many from collections taken at area churches—came in regularly. The generosity of so many in St. Ann and St. Charles warmed the Van Iseghems' hearts. Knowing that so many people had loved Elizabeth and missed her was comforting.

But there were, of course, dark clouds above every silver lining. Under Rick's instructions, his family retained control of the house on Hidden Meadow Court. To everyone's surprise, Mary was allowed to take only the children's clothing. Their toys and furniture and other possessions—all the things that could have helped them feel at home at Mary's—had to remain behind.

Georgianna was crushed, too, that she was granted none of Elizabeth's belongings. When she and Mary went to the house to collect the kids' clothing, they were watched by the police and forbidden to take any mementos. One officer begged Georgianna not to take anything; he didn't want to arrest her. She managed to sneak away only one item—a small doll in a frilly blue dress and blond yarn curls that sat above the kitchen sink—a doll that had witnessed Elizabeth's murder. If this doll could only talk, Georgianna thought later as she stared at her silent, solitary treasure.

These days also marked the start of what Mary would soon call "our second nightmare." Rick began regular collect calls from the jail to the kids at Mary's house. His calls were filled with promises that he soon would be free and they would all go back home together. Everything would go back to normal and he would buy them everything they wanted. The kids seemed to hang on to these promises that Mary found so empty and, beyond that, so cruel. How could anyone really believe Rick would ever be free again? she wondered.

But she was pleased with the early efforts to blend the members of the new family. Elizabeth's children adapted as well as could be hoped in this new town and in this new house. Mary, Phil, and their three daughters—Angela, thirteen; Colleen, eleven; and Nichole, eight—did everything they could to make the four DeCaros feel at home and an essential part of the new family.

The first day at their new school had brought tension. Mary had told nine-year-old Rachel that she could be in the same third-grade class as Nichole—a promise that had made the change less daunting and even somewhat exciting. But the school frowned on that; better that Rachel should face this on her own than to lean on her cousin. Mary and Rachel accepted that, but poor Nichole sobbed deeply in disappointment. Biil, seven and in second grade, took quickly to his new surroundings. Patrick, twelve and having a difficult time with all of this, would have preferred to live with his grandmother and attend school with his favorite thirteen-year-old aunt—Theresa. Happily, Patrick's resistance melted into exhilaration after that first day of sixth-grade classes. He returned from school bubbling over with descriptions of how "awesome" it all had been. Mary learned later that all the girls had really liked the new boy, which had provided an immediate attitude adjustment for him.

Mary shook her head at this amazing turn of events. She was now sending five of the seven children in her home to Russell Elementary School. Her oldest, Angela, attended junior high, and Elizabeth's baby, Erin, was in preschool at St. Kevin's Church.

Despite the relatively smooth going for the nine people in the newly formed household, Mary and Melanie still were concerned about what they thought to be a curious, and potentially harmful, lack of emotion among the children over their mother's death. They never talked about it to each other or to anyone else. They never asked about what had happened or what was ahead for their father. They just seemed to accept it all.

Little Erin exemplified that attitude. She once carried a stack of newspaper clippings to "show-and-tell" day at the preschool at St. Kevin's Church. She spread them across a desk and pointed to the photographs that ran with the stories. "This is my mom, and she's dead," Erin explained. "This is my dad, and they think he did it." The other kids nodded in acceptance, and that was it. It had become a fact of life.

FORTY-FIVE

The court system's first affront to the Van Iseghems' sense of justice arrived on April 23. On the motion of Don Wolff, the Missouri Court of Appeals reversed Judge Cunningham's denial of bond for Rick. Appellate judge James A. Pudlowski set the price for Rick's freedom at $1 million. The Van Iseghems were outraged. How could any judge believe that this man deserved freedom? The evidence overwhelmingly proved that he had coldly planned his wife's murder. And now the courts would free him to be with his children, communicate with his murdered wife's family, and perhaps even threaten them and other witnesses. The only saving grace—in the eyes of the Van Iseghems—was Judge Pudlowski's refusal to allow Rick to satisfy the bond by posting a small percentage in cash. He would have to put up the full $1 million.

To the Van Iseghems' unhappy surprise again, nineteen people lined up the next day and signed over their property toward Rick's $1 million goal. His father and sister were joined by Dan DeCaro's ex-wife and many of the family's friends—all committing their properties as surety that Rick would show up for trial. Their gestures were a genuine risk; if Rick fled or violated the terms of his bond, the courts could seize those properties.

One woman who put up her house—a value of $31,983—said she did not even know Rick or his family. She had been prodded to act because she believed Rick was being treated unfairly by the media.

The most notable names on the list of guarantors were Cathy and Jeff Dillon, who put up two pieces of property— including their home—worth a total of $82,650, in hopes of securing the release of Cathy's former lover. The Van Iseghems were astonished, wondering how naive Jeff Dillon could be. The only explanation they could come up with for Jeff's broad-minded attitude was his direct connection to the DeCaro family—Jeff's sister was married to Rick's brother Dan.

But all of those selfless efforts on Rick's behalf still fell short. The fund-raising campaign came up with $545,870— just over half of what was needed. For the time being, Rick would stay in jail.

While the stream of charitable property owners lined up at the courthouse in St. Charles, Braun was telling reporters at a news conference that he would take the appellate decision to the Missouri Supreme Court. Describing Rick derisively as the kind of man who used his own children to establish a murder alibi, Braun announced, "I care about keeping him in jail."

Braun also cited the concerns of Rick's neighbors in Woodfield Meadows. Several of them had called Braun to protest the possibility that Rick could be returning home; some of their children were even having nightmares about him.

But there was more going on below the surface than was reflected by the arguments over bond and by the news conferences. At family lawyer Frank Vatterott's suggestion, the Van Iseghems had complained to the authorities about Rick's contact with his children. Vatterott already had taken Mary and Phil Cordes to juvenile court in St. Charles County to apply to become foster parents, only to be told that the county did not have jurisdiction because the children now lived in St. Louis County. So Vatterott lined up an appointment there; the juvenile authorities were not only receptive to the Cordeses' application to become foster parents but were seriously disturbed by Rick's daily calls and letters. One court officer wrote in the record that

Rick's promise to sweep the kids back into their home upon his triumphant return was "not in the best interest of the children." Finally! the Van Iseghems thought. Someone who realizes that having their suspected-murderer father returning the kids to the house where their mother was murdered might not be the best idea.

Vatterott immediately petitioned for an order of protection, and juvenile court commissioner Robert H. Branom agreed. On April 24—while so many DeCaro supporters were pledging their properties—Branom stopped all calls and letters from Rick to the children "until further order of the court." Branom added that all contact between Rick and the children during visitation at the jail had to be supervised by an official from the Division of Family Services.

Braun was able to put all of that to good use when he filed his appeal with the state supreme court on Monday, April 27—as the property posted for Rick's bond approached the dangerous level of $900,000. Braun argued that Rick had endangered his children not only by using them as a murder alibi but also by secreting their mother's killer in their own house while they were home. If the court somehow believed bond was appropriate, Braun added, a figure of $10 million would be reasonable. And, even then, Rick should be allowed only bimonthly, supervised visits with his children.

The supreme court gave Braun a preliminary victory that same day, ordering Rick held for at least a week while the justices considered the case. When Wolff responded, his documents termed Braun's conditions of bond "far-reaching and onerous." Wolff also rejected the juvenile court's criticism of Rick's promises to his children. Calling them an "expression of hopefulness," Wolff argued that his client's optimism for "the reunification of this family can hardly be considered a threat against his children."

The supreme court's answer was swift. On May 11, as the fund for Rick's release rocketed to $960,000, the justices overturned the appellate court and revoked bond. Braun had won this battle.

Melanie and Mary were having dinner with their parents when the new pager bought by the Van Iseghems went off.

A hurried call to Braun brought the exciting news of success in the supreme court, a major win for the good guys. The event also proved the wisdom of the family's decision to equip everyone with pagers; sending word through the grapevine was becoming increasingly complicated, and these urgent matters needed quick attention. Getting this news on this night was worth the effort and expense.

FORTY-SIX

"March 6th will live in infamy."

As Georgianna Van Iseghem put pen to paper to unleash the pressure building in her heart, those were the first words she set free. In her new world, Elizabeth's murder was no less catastrophic than the attack on Pearl Harbor fifty years earlier that had given immortality to the phrase she now had borrowed from FDR. Georgianna added a new and essential spiritual dimension by immediately adding her prayer, "Help me, Jesus. Amen."

In the first of many, many volumes of introspection and prayer, struggle and pain, loss and triumph—all dedicated to Elizabeth's memory—Georgianna began a new practice of "journaling." Every morning that she could find the strength and the inspiration, she would pour out her heart into the diaries that would become the history of the world without Elizabeth. As Georgianna discovered in one of the very first sentences she wrote on this morning in late April, Elizabeth would seem closer as Georgianna recorded her innermost thoughts. "I can feel her with me," she wrote as she began collecting her memories. She sat in her favorite chair—looking out of the windows in the sunroom that Rick DeCaro had built for his loving in-laws so many years ago, in a different and sadly remembered world.

"I miss her smile, and the way she said, 'Hi-eee,' " Georgianna wrote that day. "She was the perfect daughter and mother and sister . . . I will never let anyone forget her."

Georgianna still talked to Elizabeth the first thing every morning, hoping to keep the bond between them strong, even though it was now strained by death—the ultimate distance. Every smile that graced Georgianna's lips was an offering to her departed daughter. Melanie and Mary had told Georgianna how important her attitude was to the rest of the family, how her quiet actions led and influenced the way everyone felt. So she tried to be sure that each look, each move, each glance, each word, provided something to cling to for everyone else who mourned Elizabeth too. That was a heavy burden for this aching mother.

She could not keep her heart from breaking on May 10, her first Mother's Day without her complete family to help celebrate. As the Van Iseghems gathered at Elizabeth's grave, her four children read special letters to their mother and seemed to be holding back their emotions, again. Georgianna remembered that their psychologist had told Mary that the children felt disloyal to their father if they openly mourned their mother. What an awful onus Rick had inflicted on his own children. As Georgianna ached on this special day, she realized anew that life for everyone in this large family puzzle that seemed so perfect just a year ago would never be the same. "One little piece will always be missing," she lamented.

When Theresa graduated from the eighth grade on May 21, she celebrated a mass in her honor by reading a poem she had written to her missing sister. In "Memories," Theresa began her reflection on the special nature of thoughts of the past:

> Memories make you laugh
> And memories make you cry.
> They make you smile
> And they make you ask why.

This young woman who missed her sister so much closed by observing:

Memories can be a person's best friend.
No matter what happens,
You will always have them.

As the youngest Van Iseghem sister poured out her grief,
her mother realized that the pain of missing Elizabeth had
rolled in again, "like a fog." Only the feeling that Elizabeth
remained close in spirit provided any solace: "I cry and cry.
I almost feel her wipe away my tears."

Mary Cordes found a more direct outlet for her grief and
anger, and it exploded directly into Rick DeCaro's ear.
After the judge's order expired, Rick resumed the daily
collect phone calls to the Cordes house to speak to his
children and his frequent letters filled with those promises
that he would be free soon. He even urged the children
not to listen to the "bad things" that Aunt Mary was saying
about him. That really angered Mary; she wasn't saying
anything bad about him, and neither was anyone else in
the family. They were going out of their way to avoid any
comment that could be construed as critical or accusatory.
They did not want the children to feel that they were being
forced to choose between their father and the Van Iseghems. The children surely sensed that Mary and the others
believed their father was guilty. But Mary had managed to
put aside her feelings about all of this and just concentrate
on what was best for the children.

Mary had even been forced to make the appointments
for the kids to see their father in jail on Thursdays. The
first time, she and Phil had taken the kids—except for the
resolute Patrick. But they decided that that system was
too hard on everyone's emotions. The county social
workers agreed to handle the visits from then on, if Mary
would set up the appointments. When she would call to
do so, the jailer would always ask the same question:
"What is your relationship to the inmate?" Mary wanted
to scream, "He killed my sister!" How could you explain
all of this to some unsuspecting clerk who just needed to
fill out a form?

The frustrations had been festering, and they erupted on

one of Rick's calls to Mary's home. "Stop calling so often," she demanded.

She could tell Rick was shocked. He shot back, "They're my kids, and I love them."

"You should have thought of that before you murdered Elizabeth."

"I didn't kill Elizabeth."

His protestation of innocence failed to impress Mary, or to deflect her fury. She ripped into him with all the passion that she had held back for so long. "I loved you like a brother. You were closer to me than my own brothers. How could you do this to me, let alone Elizabeth?"

Rick's voice cracked. "I didn't do it."

Mary's voice had taken on an edge she knew was honed by anger, a tone demeaning and eviscerating. "I don't believe you."

Rick later complained to his attorney about Mary's verbal assault, and that drew a warning to her that Rick would slap a harassment suit on her if she dared to deal with him that way again. Mary was unintimidated. Her spur-of-the-moment blast at Rick had felt good, and now he knew exactly where she stood. He probably had thought she was on his side, as he had thought his mother-in-law was on his side in the early days. Mary had tried not to say anything to him before, wanting to avoid hard feelings that would hinder her efforts to retain custody of the kids. In fact, Melanie and Mary had traded their usual roles in the family; the easygoing Melanie had become the thunderous voice of the family's outrage, while the normally outspoken Mary had remained quietly in the background. Rick had come to expect brutal truth from Mary over the years; he often told Elizabeth that her own candid comments on some subject must have followed a conversation with Mary. But in this upside-down world, Mary had held back, until that day when enough had become more than enough, and she found herself confronting this man who used to be Rick DeCaro. He surely had planned her sister's execution, and Mary could no longer sit by silently while he invaded her home to inflict even more emotional trauma on Elizabeth's children. Mary had said her piece, and it had felt good.

* * *

Georgianna could feel the stress pulsing through everyone in the family. "I pray Elizabeth's spirit will get all of us through this nightmare," she wrote in her journal. "Please, Elizabeth, send us your spirit."

Even in her pain then, Georgianna could not imagine how many times she would have to call on that spirit in the days and years ahead.

FORTY-SEVEN

A confusing initiation into the intricacies of the court system began for the Van Iseghems on Tuesday, May 26, 1992, with the first role call of witnesses in the case against Richard DeCaro and Daniel Basile. At this preliminary hearing, prosecutor Tim Braun would need Melanie Enkelmann as a witness; that, she found out to her dismay, meant she would not be allowed to sit in the courtroom and listen to testimony from the others. How infuriating that the story of her sister's murder was to be told while she sat in the hallway! Where was the fairness, the justice, in that? Georgianna had dreaded the idea of facing Rick and Basile in court for the first time, knowing Basile was the one who actually murdered Elizabeth. "I can hardly say the words," Georgianna wrote in her journal the night before.

The family never was able to grasp the real purpose for this hearing. Braun said only that it took the place of a review by a grand jury. That meant nothing to them; they weren't even sure what a grand jury was. They were never told that the so-called prelim served a vital purpose as a check on the power of the state, a procedure that grew out of English common law and kept a prosecutor from becoming a persecutor with his own abusive agenda. At a preliminary hearing, the prosecution was required to prove there was "probable cause" to believe that the defendant had committed the crime and should stand trial.

Braun would have to show Judge Jon A. Cunningham that there was enough evidence to believe that it was more likely than not that these two men had planned and carried out the murder of Elizabeth DeCaro. If Cunningham was convinced, he would bind the men over for trial; if the evidence was lacking, he would dismiss the charges. Either way, the law presumed, justice was done. But beyond that, and on the practical side, this procedure was something of a mini-trial that gave each side a chance to size up the opposition. What did the prosecutor really have to back up his charges? How would the defense attack the state's case? How did the witnesses come off when they took the stand?

It was all quite mysterious to the Van Iseghems and their supporters as they assembled in the front row of the courtroom in St. Charles that morning. When the defendants were brought in, Elizabeth's survivors found themselves staring in disbelief at this strange duo. Their first look at Daniel Basile ripped through their hearts like a chainsaw. Remorseless. Arrogant. Smirking. Swaggering. Disgusting. Mary found him simply scary-looking and, as Margie had thought, like the Devil himself.

The sisters immediately recalled the unsettling dream that had come to their friend Boo Pohlmann, just after the murder. She had relived the killing, as if she had witnessed it, and then had talked with Elizabeth's spirit about it. In exactly the language Elizabeth would have used in life, her specter told Boo that the killer had been some "scuzzball." As her sisters now looked at Daniel Basile, they knew Boo had indeed been visited by Elizabeth. Danny Basile looked exactly like the "scuzzball" she had described, just the way she would have said it.

When the Van Iseghems cast their eyes toward Rick De-Caro, he did not look back. He sat there stiffly, expressionless, like stone. They felt as if they were looking at a stranger, not someone who had once been a vital member of their loving family. On the other side of the courtroom, his family gathered behind him and the defense table. Very little conversation passed between the families across the aisle.

Braun presented his case in a straightforward manner,

and his first witness had the Van Iseghems in tears. Dr.
Mary Case, the impressive medical examiner for St. Charles
County, described the paths of the two bullets fired into
the back of Elizabeth's neck while the gun barrel was
pressed tightly against her skin—a point-blank assassination. Dr. Case—an elegant, slender, sophisticated, and confidently articulate woman—could not determine which of
the two shots was fired first. One smashed through the side
of a vertebra in the neck and—while not severing the spinal
cord—inflicted a significant injury to it. The victim would
have suffered immediate paralysis from the neck down, and
the shot probably would have been fatal. The other shot
ripped a path closer to the brain, snapped off a bone at
the bottom of the skull, and pushed that fragment into the
cerebellum—the part of the brain that controls muscle co-
ordination. The victim would have collapsed, immediately
unconscious and definitely about to die. There had been no
chance for survival; a doctor could not have saved her once
that trigger had been pulled.

Braun also had the doctor describe the old bruises she
had seen on Elizabeth's left leg. The injuries themselves
were unremarkable and unrelated to her death, but Braun
was setting the stage for the account of how Rick had
rammed Elizabeth into the garage wall with the van—certainly a telling portent of his murderous intent.

Basile's public defender, Kristine Grady, focused on Dr.
Case's inability to pinpoint the time of death more precisely
than twelve to twenty-four hours before the body was discovered. The lawyer's questions drew the mildly impatient
response the pathologist delivered when a layman demanded an answer more befitting TV's *Quincy* than a bona
fide scientist. "She hadn't been dead for two days or two
weeks. She'd been dead for less than twenty-four hours,"
Dr. Case said flatly. In the real world of medical science,
that was as precise as it got.

A very nervous Melanie Enkelmann took the witness
stand next for her first courtroom account of that terrible
day and the months that led up to it. As she testified, she
drilled Rick DeCaro with a withering stare—not unlike the
one she had delivered as he was escorted to the police

car on that Friday night ten weeks ago. But her emotional telegram was not received; Rick still did not have the courage to look at her.

Braun led Melanie through Elizabeth's last day and the search that had brought Melanie and Mike Carroll to the house on Hidden Meadow Court. She described the scene in the kitchen and painfully identified the photographs that showed the bloody mess left on the floor between the sink and the center island after Elizabeth's body was removed. The testimony got even more difficult from there. Melanie identified another photo, this one showing her sister's body on the morgue table. Braun had Melanie point out the bruises that Melanie had seen on Elizabeth's leg on the Monday night before the murder. As Elizabeth stepped out of the shower after they had played racquetball, she had shown Melanie the remains of the bruises from the van crash. By then, Melanie explained, the bruises were considerably smaller than they had been when she first saw them three weeks earlier.

When Wolff objected to Melanie's last comment, Braun explained to the judge why the testimony was important beyond establishing the condition of Elizabeth's body at the time of her death. "I would also offer it in relation to him trying to kill her by running her through the wall a couple of weeks before," Braun said. The judge overruled Wolff's objection, and Melanie described the incident that left Elizabeth with the bruises.

Braun then turned to an important witness who presented a difficult problem—the witness could not testify for himself. Braun had to use others to explain how this witness fit into the events of March 6.

"Can you tell the court about the dog that was owned by the DeCaro family?" he asked.

"He barks a lot," Melanie said. "He barks at anybody that comes to the house."

"Have you ever seen the dog with Richard DeCaro outside the house?"

"No, I haven't."

"And on March 6 the dog was gone?"

"Yes, he was."

Melanie also had to testify for her absent sister, recounting the phone call Elizabeth made to Rick while he was en route to the Ozarks that morning. "She was very upset because he had not kissed her good-bye when he left."

"And what, if anything, did she say after that phone call?"

"She got off the phone and said, 'He sounds nervous. Something's up. He's up to something. I can feel it, just like the day I went through the wall, and the day the van was blown up. Something is going to happen.'"

Braun moved next to something of value that the police had overlooked in the disappointing taped conversation between Rick and Melanie. Rick had admitted seeing Cathy Dillon in February—after their affair supposedly had ended in December—and that he had been concerned about how many times Elizabeth's amateur detectives had followed him during that period.

"So," Braun offered, "he knew that Elizabeth had known he'd met Cathy in February?"

"Yes."

To Braun, that was a critical factor that may have set the timetable for the end of Elizabeth's life. She knew Rick had continued to be unfaithful, and she could even produce an eyewitness to a rendezvous long after the affair supposedly had ended. Elizabeth now knew too much and too many things that could have been costly to Rick later in divorce and child-custody proceedings. She had to die ASAP.

Judge Cunningham broke for lunch before the defense attorneys could cross-examine Melanie. As she contemplated her testimony before returning to the stand, Melanie felt an odd uneasiness, a lack of connection to Braun's questioning. Had it been his questions? The way they were phrased? His general manner? She just didn't feel as if she had really told the story, had really explained what she knew about her sister's murder.

Don Wolff focused his cross-examination on the timing of that last day, and Melanie was insistent that she knew precisely when Elizabeth had left work to go home—2:20 P.M. Melanie had left at the same time and had checked her watch as she got into the car.

Elizabeth's two telephone calls to Rick that morning also interested Wolff, and Melanie explained that she had walked away without hearing the second one. Wolff resurrected that vague reference to a mysterious "love letter" from Elizabeth, the same unexplained reference from the bond hearing.

"Did you hear her talking to him about the fact that she had written him?"

"That she had written him?" Melanie was still confused.

"Yes."

"Not on the telephone."

Wolff dropped it; again, the family would have to wait even longer for an answer to this puzzling allusion.

Melanie's testimony about Ozzie forced Wolff to try to defuse that tidbit as an evidentiary land mine. "You don't know whether or not Rick has ever been outside the home with the dog when you weren't around. Isn't that true?"

"That's correct."

When Wolff turned his attention to the conversation between Rick and Melanie, and Rick's insistence that his affair with Cathy Dillon had ended in November or December, Braun objected to the "vague" two-month time frame. The judge agreed it could be clearer and sustained the objection. But Wolff turned back to Melanie and asked if she had understood the question.

That angered Braun. "I'm going to object. He's quibbling. I'd like to have him admonished."

The judge shook his head. "I don't think that's necessary."

Wolff shot a slightly amused, sarcastic glance at Braun. "Would you like to have me spanked?"

The judge had listened to enough. "Okay, gentlemen, move on."

Melanie's answer was a simple yes; Rick had told her the affair had ended in November or December.

And with that, Melanie's first experience on the witness stand was over. It would be far from her last.

The muscular, dark-haired man took the stand and spelled his name: James T-O-R-R-E-G-R-O-S-S-A. The story of

Rick's betrayal was about to unfold. Torregrossa told
Braun how the man he had known casually for about a
year at Gold's Gym had surprised him with two questions—
first, asking about someone to take a van off his hands, and
then about someone "to take care of someone for me."

"I said, 'What?' He said, 'You know, kill somebody.'"

"What did you tell him to that?"

"I said no."

Wolff challenged Torregrossa's memory by attacking the
date of this conversation. Records at the Old Orchard station showed he had never taken his car there in January
1992, Wolff insisted. That's right, the witness said; he had
taken his girlfriend's car that day. Wolff countered with a
police report, citing Torregrossa's claim that he had taken
his car in. Yes, he had said that at first; but he had corrected it later when he found his girlfriend's canceled check
for the tire Rick had put on her Mustang on January 10.
To Wolff, that meant Torregrossa had changed his "story."
Just a simple mistake, Torregrossa said.

Rick had complained about meeting a heavy payment on
the van? Yes. Wolff hoped that would raise a question
about the credibility of Torregrossa's whole story. Wolff
could prove that the van was leased by Old Orchard; Rick
wasn't making any payments out of his pocket.

Braun's redirect examination started with a very direct
question. "How many other times in your life has someone
asked you to get someone to kill someone for them?"

"Zero," Torregrossa snapped.

"And that was a memorable occasion from that stand-
point, wasn't it?"

"Yes, sir."

And what about "changing" the story? How long had it
taken Torregrossa to discover and correct his mistake over
which car he had taken to Rick that day? Weeks? Months?
No, just one day, the witness said.

Rick's first attempt to find someone to kill his wife was
now a documented fact; if only it had ended in that failure.
The next source tapped by Rick was called to the stand:
Craig Wells, the man who had worked for the Van Isegh-

ems and the DeCaros, the man who knew Elizabeth and Rick, the man who sent Basile to Rick.

The family-but-no-blood-relation link between Wells and Basile had almost too many curves and corners to follow as Braun tried to tie up these familial loose ends. Who was Basile?

"He's my stepmother's foster son's half brother."

"All right. Who is your stepmother?"

"R'Neil Wells."

"And who is R'Neil Wells's foster son?"

"Doug Meyer."

"And Doug Meyer is what relation?"

"He's Danny's half brother."

"So, they share the same mother. Is that right?"

"Same mother, yes, sir."

"And what have you called Daniel Basile?"

"I've called him my brother."

"You've used the term, but he is no blood relation?"

"No."

"Is Doug Meyer any blood relation to you?"

"No."

Sorting that out was almost impossible for the uninitiated. What it all meant was that Craig Wells's father, Harold, had married R'Neil Wells. She had a foster son named Doug Meyer, and he had a half brother named Daniel Basile. Basile was a half brother to Meyer, who was Wells's foster brother—and the three of them called each other brothers. Just one big, extended, convoluted family.

Once through that maze, Craig Wells described how Rick had asked him about finding someone to steal the van and how Wells had not only connected Rick and Basile but had chauffeured Basile to four meetings with Rick. After the first, Wells had been horrified to hear that Rick had asked Basile about killing Elizabeth and had offered "nice" money—about fifteen thousand dollars—for the hit. Wells had protested any thought of killing this woman he considered a friend, and he thought he had been successful in halting this "package deal" before it really got started.

Later, Basile announced that he had agreed just to steal the van. Wells drove Basile to the last two meetings with Rick but didn't have to pick him up. Rick had driven his new friend to his classes at Vatterott College after those meetings. On February 6, Rick gave Wells the envelope containing the hand-drawn map to Rick's home, keys to the van, and what Wells thought felt like a stack of money. At Rick's insistence, the reluctant Wells had looked at the map and keys, but he had not actually seen the money. Wells remembered only that the map marked the house with highlighter. Basile later told Wells he had stolen the van and burned it near Cape Girardeau. The price had been about $200, and Basile had used the money to pay off his junker car.

Wells said he hadn't known that Basile was planning the second job. He put it together after he learned that Elizabeth had been murdered and that the Blazer that Rick always drove to work had been stolen from the garage.

Braun led his witness through an account of the taped calls he had made to Rick to fish for some admission of guilt. Instead, Rick had displayed another case of amnesia; he couldn't remember ever meeting anyone named Danny Basile. Wells told the judge that he knew of at least six or seven times when Rick and Basile had met, including the time Rick arranged for Basile's old Pontiac to pass the state inspection at the service station. Rick even signed the inspection certificate, although someone else had actually looked at the car. Basile said Rick set it all up in advance.

As Braun did with all the witnesses he had extended immunity to, he had Wells explain the terms of the deal— truthful testimony in exchange for immunity on the theft of the van. But if he was involved in the murder, Wells added, Braun had vowed to prosecute him too.

Cross-examination by the defense attorneys was detailed but yielded little new information. Wells told Kristine Grady that he had left his job at Old Orchard on March 9, just three days after the murder. And he admitted a couple of convictions for drunk driving in the mid-1980s.

Wolff went immediately after Wells. Had he known that the stolen van was owned by the station, not Rick? No. After the chilling conversation in which Basile said Rick had proposed the murder of the woman Wells considered a good friend, had he talked to Rick about it? No.

"Did you go to your boss, Dan DeCaro?"

"No, sir."

"Did you go to your friend, Elizabeth DeCaro?"

"No, sir."

"Did you go to the police?"

"No, sir."

"Did you go to anybody and tell anybody else about what your brother had told you in the van?"

"No, sir."

Wolff grilled Wells about the money in the envelope. Had he seen the money? No, just felt what he thought was money. Hadn't he told the police he saw the money? Not that he recalled.

When he filled out the SCAN questionnaire the first time he talked to the police, did he tell them what he knew then? No. Hadn't he only told them the details in a later interview that lasted eight and a half hours at the police station? Yes. During Wells's calls to Rick for the police, hadn't Rick denied hiring Basile to kill Elizabeth? Yes.

When Braun returned for redirect examination, he asked why Wells hadn't called the police after Basile told him that Rick was looking for a hit man.

"It was too hard to believe. I couldn't believe that he would go through with it. I didn't believe that either one of them would do it."

Whose handwriting was on the map? "Rick DeCaro's. . . . He was still writing on it, and I know his handwriting from working with him, too."

Braun handed Wells a transcript of the recorded call to Rick. "At any time, did you ask Rick DeCaro if he killed his wife?"

"I don't believe so, sir."

"He didn't deny it in that conversation?"

"I didn't ask him in that conversation if he did it."

After all of that, the testimony by Elizabeth's friend Mary Jackson was mercifully low-key. She had stopped by the DeCaro house that Friday, between three and three-fifteen, to pick up Girl Scout cookies. She had found the overhead garage door open and the Blazer in the garage, but no one answered the doorbell. And, Braun had her add, she hadn't heard Ozzie barking.

*   *   *

The next witness hit a home run for Tim Braun. Elizabeth Burrows described her encounter with the man driving the RIK-LIZ Blazer too slowly on Interstate 70 at 4:15 P.M. the day of the murder. "I saw a person with very dark hair, and the hair was long, and then the person reached up with his right hand and pushed the hair away from his face." Was that man in court today? She pointed at the defense table as she said firmly, "That man right there with the long, dark hair and the mustache and orange suit. He's sitting next to the police officer and the lady with the purple jacket."

Kristine Grady tried to raise some doubt about how well a driver on a busy interstate in Friday afternoon traffic could see another driver, but Ms. Burrows couldn't be shaken. She had seen him clearly.

Wolff noticed she was wearing glasses—for nearsightedness she explained. And she added that she had been wearing them the day she saw Dan Basile behind the wheel.

The first day of evidence ended on that positive note for the prosecution. In the audience, the Van Iseghems had shed a lot of tears as they heard, for the first time from the witness stand, some of the participants in this insane scheme recount how Elizabeth's murder had been negotiated for a lousy fifteen thousand dollars.

FORTY-EIGHT

The word of an eyewitness no longer had to serve as the only link between Dan Basile and the murder victim's missing Blazer. After the first witness on the second day of the preliminary hearing—Wednesday, May 27—Judge Jon Cunningham knew that Basile's fingerprints had been found on some of the chopped parts of the Blazer in the garage at the condo complex. Detective Robert Frame of the St. Charles police testified that he found not only Basile's prints but some from Doug Meyer and Rick DeCaro as well.

Even before the next witness could begin her story, her testimony prompted a heated debate among the lawyers as they whispered at a "sidebar" conference at the bench. Don Wolff wanted the judge to rule that Susan Jenkins's testimony about what Dan Basile said to her was inadmissible against Rick. Braun insisted, however, that her story of serving as Basile's driver the night of the van theft made her a coconspirator. Her testimony, therefore, fell into one of the major exceptions to the ban on hearsay evidence— comments among coconspirators in furtherance of the conspiracy. Wolff disagreed again; her testimony related to the theft of the van but not to the murder. Braun countered: "We have testimony that it was a package deal."

Wolff shook his head. "We have testimony that it was not a package deal."

Kristine Grady chimed in, "I believe the testimony was that he declined to accept the package."

Braun again: "But the package was completed as a package deal."

In this legal world, Elizabeth DeCaro was a package.

The prosecutor's argument prevailed, and the judge allowed the testimony to apply to both defendants.

And then Sue Jenkins began to tell the dramatic story of her journey to the dark side with Danny Basile. As she locked him into the theft of the van, she recounted their many stops for drinks and conversation with friends before they drove to the DeCaro house. Danny was looking for a garage where he could strip the van, and he even offered one man $150 for the use of his. But he struck out; no garage. At one house, he visited a woman he called Mom, even though she was not related to him. Sue overheard Danny mention something about a TV set. Later, Sue remarked that she hoped Danny was not up to something; "Mom" responded that he was "stupid." That drew a sustained objection from Basile's lawyer.

At another stop, to visit Danny's sister, he had made a shocking comment to his brother-in-law. "He said someone had offered him fifteen thousand to kill their wife," Sue Jenkins remembered. Danny had explained later that the brother Sue had never met, Craig Wells, had arranged the whole deal and that the owner of the van worked at the same service station as Wells.

The map and directions that Danny read to her as she drove him to his destination that night had attracted her attention. She noticed that the handwritten address and the route were marked in yellow highlighter; she remembered it said, "12 Hidden Meadow Court." She kept the map that night, but—unfortunately for the authorities—later threw it away. She related all the details about stealing the van from the DeCaros' driveway; driving to the home of another of Basile's sisters, in Jackson, Missouri; scavenging some items—including a small television set—from the van; torching the van in the rural countryside; disposing of the license plate along the interstate; and stopping at his sister's again in St. Louis to unload the loot from the van that he had put in Sue's trunk. They had made another stop, too; once back in St. Louis, Danny said he had to go to the Old Orchard station to tell Craig Wells "that the job was done."

She heard from Danny again in early March, when he called to ask if she could get him some latex gloves from the doctor's office where she worked—the same kind of gloves she had seen him put on before he stole the van. He called back on Thursday, March 5, and asked if she had them.

"I said, 'What do you need the gloves for?' "

"What did he say?"

"He had a job tomorrow—a job to do tomorrow."

She never got the gloves for her old friend.

But Braun had her explain something she got from him—immunity. Once again, in exchange for her truthful testimony, she was granted immunity for her role in the van theft. If she was involved in the murder in any way, she would be prosecuted.

Kristine Grady had several important points for cross-examination. What had Danny said after he told his brother-in-law about the man's request to kill his wife? "He said he could not do it, and he said he would not get involved." Anything else? "He laughed and said, 'The money would be nice.' "

Why did she throw the map into a Dumpster? "I was scared."

"Would it be fair to say you were scared because you felt like you'd been participating in a crime?"

"I was very scared. I was very nervous. I was very panicky. I did not sleep the whole day."

When Sue called Danny for the police, what had he said when she asked if he had killed Elizabeth DeCaro? "He denied it. He said he didn't do it."

Wolff started his cross-examination by delving into the relationship between Sue and Danny. She said they were friends.

"That's how you would describe it, as friends?"

"Lovers, maybe one time."

When was that one time? "December 12, 1991."

Had Danny mentioned the name of the man who owned the van, or the name DeCaro? Never. Had he ever said he had met with the owner? No. Did he say that Craig Wells had arranged everything with the owner? Yes. And what had Danny said when he mentioned being asked to commit murder? "He said he could not do it."

Braun returned to the tape. What had Basile said about his involvement in the murder? "I believe my exact words were, 'Do you know who did this?' And he told me, 'In a weird way, maybe.'"

Weird, indeed.

Pam Hanley had listened to the descriptions of how Elizabeth had come to her death, and she couldn't hold her tongue any longer. As she sat there in the front row, not all that far the man she knew in her heart had killed her special friend, Pam began to look for an opportunity. At the next recess, an opening appeared. When Wolff left the defense table, Pam leaned forward and caught Rick's reluctant eye. With deep anger turning her voice razor-sharp, she glared into his face and spat out, "We're not finished with you. Rot in hell."

Rick turned his head abruptly. But his sister heard Pam's verbal assault and immediately informed Wolff. When court resumed, he went before the judge to complain about

Pam's "threatening comments to my client." He wanted
the judge to eject Pam from courtroom, especially since she
might be a witness at trial later. And he wanted the judge
to admonish everyone that no such threats or outbursts
would be tolerated. Ever a classy person, Wolff did not
want the judge to address the comments directly to Pam in
front of everyone else. The judge decided not to order Pam
removed, but he agreed to warn everyone in the gallery.

"Ladies and gentlemen, it's been brought to my attention
that there have been comments made by a certain person
or persons in the gallery, directed toward one of the defendants in this case. I wish to make it extremely clear to
anybody in the audience that no such comments will be
tolerated, and you are hereby ordered not to make any
such comments to either of the defendants sitting in the
courtroom here. So, thank you very much."

The warning did not embarrass Pam in the least. In fact,
she was pleased that she had bothered Rick enough to
make an issue of it. After all, she wasn't there to make
Rick happy; she was there to ensure that Elizabeth got
justice. Knowing that she had made him squirm gave her
great satisfaction, although she did vow not to cause any
more problems.

And then Tim Braun called his last witness—Doug
Meyer, the man who had seen Danny Basile and Rick De-
Caro together at the horse farm four days before the murder, had seen a stack of twenty-dollar bills and a pistol in
Danny's hands, and then had seen Danny in that garage
with the chopped-up Blazer. But before Meyer told his
story, Braun had him run through that almost hopelessly
convoluted web that connected the major players in this
story. Meyer explained that he and Basile had the same
biological mother; she had given up custody of Meyer when
he was just five, and he was raised by a foster mother,
R'Neil Wells—who had later married Craig's father, Harold
Wells. That was what had drawn Danny, Doug, and Craig
together as "brothers."

Doug Meyer described Danny's recent lifestyle: living
with Wells; working at the horse farm in exchange for the
rent-free house and trying to rehab the house in his spare

time; working for Meyer at the condos for five bucks an hour; trying to get that battered old Pontiac on the road; attending classes at Vatterott College; and always, always, broke. That had changed when Rick DeCaro showed up in that Blazer on Monday, March 2, just four days before the murder. Basile explained his sudden infusion of cash by saying he was doing a $250 job for the gentleman in the Blazer—the man Meyer identified in the courtroom as Rick DeCaro.

On Wednesday, March 4, two days before the murder, Danny had the handgun, the small-caliber revolver with the white grips that he said he bought from his father.

On Friday, March 6, the day of the murder, Danny didn't work at the condos. He said Rick was picking him up at the stables to do another job. Later that evening, Danny called and arranged for the use of the garage. When he arrived at Meyer's that night, he took Doug and his girl-friend, Iva Hanson, out for an evening of drinking and picked up the forty-dollar tab.

On Saturday, March 7, the day after the murder, Meyer asked Danny about the pistol. He said he had returned it to his father.

On Monday, March 9, three days after the murder, Meyer saw what was in the garage and realized Danny was working on the Blazer, not his old Pontiac.

"I went into a slight bit of hysterics and asked him what he was doing," Meyer testified now. "He said, 'Do not get paranoid. I'm just doing a job for someone.' " Meyer or-dered Danny to get the Blazer out of the garage and to clean up the mess. Later that night, Craig Wells's girlfriend told Meyer about the DeCaro murder and the missing Blazer. An even more nervous Meyer then confronted Danny again, demanding to know if the disassembled vehi-cle in the garage was that Blazer. "He said, yes, it was. He was doing a job and that was the Blazer, but he did not kill her."

And then Meyer dropped a bomb on the rapt courtroom. "After pushing him for quite a while, he finally said, 'It was her or me. I wasn't going back to prison.' Then he immediately turned around and said, 'No, I did not do this.

What do you think? I'm a thief, not a murderer.' He was very flippant about the whole conversation."

On Wednesday, March 11, Meyer hauled some Blazer parts to the dump. But, more important, on that night he took everything he knew to the police. Again, Braun had given him the standard deal; no charges in the vehicle theft in exchange for truthful testimony—all tempered with a vow of a charge of first-degree murder if Braun learned that Meyer was involved in Elizabeth's killing.

Kristine Grady wanted to know about that gun Meyer had seen in Danny's hand. A .22-caliber, Meyer explained.

"How do you know that?"

"I'm familiar with handguns."

That was a damning bit of memory. The crime lab had identified the two slugs taken from Elizabeth's head as .22s.

Wolff took Meyer through most of his story again and then returned to the dramatic conversation between Meyer and Basile on March 9. "It was her or me. I wasn't going back to prison . . . I'm a thief, not a murderer." Pretty incriminating stuff.

"So on March 9, when you had knowledge that the vehicle of a murdered woman was in your garage, you took no action?"

"Correct."

Wolff knew jurors had a hard time understanding why people sat on that kind of information, why they didn't tell the police when they so obviously knew they had evidence of a crime.

With Meyer's testimony, Tim Braun rested his case. The defense presented no evidence and no witnesses. And, in a move that stunned the Van Iseghems, the judge concluded the hearing with blinding speed. After two days of testimony, he didn't need legal arguments; he immediately announced his decision. The evidence established probable cause to believe that Rick DeCaro and Daniel Basile had committed the felonies of murder and stealing by deceit. He bound them over for trial and set arraignment for July 6.

The Van Iseghems were thrilled. A major victory that foretold justice for Elizabeth, they hoped. But they still found themselves a bit anxious about the prosecutor who carried their banner. Something about Tim Braun left them slightly uncomfortable, especially when they compared him to the smoother, slicker Don Wolff. Jimmy Van Iseghem—completely unschooled in the courts—had been given pause by what he had seen. During one of the recesses, he had even wondered aloud to Mary if the family should seek the appointment of a special prosecutor, perhaps the famed federal prosecutor in St. Louis, Thomas Dittmeier.

No one could imagine then how that question would echo down the courthouse hallways in the years to come.

FORTY-NINE

May 28, 1992

The day after the judge had found enough evidence to put Rick on trial for Elizabeth's murder, the Van Iseghems gathered at Memorial Gardens Cemetery to observe—one could hardly say celebrate—her twenty-ninth birthday. Her children brought a special balloon to her grave, and Georgianna vowed that next year she would continue the family tradition of blowout parties for thirtieth birthdays. For some time, she had been thinking about the soiree she would throw for Elizabeth, never dreaming that her daughter wouldn't live to celebrate even her twenty-ninth. Next year, they would have the big three-oh party, even if she would be there only in spirit. Georgianna would do everything she could to keep Elizabeth alive in all of their hearts and memories. Surely Rick and Danny Basile would have faced justice by next May, and things would be better for the family that hurt so much on this day.

But there was more than grief troubling Georgianna as she stared at her daughter's grave. What she had heard and seen during the two days of the preliminary hearing had given rise to a new and unwelcome emotion deep in her heart. For the first time in her life, she could say, "I feel real hate." She wrote that in her journal as she reflected on what was emerging as perhaps the most painful part of Elizabeth's murder: Georgianna was now convinced that Rick had been planning to kill his wife—her daughter, their children's mother—since January 1. No one had seen that storm on the horizon, even though the clouds had been forming so ominously. Georgianna had not understood what was happening, even after the sleep-shattering premonition that had come to her. All she could do now was pray for peace, she wrote. She knew that everyone in the family looked to her as a "tower of strength," but she felt like a fraud. She really wanted to collapse and cry forever, to find a way to disappear into her grief and make all the pain stop.

As the weeks and months slid through spring and summer, everyone in the family grappled with this same burden. Georgianna could find no truth in the old axiom about time healing all wounds; the one in her heart remained open and bleeding and throbbing every second of every day. She was buoyed by some wonderful letters and cards from friends and family—especially people like Pam Hanley, who wrote to urge the Van Iseghems not to let Rick's evil ways win but to live in the joy that Elizabeth had spread during her years on earth. Those words of support were essential to Georgianna, but she still spent some days lost in the hopelessness that seemed to be just below the surface every waking minute. "Elizabeth is with God in a perfect world, but we are left here, in this vale of tears," she wrote.

She began to wonder if she had found death's sting and the grave's victory, despite God's promise in the Bible.

Jim not only battled an omnipresent ache in his soul, but his new hip was giving him problems, even requiring another hospitalization. He was sometimes visited by bad dreams about Elizabeth, and about Melanie's request for him to hire a detective.

"Dad and I both missed you so much yesterday, your dad especially," Georgianna wrote one morning. "He misses you so much, I think, because he didn't get to share with you all the precious memories I did. He didn't get the opportunity to tell you how much he loved you, as I did. But you always knew that. You were always his 'little girl,' his 'Betsy.' Send him peace. Let him get rid of his hatred of Rick. That's eating him up."

Georgianna was frustrated by her failure to cleanse her heart before God. "I'm feeling such anger and rage—rage that Rick could have taken any of my precious children. *My* child! How dare he!! Not just his wife and the mother of his children, but my precious daughter. I'm feeling rage at him for violating *me*—disrupting and trying to destroy my life. I hate him."

Against her nature, Georgianna began to feel terrible anger at Rick's family—people she had loved for decades. How had they raised this monster, she wondered, and how could they continue to stand behind him? If her child had done this evil deed, she would confront and condemn him, not support him and turn a cold shoulder to his victims. She hoped her writings could exorcise her demons. "Lord, help me to vent my anger in the pages of this book, so I'm not consumed by bitterness and hate."

It was almost impossible for the Van Iseghems to control the wanderings of their hearts and minds. Georgianna was nagged by memories of how easily she had dismissed Melanie's and Mary's concerns about the dangers building in the De-Caro marriage. "We were so fooled by Rick. I'm sick to think how I defended him to Elizabeth." Georgianna even wondered if her own words had set Rick on the way to his fatal betrayal. When she confronted him after he had said he was unsure if he had ever loved Elizabeth, Georgianna had hoped to shock him back to his senses by reminding him how devastating and painful a divorce would be. "I know; I'm trapped," had been his discouraged response. Now, Georgianna looked back on that conversation with deep remorse. "Oh God, how I regret saying those words to him," she wrote. "Did I start the wheels going in his head to get rid of Elizabeth, or had he already decided that was the only way that he wouldn't lose everything? I will never know. But those words will haunt me to my dying day."

That kind of despair tormented young Theresa, as well. There were nights when the tears would not stop and she wondered how something so horrible had happened, why her sister was no longer there for her. When Theresa once wrote a letter to Margie in California, Georgianna was impressed by the maturity of her youngest daughter's words. "Theresa is so much like you, Elizabeth," Georgianna wrote in her journal. "I'm sure you're smiling down on her and guiding her. Thank you, Lord."

Half a continent away, Margie was deeply depressed; she was having problems with her husband, who still refused to consider relocating to St. Louis to be closer to the family. The distance and the solitude made her grief so much more intense. But, as was so natural for the Van Iseghem women, Margie always thought about the others. On a trip home that summer, she brought her parents a special gift—a large oil portrait of Elizabeth, taken from everyone's favorite photograph. Georgianna hung the wonderful likeness in her sunroom and stared at it for hours, shedding tears of grief and joy the whole time. This new image of their mother seemed to upset Bill and Erin. But Georgianna knew that, in time, everyone would be able to find comfort in the warmth of the smile that radiated from this new, glowing vision of Elizabeth.

Mary found herself fighting a new, raw anger—at God. How could He have let this happen to Elizabeth, to this family? And she was dealing anew with the constant letters from Rick and, even worse, the resumption of his collect calls, since a judge had dissolved the order restricting them. Mary even installed a second phone line just for the calls. Each new missive or conversation seemed to add to the kids' confusion over their futures, their lives—and their father. Any expression of grief over their mother's death, they seemed to think, was tantamount to disloyalty to their father. What a horrible place for such young children!

Rick was pressuring Patrick to visit the jail, and even some of the DeCaro family's friends made occasional comments to him about it. He was the only one who had not visited, always finding some excuse why he couldn't go. The others went faithfully, although it was far from easy. Bill once said it made him sad to see his dad there, and it always made him think more about his mom. He was afraid that he was going to forget some of the things he still could remember about her now. But Patrick had remained resolute, despite his father's pleading, and the Van Iseghems supported the boy's right to make up his own mind. After what he had been through, God knew, he had that right.

Georgianna fretted that Mary was investing all of her worry in the kids and ignoring her own pain; Georgianna prayed for Elizabeth to send peace to her sister. What happened to the children was really more important than what happened to Rick, and Georgianna tried to keep sight of that. She knew Mary and Phil would raise their nieces and nephews as well as anyone could, and she declared it her mission to aid them in any way possible. "Mary is trying so hard, Elizabeth. I know that you are very proud of her; I know I am," Georgianna observed. And as she prayed again, she offered the Lord a deal: "You keep Rick in jail, and we'll take care of the kids."

On the advice of the children's therapist, Georgianna and Mary sat down with them in mid-June and told them everything they knew about the tragic turn of events that had turned their young lives upside down—what had happened to their mother and the evidence against their father. They needed to understand everything, the doctor had urged. "I fear for the kids ten years from now—or next week or next month," Georgianna wrote. "All I can do is love them and give them security, to build a wall of love around them."

Mary threw a party for Erin's fifth birthday on June 15, trying to make it as festive as Elizabeth would have. Georgianna felt Elizabeth's spirit there but lamented that she never was able to dream about her daughter. Surely that would have brought more peace, she thought.

The first court hearing to confirm custody of the children for Mary and Phil was held on June 22. There was no opposition from the DeCaro family; even Rick wanted his children to remain in Mary's care, although he would soon hire an attorney skilled in family law to look out for his parental interests. But for now, the judge approved the

Cordeses as guardians. That also qualified them for some financial benefits from the state; the stipend hardly paid the huge expenses, but it helped. The big new family celebrated the court's recognition of this special union with a trip to the lake resort where they held a membership. That would continue to be their refuge for years.

Meanwhile, the public's interest in the DeCaro murder continued to grow. When KSDK-TV, the NBC affiliate in St. Louis, prepared a special series on the Major Case Squad, reporter Randy Jackson did a lengthy interview with Georgianna to record her glowing comments. She was more than happy to tell everyone how hard the officers had worked, and how compassionate they had been as they struggled to find justice for a woman they had never met.

Pam Hanley and her family were grappling with their own pain over their loss of Elizabeth's light in their lives. Pam's two youngest children were so upset that they began seeing their counselor at school. When Pam kept Elizabeth's children for a few weeks that summer, they all decided to make a special book of memories of "Liz": how she wrapped the girls in towels after their baths and carried them into the other room to put on their PJs; how she smiled a lot, and loved to sing along with songs on the radio; how she once fell on her butt while she was doing the limbo at the roller-skating rink, and all the kids laughed at her; how she liked to lie in the sun with Erin; and how she had a funny laugh. The last page was illustrated with a little girl under an umbrella in the rain, and said, "Although she got most of her crying done at the funeral, Amy is still sad that Liz died." In the next frame, a rainbow appears: "She loves Liz."

Pam's daughter Jenni teamed with Elizabeth's daughter Rachel to write a special poem in her memory:

> Liz was a great mom and friend.
> At age 28, her life had to end.
> Her arms were full with shopping bags,
> as she washed Erin's face with dish rags.
> She was always late

and made everyone wait.
When she died this very day,
everyone cried their tears away.

Pam decided to confront her own grief more directly, in a manner right for her. On a trip back to St. Charles in late August, Pam visited Rick at the county jail. Separated by the glass in the visitors' room, Pam still could feel the coldness that now flowed from this man's being. A woman Pam didn't know was visiting Rick and he said he wanted her to stay; he obviously didn't want to see Pam alone, she thought. As they picked up the phones, Rick asked how she was, and then added, "I was wondering when you were going to come." Rick reminded Pam that his approval had been needed for her to take the kids for the summer visit. She nodded, "I know. That was real nice, Rick."

And then she was ready to tell him why she was there.

"I just had to come because I want you to know that I know you killed Elizabeth," Pam said firmly, drilling him with angry eyes as his witness fled the area. "And I want you to know that I do love you, but I can't talk to you anymore, and I will have nothing to do with you until you show some regret and until you apologize."

Finally Pam saw some emotion from this man. He was furious. "How can you say you love me?" he spat out angrily.

She had said her piece. She hung up the telephone and walked away, leaving Rick to stare at her back and ponder the message in her silence.

When Pam described what had happened, Georgianna flashed back to that new and hideous chill in Rick's voice the night he threatened to keep her grandchildren from her if she dared approach him with any suspicion. "I knew in that instant that he had killed Elizabeth," she recalled. "There is a dark side to Rick that came out in the last months before Elizabeth died. That's the Rick the prosecution has to bring out."

While the others struggled with their feelings, Melanie Enkelmann channeled her pain in yet a different way—

finding in it the strength to pursue what she now saw as her mission. The discomfort from her experiences with prosecuting attorney Tim Braun at the preliminary hearing now empowered her secret career as a detective. She became convinced that the almost purely circumstantial case against Rick and Basile needed real, conclusive physical evidence, and she saw no effort by the prosecution to develop that. The lack of a murder weapon seemed to weaken the case seriously, and so she set about finding it. She rented a metal detector and one rainy fall day she and Margie searched the yard around their sister's now vacant and forlorn house, concentrating on the vicinity of the wooden deck at the back. The possibility that Basile had hidden the gun somewhere outside the house seemed very real to them. After all, one of Elizabeth's earrings had been found on the glass-topped table on the deck. That could mean her killer had been out there for some reason. Was it to hide the gun in some prearranged place so Rick could retrieve it later? Was it still there, overlooked by the police and waiting for Melanie and Margie to find it and seal the fate of Rick and Basile?

When the search proved fruitless, Melanie even resorted to her last option—psychics. Convinced that she had nothing to lose, she consulted several in hopes that one would offer some useful clue. One did, in fact, describe to a T a place that Basile had known intimately—the horse farm on Fuchs Road where Basile had planned to live as soon as the dilapidated old shack was rehabbed. She and Margie screwed up their courage and shifted the search to that more dangerous location; they slipped onto the property without the owner's permission and swept it with the metal detector. But again, nothing useful set off a hopeful beeping.

They found a quarry not far from the farm, and their hearts sank as they thought what a terrific and convenient— not to mention unyielding—burial place that would have been for the small instrument of their sister's death. The St. Charles Underwater Recovery Team had already combed the murky bottom of the lake at the quarry for the police, with no success.

Rick and Elizabeth's wedding day, January 16, 1981. (Photo courtesy of McCarty Photography)

Rick and Elizabeth DeCaro in 1988. (Photo courtesy of Olan Mills)

Rick and Elizabeth with their childern (from left to right), Erin, Bill, and Rachel, in 1991.

Childhood sweethearts:
Elizabeth Van Iseghem,
age 13, and
Rick DeCaro, age 14,
in 1976.

Elizabeth with
her sister,
Theresa,
in 1980.

Elizabeth with her friend Pam Hanley (left) and her
sister Mary Cordes (right) in 1990.

The Van Iseghem family: Standing, Jimmy Van Iseghem.
From left to right, Melanie Enkelmann, Mary Cordes,
Georgianna Van Iseghem, Jim Van Iseghem,
Theresa Van Iseghem. On the floor, Marge Ugalde
and Elizabeth DeCaro. (1992).

Elizabeth's parents,
Jim and Georgianna Van
Iseghem, in 1990.

Rick and Elizabeth
DeCaro in 1990.

The DeCaros' house on Hidden Meadow Court in St. Charles, Missouri. (Courtesy of the St. Charles Police Department)

The murder scene: Elizabeth's body was found between the sink and the island. (Courtesy of the St. Charles Police Department)

The basement workroom of the DeCaros' home, where Daniel Basile may have hidden in the hours before the murder. (Courtesy of the St. Charles Police Department)

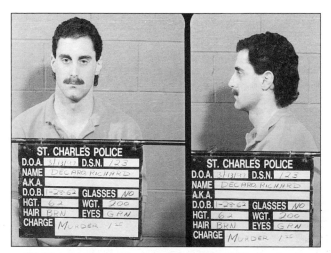

Rick's mug shots, taken on March 13, 1992, the day he
was arrested for hiring a man to shoot his wife to death.
(Courtesy of the St. Charles Police Department)

The mug shot of
Daniel Basile,
the man Rick hired
to murder his wife.
(Courtesy of the
St. Charles Police
Department)

Tom O'Connor, the commander of the St. Louis Major Case Squad. (Photo by Charles Bosworth)

St. Charles Prosecuting Attorney Tim Braun. (Larry Williams, *St. Louis Post-Dispatch*)

St. Charles Police Chief David King. (Courtesy of Amy Westermann, *St. Charles Courier-Post*)

Richard DeCaro leaves the St. Charles Jail after his acquittal
on September 14, 1994. He is accompanied by his mother,
Grace DeCaro (left), and his sister, Patricia Fiehler (right).
(Larry Williams, *St. Louis Post-Dispatch*)

Demonstrators protesting the acquittal of Rick DeCaro outside
the St. Charles County Court House on September 16, 1994.
(Larry Williams, *St. Louis Post-Dispatch*)

Rick DeCaro accompanied by defense attorney
Scott Rosenblum outside Federal Court in Cape Girardeau,
Missouri, during the second trial in 1996.
(Odell Mitchell, Jr., *St. Louis Post-Dispatch*)

Federal marshals escort Rick DeCaro (center, white shirt)
and Dan Basile (left, partly obscured) to a van bound for jail
after their convictions in Federal Court in Cape Girardeau,
Missouri, on March 7, 1996. Both men are handcuffed
and shackled. (Photo by Fred Lynch)

Melanie always offered to keep her friends with the St. Charles police informed of her activities, but each time their response was wary: "We don't want to know what you're doing."

Even the imprisoned Rick DeCaro was not immune from the realities of life outside the cellblock. In August 1992 a bank sued him for failing to make the payments on the Blazer. What irony! The vehicle that had become such a strong link between him and Danny Basile had now become a financial albatross as well. The bank didn't care that the Blazer was now chopped beyond recognition as part of this murder conspiracy. The bank simply wanted its unpaid balance of $6,506.54, plus interest, attorney's fees, and court costs. There was a bank note in Rick's name, and somebody had to pay it.

In late September, Tim Braun announced a major decision. For this cold-hearted, calculated, ruthless execution in the sanctity of Elizabeth's own kitchen, he would seek the ultimate penalty; Rick DeCaro and Danny Basile would face a death sentence—by lethal injection.

The Van Iseghems agreed wholeheartedly, and Jim more than once expressed his willingness to carry out the sentence with his bare hands. But the family found more in the ultimate penalty than simple vengeance. For the two men who had ruined so many other lives when they murdered Elizabeth, forfeiting their own lives seemed the only just punishment.

The other family in this Greek tragedy took the news differently, of course. Georgianna heard that Rick's mother and sister were so shaken that they fled to Florida.

As the remaining days of 1992 dragged by, Georgianna searched for new ways to return to her faith, often by reflecting on how this family's struggle with adversity would be recorded. "The real story will be how the love of family and friends, and the love of God, transcends all circumstances. Our family is going to be living proof of what God and love in the lives of all of us can do. Elizabeth's spirit and goodness will live on forever in all of us."

FIFTY

Rick DeCaro had planned the murder of his wife in great detail, and Danny Basile was the man Rick had paid to pull the trigger. These two beasts were bonded together by those bare facts—this simple description of their terrible crime against Elizabeth DeCaro, her children, her family, and friends.

Surely, prosecuting attorney Tim Braun knew, the coconspirators in this grievous murder should be tried together, side by side, to be judged for their common crime, each of them an integral factor in the death of this good woman. A jury should see these two men as halves of the whole, the trigger and the bullet.

But case law in Missouri was clear; they had to have separate trials. Under Braun's analysis, Basile's criminal record and DeCaro's clean past caused an insurmountable conflict and mandated individual trials. If they were tried together and convicted of second-degree murder, Basile's record required sentencing by a judge, while DeCaro had a right to stay with a jury. With no way for a judge to instruct the jury for that two-pronged complication, the courts had ruled that separate trials were necessary—for Braun, a disappointing reality. He would have to mount two trials for the same murder—twice the work, twice the challenge, twice the risk. How much easier it would have been for a jury to understand this plot if the jurors could see these men at the same table. Separating them definitely cut in favor of the defense. But Braun was confident that the evidence was there to convict both of them, no matter how their trials arrived.

Braun had developed a timetable for Elizabeth's last day—a scenario that he felt the evidence proved entirely. Friday, March 6, 1992, began at 4:30 A.M., when Rick left the house without a kiss or even a quiet good-bye for the woman he knew would be dead within hours.

At 5:00 A.M., Basile was telling Doug Meyer that he was going to the stables to be picked up for a job by a "Rick or Richard."

Elizabeth left for the car pool about 7:25 A.M., dropping Erin at the baby-sitting neighbors—the McKays—and then driving Patrick and his friends to school. At 8 A.M., a distressed, worried Elizabeth was pouring out her heart to Mike Carroll at his home.

By 9:25, she was at work at the corporate training center.

Rick left his job about 10:30 A.M. to drive to the stables, pick Basile up around 11, and deliver him to the DeCaro home. On the way—at 11:07—Rick called his house from the van to make sure Elizabeth hadn't come home unexpectedly. They arrived about 11:30, and Rick slipped Basile into the basement work room. At 11:35 or so, Rick put the barking Ozzie into the van and packed for the trip.

At 11:50, Erin was dropped off at home, and Rick left with her to pick up Patrick's gang at school. He arrived back at the house about noon so the kids could change clothes. Ozzie stayed in the van and, as soon as the kids were ready, they headed for the lake, leaving Basile there alone.

At 12:17 and 12:28, Elizabeth called Rick as he drove west. She left work at 2:20, was seen by a friend on the way home at 2:28, and arrived about 2:45 P.M. Braun was absolutely certain that Basile murdered her immediately.

Just minutes later, at 2:59, Rick and his children checked in at the Holiday Inn—ready for "Daddy's weekend," indeed.

Between 3:00 and 3:05, a friend of the DeCaros' saw the garage door open and the Blazer there. About 3:15, another friend stopped by to pick up Girl Scout cookies, found the open garage and the Blazer but got no response to the doorbell. She couldn't know that Elizabeth had just been murdered—or was about to be.

At 4:00 P.M., Rick and the kids stopped by a real estate office to confirm an appointment for the next day to look at condos. Rick wanted an airtight, locked-down alibi.

Basile loaded his loot into the Blazer and left the house quietly. He drove onto I-70 and was spotted by an amazingly observant Elizabeth Burrows at 4:18 P.M.

Tim Braun was pleased when the pretrial motions by the defense attorneys arrived in fairly predictable fashion. With no confessions from Rick or Basile, the defenders concentrated on other matters. They challenged the constitutionality of Missouri's death penalty law and tried to suppress the identification of Basile by Elizabeth Burrows. They wanted the tape recordings of conversations with Rick banned from trial. And they attacked every incriminating statement by every witness. For Braun—long a defense attorney, after all—the motions brought no surprises and no insurmountable obstacles.

At one hearing, a judge agreed to a motion by Basile's lawyer that jurors for his trial be chosen from outside St. Charles County. A survey by Kenneth Warren, a pollster and professor at St. Louis University, showed that 69 percent of those asked were familiar with the DeCaro murder. Given a little more information, 87 percent of those polled recalled the allegations against Rick. Only 6 percent could name Basile as the accused hit man, but 37 percent thought he was guilty. Pretty heavy numbers, all weighing against finding an impartial jury on the home field.

Braun agreed with the defense. The survey proved the need for special precautions, and even the worst killer was entitled to a fair trial. Braun didn't want to violate that right, and he certainly didn't want to retry a conviction after an appellate court had found the first trial unfair.

The judge ordered the defense and prosecution to prepare lists of three counties each. The Missouri Supreme Court would choose the county from which the jurors would eventually be selected.

But even that step forward did not mean that Rick and Danny were on the slippery slope toward quick trials. Months more dragged by with little progress. Basile ate up some time on the calendar by demanding a new attorney. He eventually acquired the assistance of an experienced attorney in the capital division of the public defender's office, Caterina "Cathy" DiTraglia, and another assistant who specialized in death cases, Beth Davis.

Braun caused a lengthy delay himself, but he had little choice. A chronic problem forced him into surgery for a hip replacement, and that sidelined him for six months.

In the meantime, Basile's teenage girlfriend delivered his baby; the Van Iseghems hoped this would be a better generation.

Amid those official delays in the criminal courts, the Van Iseghems continued to fight their own special battles.

The DeCaro family filed a petition in juvenile court asking for visitation with Rick's children every other weekend. Mary was outraged. There hadn't been a divorce, she fumed; there had been a damned murder. This wasn't one weekend with Mom and the next with Dad. Mom was dead and Dad was in jail for hiring someone to kill her. Mary would not oppose visits with the DeCaros, but they hadn't even asked for any. As Mary and Phil ran nonstop to keep up with the school programs and sports games of seven active kids, she did not want a court order hanging over her head. How could she comply with an order to have the kids ready to be picked up at some arbitrarily appointed hour for the DeCaros' convenience? Would she and Phil face a citation for contempt of court if they couldn't pull it all together some busy Friday night? The whole "visitation" idea not only irritated Mary and the rest of her family, but it seemed almost impossible to accomplish. And more important to Mary, she found the concept of enforced visitation a threat to the kids' sense of security, of stability. She never wanted them to wonder where they belonged, and she feared that even a brief, temporary shift in their residence would leave them unsure. Her home was their home now, and she would fight anything that even remotely threatened that concept.

She fought and won. A judge denied the DeCaros' request.

The children, meanwhile, continued to amaze everyone at the way they adapted to such life-shattering upheaval. There were moments of pain and uncertainty, to be sure.

Patrick was bothered for a while by recurring nightmares about two people fighting in a dark room. The symbolism in that dream was not difficult to discern for anyone, and the children's therapist confirmed that Patrick surely was thinking about his parents' battles. He once had confided in Georgianna that all he could remember from that horrible weekend was his father's bizarre reaction to the news of their mother's murder. While Erin was still asleep in the motel, Rick had asked Patrick, Rachel, and Bill if they wanted to stay another day and do some "fun things" before returning home on Sunday. The three siblings were young, but this suggestion from their father had stunned them. We want to go home now, they had said.

They still spoke rarely about what had happened. Erin and Bill seemed to hang on Rick's vows of victory and promises to sweep them all back to a happy home someday soon. Rachel sometimes revealed her deepest thoughts: she once asked her grandmother for help with a homework assignment that required her to list the significant events in each year of her life. When she reached 1992, she found herself in a quandary. "Grandma," she said, "I don't want to say that in 1992 my mom died. That would be embarrassing." They decided that she should just say that 1992 was the year she went to live with the Cordeses.

About a year after Elizabeth's death, Rachel revealed to her Aunt Melanie that she had concluded her father was guilty.

When the painful, one-year anniversary arrived, Georgianna decided to mark it the way the Van Iseghems always observed important dates. She scheduled a memorial mass on March 6, 1993. That could never replace the thirtieth birthday party that would have been held for Elizabeth in May, but it was all Georgianna could do. For the crowd of 300 who attended the mass, Mary and Margie read passages from the Bible, and Elizabeth's children read letters they had written to their missing mother, remembering her in sweet, childish terms that brought tears to everyone's eyes. After the service, Georgianna and Jim hosted a dinner at the house on St. Francis Lane, and it was packed with 150 guests who gathered to share their bittersweet memories of Elizabeth. The crowd frightened five-year-old Erin; she cried and said she just wanted everyone to go home. After they had left, Georgianna and Pam Hanley cried together, aching so deeply for the one person who could not be there that night.

The Van Iseghems kept in regular contact with Tim Braun, calling often to see if the cases were headed toward trial anytime soon. When no trials were on the calendar by September, Margie wrote a letter that the family members signed and sent to Braun by certified mail. In no uncertain terms, they expressed their concern about the lack of progress and even threatened to go to the media with their frustrations if these cases did not move off the dime. Was a special prosecutor needed? they asked. Were the cynical concerns of some valid? Was Braun delaying on purpose, to use the trials to his political advantage closer to his reelection campaign in 1994?

Braun quickly called a meeting with the Van Iseghems to assure them that he was pushing the cases as hard as he could and would do everything possible to get them to trial.

FIFTY-ONE

Daniel Basile would be first to go before a jury.

Trial dates were set; dates were delayed; dates were changed. The Van Iseghems rode the ups and downs as if they were tiny lifeboats adrift and buffeted by a merciless North Atlantic sea. Hopes and fears and anxieties careened up and down as the day of reckoning neared, only to wash off into the distance again. "What haunts me now, more than ever, is the fear that Rick will be freed, that his smart and cunning lawyer somehow will convince the jury that he is innocent," Georgianna fretted in her journal.

Finally—on Monday, April 25, 1994, more than two years

after Elizabeth's murder—the man who so many believed had pulled the trigger was brought into court to face judgment. He would be tried before Judge Lucy D. Rauch—a distinguished woman with gray hair and a demeanor that quietly assured integrity, morality, and fairness.

Braun was cautiously confident about the evidence amassed by the police in their excellent investigation. And he was glad to be backed up by veteran prosecutor Jim Gregory, who some thought a dead ringer for actor Andy Griffith's television lawyer in *Matlock*. As Braun compared the cases against Basile and Rick DeCaro, he was actually a little less confident about the evidence against the trigger man. To convict Basile, Braun would have to use the defendant's own brother, Doug Meyer; his own foster brother and best friend, Craig Wells; and his former girlfriend, Susan Jenkins—all of them testifying under immunity deals because of their own involvement in some aspect of the crimes. And Braun would be using several of Basile's friends, including Carl Swanson and a couple more that the St. Charles police had turned up during their continuing investigation. Calling those kinds of witnesses was always a delicate proposition; some jurors seemed to resent being asked to convict on the say-so of people who had been friends or participants in the misdeeds. Braun recognized a natural bias against "snitches," even when they were serving justice. He sometimes reminded jurors that he would rather have testimony from ministers and others of spotless repute, but they seldom hung out with killers.

Basile's jury was to be chosen from the residents of Montgomery County—a mostly rural community some fifty miles and two counties west of St. Charles, and the Van Iseghems and their band of supporters made the trip for the jury selection. Georgianna and her daughters could not believe their eyes when they arrived at the facility that would host this activity—it was little more than a huge barn. In reality it was the county fair's exposition hall, the only place with enough space to hold three hundred people. Poor Melanie was excluded from the proceedings—she would be a witness in the trial and could not even watch jury selection. She sulked outside—"pissed," as she described it.

Georgianna stared at Daniel Basile as he sat at the defense table, looking deceptively normal with a fresh shave, bath, and haircut. She felt a new and even more overwhelming hate. All she could think was that if she had a gun, she would shoot him right there and then and be done with it. She couldn't believe that she had been so focused on Rick that she had spent amazingly little time thinking about this man who had actually killed her daughter. How could he have done that to Elizabeth? Didn't he feel the love that filled that house? Didn't he see the kids' photographs covering the walls? Didn't he notice the toys scattered through the rooms? Didn't he realize he would be taking the life of someone who was loved by so many and gave so much love in return? Couldn't he have backed out of this awful "job" he had to do for this man he knew so slightly? My God, Georgianna thought again, this man surely deserves the death penalty for this crime that seemed more heinous as every day passed. And if he was executed someday, at least he would have time to say his good-byes to his family and to ask God for forgiveness and mercy. That was more than he gave Elizabeth.

When Mary Cordes grew more familiar with the sheriff's deputies guarding Basile, she cracked to one that she wished Basile would make a break for it so they could shoot him down. She got a wry, knowing grin in return.

As the first day wore on, Georgianna became aware that Basile had begun to stare at her and the others; she ignored him. Later, Braun surprised the Van Iseghems by asking them not to stare at Basile, warning that they might be asked to leave the courtroom. Georgianna was insulted. "He's staring at us," she protested. Braun passed her response along, and the defense table was shifted around until Basile faced away from the audience and more directly toward Judge Rauch.

The jury selection process fascinated the Van Iseghems at first. Mary was surprised that so many of the people said they would not hesitate to impose the death penalty if a crime warranted it; she would have expected more reluc-

tance in the political climate of the time. She was struck
by how many offered the same reason for wanting to be
excused from service: they were farmers who couldn't be
away from the fields that long. By the end of the first day,
the judge and lawyers had questioned 160 potential jurors
and were ready to call in another 100 for Tuesday.

With the cast changing slightly from day to day, the Van
Iseghems faithfully watched the process drag out over five
days in that barn. Jim came one day and, after a few hours,
leaned incredulously over to his wife and asked, "THIS is
what you've been doing all day every day?" By Friday the
lawyers had chosen the jury of eight women and four
men—a group the Van Iseghems found completely satisfac-
tory for the trial in St. Charles. These jurors seemed to be
good, solid, down-to-earth, country people—exactly the
right folks to decide whether all the evidence against
Danny Basile was enough to convict him—and perhaps
even to claim his life.

FIFTY-TWO

"Richard DeCaro . . . saddled with debt . . . unhappy with
his marital situation . . . having an affair . . . just wanting
to get divorced . . . takes the timeworn, weary method to
solve that problem.

"He wants to kill his wife."

With those staccato phrases, prosecuting attorney Tim
Braun began to tell the jurors the story of how the disinte-
gration of a marriage led to the murder of Elizabeth De-
Caro and how Daniel Basile became a pivotal character in
that tale. In his opening statement on Monday, May 2,
1994, Braun walked a straight line toward the point of this
trial, without straining to be fancy or profound along the
way. The premise was simple and basic: Rick had decided
to solve his financial problems with an insurance policy on
his wife, and to remove her as a complication in his life.

He had found the means to do that through a curious plot using two vehicle thefts as a cover-up for murder. It was all designed to look as if "some maniac car thief" had stolen the first vehicle, returned a month later to steal the second, and had to kill Elizabeth when she interrupted him.

After barely thirty minutes with the jurors, Braun summed up what he hoped to prove about Danny Basile: "That this man is not just a thief—which he professes that he is—but that he is a cold-blooded, lying-in-wait, contract killer who stayed in this woman's house for two and a half hours, and shot her in the back of the neck with two bullets, and drove around in her Blazer because he didn't expect her body to be found until Sunday, because he knew her husband wasn't coming home." First, Braun would ask the jurors to return a verdict of guilty of murder in the first degree, and then he would come back and ask them to sentence Basile to death.

Cathy DiTraglia—a petite woman with dishwater-blond hair and what struck the Van Iseghems as a slightly disheveled appearance—took the stage to argue for Danny Basile, and to fillet Rick DeCaro like a flounder.

"The evidence in the trial you are about to hear is all about greed," she began, ". . . of Richard DeCaro. You will hear evidence that this was a man who had everything anyone could want, and more. He had a beautiful home, children, a wife, an eighty-thousand-dollar-a-year job. He had cars and vans. He had a boat. He was going to buy some lakefront property at the Lake of the Ozarks. He went out every day, two or three times a week, to work out at Gold's Gym, morning and evening. He went out to the bars until all hours of the night, whenever he pleased. He had more stereo equipment than most of us will ever have in a lifetime. He had it all. But the evidence, ladies and gentlemen, will show you that Rick DeCaro wanted more. And he knew plenty of people in his life, who he dealt with, who could set things up for him the way he wanted it."

But, DiTraglia cautioned, there was more to this than Rick DeCaro's all-consuming desires. Her client did, indeed, bear some responsibility. "This case is also about

Dan Basile's greed. He had just gotten out of jail for a
burglary, and he was getting his life together. He had a job
working for Doug Meyer and a job working on a farm—
putting together a little house there where he was going to
live. And he goes to school. But Craig Wells dangles a
chance for him to make some quick cash."

The bait, of course, was the seemingly simple plan to
steal Rick's van to help him get out from under its expensive upkeep. Basile took the van, DiTraglia admitted, "for
the bargain price of two hundred dollars. And he agreed
to do the same bargain for the Blazer."

That was where the road had turned toward murder.
Rick's greed could be satisfied only by Elizabeth's death,
which would protect his money, his lifestyle, and his freedom—all at her expense. When Basile refused to become
a killer, Rick found another way. "He tried to kill her himself, but he failed. Still—and you will probably realize this
about him—he is the kind of guy who's going to get the
job done."

The defender moved toward the close of her story: Rick
had indeed gotten the job done, using his money to set it
up "with the kind of people who don't get caught, and who
know how to protect themselves by setting Dan up for a
murder that he did not commit."

There it was. Basile was Rick's fall guy—the simpleton
suckered into a cheap van theft, only to be left holding the
smoking gun and wearing a look of surprise after someone
else pulled the trigger. DiTraglia told the jurors that finding
Basile innocent would be the only verdict possible after
they waded through all of the lies and the deals cut with
prosecutors.

And then, as the Van Iseghems took deep breaths, the
trial began. Melanie was the first on the stand, and she
described Elizabeth for the jury in hauntingly pure terms:
"She was my sister and my very best friend. I don't think
sisters could be any closer. I don't think there are words
to describe how close we were."

Melanie's heart began to break again, and her mother
felt it as she watched from the first row of the gallery.
Braun knew this was painful, but he had to ask Melanie to

relive the horror of finding her sister's body on the first day Elizabeth had ever been home alone. Braun used Melanie to tell the jurors about the bizarre van crash and the huge bruise it had left on Elizabeth's left thigh. Braun asked about Rick's reaction after he had abandoned Elizabeth in the garage and then turned around to see her standing in the kitchen, a flesh-and-blood apparition. "He was shocked that she was alive," Melanie said.

On cross-examination, DiTraglia tried to mine Rick's claim that he was paranoid about being followed because he had been setting up a drug deal. Melanie explained that the story was trumped up by Rick to cover his parking-lot assignations with Cathy Dillon. But the defender was not easily detoured. She asked repeatedly if Rick had not, in fact, been setting up a drug deal; that would fit nicely, after all, with her "greedy-Rick-on-the-edge" theory. Melanie had to insist that the drug story was a sham.

On redirect, Braun helped Melanie refute the drug angle. After all, hadn't her husband actually seen Rick meeting Cathy, not drug dealers? Yes.

Day One of the trial ended as a hurting, drained Melanie left the stand, and the Van Iseghems wondered how they had become part of what seemed to be some dramatic television show. How could this have become their lives, their world?

James Torregrossa told the jury how Rick's extraordinary question shattered what had been a fairly normal conversation between a couple of guys sitting around a service station, bitching about their cars. As court reconvened for a second day on Tuesday, May 3, those in the courtroom were riveted by Torregrossa's memory of Rick's first venture into the underworld of car thieves and hit men, on a Friday afternoon in January 1992. Tim Braun wanted to put this event into the proper perspective. "How many times in your life had someone asked you to get someone to do a hit for them?" he asked.

"Zero."

"So, that was a memorable occasion, when he asked you that?"

"Yes, it was. . . . No one had ever asked me that question before."

Torregrossa explained how the police had him call Rick and pretend to be nervous about all the pressure being applied to him by the aggressive cops. Rick had suggested that Torregrossa say they had gone out for a few drinks. "He was essentially telling me to lie, because we have never had any beers together."

On cross-examination, DiTraglia focused first on an "arrangement" between Torregrossa and DeCaro; Rick did some work on Torregrossa's car in exchange for some breaks on the cost of vitamins at the gym and maybe even a free tanning session there. As part of the atmosphere at the gym, DiTraglia wondered, didn't men often talk about their wives and girlfriends? Yes. Hadn't Rick said that his wife wanted him to stay home more? Yes. Could Rick's question about "taking the van off his hands" really have been about someone assuming the lease? "I can't say for sure I 'knew' he wanted someone to steal it, but at the time I assumed he did."

Boo Pohlman—Elizabeth's dear friend who was now using her new married name of Marchetto—had two pieces of the puzzle that would show the jury scenes from a deteriorating marriage. Questioned by assistant prosecutor Jim Gregory, Boo quoted Elizabeth as saying in January that Rick was exhibiting wild and scary mood swings, wasn't coming home from work until late, and had admitted to having an affair. "He even ran me over with the van," Elizabeth had disclosed. As Boo listened, mouth agape, her friend described how Rick had seemed to floor the van's accelerator, careening into her and driving her nearly into the kitchen on the other side of the garage wall.

"She said she was stuck between two bicycles and the van, and she said she was screaming, 'Rick, help me! Rick, help me!' She said he got out of the van, didn't come right there, but went out of the garage, into the front door, and ran upstairs." When Elizabeth dragged herself out of the wreckage and limped inside, she found him in the kitchen.

"She said, 'Why didn't you help me?' He said, 'I thought you were dead. I wanted to go upstairs and make sure the kids didn't come downstairs.' "

Gregory also wanted to know about February 7, the night of Boo's birthday party when the DeCaros left unusually early. Elizabeth had told Boo later that she was surprised when Rick backed the van into the driveway and left it there—after cleaning out valuables like the Nintendo game and cellular phone. What had Elizabeth told Boo about that? "She said, 'Probably, that's why he wanted to leave so early. He probably had it stolen.' "

DiTraglia had no questions for Boo.

Tim Braun pointed to the people sitting in the front row and asked witness Craig Wells if he knew them. Yes, they were the Van Iseghems—whose home he had worked on, whose yard he had landscaped, whose delicatessen he had helped remodel, whose catering service had employed him for a while. Did Wells know Daniel Basile? Yes, he was the man sitting at the defense table. Were Wells and Basile related? Not exactly, even though Wells called him a brother; Basile was a half brother to Doug Meyer, who was a foster son to Wells's stepmother, R'Neil Wells. With these relationships defined, Braun moved directly to Rick DeCaro's second—and successful—attempt to find someone to do his dirty work. "I introduced him to Dan Basile," Wells told the jury.

The plot thickened, and Wells recounted the meetings where Rick recruited Basile as a hit man for $15,000; Wells had tried to protect his friend Elizabeth. Braun wanted the jury to understand what had happened. "So, you didn't want the murder done, and they started working around you. Is that right?" DiTraglia's objection was sustained, but Braun had already rung the bell.

Now it was time for Braun to test part of his theory about the dynamics of this evil plot. "Did you know that Elizabeth DeCaro was going to come forward—as part of a divorce—and reveal that Basile had done the van with Rick the first time?"

Wells was puzzled. "No, I wasn't aware of that."

DiTraglia immediately called for a sidebar conference at the judge's bench to protest the question and ask that it be stricken. "He knew that this witness did not know anything about that," the defender charged. "By suggesting that in a question, the jury may think there is some evidence of that, and there is not."

Braun shook his head. "I'm trying to show that the witness is not part of the murder."

Judge Rauch sided with DiTraglia, ordered the question stricken, and instructed the jury to disregard it. Braun's theory on that point would have to wait until closing arguments.

Braun decided to demonstrate the weaknesses of his own witness before the defense could. Why hadn't Wells called the police as soon as he knew Elizabeth had been killed, as soon as he realized the target of a murder plot discussed by Rick and Danny had indeed been gunned down?

"I couldn't have said that either one of them did something like that. At that time, I didn't—couldn't—think so."

And on Monday, why had Wells lied repeatedly on the SCAN questionnaire he filled out for the police? "Were you doing this to cover for yourself?"

"No, I wasn't, because I still didn't believe that Dan Basile had murdered . . ." He hesitated, unable to speak her name. ". . . had done it," he said finally.

DiTraglia went right for the throat on cross-examination, hoping to reveal someone completely untrustworthy. She reminded him that when the police interviewed him at the Amoco station the Monday after the murder, he said he didn't know anything about it. In fact, he had lied to the police about everything that day, then lied on every question of the SCAN test, and then signed it. He had even lied or withheld the truth from the police in the next interview at the station. Yes, he said, all true. DiTraglia offered her own testimony about Wells's background by referring to Rick's unexpected request for Wells to find a car thief. "And the reason why Rick asked you was because you had been involved in the drug and alcohol scene before, and he knew that?"

"Yes."

"And he thought you might know somebody?"

"He thought I might know somebody, yes."

Unfortunately, Rick had been very right about that.

FIFTY-THREE

In pink highlighter, Susan Jenkins traced the route she had driven with Danny Basile that night to the house where the white GMC van was waiting to be stolen, the opening gambit in this two-part murder conspiracy. As the jurors watched, Susan used the neon-bright marker on a large map to denote the roads she followed under the instructions Danny read from his little map. That map, she recalled, had been marked in yellow highlighter.

As the Van Iseghems listened, they felt sorry for this witness. They were convinced she had been a most reluctant participant in all of this, sucked into it by her friendship with a man she probably knew she should avoid. As she testified, she seemed genuinely sorry that she had ever let herself become part of this ugly story. Braun felt very much the same way about his witness. He thought of her as heroic, even though she had been part of the van theft and had been close to Basile and his sordid life. Still, she had come forward to tell what she knew.

"How did you feel about your part with this van?" he asked.

"Ashamed," Susan Jenkins said softly.

Roberta Paulus had seen Daniel Basile many times when she went to the South County Stables to care for her horses, and he looked different in court. "Today, he has a nice haircut. When I saw him out there at the stables, he had long, stringy hair."

Had she seen another man out there the first week of March 1992, asking for Danny Basile? Yes, and she had later picked that man out of a lineup. He was Richard DeCaro.

"What, if anything, did you notice about his tone of voice?"

"I heard an urgency in it."

She had been quite sure the man in the lineup was the one she had seen that day.

"Was your heart pounding at the time?"

"Yes, it was."

The last witness of the day was Lloyd Nichols,* one of two half brothers who had brought some valuable information to the St. Charles police after Basile was arrested. Assistant prosecutor Gregory wanted to get this witness's weakness out of the way first; Nichols confirmed that he had convictions for burglary and receiving stolen property. With that said, he explained that Basile had lived with him for several months in 1991, before Basile moved to Craig Wells's trailer. When Nichols and Basile bumped into each other in January 1992, Basile mentioned that he was about to steal a van "for insurance purposes" and wondered if Nichols wanted any of the parts for the similar van he owned.

Had there been more to the van owner's plans? Nichols nodded; Basile said the owner "wanted his wife removed from the picture completely—on the basis of a contract-type thing—to remove her completely out of the picture for reasons that she was possibly going to divorce him, and he was in fear for how much damage financially she could do to him."

There it was; Rick had arranged the murder to keep Elizabeth from cutting into the lifestyle he had worked so hard to acquire. She was expendable; his financial security was not.

DiTraglia had no questions, and the second day of trial ended.

Danny Basile had described this van theft as "pre-set up scam" when he called his friend Eddie Bonds, and Bonds was now recalling that conversation for the jury on

Wednesday, the third day of trial. Jim Gregory once again got the problem of a criminal record out of the way first, having Bonds reveal his probation for resisting arrest. The important thing here was Basile's calls to Bonds—looking for a garage where he could strip down this van, and then for a "throwaway" gun that couldn't be traced. Basile said this was all worth "double digits," the slang term for an amount over $10,000. The third call came on March 6, sometime between six-thirty and seven o'clock, when Basile was looking for a ride and sounding "pretty shook up."

"He said things went wrong. It wasn't supposed to happen this way. . . . 'Things went down. I did what I had to do.' "

DiTraglia knew a little more about Bonds's background. Hadn't he had problems with drugs and alcohol? Yes. Hadn't he gotten in trouble when he lived in Illinois? Yes, a teenager showed up at a party Bonds threw, and Bonds ended up on probation for contributing to the delinquency of a minor. But DiTraglia didn't do much damage to Bonds's stories about Basile.

Braun was then ready for the second half of the Nichols saga. He called Ray Nichols,* Lloyd's half brother, to describe his visit with his old friend Basile in January 1992. Basile had mentioned that he knew someone who wanted his van to disappear for an insurance claim. "And then he said he wanted his wife to go with it." Nichols had urged Basile to get completely away from that trouble; if he needed money that bad, he should pick up aluminum cans along the highway.

In February, Basile had called Nichols to ask if he knew where Basile could get a gun. Nichols said no, and Basile's response had been, "My dad's got one I might be able to get a hold of. I might be able to buy it off him." He mentioned a price of $100. Later, Basile left a message on Nichols's answering machine: "I got what I want. Never mind."

Had Nichols seen Basile again?

"Yeah. It was kind of scary." At two-fifteen in the morning on Thursday, March 12—almost a week after the murder—a "real shook-up, upset" Basile had knocked on Nichols's front door. He came in and sat on the floor, smoked a cigarette, and told Nichols, "I'm in deep shit." The police were after him, he explained, because they thought he had done "the van and the lady."

Nichols panicked and asked Basile to leave; with kids in the house, Nichols couldn't afford any trouble. He urged Basile to surrender to the police, and Basile left. Nichols learned the next day that Basile had been arrested for Elizabeth's murder. That was when he went to his brother and they decided to call the police.

DiTraglia tried to perform some damage control. After the first conversation, hadn't Basile said he had told the guy proposing the murder to go to hell? Yes. Did Basile offer a reason for needing a gun? Yes, he had to meet with someone he didn't trust; Nichols had taken that as a reference to the guy Basile said had given him a black eye in a fight in February.

The Van Iseghems had dreaded the appearances by the next two witnesses, but not for what they might say. They just hated to see Rachel and Patrick DeCaro put through the frightening experience of testifying against the man who had killed their mother. The family members sat with lumps in their throats as they watched the children take their turns on the stand. Rachel, now eleven, told the jury her father had already left for work when she got up on March 6, but her mom was home.

"Was the last time you saw your mom that morning?"

"Yes," she said softly.

Braun turned his attention toward the canine member of the DeCaro family, Ozzie. Rachel described him as "part beagle, part poodle" and explained, "When any strangers came up, he would go crazy, jump on them, and start barking."

She couldn't remember which of the other parents in the car pool had driven her and seven-year-old Bill home from school that day. They got home just before noon, before their father returned from his car-pool duties for Erin and Patrick. No one was home then, not even Ozzie. Rachel and Bill went into the house through the unlocked side door into the garage and then through the unlocked door that led through the laundry room. She went to her bedroom and got out the clothes she was taking to the Ozarks. Then she and Bill hung some pictures they had made at school on the wall halfway down the basement stairs. That was an important point in Braun's theory. He gave Rachel a photograph of the wall to show the jury where the kids always hung their school artwork.

Braun then showed Rachel the Sony boom box that had been taken from Patrick's room. She said she had been using it to listen to Patrick's compact disc by The Artist Formerly Known As Prince. Drawing some gentle smiles from spectators, she explained that when she had listened to the boom box at the courthouse earlier, it still had that same CD in it.

Cathy DiTraglia had to tread softly here. She really just wanted to know if Bill had jiggled the lock to get in that day, using that special talent he had developed for getting into the house when it was locked up. No, Rachel said, she had watched him as he just turned the unlocked doorknob on the garage door and walked in; Bill only knew how to pop open the lock on the sliding door on the back of the house—not the door into the garage.

Patrick, now fourteen, followed his sister to the stand. He explained that he had been going to a different school from Rachel and Bill on that Friday two years ago. His dad had picked up him and the others in the car pool—Ozzie and Erin were with Rick already—and then they went home to pack the van and take off for the Ozarks. When they returned home in sorrow on Saturday, Patrick had found his television and boom box missing. He identified his boom box for the jurors and explained, just as Rachel had, about his Prince CD. That drew smiles from the Van Iseghems; he had told them how the police had met with him before the trial, how he had checked the boom box, and—to everyone's surprise—had found the Prince disc. He had smiled and said, "I wondered where that went."

Braun then had Patrick identify photos of the basement, showing the two rooms there—one a workroom and the other a storeroom where his parents always hid the kids'

Christmas presents. Braun showed Patrick a photo of the door to the workroom. Did it lock from the inside? Yes.

Braun wondered if anyone had caught his drift yet. In Braun's theory, Basile had locked himself in that room to hide while the children were home. After that, he had lain in wait for Elizabeth.

Braun had more for Patrick to accomplish. The prosecutor showed him a photograph of the inside of the garage. What wall was that? Braun asked. In the way only a child could, Patrick explained, "The wall my mom went through." He could recall that night, he told the jurors. "I remember hearing a lot of noise, and then my dad came upstairs and went into my brother's room. He came back out and I asked him what happened. And he said, 'Nothing.' And I said, 'What really happened, Dad?' He said, 'Nothing happened. I was just shutting windows upstairs.' "

"And when did you find out that your mom had been run through the wall?"

"The next morning."

DiTraglia was careful again. Had Bill said he "jimmied" the door to get into the house that day? No, he told Patrick they went through the garage door.

With that, the testimony Georgianna had feared the most was over. Her grandchildren had done so well, delivering riveting accounts of that last day, stories that surely had made Elizabeth more real for the jurors, a flesh-and-blood woman who had left these precious children behind to grieve over their father's sins.

A quick series of witnesses established the time parameters for the murder. No one answered the door when the milk was delivered between two and two-thirty. Mary Jackson tried to pick up her daughter's Girl Scout cookies at three-fifteen and found the overhead garage door open and the Blazer still there. But no one answered the front doorbell. And even more unusual than that, Mary didn't hear good ol' Ozzie barking. Neighbor Bruce Dike had noticed the blinds closed on the DeCaros' patio doors—the only time in years.

After Lieutenant Pat McCarrick provided a general overview of the investigation, Braun put on his favorite witness—

Elizabeth Burrows. She confidently identified Basile as the man driving the vehicle with the RIK-LIZ license plates. How sure was she that he was the man she saw that day? "I am very sure." Musical words to Tim Braun's ears. In his years as a defense attorney, he would have challenged such an identification as preposterous. He would have refused to believe that someone could be so certain from just a moment's exposure on an interstate highway. But that was before he had talked to Elizabeth Burrows. She had convinced him beyond any doubt that she knew exactly what she was talking about, and exactly whom she was talking about.

DiTraglia's cross-examination was brief, and fruitless.

"I did this lady."

With the testimony from Carl Swanson, Prosecutor Jim Gregory was able to give the jury a direct confession by Danny Basile. He had surprised his pal Carl Swanson with the boom box birthday present and then had wrapped it in a murder confession. True, this witness was on probation for selling marijuana, but the prosecutors thought his story rang true.

What happened when Swanson leaned against the shiny black-and-silver Blazer that Basile said belonged to his brother-in-law?

"He told me not to," Swanson remembered. "Where I was leaning, he wiped it off."

Then, amid a general conversation about Swanson's birthday plans, Basile had said, "I did this lady." Swanson had stared at his friend in shock. "And then he stopped for a second, and then he changed the subject totally and went back to my birthday party. And he apologized he wasn't going to make it."

DiTraglia asked the court to recess until the next morning. Bright and early on Thursday, she came at Swanson with her fangs bared and ripped into his criminal record with vigor. He agreed that beyond the drug-sale conviction, he had records for carrying a concealed weapon—a pocket-knife—and marijuana possession, both in 1976. A weapons charge in 1983 came after neighbors complained about the noise when he and some friends staged a mock western gunfight using their black-powder pistols but no bullets. In 1987, DiTraglia asked, didn't the police find marijuana and cocaine in his house? Just marijuana, and he got a suspended sentence for that. Between the arrest and the sentence in that case, he explained, he had been picked up on a drug-sale charge.

He offered a frustrated defense for his past life. "The thing is, you make it sound so bad that I sold it. You don't live where I did. You don't got to make your bills. You got a good job."

DiTraglia seemed almost flustered as she shot back defensively, "No, I don't!"

The courtroom crowd burst into laughter, but DiTraglia kept after the witness. Yes, he agreed, he had pleaded guilty to the drug-sale charge in 1992 and was still on probation. She wanted the jury to see why Swanson might cooperate with the police after he was found in possession of a stolen boom box. If his probation was violated, he could have faced seven years in prison.

She reminded Swanson of his claim that he had shaken off his clouded past and was now "Mr. Joe Legal." She led him through a long series of Qs and As about the illegality of marijuana. If he used it, he granted her, he would go to jail. And then she blindsided him with a letter he had written to his jailed pal Dago Basile. Swanson wrote that he had smoked marijuana with a barmaid also every night at a nightclub he ran. Now, he claimed he had only written that in an attempt to buoy the spirits of his imprisoned pal by describing fun events at the club.

At the prosecutor's table, Tim Braun had to hand it to DiTraglia; she had set Swanson up quite nicely and then knocked the props out from under him. But she wasn't finished yet. Just a month ago, hadn't the police accused Swanson of holding out on them? Yes. Wasn't it really true that Dan Basile never said anything like, "I did this lady"?

"He did say that."

DiTraglia unholstered another big gun. Hadn't Swanson told the police just last month that Basile never said that? Yes. And hadn't the police brought in Lloyd Nichols to claim Swanson had quoted Basile as saying, "I did this lady"? Yes. And hadn't Swanson called Nichols a liar? Yes. Didn't the police threaten to charge Swanson with perjury? Yes, but Swanson insisted he had told the truth after the police "backed me in the corner."

Gregory had some serious damage control to do on redirect. Hadn't Swanson been reluctant to inform on Basile and endanger himself with the police? Yes. Hadn't Swanson been scared? Yes. Hadn't he really told Nichols about Basile's comments? Yes. And hadn't Swanson finally agreed to tell the truth? Yes.

FIFTY-FOUR

Melanie Enkelmann was putting her time in the courthouse hallways to good use as the trial plodded on without her. Even after she had testified, she remained on call as a potential rebuttal witness. She soon struck up a surprisingly good relationship with Doug Meyer and Iva Hanson—other barred witnesses. Melanie and Iva hit it off; Iva's brother had been murdered, and the women forged a bond out of their common pain. They passed the long hours in comfortable conversation. As they became friends, Iva even promised to let Melanie know if she learned anything else useful about the case from Doug or Craig Wells.

Melanie made another amazing discovery too. From the courthouse hallway she could see across the street into the county jail—and directly into Rick DeCaro's cell. She could stand there and look at the man who had brought them all to these buildings for these activities. He looked like hell, Melanie thought, like the Devil himself. He had lost a lot of weight, and his gaunt face reflected the evil that Melanie knew dwelled inside. His dramatic weight loss, she thought, supported suspicions that he had been taking steroids to supplement his weight lifting. As the days passed, Melanie was so bothered by the vision of Rick pacing and making frequent trips to the window that she asked a friend with connections at the jail if he could help. Before long, Rick was relocated to a different cell—one that was conveniently out of sight.

FIFTY-FIVE

Douglas Lee Meyer looked across the courtroom at his half-brother, Daniel Basile, as Tim Braun asked, "It's painful for you to be here today, testifying about him?"

Meyer nodded, "Yes, it is."

Of all of his blood relatives, Meyer had the most contact with Basile. Their biological mother was not even in the courtroom; Meyer hadn't talked to her for several years. But the woman he called Mother—his foster mother, R'Neil Wells—was there, sitting behind the prosecutors' table. Meyer looked at her softly as he explained, "She took me when I was approximately five or six."

And then he began to tell his story, reluctantly tying Basile to Richard DeCaro and the Blazer and the money and the gun and the murder. The tale began Monday, March 2, 1992, as Meyer and Basile worked on the ramshackle house at South County Stables. A man in "a real beautiful Blazer" drove up, chatted with Basile, and then left. The always-busted Basile suddenly had a small stack of $20 bills—enough to repay Meyer about $35 for the day's electrical supplies. Basile said he got the money from the man in the Blazer—payment for a job. A week later—on Monday, March 9, after Meyer found the Blazer in the garage—Basile explained that the $250 from the man at the stables had been for "doing an insurance job on the Blazer."

Braun interrupted Meyer at that point to take testimony from another witness, out of order. Dr. Mary Case—the forensic pathologist and medical examiner for St. Charles County who performed the autopsy on Elizabeth's body—had to testify then so she could leave for an appointment.

Such a procedure was a bit unusual, but certainly not un-heard of.

As the doctor described the two point-blank contact bul-let wounds to the back of Elizabeth's neck, Braun handed her a series of autopsy photographs. They were not shock-ing scenes for Dr. Case or the prosecutor, but two people in the audience were devastated as they caught an unintended glimpse. Georgianna and Jim thought their hearts would explode at the sight. She had successfully battled for two years to put that vision out of her imagination and her mind, but now she had seen the violence of Elizabeth's death in full color. "This sweet, innocent person, who never knowingly did an unkind thing in her life, did not deserve to die like this," a weeping Georgianna wrote in her jour-nal. "Help me, Lord, to replace this image in my mind." Georgianna and Jim left the courtroom, and Mary followed. This was just too much to abide.

The doctor also noted the bruises on Elizabeth's left thigh. She described them as "older." Braun wanted to know if they could have been five weeks old—asking with-out asking if they had been the remnant of Elizabeth's close encounter with the van driven by her husband. Dr. Case couldn't say for sure.

She also was unable to offer an exact time of death but agreed with Braun that the evidence was consistent with about eight hours before Elizabeth was pronounced dead at the hospital at 8:38 P.M. DiTraglia wanted to know if death could have come at 3:30.

"There is no difference between three and three-thirty," the doctor said.

"Or four?"

"Four, no."

"Or five?"

"No."

"Or six?"

"No."

The doctor finally explained that she really had not tried to estimate the time of death, something that rarely pro-duces an exact answer anyway. She had simply said that nothing contradicted a time of three o'clock or so.

And then Doug Meyer returned to the stand to resume his account of Danny Basile's activities in the borrowed garage. While checking a resident's complaint of leaking antifreeze on Monday, Meyer had found the chopped-up Blazer. The result was an angry confrontation, with Meyer ordering Basile to get rid of the stolen vehicle. Basile explained that he was just doing an insurance job for a friend; he told his brother to lighten up.

Why hadn't Meyer called the police? Braun asked.

"Number one, he was my brother. Number two, this would destroy his life. Number three, it would destroy my life for being involved in any type of criminal activity. I would lose my job and my home. And, it was just a very difficult decision to make."

"You ended up losing your job and your home anyway. Didn't you?"

"Yes, I did," he said sadly.

After Meyer heard about Elizabeth's murder and the missing Blazer, he put it all together. The possibility that his brother was not just a car thief but a murderer left Meyer numb. When he saw Basile later that evening, he charged at him again with a new set of allegations. Basile admitted that the disjointed vehicle was the DeCaro Blazer, and he offered a vague explanation for the rest of the crime.

"He said that it was him or her, and he wasn't going back to jail. He was very flippant about it at that time— very flippant. He said he was a thief, and not a murderer."

Braun was nodding his head. Here was the essence of his theory about the timing of Elizabeth's murder. Braun believed Rick was so cool, clever, and calculating that he had lured Basile into the black center of this plot with the easy van theft. When Basile then balked at carrying out Rick's murder contract, Rick explained why Elizabeth *had* to be removed. She knew Rick had arranged the theft of the van, and she had threatened to expose him—and therefore Basile—to gain the upper hand in the coming divorce and custody battle. Braun believed Rick had given Basile a simple choice. Kill Elizabeth, or go back to prison. Basile had realized, "It was me or her," and he had decided, "I'm not going back to jail."

Braun hoped a subtle point would negate Basile's claim to be a thief but not a murderer. Hadn't Basile told Meyer that Rick gave him the keys to the Blazer? Yes.

"You don't need a gun if you've got the keys, do you?"

"No."

DiTraglia objected and the judge sustained it, but Braun had already let that horse out of the barn.

DiTraglia's cross-examination zeroed in immediately on the singular weakness in the prosecution's case. Doug Meyer, like many of Braun's witnesses, had lied to the police at first. He had originally told them he didn't know about the Blazer in the garage until Wednesday.

"That was a lie?"

"Correct."

She moved immediately to a couple of unexplained pieces of evidence—the .22-caliber bullets found in Meyer's apartment, where he kept his .25-caliber pistol. Are the handles on Meyer's gun white? No. Hadn't Meyer claimed that he had cleaned the old, worn pistol Danny showed him? Yes.

"You expressed, at some point, some question about whether it would even work?"

"That is correct."

DiTraglia offered an alternative use for Danny's gun. Hadn't he been sporting a black eye from a fight when he said he needed the gun for protection? Yes. Hadn't he denied repeatedly that he had killed Elizabeth? Yes. And hadn't he seemed flippant about the one comment "It was either her or me?" Yes.

"Like joking?"

"Exactly," Meyer said.

Tim Braun rested the prosecution's case after presenting the testimony of Thomas Buel, the criminalist for the forensic laboratory for the Missouri Highway Patrol. Buel—an expert with twenty-nine years' experience in the examination of firearms, tool marks, and footwear—had analyzed the two bullets removed from Elizabeth's body and found them severely damaged and distorted. He also tested the .22-caliber revolver that Craig Wells had given the police.

He was unable to say whether those bullets were fired by that pistol.

Cathy DiTraglia opened her defense of Danny Basile by calling Detective Robert Frame, the officer in charge of the crime scene unit for the St. Charles police. His examination of the chopped-up Blazer found Rick DeCaro's fingerprints—naturally enough—but it also found Doug Meyer's prints on the hood and on a shop light in the garage. Danny Basile's prints were found in the garage as well, on a toolbox and a half-empty can of Busch beer.

Jim Gregory really needed to address only one point on cross-examination.

"If a person was wearing latex gloves and if a person was wearing brown work gloves over that, would you expect to find fingerprints?"

"No sir."

"Do thieves normally wear that kind of stuff?"

"It's common, yes, sir."

The prosecutors thought their case, and day four of the trial, had ended well.

Friday, May 6, 1994. Cathy DiTraglia called her second witness—Doug Meyer's boss at the condo complex, Mary Reinhold. She confirmed that she had allowed Meyer to use a vacant garage for his brother's mechanical work that Friday night. And then DiTraglia directed Mrs. Reinhold through an examination of the three work orders that Meyer claimed to have completed at the condos the day of the murder—some painting, some electrical work, changing some locks. Reinhold was unable to say for sure when the work was done, but she thought it was too much to do in one day. And she noted that the third order was in Meyer's handwriting, not hers.

If DiTraglia was suggesting that Meyer may have had the time to commit the murder himself, Braun wanted to nip that in the bud. When did Meyer pick up his paycheck? On Fridays, usually between four-thirty and five. Did he pick up at that time on that Friday? Couldn't say for sure.

And then the evidence was complete. DiTraglia rested her case after just two witnesses.

FIFTY-SIX

"Ladies and gentlemen, this is a case of a dumb, but cold-blooded, lying-in-wait, contract murderer who wants only to be a thief."

Tim Braun began his closing argument to the jury with the most direct description he could summon for this twisted case.

In the front row sat the entire Van Iseghem family, including the DeCaro children. Everyone was there for the final curtain. The kids wanted to see Basile convicted; even Rick had told them that this man had killed their mother. Rachel looked at Basile across the courtroom and whispered, "He's scary-looking." They all held hands as Braun began his final assault.

"This is the case of a contract killer who brags so much, who talked about the crime so much, that he got caught. This is the case of the contract killer who says he only wants to be a thief, but begged his friends for a gun and finally got one from his father—a gun he used to kill Elizabeth DeCaro. This is the case in which the dog never got to bark, so that Elizabeth got killed. This is the case in which the contract killer was observed in what I call the 'smoking Blazer,' because we don't have the smoking gun. We've got the next best thing to it, because of a keen-eyed citizen observer. And this is the case in which a contract killer who only wants to be a thief admits that he's a killer to those who know best—a friend and a half brother.

"The case," Braun said simply, "is overwhelming against him."

The prosecutor was thrilled to make his closing argument, to finally be able to use his theories to string together the facts. All of the evidence showed how Rick had molded an amazing plan and Basile had carried it out. "He's in that house to kill that woman. And he's there with a white-handled, semiautomatic gun—maybe it doesn't look new, according to Doug Meyer—waiting for Elizabeth DeCaro to come home. In the meantime, her husband is driving with the four children and the dog to the Lake of the Ozarks. And every minute he's driving is a minute closer to the death of Elizabeth DeCaro."

She probably arrived home about two-forty-five. While she stood at the sink, Basile made his move from the basement door. He slipped up behind her, grabbed her, maybe even made her kneel down, pressed the gun barrel against the back of her head and neck, and fired twice as fast as he could.

"It doesn't get any colder. It doesn't get any meaner. It doesn't get any more vicious. It's outrageous."

He gathered up enough booty to fake a burglary-gone-to-murder, waited until the coast was clear outside, and cruised out of the subdivision in that black-and-silver Blazer. He just didn't plan on encountering Elizabeth Burrows on Interstate 70, and he didn't plan on her being the perfect witness.

The jury knew the story from there. A visit to Carl Swanson in the stolen Blazer to deliver the stolen boom box and a fatal admission: "I did this lady." A call to Eddie Bonds and another sloppy confession: "I did what I had to do." On Monday, Basile told Meyer, "It was her or me, and I wasn't going back to jail."

Braun now was able to explain his theory that Elizabeth had threatened Rick with a divorce but had played her trump card too soon. She may have warned him that she would expose his insurance scam on the van if he tried to get custody of the kids or refused to pay adequate support. Once that was out in the open, her days were numbered, and Rick quickly put his plan into action.

"The dog is more important than any of us think," Braun reminded the jurors. Rick had to take Ozzie along. He couldn't leave him there—"barking his fool head off"—at the man hiding in the basement.

Braun concluded the first part of his argument by stressing that his witnesses weren't lying—Swanson and Meyer and Wells and Jenkins were telling the truth. And that was enough evidence to convict Dan Basile of "deliberate, premeditated murder."

The Van Iseghems thought that Braun had made his case well and that the week had been wearing on Cathy DiTraglia. As she began her closing arguments, they thought she looked tired and frazzled.

"This case is not about whether or not you like Dan Basile," she said. "Because I submit that you shouldn't—and that he should and will be punished for what he has done. This case is not about how you feel about what happened to Elizabeth DeCaro. Because it is horrible; it is a tragedy. But you are not here to contemplate that issue. You are here to contemplate the evidence before you."

And that evidence, she insisted, did not support Braun's "very nice story." What about Rick and the drug dealing? He told Elizabeth about it more than once, but Braun called it a lie. He wanted to say that Rick was telling the truth only when he disavowed drug dealing. So when was he telling the truth and when was he lying? "You are supposed to know by some miracle," she marveled. She offered her scenario: Rick was dealing drugs and was scared; he told Elizabeth so she wouldn't follow him and perhaps unmask his dangerous contacts.

DiTraglia was unimpressed with the state's witnesses, ticking them off one by one and calling them liars with unbelievable stories. Amid all these lies, she wondered, how could the jury know what the truth really was?

"Mr. DeCaro certainly had a motive to get this thing taken care of, and to take care of Dan Basile at the same time. And he is certainly diabolical enough, and smart enough, to do it."

That was DiTraglia's theme. DeCaro had set up his wife and Basile at the same time, and he had used his money and his unknown, dangerous friends to do it. Dan Basile was a car thief, indeed, but not a killer.

"Ladies and gentlemen, the only verdict that makes any sense in this case, the only verdict not based on lies and deception, is not guilty."

Tim Braun's rebuttal argument would be tough and direct. The witnesses criticized by DiTraglia didn't kill Elizabeth DeCaro; DiTraglia's client did, and the evidence proved it. This was no insurance scam, he insisted; the van was owned by the service station, so Rick had not made any profit from its destruction.

"The only 'insurance scam' was on Daniel Basile," Braun suggested. The van job got Dan on the hook. "That was the 'insurance' that he would do the murder."

Did Sue Jenkins tell the truth? Braun held up the license plate the police had found on the highway, exactly where she told them it would be. The testimony of all of his witnesses was backed up with independent evidence, such as the boom box that Basile had given Swanson, the boom box bearing Rick DeCaro's fingerprints. But who really provided the evidence that should convict Basile? He did, with his own mouth. He had confessed or disclosed some detail of the murder plot to Craig Wells, Sue Jenkins, Doug Meyer, Ray Nichols, Lloyd Nichols, and Carl Swanson.

Braun rejected the "frame-up" suggested by DiTraglia. What kind of sense did that make? Would DeCaro set up Basile, the killer who would point directly back to DeCaro? Of course not.

How many chances did Basile have to walk away and allow that woman to live out her life? Hadn't he sat there, just feet from her children as they hung their school artwork on the basement stairway wall? Hadn't he known that in just a couple of hours he would be killing their mother? Think of that cold deliberation, Braun urged the jurors.

As the jurors filed out to debate their verdict, about three o'clock, the Van Iseghems felt pleased about the way the trial had gone. Braun's closing statement had been too much for Erin, however; the graphic remarks about her mother's death had brought her to tears and she wanted to leave. But the rest of the family thought Braun had delivered a dramatic argument. DiTraglia had done well too, but her case ultimately failed to hold water. Melanie was surprised that there was so little defense presented.

The trial had come as a revelation to Mary. She had expected to hear the whole, complete, every-question-answered truth. She now understood how naive she had been; trials were really about making a theory fit what the witnesses were saying. But she was pleased with two observations. She thought the jurors had made a lot of eye contact with the family, and she hoped that was a good sign. And she knew the jury had watched Basile sweep his hair off his forehead repeatedly with the same motion that Elizabeth Burrows had described so definitively. To Mary, that seemed to put the gun in Basile's hand as surely as it put him behind the Blazer's steering wheel.

By the time the hubbub in the courtroom died down and everyone drifted away to await the eventual verdict, Mary decided the kids and even the adults would appreciate some pizza. She counted heads and was in Braun's office placing a telephone order for nine pizzas when a bailiff called with a message for the prosecutor: the jury was coming back with a verdict. Mary checked her watch—just after four-thirty—less than two hours, just barely more than ninety minutes since deliberations began.

The Van Iseghem clan—numbering in the dozens of family and friends—crowded into the elevator for the ride to the courtroom. They all seemed in shock at the speed of the verdict. Had the jurors rejected the evidence so quickly? Had they found the state's witnesses simply unbelievable? Had they refused to believe that someone in small-town St. Charles would so carefully plot and execute his wife just to protect his finances in a divorce?

Once again those who loved and missed Elizabeth lined up on the benches and held hands. Mary and Melanie looked at their sister's children; they still seemed uncertain about how they should be feeling, as if they needed someone to tell them. Melanie thought again about this verdict; they had to get Basile to get to Rick—and he was certainly the ultimate target. Could they convict Rick if Basile were acquitted?

Judge Rauch delivered an adamant warning against any emotional outburst, and then the jury foreman handed the verdict form to the court clerk. The moments before the clerk read the decision seemed hours to Melanie, Mary, and the others—as if their lives were hanging in the balance.

"On Count One, first-degree murder, we, the jury, find the defendant . . ."

They all held their breath, as if one.

". . . guilty."

The Van Iseghems dissolved into tears of joy, hugging each other and sharing this first moment of victory and justice, this first glimpse of relief since the nightmare had begun, so long ago. The timing seemed so fitting—that Basile should be convicted on Friday the sixth, the same day of the week and month that he had killed Elizabeth exactly twenty-six months before.

Dan Basile's face remained emotionless, but he put his head into his hands. Georgianna could see that he was beginning to realize what had really happened to him. But she still could find no sign of remorse for what he had done.

Despite the surge of excitement through the family, they all knew that their pursuit of justice for Basile was not finished. The conviction meant that court would resume the very next morning for the same jurors to decide whether he should die.

And step two was to deliver the same justice to Rick, who deserved it even more. Jim Van Iseghem had said it well for everyone when he summed up the verdict: "One down, one to go."

FIFTY-SEVEN

As Tim Braun faced the jurors on Saturday morning, May 7, he could feel the heavy weight of what he was about to do. For the first time he was going to ask a jury to send a man to his death. As a defense attorney, he had beseeched jurors not to do that twenty-three times, and they had always spared his clients. Now he stood on the other side of the aisle, on the other side of the issue of capital punishment. For the first time he believed in his heart that execution was indeed the appropriate punishment for the crime and the man before the jury.

He explained that he was about to prove four aggravating factors that the law said justified the death penalty. Did Basile receive money or something of value? Did he murder Elizabeth while acting as an agent or employee of Rick DeCaro? Did the murder involve torture or depravity that made it outrageously horrible, vile, or inhumane? Was Elizabeth a potential witness in a separate criminal act—in this case, the theft of the van? To impose death, the jury only needed to find that one of those factors applied. Braun said he would prove all four beyond a reasonable doubt.

And there would be evidence of other circumstances the jurors could now consider—Basile's previous criminal record and his long list of violations while in prison; his propensity toward violence against women and others; and the impact of Elizabeth's death on her family and friends. There would be some chilling insight into the evil mind and heart of Daniel Basile and how he had shattered the lives of the Van Iseghems. Once the jurors had heard all of that, Braun would ask them to agree to a simple, but painful, proposition: "The only penalty is death."

In defense of Dan Basile's life, assistant public defender Beth Davis spoke for the first time. She had hoped that her voice seeking to spare his life would not be needed. But now she had to speak, because the jurors had arrived at a profound choice. They could decide to give Basile a sentence of life without parole, or they could order his execution. Since his life was at stake, Beth Davis wanted the jurors to know more about that life.

Dan's story would be told by his sister, Sherry Keller. At just seven, she became the closest thing to a mother her little brother would ever know. She had no parental figure either, and she didn't know how to raise him. She would tell the jury about the abuse she and Danny and their mother suffered from Dan's father. The jury's decision would affect Sherry too.

Even Doug Meyer would be affected. He had testified against Dan—his brother—and that had been painful. He would tell the jury about Sherry's attempts to raise him

too, and about the abuse. Doug would explain that Dan
had never learned how to love; he learned only that life
was meaningless, because that was what he was repeatedly
told about his own.

There wouldn't be a lot of people in Dan's corner, Beth
Davis said, unlike the loving, supportive family members
who would testify about Elizabeth. And that, too, was
something the jurors could consider. When all of the evidence about heartache and tragedy was in, she would come
back and ask the jurors: "Is it enough?" And then she
would ask for a sentence of life without parole.

Marie McCormack was sixteen when she met Dan Basile
in 1984, she told the jurors as Braun opened his case. She lived
in Florissant, the St. Louis suburb where Mary lived now, and
Dan hung out with some neighbor kids across the back from
her house. One summer day, seventeen-year-old Basile had
suddenly begun screaming at her, calling her a bitch and using
the "F" word. When she walked toward the neighbor's yard to
tell him to stop, he leaped over the fence and began choking
her. Even when she collapsed to the ground, he kept stran-
gling the breath out of her; finally, she passed out. Her father
had run to her rescue. She had testified against Basile in court
and he was convicted of assault. What was his sentence?
Braun asked. Thirty days in jail, on weekends.

On cross-examination, Ms. McCormack couldn't tell Beth
Davis whether Basile's parents went to court with him—as
her parents had gone with her—or whether he even had a
lawyer to defend him.

The second witness was Lisa Marie Carr, who was fourteen some ten years ago when she had begun dating the
eighteen-year-old Basile. But while Basile was in prison in
1990, she married another man. She wrote Basile about her
marriage, about her new husband's wish for her to stay
away from Basile, and about her need to move on with her
life. Basile's response was to write back and threaten to
kill her husband for taking the one thing Basile ever cared
about. He wouldn't be in jail much longer, and when he
got out, he would enjoy finding out how much of a "bad-

ass" her husband was. "Cause I'm not going to just kick his ass," Basile wrote. "I plan on killing him."

Convinced that Basile's threat was serious—and that perhaps he had "cracked" in prison—Lisa Carr and her husband showed the letter to the police and bought a gun to keep in their house. After the authorities contacted Basile about his threat, he responded with another, even angrier letter. Braun handed Lisa two pages to identify. Basile's hand-drawn letterhead presented the horned face of a menacing demon that sported a long mustache and goatee. And in a sinister twist on corporate memos, it bore the notation "Desk of EVIL."

It was, quite simply, a prosecutor's dream.

"I've changed in quite a few ways over the past years, Lisa, and all of it hasn't been for the better," Basile wrote. "I've got a very black heart now, and I can be very cold, too. I've come to that point in my life where I just quit giving a shit about other people."

Braun couldn't have said it better. "Black heart. Very cold."

Beth Davis established immediately that there had been no attempt by Basile to enforce his threat after he got out of prison, even though Lisa had seen him a few times. And Lisa agreed that Dan's angry words may just have been his way of expressing his hurt and resentment over her marriage, and his fear of losing the only person he ever loved.

Braun then introduced Basile's prison disciplinary records, showing more than twenty violations—as petty as refusing to cut his hair, as serious as fighting.

Georgianna would spend more than an hour on the witness stand that day as Braun presented what had come to be known as "victim-impact evidence." The idea of giving the victims of crime, or their survivors, the opportunity to describe the effects of the crime on their lives was just beginning to take hold in Missouri, and Braun knew he could be pushing the envelope. But this case, and this family, deserved all the voice he could offer. The defense attorneys had objected and had called for strict limits. But the judge had given Braun some latitude, and he was going to put it to good use.

Georgianna told the jurors about her Elizabeth, from birth through her school years and on to her own blos-

soming motherhood. Georgianna even disclosed that she
had made a promise to God while she was pregnant: if she
delivered a daughter, she would name her for St. Elizabeth
Ann Seton. In treasured photographs and heartfelt words,
Georgianna delivered a touching portrait of the one she
could only describe as "a perfect daughter." Her father had
called her Betsy, and brother Randy had nicknamed her
Lizard. But everyone had known she was special—extraordinary in so many ways. Georgianna depicted each of Elizabeth's four children as only a grandmother could. A group
photograph of the kids in their school uniforms made them
look like the Von Trapp family, she said with a soft smile.

"Every morning I get up and talk to Elizabeth," she said.
"I tell her how much I love her, and every smile all day
long is for her. I will never let anyone forget her."

Tim Braun could feel the emotion rising in his throat
and washing into his eyes. He showed Georgianna the large
portrait of Elizabeth commissioned by Margie.

"Does that capture the smile?" Braun asked, his voice
choking.

"Yes," Georgianna said softly.

Beth Davis called for a sidebar conference with the judge
and suggested that Braun needed a recess to "contain himself." The judge deemed that wise and sent the jury out.
DiTraglia then complained that weeping by Braun and the
Van Iseghems "was getting a little bit much." Those who
couldn't restrain themselves should leave, she demanded.

Braun nodded knowingly and admitted that this case had
brought out unexpected emotions. "All I can tell you is,
when I went through this last night, I cried for two hours."

DiTraglia was not sympathetic to conditions that she
knew were storm clouds gathering over her client's head.
"Will you let us know if you are going to cry, and we can
take a recess?"

"Believe me, I'm not staging this," Braun insisted.

When Georgianna returned to the stand, she described
how it hurt to think that Elizabeth wouldn't be there to buy
Rachel's first prom dress, attend Erin's first communion, or
share in all the special activities of Patrick and Bill. And

worst of all, Erin was already fretting about losing her memories of her mother.

Georgianna closed her testimony by going through the special scrapbook she had prepared, documenting each part of Elizabeth's life and the lives that she had brought into the world. And then she showed some of the photographs taken at the holidays since Elizabeth's death—the ones missing someone special.

Beth Davis had no cross-examination.

And then Braun called Melanie Enkelmann. Not far into her testimony about Elizabeth, Melanie read Theresa's poem titled "Now and Then." It began:

I can see your face

Your smile all aglow
It reminds me of the times I used to know
The cheeriness of your laughter
The brightness of your eyes
All this is gone now
Too late to say goodbye.

That tender beginning built to a crushing ending.

I hate the way you had to die
I hate that I will never know why
These feelings are real
There is no doubt
This is how I feel
Then and now

Melanie offered her own thoughts of her sister, of their childhood, of their amazingly close relationship as adults, of the way their children were all so close to each other and their special aunt, of their wonderful hours spent working together, and especially of their almost telepathic ability to look at each other and know exactly what was going on in the other's mind.

And then Melanie turned directly to Dan Basile and stared angrily into his eyes. "Her life had just begun and nobody had the right to take it away. Her last feelings were in fear, and all she ever did in life was good."

She told Basile he had injured every member of the family by taking Elizabeth away from them. "What you did to my family is unforgivable, but we will survive with love, because we will not allow someone like you to destroy us."

Melanie set her jaw and glared at Basile, and as tears ran down her cheeks, her voice edged into a new level of outrage.

"You see, I saw what you did. Where everyone else here has just heard what you did, I saw Elizabeth lying on the floor. I saw her not breathing. I saw them turning her over, and the blood on her face."

In the audience, Margie Ugalde could not stand the pain. As her deep sobs took control, she fled the courtroom, with Georgianna close behind.

But Melanie still wasn't finished. "I saw them try to save her. I saw them lift her up, and I saw her neck—red as fire. I saw them put her on that stretcher, with the tubes in her. And I knew then that she was dead. But I prayed to God that somehow she would live. And I pray to God now that justice will be served."

Nearly everyone in the courtroom was now in tears. Many in the Van Iseghem family were crying harder than they had in some time as the crushing reality of Elizabeth's death caved in on them. Beth Davis offered no cross-examination and Judge Rauch—her eyes also strained—called a recess.

At another sidebar conference, DiTraglia again sought a mistrial. Basile's right to a fair trial had been violated by what had just occurred. "I would like the record to reflect that this witness testified angrily, looked at the defendant, that there were outbursts in the courtroom of weeping, and emotions of anger about what she feels is his responsibility in this case." Jurors had even leaned forward in their chairs and wept, DiTraglia charged, and she had heard sobbing from all parts of the courtroom. This victim-impact evidence had become so prejudicial as to render the trial fundamentally unfair and so inflammatory as to risk a verdict based on passion, not deliberation. Melanie's testimony had "obliterated" any hope of fair deliberation by the jury.

Assistant prosecutor Jim Gregory disagreed. This was an emotional case and Melanie had testified to what she had seen, as was her right. And he defended the Van Iseghems, who were seated directly behind him; he had heard none of the extreme conduct DiTraglia had described. The court had even recessed to allow for the release of emotions; a mistrial was unjustified.

The judge agreed. People had indeed cried, but she would not categorize that as "emotional outbursts." And after those incredible moments, the judge recessed court until Monday morning.

Despite Jim Gregory's defense of Melanie before the judge, he angrily confronted her in the hallway. She might have handed Basile a valuable appeal point by injecting such emotion into what the law required to be dispassionate deliberations. But Melanie was not about to stand for that. She snapped back that she had done this by the book; Gregory and even the judge had approved her statement before she read it. The judge had excised only one line, forbidding Melanie to call for the death sentence.

She had wanted to push the envelope, and it had been the most dramatic moment of her life. And only after she had finished, and realized that everyone in the courtroom was crying, did she understand just how dramatic it had been.

FIFTY-EIGHT

Daniel Basile had been raised—if that term can apply to what some parents inflict on their children—in a world without love and without hope, in a world of abandonment, neglect, and abuse. Beth Davis wanted these jurors to understand the past that lay behind Dan so they could decide the future that would lie ahead of him. Davis called the witnesses who knew this sad story better than anyone else—Dan's half sister, Sherry Keller, and his half brother and star prosecution witness, Doug Meyer.

According to them, the story began with the woman who had given birth and little else to these children. Amid her many marriages and boyfriends, the children were shuffled from one relative to another, sometimes living with their mother, other times not. They never "belonged" anywhere or to anyone. They recalled changing houses the way other families changed clothes. When their mother was there, they said, she was usually locked in her bedroom reading romance novels. Dan was the youngest of the three children, born when Sherry was only five. The little girl became the default mother for the brood. Dinner was often cold SpaghettiOs from the can.

And those were the good times. The bad times came when one of their mother's boyfriends or husbands—even Dan's natural father, according to this testimony—decided to abuse the children. These were the kind of men typified by a temper tantrum that concluded when one of them threw a kitten against the wall and killed it. Doug and Sherry told the jurors of sexual abuse and physical abuse and mental abuse and verbal abuse. Beaten, held under water, forced to stand for hours in corners and closets. No one protected them. One of these men repeatedly called little Danny the "punk," and most people know how parents' prophesies sometimes become self-fulfilling.

R'Neil Wells had rescued the middle child—Doug Meyer—from that hell, taking him as her foster child. She wished, she told the jurors through her tears, that she could have done the same for Dan and Sherry.

But no one helped little Daniel Basile. And everyone in the courtroom knew where that childhood had taken that man.

FIFTY-NINE

As Tim Braun began to sum up his case for the execution of Daniel Basile, he invoked the name of someone he knew his fellow Missourians would revere. He reminded them that the day before had been the birthday of Harry S Truman, the Democratic president from the Show Me State.

"And of all the presidents we've had, he was the one who taught us the most about individual responsibility. He said, 'The buck stops here.' "

As Braun pointed directly at Daniel Basile, he added, "And the buck stops with that young man."

The prosecutor's first job was to convince the jurors that this crime was accompanied by the aggravating factors that state law said warranted death. Obviously, the murder was committed for money or something of value; there were witnesses to two cash payments from Rick to Basile—$200 once and $250 another time. Beyond that, Braun argued, Basile was expecting to get $15,000 after Rick collected the $100,000 in life insurance on Elizabeth's head. That was the "double-digit, nice money . . . almost too good to pass up" that Basile mentioned to Wells, Swanson, and others. And Basile obviously got the benefit—a down payment, perhaps—of the van and Blazer that he stole.

The second factor asked if Basile was acting as an agent or employee of Rick DeCaro. The jurors had already ruled that Basile had been exactly that in this murder plot.

Did the defendant have prior criminal convictions? Absolutely. And Braun had provided additional, and chilling, evidence of Basile's criminal nature—his death-threat, demon-topped letters from the "Desk of EVIL." Those letters offered a rare glimpse "into the mind of a killer." A cold, black heart, indeed.

Braun rejected the defense claims of an abusive childhood. Where was the evidence to support the allegations?

And beyond that, did the jurors think that—during the hours when Basile was lurking in Elizabeth's basement, waiting for her to come home so he could kill her—he was thinking about his childhood? Braun mocked that idea. "Oh, I'm here because my family mistreated me. I'm here because I didn't get supper when I was seven years old. I'm here because my parents didn't love me. I'm going to kill this woman because I was abused as a child."

What about Dan Basile's free will? If he was abused, that was a shame. It was not, however, an excuse for murder.

"You know what he was thinking about in those three hours? It was greed. 'Boy, I would sure like to have that $15,000. Boy, I'm glad I got that $250 last week. Man, I'm going to get to cut up that Blazer.' "

Many people had tried to help Dan Basile, especially Doug Meyer and Craig Wells. Basile had the ability and the opportunity to make something of himself. Instead, he *chose* to destroy someone else.

Before Braun yielded to the defense for its argument, he told the jurors, "This is one of the most vicious, cold-blooded, premeditated murders that this community has ever seen. And the only appropriate punishment is death."

As Braun sat down, he thought one of his shining moments had been his reference to Truman—a clever blend of history, civics, and Missouri pride. But Jim Gregory delivered a splash of cold water. He had served as the elected prosecuting attorney in Montgomery County for years, and as a Republican, Gregory knew his Democratic boss had just committed an egregious political faux pas.

"Tim, that might have been the wrong argument."

Braun was shocked. "Why?"

"Montgomery County is Republican, and these people probably all voted for Tom Dewey."

Braun scanned the jury box. Yeah, he thought, most of them were old enough—they probably had voted for Dewey.

Beth Davis wanted the jurors to understand that they had heard a story about life in two different worlds, "about two very different types of families."

On the one hand there were the Van Iseghems. A large family, united and strong in love and faith. This tragedy actually had brought them closer together. "They are survivors. They have shown us that they have survived with love and grace."

She turned toward her client. "The other family—Dan's family—fractured and fragmented as it is. They are a little family that has come together. Dan's family is not a family of survivors. . . . Just this week, you have seen his mother leave him. She was here; Mr. Braun pointed her out to you last week. She is not here now. She walked out on him—once again—ladies and gentlemen. When the going got tough, she got the hell out of Dodge."

Davis presented a devastating and seemingly endless series of tragic parallels between the families.

"When the Van Iseghems were raising five children, Dan's mother was going through the first five marriages and a variety of boyfriends. When the Van Iseghems were moving into a larger house in the same neighborhood, Danny and Sherry and Doug were moving to their sixth or seventh house." While the Van Iseghems kept their children protected under an umbrella of love, Dan's mother "shuffled off" her children "willy-nilly" to others to care for, until she decided to "play family" again and jerked them back home.

"I was thinking," Davis said, "when Elizabeth was being cradled by her mother, Dan was being hit. When Elizabeth was being fed by her mother, Dan was being raised by Sherry. . . . You know, no one cradled Dan and no one taught Sherry how to be a good mother."

Dan's abusive childhood was no excuse for crime, but Beth Davis was convinced he wouldn't be sitting in that courtroom if he had received the love and guidance every child needs. Elizabeth and Dan were three years apart in age, but their lives were light-years apart.

"Elizabeth was a product of love, and he was a product of abuse and fear."

Davis held up the "Desk of EVIL" letter. To her that letter revealed not a criminal mind, but a wounded heart lashing out because he felt abandoned by the one person he had loved.

Dan's family had only a couple of photos to illustrate his life, including one in prison. They didn't have the scrapbook and the dozens of photographs the Van Iseghems had to document happier times; there had been none for Dan Basile and his family.

She urged the jurors to remember that Dan was just as important to his family as Elizabeth had been to hers. His family may just be learning to love again because of this tragedy.

"Sentencing Dan to death is not going to bring Elizabeth back, and will not make her light burn any brighter. A sentence of death would finally destroy what's left of Dan's family, the people who still love Dan and still want him in their lives. You can put an end to this tragedy with a sentence of life without parole. And if you do that, you know that both families are going to walk out of here surviving."

Beth Davis had been fairly effective, but Braun opened his rebuttal by arguing that Basile's relatives were not on trial. No matter what they did to him, they had not put two bullets in the back of Elizabeth's head. The system had given Basile too many chances already. "We let him out on parole, and less than a year later, Elizabeth DeCaro is dead, killed in her kitchen by Mr. Evil."

Braun tried to reconstruct Elizabeth's last moments as she came home to her empty, sad house, but still a place that should have been a safe haven, a sanctuary for this woman.

"Just imagine the terror when she was aware of this person behind her, this person grabbing her, even if it's just for a few seconds of terror that rippled through her body and wracked her. And then what? Cold steel, searing heat, and eternity."

A murder with a gun allows a killer some distance from the victim. But not in this case. Braun pointed an accusing finger at Dan Basile.

"He had to get close enough to put two bullets in the back of her head. She smelled the stench of evil. She felt the sweat of evil. Elizabeth DeCaro died in his grimy hands. Either he was holding her up when he shot her, or had her down, which is worse, on her knees, or lying on the ground as he bent over her and put two shots into her."

Braun then pointed to the two photos he had placed on easels in front of the jurors—one a lovely portrait of a smiling Elizabeth, the other from her autopsy. He pointed to the image of Elizabeth in death.

"Mr. Evil watched her die. This is what he saw after he did this. And he let her die while he went around the house faking up this burglary." Braun pointed to the two photos again. "You know, the difference between this, and this, is Mr. Evil. No amount of child abuse justifies this."

Braun ended his charge to the jury. "Justice is now at the Desk of EVIL. And when justice meets evil, justice shall prevail. And the only justice here, under the facts and evidence, is a sentence of death."

About three-thirty on Monday, May 8, 1994, the second round of jury deliberations began—this time on the pure issue of life and death.

Mary Cordes thought about what she had heard in the courtroom in the moments before the jury filed out. She had been strangely touched by what she had heard about Basile's deprived childhood; she hadn't heard any of that before, and it was a horrible way to grow up. Mary thought that perhaps Basile's mother should be sentenced with him. The Van Iseghems looked like the Waltons compared to the lives on the other side of the aisle. But Mary still found the tactic of trying to use his background as a defense sickening. She could find in that no reason to spare Basile the ultimate penalty for inflicting the ultimate injustice on Elizabeth.

This time the jurors took six hours to arrive at a verdict, returning to the courtroom just before ten o'clock that evening. The Van Iseghems were anxious about the decision, of course, and they wanted Basile sentenced to death. But the tension in the courtroom was simply not so acute as it had been some seventy-two hours before. Basile was doomed forever by the guilty verdict; that could not be undone. At stake now was the magnitude of his punishment.

And for the second time, this jury of good and decent people delivered the justice the Van Iseghems sought. The jury recommended that Daniel Basile die by lethal injection.

He looked down at his hands, but offered no other reaction. Judge Lucy Rauch set the formal sentencing for July 1, and then the solemn, shackled Basile was led from the courtroom.

For Melanie, this final verdict was a very powerful moment—to actually hear a panel of responsible, thoughtful citizens recommend death for another man. Surely this proved that the Van Iseghems were not vengeful, bloodthirsty brutes. They were simply honest, God-fearing people who demanded real justice—fitting, absolute, and supreme justice—for their beloved Elizabeth.

But for Georgianna and Jim, the night's victory was hollow. As they had heard so many say before, executing Basile would not bring back Elizabeth. It was justice, but it didn't stop the pain or repair the wounds. Georgianna just hoped it was a victory for some future victim, perhaps a warning that would convince someone somewhere that committing a murder was not worth the risk to his or her own life.

The Van Iseghems and their supporters gathered at a restaurant down the block from the courthouse, and unashamedly celebrated this recognition of justice. Tim Braun joined them and, as they began to look ahead toward another trial for another man, they dedicated this victory to Elizabeth's memory.

Daniel Basile had taken his first step toward death row in Missouri on this night, but in the state just east and across the Mississippi River—in Illinois—the end had finally come to a celebrated murderer who had been sentenced to death more than fifteen years earlier. Just three hours after the jury recommended execution for Basile, a lethal injection ended the life of serial killer John Wayne Gacy at Stateville Correctional Center in Joliet, Illinois. He had sexually abused and murdered thirty-three young men—some of them so young that Gacy was on death row more years than they had lived. Most of the bodies were found in his gruesome makeshift graveyard—the crawl space under the ranch-style home in Chicago owned by this contractor who liked to dress up as a clown and entertain children.

KMOX Radio in St. Louis conducted a call-in poll that night to gauge public sentiment on the death penalty. One of the callers was a young woman with a personal perspective on the subject. Her name was Melanie Enkelmann. In the candid and biting style that was her trademark, she gave the listeners a firsthand account of why the death penalty was an essential part of American justice.

And she rocked them with one of her typically incisive observations. Wasn't it disgusting that the state—its taxpayers, including the Van Iseghems—had paid for the suit that Basile wore to the trial?

SIXTY

Richard DeCaro looked like death warmed over as he sat at the defense table. His dramatic weight loss—fifty pounds, the Van Iseghems were certain—had left him gaunt and emaciated. Dark circles ringed his sunken eyes. His cheeks were hollow, emphasizing a protruding chin that had not seemed so prominent before. Even a crisp white shirt and a red "power" tie failed to divert attention from his ghostly appearance. Despite Mary's hatred for him, she couldn't help but find him pathetic. Melanie wondered, however, if this withered appearance wasn't exaggerated as a tactic to elicit sympathy from the jurors who would try him for murder.

As jury selection began on August 22, 1994, the Van Iseghems prayed that they were nearing the end of this seemingly eternal nightmare. The nearly four months since

Basile's conviction had been incredibly difficult for everyone. They had been there July 1 when Judge Rauch affirmed the jury's recommendation and ordered execution for Dan Basile. A hollow victory after a hollow loss, as Jim Van Iseghem had described it for reporters.

Rick continued to call and write his children regularly, proclaiming his innocence and vowing that he would soon prevail over these unjust charges. He would return to the kids in victory, and they would all live together again. He would buy them everything they ever wanted, from water beds to St. Louis Blues hockey tickets. "Stay strong for me," he exhorted his little troops. They still were visiting him every three weeks at the county jail, although Patrick continued to resist this contact with his father. He had gone only twice during the entire twenty-nine months Rick had spent behind bars.

Erin and Bill were young enough to be caught up in their daddy's promises. Erin was still so innocent that she once remarked that orange must be Dad's favorite color; that's what he always wore when they visited him in jail. Patrick and Rachel were enough older to be sadly wiser; in private moments they had confided to trusted family members that they had reached their own conclusion: their father was guilty of their mother's murder.

The children continued to get counseling, but the subject of what had happened to their parents remained unbroached in the Cordes house. Mary likened it to a shameful case of incest—everyone knew it was there, but no one talked about it. And she didn't want to rock that boat. Her goal was to take over where her sister had left off and to provide the children with the most secure home possible, filled with love and an undoubted assurance of belonging. Everyone scrupulously avoided any critical remark about Rick or any other DeCaro. They never tried to shame the kids for loving their father. They knew that Rick and the DeCaros assumed the Van Iseghems were bad-mouthing them constantly, but nothing could have been further from the truth. They did not hide their feelings about Rick, but they would never have used that to batter the kids.

Everyone respected everyone else's opinions. They just didn't discuss it.

In the middle of June 1994, as Georgianna prepared herself for Rick's trial, she was struck by amazing similarities between him and another husband who had just rocketed into the national news—O. J. Simpson. "The only difference is," she wrote in her journal, "O. J. didn't pay someone else. He did it himself. He went to the funeral; he went to her parents' home; he has been claiming his innocence all week. But who else but him would want her dead? He's claiming he was framed (sound familiar?). He clams he loved her. He was very jealous and had already been convicted of abuse five years ago. It sounds so much like Rick that it's helped me to understand how Rick had been able to maintain his innocence in spite of all the overwhelming evidence."

The torrent of publicity about the murders of Nicole Brown Simpson and Ronald Goldman forced Georgianna to relive a lot of the pain she had been trying to put behind her. Amid all of that, she suddenly lost the feeling that Elizabeth was still close to her. Was she was learning to cope with her daughter's death, perhaps nearing the point when she could let go of Elizabeth and get on with life? That had been the Van Iseghems' unofficial mantra for months—"Life goes on." But Georgianna still found herself dealing with a lot of anger, and O. J.'s case seemed to aggravate it. She was becoming increasingly disturbed by the public support for O. J. To Georgianna, everyone was forgetting about the vicious crime that had taken the mother of two innocent children. Even from halfway across the country, that hit too close to home for her.

Tim Braun's campaign for a second term as prosecuting attorney was in full swing by summer, and he found himself defending his handling of the DeCaro case. While he ran on the catchy slogan "A man of convictions," his opponent in the Democratic primary on August 2 accused Braun of scheduling Rick's trial in late August for political advantage. Braun shot back that he had been pushing for faster trials, but the delays had been beyond his control. When the votes were tallied on August 2, Braun had won the nomination; in November he would run against the Republican he had defeated four years earlier, William J. Hannah.

Braun was cautiously confident about the trial of Rick DeCaro; the evidence against him was stronger than what had sent Dan Basile to death row. And Braun's optimism was bolstered when defense attorney Don Wolff proposed a plea bargain: he would try to get his client to plead guilty to first-degree murder in return for Braun's dropping the demand for the death penalty. Braun met with the Van Iseghems, and they all agreed to reject such a deal for Rick. He richly deserved the ultimate penalty. So, it was on to trial.

But as that date neared, Braun frustrated the Van Iseghems by telling them that Melanie would not be allowed to testify the way she had at Basile's death-sentence hearing. Missouri's victims-rights law had not been tested in court yet, and Braun did not want to hand Rick an appeal issue. Melanie and Mary were furious. What good was the law if it did not work for the victims?

And then Don Wolff angered everyone in the family by subpoenaing nearly all of them as witnesses, which would bar them from the trial. The Van Iseghems threatened to challenge the subpoenas, but Braun asked them not to; that could delay the trial, require the sequestration of the jury, and cost the county a lot of money. Georgianna and the others were in no mood to care about any of that. They vowed to fight all the way to the Supreme Court if Wolff persisted in drowning them with subpoenas. Braun delivered that message to the defense and the judge, and it had some effect. Wolff agreed to subpoena only Georgianna, Melanie, and her husband, John, and added that the defense would not oppose Georgianna and Melanie's watching jury selection.

On August 22, a process reminiscent of picking the jurors for Basile began anew. Everyone traveled to Platt County, just north of Kansas City, to find the panel to take back to St. Charles for the first trial in the county's new courthouse. The Van Iseghems and the DeCaros felt awkward when they saw each other for the first time in so long. But the third time they passed in the hall, Grace and Georgianna hugged each other warmly. Georgianna thought she could read in Grace's eyes a sad, weary recognition of what was about to happen to her son. Jim Van Iseghem spoke for both families when he said, "I'll tell you one thing, Grace. Regardless of how this turns out, there is no winner here."

Georgianna found herself staring at Rick's back as they sat in the crowded courtroom; she was almost glad she couldn't see his face. She sensed a peculiar jealousy as she thought about those days that seemed so long ago now, days when the world seemed safe and secure and loving, and she was surrounded by her unbroken chain of children. As she sat there and thought about Rick's vow to beat the charges, she wrote in her journal, "He will be convicted. I'm so certain of this that I'm calling on all my powers of positive thinking, and on the spirit of Elizabeth."

By the second day of jury selection, Georgianna had noticed a disturbing trend. She thought Judge William T. Lohmar was agreeing with Don Wolff more than with Tim Braun. "I hope this doesn't mean anything ominous," she worried in her private writings. Mary and Mel were more concerned about the jurors themselves; they seemed almost flippant about the whole process. Most of them wanted little to do with this civic duty; one even asked about a hung jury—not exactly a concern the Van Iseghems wanted to hear expressed at this early juncture. When the final group had been selected on Friday, the Van Iseghems were not happy; something about the panel bothered them all. In Melanie's opinion, it was just a bad bunch.

But the week of contact with Wolff had proved again just what a classy man he was. Despite positions that could not have been farther apart, Wolff granted a special wish from Georgianna. On his Saturday night radio jazz show, Wolff played her favorite song—"Sophisticated Lady."

SIXTY-ONE

They were young sweethearts—Liz and Rick—the loves of each other's lives. And from that love a first child was born before they were even old enough to marry. They waited a year, married, and built a joyous life together with a family of four children. A happy Catholic family destined for great times.

The Rick DeCaro in defense attorney Don Wolff's opening statement differed from the man the jurors had just heard described by Tim Braun as a philanderer trapped in an unhappy marriage, so desperate for a solution to his financial woes that he decided that killing his wife was the answer to all of his problems. Braun had taken the jury on the same route he had traveled at Basile's trial, adding the details from the extra witnesses who would have special testimony to offer about a cold, calculating Rick DeCaro and his carefully designed plan to kill his wife.

Wolff followed that with a different view of the same man—this one a devoted husband and a dedicated father who coached his kids' sports teams. He had worked hard to support his family and showered his wife with constant attention and flowers and gifts.

And then the clouds rolled in. Elizabeth began to feel smothered, eventually losing her appreciation of her husband's constant affection and wanting "some space." A confused Rick found the emotional pendulum swinging the other way; he pulled back, creating a uncomfortable distance between the spouses. Adrift without the anchor of his relationship with Elizabeth, he found himself overwhelmed by the advances of the secretary who had her own troubled marriage and was looking for someone to listen to her problems. They had a short affair, but Rick ended it and confessed his transgression to Elizabeth. That, unfortunately, had shattered "the trust factor" so vital to a marriage.

With that background, Wolff offered reasonable explanations for the state's evidence. The $100,000 insurance policy on Elizabeth's life? A normal, prudent financial step that grew out of a review of his insurance when he bought the new Camaro in 1991. Financially desperate? Hardly; they had bills and debt, but they weren't drowning in red ink. Rick's income had risen steadily, to $73,000 by 1991. They paid their bills on time and in full. They were looking at lake property in the Ozarks, even with their financial situation and in the wake of Rick's affair.

Rick's weekender to the Ozarks with the kids? Simply a chance for him to spend more time with his children. He didn't want Elizabeth to go along because she didn't really want to be with him and didn't trust him.

The van crash? Even Elizabeth told everyone that was an accident. She had described repeatedly how upset Rick had been as he held her for hours and apologized again and again.

The theft of the van? He had left it in the driveway because the garage still held the material from the repairs to the wall after the accident. He backed the van in to unload some supplies—toilet paper, towels, and such.

James Torregrossa? A story full of holes. Rick's solicitation for a hit man was so shocking that Torregrossa turned right around and asked him out for a beer?

Craig Wells? Too many inconsistencies and lies.

Doug Meyer? He was the guy who helped Basile rent the equipment to cut up the Blazer and then helped him dump the trash from the job.

What about Rick's unemotional response when the detectives told him his wife was dead? This man doesn't show emotion well; he was in shock, and he didn't yell or scream or cry. But he cooperated with the police, giving them interviews and signing every consent form for searches and documents.

What about Basile? All the phone records checked by police had failed to show a single call from Rick to Basile.

Rick didn't have access to any large amounts of money to pay this alleged hit man.

A lot of people had failed to tell the truth, Wolff warned the jurors. Some had lied about the relationship between Elizabeth and Mike Carroll, including Mike. This would be a long and convoluted case, and Wolff asked them to keep their minds open throughout all of the evidence. They would find more than enough reasonable doubt to justify the only proper verdict—not guilty.

SIXTY-TWO

Don Wolff's defense strategy became apparent the next morning, with his cross-examination of the first prosecution witness—Melanie Enkelmann. In a tactic he would wield like a jackhammer, Wolff drilled in on even the smallest point that he could argue was an inconsistency between the testimony on this Tuesday, August 30, 1994, and what had been said to police more than two years ago. Hadn't Melanie told the police that Elizabeth was going to work out at Vic Tanny's on St. Charles Rock Road in St. Louis County? No, she told the police Elizabeth worked out at Vic Tanny's in St. Charles. Had Melanie read the police reports from her interviews? Some of them. Didn't the police quote her as saying Elizabeth was going to the Vic Tanny's on St. Charles Rock Road? Melanie tried repeatedly to explain that if the police wrote that, they were confused or mistaken. Did she ever read the reports and tell the police they were wrong? She hadn't seen any reports until months after the murder, didn't remember seeing that one at all, and didn't even know she could have them corrected.

Braun objected several times, but the judge gave Wolff great latitude on cross-examination, and he was relentless. Hadn't Melanie told the police Elizabeth was going to Boo's house that afternoon? No, she said she was going to call Boo. Did Melanie want to see the police report that quoted her as saying Elizabeth was going to Boo's house? It didn't matter; if the report said that, it was wrong. That's not what I asked, Wolff would retort.

Had Melanie told the police about Elizabeth's affair with Mike Carroll? No. But she had admitted to them later that there had been an affair, hadn't she? No. Wolff was surprised this time. "You did not?" he asked, his voice reflecting his shock.

"No." After they sparred a bit more, Melanie finally explained, "I have never considered what Elizabeth had an 'affair.' My definition of 'affair' is not what Elizabeth had."

By the time she ended her testimony, Melanie was terribly frustrated. The judge had been overly restrictive, allowing Braun to ask her about barely 20 percent of Rick's manipulative and murderous behavior. So many of the things Elizabeth had said about Rick were stricken even before Braun could ask. And Wolff had been given much too much leeway to twist her testimony. Her only consolation was her confidence in the system and the certainty of justice. They had made it into court, and the truth would prevail.

In emotional and effective testimony, Georgianna described her daughter and the events that had led to those final awful months. On cross-examination, Wolff wasted no time in setting up his theory of the case. He asked her to describe the DeCaro marriage before 1992. "They were the perfect couple. They had the perfect family. Just a beautiful family—a beautiful family," she said sadly.

Wolff tried to guide her down the road he had mapped out. She agreed that Rick had been a hard worker and an active, dedicated father. She managed to get in a shot, however, when Wolff asked if Rick had been the school's basketball coordinator. "Yes, but he hated that," Georgianna said as she realized what was happening.

Wasn't that "perfect" relationship between Rick and Elizabeth just another way of saying that Rick was a "caring, loving, attentive, warm husband"? Georgianna couldn't let that go unchallenged. "He was never warm. He was caring and he loved Elizabeth. That was why it was so difficult for me when all of this changed. But he was never a warm person."

But he was very attentive, Wolff insisted, to the point that Elizabeth finally complained that he was smothering her, that she wanted some space. Yes, Georgianna agreed, but part of that was because he was so insecure, even threatened by her return to school to get her G.E.D.

Wolff began testifying as he set up what he hoped the jury would believe was the real truth about Rick's relationship with Elizabeth. "He was also, I think, concerned that the attention he had been giving to her, that she didn't want so much of it anymore. He didn't know how to handle it?"

"No, he didn't."

"He found it difficult to back off from somebody whom he had been overly attentive to, if not very attentive to? Is that a fair summary?"

"I'm not really sure," Georgianna said as she tried to pull back from Wolff's warped scenario.

"But he had a hard time coping with her telling him to 'Give me some space; back off a little'?"

"Yes."

Wolff was ready to move to the next step. Hadn't Rick voluntarily admitted his affair to Elizabeth and even Georgianna? Yes. Hadn't he said he found Cathy Dillon to be someone who would talk to him and listen to him, make him feel important? Yes. And hadn't Georgianna insisted that this all had been just a fling that didn't have to threaten the marriage? She had felt that way, yes, but she didn't think Rick saw his relationship with Cathy that way. Hadn't Rick told Georgianna that the affair was over and he wanted his marriage to Elizabeth to work? Georgianna struggled to resist Wolff's directions. "Yes, I guess. I am trying to remember." This didn't sound right to her. Wolff seemed to be spinning the facts to make Rick sound good, but it was difficult to find the right way to disagree with this very good lawyer.

Hadn't Rick complained that Elizabeth wasn't trusting him anymore, wasn't believing him anymore, wasn't forgiving him? Georgianna wouldn't go there. "No, I don't remember that because Elizabeth wanted to believe him so bad."

But wasn't Elizabeth avoiding Rick? Well, yes, but that was later, in February. But still, Wolff insisted, it was after Rick had vowed that the affair was over and he wanted the marriage to work. Wasn't Elizabeth still having nothing to do with Rick? "How could she?" Georgianna sputtered. Wasn't Elizabeth frustrated because Cathy hadn't been fired? Yes. And when she told Rick she was going to leave, hadn't Rick threatened to leave? Yes. And hadn't that changed her mind, and she asked him not to leave? "Yes. He scared her to death."

In the heat of the moment, the irony of her answer failed to register.

Hadn't Georgianna told the police that Elizabeth was looking forward to this "mini-vacation" without the kids while they were gone with Rick? The implication that Elizabeth was a less-than-happy mother who wanted to unload her children infuriated Georgianna. "No, she didn't say that to me, and that police report is wrong. I did not say that." She was steamed now. "I never said 'mini-vacation.' I don't know where those words came from. I know that I did not say she was looking forward to this, because I know she wasn't."

Hadn't Elizabeth described Rick as terribly upset about the van accident? Yes. Hadn't he held her all night and then taken her to the hospital? Yes. Hadn't she said it was almost worth it to see him show that he cared? "Yes, I thought so, too—for about three days."

After Rick admitted his affair, hadn't he said he loved Elizabeth and wanted their marriage to work? Now it was Georgianna's turn to answer in a cold voice. "He never told me that."

As daughter Margie watched from the audience, she felt great pride in her mother and her sister. They had done well under Wolff's powerful assault, and Margie thought they had inflicted serious damage on his opening statement's claims about a loving and dedicated husband striving toward a recovered marriage.

*   *   *

Don Wolff tore into James Torregrossa on Wednesday morning. After Braun drew the details about Rick's mind-blowing murder solicitation and played the profanity-laden tapes of their telephone conversations, Wolff bore in on every contradiction he could find. Torregrossa had told the jury that Rick had complained about matrimony and its effect on his wallet during their talk in Rick's office. Hadn't Torregrossa told the police that happened at the gym? He couldn't remember. Hadn't he read the police reports before trial? Not lately. Wolff showed him the reports. Okay, that refreshed his recollection; yes, the conversation about marriage had been at the gym.

After this shocking conversation about having someone killed, hadn't Torregrossa asked Rick to have a beer with him? Yes, probably because he was so shocked. Weren't there other times he had invited Rick for a beer? No. Was he sure about that? Yes.

Wolff closed by trying to put some perspective on this bizarre event. Was Rick a friend of Torregrossa's, or merely an acquaintance? An acquaintance. That was the answer Wolff had wanted; he could argue later that it made no sense for a husband looking for a hit man to pop that question to a person who was really just some guy from the gym.

Braun knew that what he had to do was rehabilitate his witness on redirect. If Torregrossa had been mistaken about the location of the conversation about marriage, was there anything specific he remembered Rick saying at the station?

"Yes . . . If I knew anybody that could kill somebody."

Why had Torregrossa used such vulgar language when he recorded his calls to Rick? "Because obviously, I was talking to somebody that had just had his wife killed."

Wolff objected, and the judge struck the comment.

Debbie Brennan answered a question few people had thought about. Where was Ozzie the dog now? Her family had taken him in, she told Braun, and he still barks incessantly. "He keeps going," she said, conjuring up a strange canine version of the Energizer Bunny from TV commercials. Had Rick ever taken Ozzie to the lake when their families vacationed together? Never.

Braun had an even more important question for Debbie. When she went to the DeCaros' house the day after the van crash, what was the condition of the wall? It had been repaired completely, except for the wallpaper in the kitchen. Braun hoped that would trump Wolff's claim that a pile of building material had forced Rick to park the van outside some twelve days after the crash.

Wolff had two points of his own to make on cross-examination. Hadn't Elizabeth herself termed the van crash "an accident"? Yes. Had the Brennans ever taken their dog when they went to the lake with the DeCaros? No.

Why, Tim Braun wanted to know, had Rick DeCaro asked Craig Wells about finding someone to steal his vehicle? "Because of the people I had known in the past," Wells explained.

"What kind?"

"Well, I had been involved in drugs and alcohol, and hung around with the rough crowd when I was younger."

In agonizing detail, Wells described his role as the connection between Rick and Basile. How did he feel when he heard that Rick wanted Basile to kill Elizabeth and had offered so much money that it was almost too good to pass up? "I was nervous, sick. I was upset."

Wolff's request for a recess because he was ill ended testimony early on Wednesday, and Craig Wells returned to his direct testimony first thing Thursday morning, September 1. Why hadn't Wells gone to the police right after he learned about Elizabeth's murder? Braun wanted to know.

"I was nervous about the van. I had known that Rick had asked Danny to kill his wife. I didn't want to accept that they had done it. I was scared. I was nervous for myself. I was nervous for Rick, and I was nervous for Danny. I didn't know what to do."

"Who were those two people to you?"

"Dan Basile was a friend of mine. Rick DeCaro was my boss."

Wolff followed true to form, with a brutal, lengthy cross-examination that focused on Wells's early lies to police and every inconsistency the defender could find. Hadn't he lied until his attorney cut a deal with the prosecution? He was cooperating before that, but he tried to be completely honest after the deal. Wolff pointed out some other omissions of facts after that. "I missed a couple of things in there, but I was honest," Wells insisted.

Hadn't Wells driven the Blazer on an errand for the service station the day before Elizabeth's murder, the same day that Roberta Paulus thought she had seen Rick DeCaro looking for Basile at the stables? Yes. Hadn't Wells driven to a Sam's discount store about thirty minutes away, even though there was another Sam's much closer? Wells disagreed with Wolff's assessment of the distances; and besides, Wells liked the other store better. Wolff had Wells use colored pushpins to mark all of the spots on a map. Wolff wanted the jurors to see how close Wells had driven to the stables on what he said was an errand to pick up soda pop and candy for the station. Wolff couldn't come right out and accuse Wells of being the man who was urgently looking for Basile that day. But he could let the jurors draw their own inferences.

Didn't everyone at the station use the Blazer for errands? Yes. Didn't everyone know that a set of keys was kept in the pocket on the driver's door? That's where they were when Wells drove it. And then Wolff eased Wells a little farther into the case. Hadn't Dan Basile given Wells a speaker from Rick's stolen van, and hadn't Wells tried unsuccessfully to install it in his own car? Yes.

Wolff handed Wells his time card from work. What time did he sign out on Friday, March 6? "Didn't sign out," Wells said as he studied the card. Weren't his hours on the day of the murder and the next day written in pencil, while all of the other days that week were stamped by the time clock? Yes.

Wolff was slowly building his theory of the murder.

Dan Basile had called Susan Jenkins the night after their grotesque journey into his world of larceny, just to pose a question with its own peculiar pathology. "He asked me if I was having nightmares about vans," she told the jurors.

"What did you tell him then?" Braun asked.

"I told him, yes, that I would for a long time."

Sue Jenkins hesitated before saying solemnly, "That was the last time that I saw him. I never saw him after that."

Wolff returned to his theme. What had Dan told her about how the van theft was set up? "He told me that everything had been arranged through Craig, that he worked with the owner of the van at the gas station. Everything had passed through Craig—the keys to the van, the directions. I don't know about the money." Basile never mentioned the DeCaro name, did he? "No, he did not."

SIXTY-THREE

Have you heard the one about the hockey game and the unfaithful husband?

The testimony that opened Friday, Day Five of the trial, was not a joke. It was a tragedy.

Mary "Boo" Marchetto recalled a lunch in January 1992 when Elizabeth filled her in on all of the disturbing developments, including Rick's admission that he had been having an affair. That jarred Boo's memory; one Saturday night in November, Boo had encountered Rick with an unfamiliar woman at a Blues hockey game. Rick introduced his blond companion; Boo couldn't remember her name, just that she and Rick worked together. Elizabeth had nodded; that was Rick's lover, Cathy. They worked together, all right.

Jackie Balunek, a DeCaro neighbor and friend, had a story for the jury about seeing Rick and Elizabeth together. She recalled their arrival at the New Year's Eve dance, when Elizabeth had held Rick's arm and had tried to look as normal as possible. How did Rick look? "He was as cold as ice." After he stormed out and left Elizabeth standing at the dance alone, the women had met in the powder room. Elizabeth had cried as she told Jackie, "He says he doesn't love me anymore. He doesn't know if he ever did, and everything was an act. This is the real him."

Wolff wanted to know what Rick had told Jackie three weeks after the murder, when she asked if he knew Basile. Rick denied knowing the guy, ever hearing of him before. And Rick denied having anything to do with Elizabeth's murder; he said he was being framed.

Pam Hanley shot an arrow right through the heart—the essence—of the way Rick had changed toward Elizabeth. He used to be attentive and affectionate. By the end? "He couldn't have cared less where she was or what she did."

Pam also had evidence of an important contradiction. When she talked to Rick on the phone to try to convince him to accompany his wife and children to Kansas City on that fateful weekend, he begged off. They were way too busy at work for him to get away, he explained. But obviously he had found a way to get to the Ozarks.

Braun also plucked the jury's heartstrings by having Pam read the card Elizabeth had sent when they still expected to spend the weekend together. As Pam recited the "star light, star bright" verse and Elizabeth's special note—"Can't wait to see you. I love you. Liz."—Pam cried unashamedly. Don Wolff had no cross-examination.

The next witness would not be so lucky. Doug Meyer recited the story of his half brother's downfall in detail. "It was her or me, and I wasn't going back to prison" had been Basile's flippant description of what happened at the DeCaro house. Finally, Meyer had made the tough decision to call the police. Why hadn't he done it before? "This wasn't somebody I just met off the street. This is my brother. He had been in enough trouble all of his life. This was his life. He could die over this."

Wolff was merciless again. Hadn't Meyer gone to the police only after he had noticed their helicopter and surveillance cars while he was taking the Blazer parts to the dump? No. Hadn't he at first told the police that he "possibly" had some information on the missing Blazer, even though he knew absolutely that he did? Yes. Hadn't he said Dan "apparently" had been working on the Blazer in the garage, when he really knew absolutely that he had been? Yes, but that was just wording. "Just wording," Wolff repeated thoughtfully. Hadn't he lied about why he wanted to borrow a garage, claiming he wanted to work on his own car? That was possible, yes. Hadn't he lied to the police, telling them he only discovered the chopped-up Blazer on Wednesday, when he had known about it about since at least Monday? Yes.

Court recessed Friday afternoon, and Wolff resumed his assault at a rare Saturday-morning session. Was Meyer just protecting Danny with his lies? "As well as myself," Meyer admitted. Wolff ripped into Meyer at length over what he told the police and when, using reports and statements—line by line—to document every contradiction. Hadn't Basile offered to sell Meyer the doors to the Blazer on Sunday? Yes. Basile showed the doors to Meyer on Monday? Yes. The Blazer questions seemed endless.

Hadn't Meyer asked Jerry Gromer to lie for him, to tell anyone who asked that Meyer had been working on his truck on the Wednesday that they had actually hauled Blazer parts to the dump? Yes, but he had done that only to keep Gromer out of this dangerous situation.

"And all of these statements that were less than truthful, they were made to protect your brother, Danny?"

"To some degree, yes. He was facing death . . ."

Wolff's objection froze Meyer's thought, and Judge Lohmar ordered the jury to disregard it.

But Braun took up the issue on redirect. Why had Meyer asked Gromer to lie? Because Meyer knew Danny was into something bad, and Meyer didn't want his friend Gromer involved. Meyer realized he would eventually get into trouble because he had known something illegal was going on for at least two days and hadn't reported it. He told Gromer he was trying to cover up something for Danny and would surely regret it.

The prosecution ended the Saturday session with a rapid run of young witnesses, an unusual cast of characters for a criminal trial. Braun called all four teenage members of the DeCaro car pool, counting on them to offer their recollections with an innocence that Braun thought could be devas-

tating to Rick. Each one of them told the jury they could
remember well that Friday in March, more than two years
ago. Why? Because that was the day Liz had died.

Andrea Ledwon was fourteen and had been in the sixth
grade at St. Robert's School with Patrick in 1992; she had
never seen yappy, hyperactive Ozzie in the car pool before
Mr. DeCaro picked her and Patrick up that day.

Ryan McTague, sixteen, an eighth grader then, remembered Patrick and his dad talking about how to get Ozzie
into their motel that night; Mr. DeCaro said they would
sneak him in. Whose idea had it been to bring Ozzie along?
"I think it was Mr. DeCaro's." Wolff challenged that, suggesting Ryan wasn't really sure. The attorney didn't get the
answer he had wanted. "I know it was Mr. DeCaro's idea
because Patrick was arguing with him over if the dog would
be allowed into the hotel room," Ryan explained.

Braun's last witness for the week was Stephanie Brennan.
She had been twelve on that day and remembered Mr.
DeCaro and the kids wondering if they could sneak Ozzie
into the motel room.

The defense attorney smiled. "Stephanie, I'm Don Wolff.
I represent Rick. Would it be okay with you if I didn't ask
you any questions?"

"Fine with me."

SIXTY-FOUR

It was just a fling, Mike Carroll explained. He and Elizabeth had been good friends who became lovers even
though they were not in love. They had sex three times,
and then they ended it because she wanted to make her
marriage work and he didn't want to be the other man in
a divorce. He had just endured that with his wife.

The story of Elizabeth's brief refuge in another man's
arms opened the second week of trial on Tuesday, September 6, after the holiday weekend—a combination of Labor

Day and Rosh Hashanah—had flown by. For Mike Carroll, telling this painful story to this audience, exposing some things he was not proud of to a courtroom full of strangers, was very difficult. And it was especially uncomfortable as Rick DeCaro stared at him.

Wolff's cross-examination intensified Mike's nervousness. Hadn't Mike lied to the police at first? Yes. Hadn't he been just about to walk out of the door before he told them the truth about his relationship with Elizabeth? Yes. Hadn't he finally told the police he had sex with Elizabeth "at least" three times? Mike didn't remember saying "at least." Wolff showed him the police report. Yes, it said "at least." Did the report say Mike called it a "fling" or an "affair"? An affair. Hadn't Elizabeth spoken of Rick as a good husband and father? Yes. Hadn't she said that in a conversation sometime before "the little accident" happened?

Braun jumped in. "Judge, that is a trick question. She wasn't involved in any accident."

Wolff objected to Braun's comment; the judge ordered it stricken and the jury to disregard it. Wolff turned back to Mike. Hadn't Elizabeth referred to the garage incident as "a little accident"? An accident, yes. Hadn't Elizabeth said Rick was sorry about it? Yes. Hadn't Elizabeth said Rick wanted to make their marriage work? Yes. When Mike followed Rick that night, had he seen Rick meeting Cathy? No, Mike had lost him.

On redirect, Tim Braun handed Mike a photograph showing the recent repairs to the garage wall damaged when Rick smashed into Elizabeth with the van.

"Would you call that 'a little accident,' that whole section of the wall?"

Wolff objected to the leading and suggestive question; Judge Lohmar sustained the objection.

Wolff stayed with his theme as he cross-examined the DeCaros' neighbor, Jenny McKay. She had just testified that Rick repaired the garage wall within days, a week at the most. Wolff wanted to know if Elizabeth hadn't said Rick had cried all night after the accident. He cried, Elizabeth said, but not all night. Had she seen the report on her interview with police? Yes. Didn't it quote her as saying

Rick had cried all night? Yes. And hadn't Elizabeth even hoped that something positive in their relationship might somehow come out of the accident? Yes.

The next witness had one terribly important piece of information. Diane Ledwon, who lived just around the corner from the DeCaros and shared car pools with them, had seen Elizabeth not far from their subdivision at 2:38 P.M. that Friday—obviously headed home. Braun knew that Diane—more than any other witness—offered the best evidence of the time when death had come to Elizabeth. At 2:38 she had been only minutes from home. Wolff had no cross-examination.

By Wednesday, September 7, Braun was moving into some new areas. Ronald Stevens, who lived at 10 Hidden Meadow Court, offered some surprising memories about both crimes at 12 Hidden Meadow Court. On the night of February 8, Stevens had noticed that the streetlight in front of the DeCaro house had been broken out—convenient for a wily thief about to steal that van in the driveway. And on March 6, sometime between 2:45 and 2:50 P.M., Stevens had heard a "popping" noise outside, a noise so suspicious that he stepped outside to check the neighborhood. He hadn't seen anything and had forgotten about it until he heard what had happened to Liz DeCaro. He had mentioned it to the police that night, but he never saw anyone write it down.

Braun also used Ron Stevens to begin the discourse about one of Braun's pet theories—the traffic patterns that he believed had been of great concern to Rick DeCaro. Braun had Stevens describe the route to his home from Interstate 70: the Zumbehl Road exit, a right onto Bogey Road, left onto Country Club and another left where it became Tree Top, follow that onto Muegge Road; and finally, a right turn into their subdivision on Hidden Meadow. Now Braun wanted him to back up, going back to the highway. On a Friday afternoon, Braun wondered, how many stoplights would a driver on Country Club have to sit through while waiting to get through the Zumbehl exit and onto eastbound I-70 toward St. Louis? Four or five, said Stevens in the voice of experience.

Wolff followed his game plan. Police reports of interviews with Stevens didn't contain any comments about broken streetlights or popping noises, did they? No, they didn't. Wolff then challenged Stevens's knowledge of his route home. Why didn't he use the Cave Springs exit onto I-70? It looked shorter to Wolff. Stevens disagreed; he had tried several routes after he first moved there and found the one he had described to be the fastest.

On redirect, Braun decided to explain to everyone why this was so important. "Now," he began his question, "if you had just killed a woman, you are driving a Blazer with personalized plates—which the neighbors know—would you want to be sitting in this traffic at three o'clock on a Friday afternoon?"

Wolff's immediate objection was sustained and the jurors were, once again, ordered to disregard the question. That was okay with Braun, because he was about to call to the stand the other woman named Elizabeth who was so important to this case—Elizabeth Burrows. When she saw Basile driving eastbound on I-70—toward St. Louis—he was just east of the Cave Springs exit. That meant he had taken Wolff's route, not the direct route described by Ron Stevens. Braun was absolutely convinced that Rick had sent Basile the long way around, taking the Cave Springs exit to get onto eastbound I-70. Rick had routed the hit man's getaway specifically to avoid the long traffic backup at Zumbehl, where someone might notice a hired killer in the noticeable Blazer.

The prosecutor even called a state traffic-studies engineer to follow Elizabeth Burrows to the stand. Richard A. Schmidt, of the Missouri Highway and Transportation Department, said the traffic light at Zumbehl Road had been designed to favor drivers coming off of I-70 at rush hour, when that intersection averaged a lane-jamming 760 cars per hour. Drivers trying to get onto the highway would have to sit through two or three cycles of a light that stayed red for more than two minutes. If Schmidt was right, that meant more than six minutes of sitting in traffic and as long as ten and a half minutes if experienced driver Ron Stevens was correct. That's a long time to sit when you're fleeing from a murder scene in a very visible vehicle, Braun thought.

Don Wolff thought Tim Braun was "overtrying" the case, and he told him so at a recess. The kids from the car pool. Neighbors who stopped by. Baby-sitters. Traffic engineers. Wolff knew that jurors could be so overwhelmed by a forest of evidence that they lost sight of the trees. Braun disagreed; he had amassed a lot of evidence, true, but it all was essential to a very complicated story of a man who had masterminded a very complicated plot. Braun was sure the jurors could follow the trail he was leaving, and the next witness called by Jim Gregory was a perfect example.

"I did this lady," Dan Basile had told Carl Swanson in that unexpected birthday visit in the Blazer just hours after Elizabeth's murder. And, almost as odd, when Swanson leaned against the Blazer, Basile told him not to touch it and then wiped it off.

Although Gregory had been careful to get the negatives about his witness out in the open before Wolff began his cross, that didn't deter the defender. He hammered Swanson repeatedly about his convictions for marijuana sale and possession, and then for lying to the police.

"I didn't," Swanson protested. "I just, you know, told them what they asked. I didn't volunteer any information."

Wolff didn't appreciate the distinction. Hadn't Swanson lied at first when the police asked if he had seen the Blazer? "Initially, yes," Swanson now admitted. Hadn't he denied seeing the stolen property? Yes. When the police asked if Basile had said anything about killing a woman, hadn't Swanson lied to them again? "I hedged the truth," he offered this time.

Wolff still was buying. "Hedging the truth is different than lying, in your judgment, sir?"

"Yes, sir."

Braun ended the day with a catchy comment from neighbor Bruce Dike. What did he know about Ozzie, the dog that barked at him all the time?

"Small dog, but it made a lot of noise."

SIXTY-FIVE

Yes, Dr. Mary Case told the prosecutor on Thursday morning, the wounds would be consistent with an "execution-style killing." The forensic pathologist couldn't say which bullet struck first, or what position Elizabeth was in when she was shot. Standing up, perhaps even held up from behind as the killer fired the fatal shots in rapid succession. On her knees, as if she were being executed by the Nazis or the Khmer Rouge. Even lying on the floor. All of those positions were consistent with an execution-style killing.

None of those were offered in her autopsy report, Don Wolff noted. Such speculations were not part of such a report, she explained. Wolff moved quickly to the bruises on Elizabeth's leg. The larger one that Dr. Case had just described was not shown in the report from the hospital the morning after the van crash; Wolff wondered why. A bruise that deep could take longer to form, she said. Her own report, Wolff noted, suggested the bruise was three or four days old on March 6. If the van crash was January 26, why the discrepancy? There is not much difference in the pathology of a bruise three or four days old and one forty days old, Dr. Case explained. Was it a "minor injury"? Wolff wondered. Dr. Case was not willing to go that far. A minor injury probably wouldn't necessitate a trip to the emergency room, as this had.

Braun couldn't allow Wolff's suggestion to go unanswered. Would Dr. Case call it a "minor injury" if a woman were struck by a van with enough force to knock her through a wall? Dr. Case considered that "a highly significant event."

But, Wolff countered on recross, didn't the emergency room report quote Elizabeth as saying her husband "inadvertently drove van into patient yesterday, pinning her against wall"? Dr. Case nodded, "That is what it says."

Braun charged back. "Ma'am, are you familiar with the battered spouse syndrome?"

Wolff objected on relevance. Braun tried to explain that the syndrome could demonstrate why a battered spouse would try to minimize an injury when talking to authorities, but the judge cut him off in midsentence and sustained the objection.

Lieutenant Patrick McCarrick returned to the witness stand Thursday to tell the jury that he had never seen a burglary committed like this: no forced entry, too neat, a vehicle stolen from the home. That was really unusual; few burglars walked to the crime scene, counting on stealing transportation for the getaway.

What about the intersection at Zumbehl Road? Braun asked. One of the busiest in St. Charles. McCarrick gave Braun what he wanted but really didn't agree with the prosecutor's theory on why Basile had used the Cave Springs exit. McCarrick thought the simplest explanation was the best. Basile had merely gotten lost on his way out of the DeCaro subdivision and ended up there. Making it part of Rick's plan was too complicated and was pure speculation.

On cross, Wolff charged at the burly lieutenant. Hadn't the police found some keys near Elizabeth's overturned purse? Yes. Were they the keys to the family's van? Yes. Did you ever find Elizabeth's keys to the Blazer? No. Hadn't McCarrick ever seen a burglary with no forced entry? Rarely, but yes. Don't some burglars hit houses when they know the residents are out of town, making the thieves less worried about capture? Yes. If there were two burglars, couldn't one of them steal a vehicle to help haul away the loot? "Extremely rare, but I have seen it happen, yes."

Wasn't it true that Elizabeth's body bore no jewelry other than earrings? McCarrick couldn't say.

"So, is it your testimony that you are not aware of any of the records that deal with the fact that Elizabeth DeCaro was observed not to have any rings?"

McCarrick hated the semantic games that lawyers played as they tried to spin things their way—in this case, trying to suggest that a legitimate robbery had occurred. McCarrick gritted his teeth as he shot back, "It is my testimony that I don't recall whether she did or not, sir."

Wolff had another line of questions ready. Hadn't Doug Meyer lied to the police at first? Yes. Hadn't someone claimed to see Doug Meyer on Sunday at the garage where Basile was chopping up the Blazer? Yes. Hadn't Meyer first said he discovered the Blazer on Wednesday, and only later admitted it was on Monday? Yes. Hadn't the police found .22-caliber bullets—the same caliber as the murder weapon—at Doug's house? Yes.

The next witness fit into Wolff's plan pretty well. After former detective Robert Frame testified about his fingerprint examinations, Wolff had him stress that Doug Meyer's prints were found on a shop light in the garage, as well as on pieces of the Blazer's hood, air cleaner, and roof that were also there. Basile's prints were found on a toolbox and beer can, and Rick's prints, predictably, were on the Blazer.

Braun had Frame identify something else, too. Frame showed the jury a photograph he took of the workroom in the DeCaros' basement and explained that the room could be locked from the inside. Braun was sure that had been Basile's hiding place while he waited for Elizabeth's return.

As Day Ten of the trial began Friday morning, Georgianna Van Iseghem's stomach was in knots. She knew the end of the state's case was approaching, and she was now haunted by doubts. She hadn't even had the strength to write in her journal for the last two weeks, but on this day she finally wrote, "I think about the outcome and I get so scared. When people realize how worried I am, they act surprised because they feel it's a 'sure thing'—that he'll be found guilty. I just don't feel that way. I'm so nervous that Don Wolff will pull a cat out of the hat."

Edward Weindel had a very limited role to play in this trial, but Tim Braun thought this witness could tell a very revealing story. Weindel knew the DeCaros from church, and he was quite surprised to see Rick at the Country Club Car Wash sometime after mass on Sunday, March 8. Weindel offered his condolences to this new widower, and then they chatted about what a good job the car wash did. Rick had some extra time, he had explained, because a cleaning crew he had hired was working at his home—the murder scene—while he was getting the van washed.

Braun's case was traveling headlong toward completion as he called two employees from the Old Orchard Amoco Station. Robert Burres and John Stuber had seen the guy they knew only as Craig Wells's relative Dan hanging around the station on a lot of early mornings in the summer of 1991. Burres had complained to Rick that Dan's dirty mouth was offending the customers. Rick had shrugged it off; he was an employee's relative and there wasn't much they could do. Burres later saw Basile, Wells, and Rick talking on the day that Dan's car was inspected.

On cross-examination, Burres said he hadn't known Basile's last name until the murder. And, Burres thought, Basile usually had left the station by the time Rick got to work.

Stuber thought Basile had been at the station somewhere more than twenty and fewer than fifty times that summer. Stuber had even asked him to leave because of his offensive mouth. Stuber remembered that Rick had signed Dan's car inspection certificate, but only after requiring Dan to put an air cleaner on his car and mounting two used tires that Rick had furnished.

Wolff used Stuber to launch a direct attack on Craig Wells's credibility. What was Craig's reputation for truthfulness among employees at the station? "My opinion, sir, is that his reputation was pretty bad for truthfulness, yes, sir," Stuber said.

Detective Mike Miller had delivered bad news to a lot of people, among them Rick DeCaro in that motel hallway. What did Rick do? Braun asked.

"He leaned his head back against the wall, and then asked what had happened."

"What was his demeanor then?"

"I would describe it as cool and calm."

"What did you think of this?"

"I was surprised by his reaction."

"When, if ever, have you seen someone react like this?"

"I have never seen anyone react like that—so calm."

What did Rick say when the police offered to drive his van back to St. Charles so he and the kids could grieve or rest? He said no, that they might stay another day at the lake.

"Did you think that was unusual?"

"Very."

Braun then had Miller fill in another blank in the equation. Miller had driven the route Rick might have taken the day he hid Basile to await Elizabeth's fatal return home. At ten o'clock Friday morning, April 22, 1994, Miller drove from the Old Orchard Station in Webster Groves to the South County Stables—nine miles and nineteen minutes—and then from the stables to the DeCaro house—twenty-nine miles and thirty-three minutes. Total trip? Thirty-eight miles and fifty-two minutes. Braun hoped the jurors would see that there was plenty of time for Rick to pick up Basile at the stables and deliver him to the house.

Miller offered one other tantalizing detail. From the phone in his van, Rick had called his home at 11:07 A.M. Clearly a precautionary call, just making sure Elizabeth hadn't come home unexpectedly before Rick could deliver her murderer.

Wolff began his cross-examination of Detective Miller with a long list of details that Rick had volunteered to the police in those first hours at the Lake Ozark Police Station. He had accurately described the activities of the day, from driving the car pool, to his wife's two phone calls to him on the trip to the lake, to the family's arrival at the motel, to their activities in Osage Beach. He had volunteered that he was having an affair and that he had ended it because he loved his family. He volunteered that he had taken out life insurance on Elizabeth that he was unsure had gone into effect. Finally, Braun objected to the self-serving recitation of information that had been provided to the police, especially since statements by the defendant are inadmissible. "Sustained."

But Wolff pressed the same tack. Hadn't Rick agreed to let the police awaken and interview Patrick alone that morning? Yes. Hadn't Rick given them the shirt and pants he had worn that day? Yes. Hadn't Rick signed the form giving the police the right to search his van and house, and to get his business records? Yes. Hadn't Rick submitted to a gunshot-residue test that was negative? Yes. And later, hadn't Rick accompanied the police on a search of his home to identify which items were missing? Yes.

And then Braun called Christina Byrd as his sixty-first—and final—witness. Georgianna's niece described Rick's denials that he knew Basile as she and Rick watched TV together the night of Basile's arrest.

And then, on the afternoon of Friday, September 9, 1994, the tenth day of trial—the state rested its case against Richard DeCaro.

The Van Iseghems remained confident—as confident as they could—that Braun's case against Rick had gone well. The sisters were sure that Wolff's pit-bull cross-examinations had failed to damage the witnesses who so certainly had put Basile and Rick together in this plot to kill Elizabeth.

SIXTY-SIX

The defense case for Rick DeCaro began with an intriguing suggestion. Had Craig Wells been missing from work the entire afternoon on the day of Elizabeth's murder? The cashier at Old Orchard Amoco, Vickie Hauser, testified Friday afternoon as Don Wolff's first witness that she had not been able to find Wells all afternoon. He and his car were gone when she began searching for him around lunchtime, she said, and he was still missing in action when she left for the day about two-thirty.

Tim Braun thought that testimony quite odd. Had she mentioned that to the police when they interviewed her shortly after the murder? No. When did she first tell the police about Craig's supposed disappearance? Just two weeks ago.

Wolff was trying to fortify his suggestion that there was someone else with enough opportunity to commit this murder. The Van Iseghems wondered if anyone would really believe this flimsy alternative to Rick's guilt. Could Wolff raise enough reasonable doubt to sway the jurors?

Wolff's second witness was a different story, and the wheels came off in a hurry. Gayle Dorman—Craig Wells's fiancée—immediately contradicted her report to police that she had seen Dan Basile sleeping in a chair at Wells's house about six-thirty the morning after the murder—still wearing the blue shirt and white painter's pants he had had on the morning before. Wolff was shocked by Gayle's reversal and tried to get her back on the flight path. Yes, she knew she had said all that, but she had realized later that she was wrong. Basile had indeed left early on Friday, March 6, but she now was sure she had not seen him again before late Saturday or Sunday. Wolff was stymied.

On cross, she told Jim Gregory that she had realized her error when she was talking to him and Detective Miller just before Basile's trial. When Gregory mentioned that Basile had returned from the van theft in February 1992 reeking of gasoline, she remembered that that was the morning Basile was asleep in the chair—not the Saturday after the murder.

But she had remembered another detail correctly, she told Gregory. The morning after the van theft, the perpetually busted Basile was carrying an uncharacteristically thick wad of cash—some fifties, twenties, and tens in his wallet.

Any redirect examination? the judge asked Wolff. "Nooooo," he groaned, sending giggles through the courtroom. Is she dismissed? "She certainly is by me," Wolff mumbled.

His next few witnesses added little to the case. One of Elizabeth's friends recalled Elizabeth theorizing that the van was stolen by someone who followed them home. They had left it in the driveway because the garage was full of building materials. That certainly was not the story others told about a wife suspicious of her husband, Wolff hoped the jurors would agree. On cross, however, the friend admitted that she had heard that the garage wall had been fixed well before that night. Braun's question about whether Elizabeth might lie to cover for Rick went unanswered after a sustained objection.

On Saturday, the eleventh day of trial, Wolff called Doug Meyer's boss, Mary Reinhold. In some detail, Wolff took her over the work orders that Meyer had filled at the condos on the day of the murder. Wolff wanted to know if Meyer had really been working. The result? Meyer definitely had completed several orders that day, but one—checking the fit of some French doors—may have been done earlier that week. Hardly earth-shattering news.

Wolff's eighth witness came very close to putting Meyer at the temporary chop shop in the garage on Sunday—a full day earlier than he had ever told the police. A woman visiting her parents at their condo heard some men at the garage talking about changing an engine, and she noticed something dark inside the garage—perhaps a vague reference to the Blazer.

Another resident recalled Meyer asking her on Saturday if the noise in the garage below was bothersome; he came back a couple of times that Saturday and Sunday to ask again.

As a part-time insurance salesman, Rich Fiehler had counseled his brother-in-law, Rick DeCaro, to buy term life insurance policies. Fiehler—married to Rick's sister, Patty—said Rick hadn't thought there was any point to insuring Elizabeth. But Fiehler had pointed out how much help the proceeds from a policy could be to the four De-Caro children if something horrible ever happened to Elizabeth. Rick relented and took out the $100,000 policy—the same amount Fiehler had on his own wife.

Fiehler was a useful witness for Don Wolff—the first person close to Rick DeCaro who had much good to say about him and who could explain several of the small points that Wolff needed to hit. With a fourteen-year relationship between them, Rich F. described Rick D. as a good father, an active dad who coached his kids' sports teams. Rick and Rich together had coached Bill DeCaro's basketball team in the months before the murder.

Fiehler recalled that the DeCaro garage had been full of building materials the night the van was stolen; that was why Rick had parked in the driveway. A logical explanation to what prosecutors had presented as damning evidence of a criminal conspiracy.

Braun tried a subtle question. Which of the DeCaros' vehicles was worth more—the '85 Blazer or the '92 Vandura van? The van, of course; it was brand-new. Braun hoped the jurors would see the obvious. Wouldn't Rick— a fanatic about the condition of his vehicles—park the new van in the garage and leave the Blazer in the driveway?

Bonnie Dike, the wife of one of the neighbors who tried to revive Elizabeth, offered Wolff and Rick some badly needed support. She told the jurors she had seen Rick arrive home from work between eleven-fifteen and eleven-thirty that Friday morning, and he had parked the van in the street under the kids' basketball hoop. He went into the garage through the side door—all alone. Here, Wolff was sure, was the witness who could testify that Rick had not brought a killer home to await Elizabeth's arrival.

But Braun wasn't overly concerned. On cross, Bonnie admitted that she had not watched Rick constantly over the next fifteen minutes or so. While she wasn't watching, Braun was sure, Rick had returned to the van, pulled it into the garage, and unloaded his deadly cargo.

On Monday, Wolff called perhaps his most important witness—the brother of the defendant. Dan DeCaro would testify for hours and hours—and provide little evidence that the Van Iseghems thought accomplished anything. Dan slowly went through the insurance claims from the van theft, showing how little of the settlement had gone to Rick for the van that the Old Orchard Amoco Station leased for him. The Blazer was often used by station employees for work-related errands; a set of keys was kept in the pocket on the driver's door. They had done a lot of repairs on the Blazer shortly after Rick bought it—engine replacement and transmission work—and it was scheduled for more when it was stolen. Parts for the front suspension and steer-

ing—to correct a pull to one side—were ordered the day
of the murder, but, obviously, never installed.

Wolff guided Dan DeCaro through what seemed like
endless testimony about payroll records and time cards.
Wolff paid particular attention to the work hours for Rick,
Craig Wells, and Cathy Dillon on all the important dates.
It was clear that Wolff hoped to prove that Wells had the
time to meet with Basile and chart this fatal course.

When were the paychecks issued and who handled them?
On Fridays, by Cathy Dillon—who was married to the
brother of Dan's wife. Wolff had Dan testify that the bank
had stamped Craig Wells's paychecks for January 1991 as
deposited on Fridays or Mondays; Wolff aimed that
squarely at Wells's contention that he had deposited his
paycheck on the Thursday night that he ferried Basile to
the first murder meeting with Rick.

When did Dan find out about the affair between Rick
and Cathy? Just after Christmas; Dan had suspected Rick
was seeing someone but only then did he learn who was
involved and just how close the affair had been to family
and work. Had Dan wanted to fire Cathy? No; the affair
hadn't affected her performance at work.

How did Rick handle emotions? He was very quiet and
didn't display his feelings to anyone outside the family.
Wolff hoped that would help explain what others saw as
Rick's inappropriately blank reaction to his wife's death.

Rick's time card showed his schedule on the day of the
murder as 7:00 A.M. to 11:00 A.M. When did he leave for
the lake? Dan remembered conferring with Rick and Craig
Wells about the day's orders about 10:30, so it was after
that—probably about 11:00.

Braun's turn. If the paychecks that Cathy Dillon prepared on Thursday were obtained by a manager that evening and deposited that night, they still would be stamped
by the bank on Friday? Yes. So Dan really couldn't tell
from the checks when Craig Wells had deposited them? No.

Had Dan DeCaro ever seen Basile at the station? Yes.
Had anyone complained about Basile's foul language? Not
that Dan DeCaro could remember.

Hadn't Dan DeCaro told police that Rick left work the

morning of the murder between 10:30 and 10:45 A.M.? Dan didn't remember giving the police the earlier times, but he did remember talking to Rick at 10:30. Hadn't Dan told the police he had worked with Craig Wells until 4:45 P.M. that day? Not side by side, no. Wouldn't Dan have told the police if Craig had been gone in the middle of that day? He would have if he had known.

Had Dan told Jeff Dillon about his wife's affair? No. Wasn't Jeff his best friend? No, they were just brothers-in-law.

Braun wanted to know if Dan was paying Rick's legal defense fees. Wolff objected. Braun said he was going after a point of bias by the witness, but the judge sustained the objection.

The next witness was something of a surprise to the Van Iseghems, but they had no idea how deeply his testimony would wound them.

Rick's first lawyer, Ronald Jenkins, took the stand to explain that he had kept the sack lunch that Elizabeth had packed for Rick that morning—Rick had left it untouched at the station. Jenkins had thrown away the food, but kept the bag and what appeared to be a greeting card that was in it—a card addressed to Rick. Had Jenkins opened the sealed envelope? No. When was it opened? At a court hearing just last Thursday, September 8, 1994.

Wolff handed Jenkins the card and asked him to read it for the first time. In almost unbearable irony, the cover of the card that Elizabeth had given to Rick just hours before she was murdered read, "Who knows what tomorrow will bring?" Inside, it said, "Let's just enjoy each other, one today at a time."

And Elizabeth had added in her unmistakable, lyrical handwriting, "Have a nice weekend, Rick. Looking forward to really starting over and loving again, one day at a time. Love to you always, Liz."

In the audience, the Van Iseghems dissolved into tears as they were overwhelmed by Elizabeth's last words to the husband she didn't know was planning her murder that day. So this was the "love letter" that Wolff had referred to so

mysteriously at the bond hearing and preliminary hearing
more than two years ago. Georgianna and Mary and Melanie and Margie were wounded and stunned; they knew how
angry and distrustful Elizabeth had been toward Rick that
day. She had seemed to be accepting the failure of her
marriage and the reality of an impending divorce from a
man she couldn't trust, a man she couldn't even stand to
look at anymore. So, why had she written such a lovely,
hopeful sentiment to him? Only years later, as the Van
Iseghem women sat together one night and talked of that
card would they begin to piece together what had been in
Elizabeth's mind. Melanie and Mary decided that Elizabeth
had probably slipped the card into Rick's lunch as something of a peace offering because of her angry outburst at
him on the telephone on Thursday. She had shredded him
mercilessly in the mistaken belief that he and Cathy Dillon
had been absent from the station at the same time, leading
Elizabeth to assume they had been trysting elsewhere. Then
she had learned that she was wrong; Rick had been gone,
but Cathy was there. A card like this would be Elizabeth's
trademark gesture if she were offering an apology, perhaps
even suggesting a real effort to revive their marriage in the
shadow of such a terrible mistake.

And now the ones Elizabeth left behind were hearing
another example of her loving heart from the witness stand
in her murderer's trial. How much, Georgianna asked
again, would they have to bear?

Wolff was still questioning his colleague. Jenkins explained that Rick had called him twice during the ten
o'clock news the night Basile was arrested. Rick had been
calling Jenkins from his van when Christina Byrd surprised
him. Jenkins had met with Rick for two hours later that
night and had asked if Rick knew Basile. Jenkins quoted
Rick as saying, "No, I don't. But I'm concerned that I've
seen him before; I don't know where."

On cross, Jenkins reaffirmed his testimony that the card
had remained unopened by anyone until a hearing on the
evidence just the week before. Jenkins had thought it was
a risk, but that had been Wolff's strategy. If the card had
not been opened until last week, Braun demanded, how

had Wolff known to call it a "love letter" when he questioned Lieutenant McCarrick about it more than two years ago?

"I assume because the envelope had hearts on it," Jenkins said. A woman probably wouldn't use a romantic, heart-covered envelope if it contained anything but a love letter.

Braun read the cover of the card again. "Who knows what tomorrow will bring?" He looked back at Jenkins. "And you know what tomorrow brought?"

Wolff objected. Sustained.

Braun was undeterred. He offered the answer himself, using the familiar lawyer's device—a statement with a question mark at the end. "As a matter of fact, she was dead the same day?"

Objection. Sustained.

SIXTY-SEVEN

"We had an affair."

Cathy Dillon's soft voice explained candidly from the witness stand what had happened when two people wounded by unhappy marriages found companionship and solace in each other. The blonde's relationship with the raven-haired Rick had been "strictly business" at Old Orchard before November 1991, but that changed after dinner and a hockey game. The affair had lasted roughly from Thanksgiving to Christmas. Were they intimate? Don Wolff asked gently. Four or five times. And then, a few days before Christmas, Rick had ended it; he wanted to work things out with Liz. They had remained friends, and even met once in a parking lot in February just to talk. Rick was still confused; he was looking for advice because his marriage still wasn't going well. Did they have sex that time? No.

Cathy had agreed to look for another job after Elizabeth demanded that Rick fire her. He had even been helping

her look through the classifieds for another job. Had she
told her husband about her affair? No; why cause more
problems? She and Jeff still were working on their marriage too.

A business question. Did anyone at Old Orchard get
their paychecks on Thursday? Not normally.

Jim Gregory picked up where Wolff had left off. Could
employees get their paychecks on Thursday if they asked?
Yes; she prepared them before noon. Had Cathy known
about Rick's plans to buy property in the Ozarks? Yes, that
was his dream.

Back to the affair. Had Rick and Cathy met Elizabeth's
friend Boo at the hockey game? No. Was Boo lying if she
said they did? Yes.

Did Rick and Cathy have sex in the car? Yes. Did they
have sex at the Dillons' house? Yes. In the Dillons' bedroom? Yes. In her husband's bed? Yes. Did Rick tell her
he loved her? Yes. Did he tell her that breaking up with
her was the hardest thing he had ever done? No. Did he
send her flowers that Christmas? Yes. Why had they met
in the parking lot in February instead of just talking at
work? There were too many people around the office. How
many times had she met Rick after Christmas? Just that
once. Had she noticed John Enkelmann following Rick that
night? No.

The Van Iseghem sisters could barely contain themselves
in the audience. They couldn't believe that Cathy expected
the jury to believe she and Rick had met just once—and
that had been the only night that amateur sleuth John Enkelmann had been spying on Rick for Elizabeth. Mary
thought Jim Gregory had just destroyed any claim Cathy
had to respectability. What kind of woman had sex with
another man in her husband's bed?

Gregory asked if Cathy had recognized Basile when she
saw his photograph on TV. Yes, she had seen him at the
station. Had she seen Basile and Rick together? Yes, when
Basile's car was inspected.

What had Rick given her as the reason he went into the
house without checking on Elizabeth after he had hit her

with the van? He said he had struck a support beam in the garage and was afraid the house would collapse.

In the audience, Georgianna Van Iseghem stared at the woman she held partly responsible for this tragedy. This was the woman Rick had "loved" so completely? Why didn't Georgianna want to kill her? Where was her rage? Was it all bottled up somewhere deep, awaiting a destructive explosion later? All Georgianna knew at that moment was that she was now ready to return to the witness stand to tell this jury about Elizabeth in the penalty phase, as she had done in Basile's trial. Perhaps that would be when her rage would find its voice.

Jeff Dillon had little to add to this sordid story, but he answered an important question. He had learned about his wife's affair only when she told him—the day after the murder. She had been home with him for several hours the afternoon Elizabeth died.

Jeff didn't know Rick DeCaro well—only from Cathy's job. Jeff was good friends, however, with Dan DeCaro, his brother-in-law. Dan was married to Jeff's sister.

Braun had no cross-examination for Jeff Dillon.

The last witness for Rick DeCaro was his sister, Patty Fiehler. She spoke of how close she and her husband had been to Elizabeth and Rick; Elizabeth was the sister Patty never had. They had planned to buy a condo at Lake of the Ozarks together—the DeCaros, the Fiehlers, and a third couple.

But the DeCaro marriage began hitting rough waters in October 1991. Elizabeth talked to Patty about suspicions that Rick was having an affair. Elizabeth didn't know who was involved, but she suspected it was related to the De-Caros' growing marital problems. Elizabeth had felt she needed more space, had felt smothered by the constant gifts and flowers she didn't want from Rick anymore. That confused him and, feeling rejected, he had pulled back emotionally. He told Patty that if Elizabeth could not put her family and children first, that was her problem.

Elizabeth had been hurt by the affair, Patty knew; but

Elizabeth had said she was glad Rick loved her enough to admit it and end it. Even so, she was having a hard time forgiving him. By Christmas 1991, Patty believed the roles had reversed; Rick wanted the marriage to work, and Elizabeth was pulling back.

Patty also vouched for Rick's valid reason to park the van in the driveway on February 8. She didn't remember the date, but she knew there were building materials stacked up in the garage the night the van was stolen.

The morning after the murder, Rick had called Patty from the Ozarks between four and four-thirty. When he arrived at her house a few hours later, his face showed his troubles and he had tears in his eyes. They hugged. "We all cried," Patty said. She described him as very worried about his children; he was concerned about their feelings and wondered who would take care of them now.

Did the DeCaros have two video cameras and two Nintendo games, Wolff asked. Yes, she had seen them.

Braun opened his cross-examination with Patty's portrayal of Rick as the devoted, concerned father. Didn't the kids love going to their Catholic parochial schools? Patty hadn't heard them say that. Didn't Rick immediately sign them up for public schools? He had talked about that, but Patty wasn't sure if he had done it. Braun was building his righteous indignation. This loving father, this concerned father, killed their mother and then changed them to public schools in the middle of the year? Wolff objected; that was for the jury to decide.

Braun returned to the prosecution's table, and Don Wolff rested the defense of Rick DeCaro.

The Van Iseghems could find little in Rick's case to threaten the mountain of evidence the prosecution had presented. Surely, they thought, the jury could see the truth around the few obstacles erected by the smooth Don Wolff.

With time remaining on this Monday afternoon, Braun countered some of the claims by defense witnesses. He opened his rebuttal by presenting the jury with some "stipulations of fact"—evidence agreed to by both sides. If Melanie was called to the stand again, she would testify that

Elizabeth had been carrying her wedding and engagement rings in her purse. Although she had good reason to hide them, she had just stopped wearing them because her dramatic weight loss had made her finger so small they wouldn't stay on. They had been found on the table by her overturned purse the night of the murder. So much, Braun thought, for the suggestion that a murderous robber had taken Elizabeth's jewelry.

The lawyers also stipulated to the secretly recorded conversation between Melanie and Rick, and Braun read the jury the transcript of that long talk.

Braun's first rebuttal witness was Officer Mark Ehrhard of St. Charles. He had helped search the DeCaro house, finding a Nintendo game in a hall closet near the master bedroom and a video camera in the workroom, in a corner behind the workbench. Braun was hoping the jury would see that Rick had hidden the items he had falsely reported stolen with the van.

Wolff asked if Ehrhard knew whether Rick had two of each of those items? No. Was there Velcro on the Nintendo unit, he asked, the kind used to secure it in a van? Yes.

Braun next hoped to expand the time frame for Rick to pick up Basile that morning. Braun called Officer Gary Schwendemann, who had interviewed Dan DeCaro the night of the murder. Hadn't Dan said that Rick left work between 10:30 and 10:45 A.M.? Yes. Did Schwendemann have his original notes from that interview? Yes. Hadn't Dan quoted Rick as saying Elizabeth was spending too much time with the kids and sports, and not enough at home? Yes. Hadn't Dan said Rick had refused to go to counseling? Yes.

Wasn't it Schwendemann's experience, Wolff wondered, that in the midst of crisis, people have things other than exact times on their minds? That's possible. Would Schwendemann say Dan DeCaro was lying if he denied saying those things? Objection; sustained.

Braun then called Mike Miller to testify about his interview with Vickie Hauser shortly before this trial. That was when she first offered her recollection that Craig Wells was missing from the station the afternoon of the murder. "I was shocked. That was the first time I had heard that," Miller explained. Wolff's objection was sustained. Braun showed Miller a Nintendo game. Patrick had identified it, Miller said, as the one reported stolen with the van.

Wolff asked if Miller had tried to operate that Nintendo. No. Did he know if it was broken? No. Did he try to operate the video camera? No. Did he know if it was broken? No.

By late Monday afternoon, September 12, 1994, the jury had heard the last of the evidence in the murder trial of Rick DeCaro. The next day, the lawyers would make their closing arguments and the jurors would deliberate on the fates of Rick DeCaro, the entire Van Iseghem family, and Elizabeth Van Iseghem DeCaro's memory.

SIXTY-EIGHT

Tuesday, September 13, 1994

It was simply the meanest, most selfish murder St. Charles County had ever seen, prosecuting attorney Tim Braun told the jurors as he closed what he hoped would be the final chapter in the DeCaro case. Instead of reconciling with his wife and preserving his family, Richard DeCaro had bought an insurance policy and gone in search of a hit man. He had found one, but his hired gun had turned out to be dumb *and* talkative—an unfortunate combination in the professional assassin business. Dan Basile had pulled off the crime fairly well—exhibiting some degree of cold-blooded proficiency at his first murder—but he had been unable to keep his mouth shut about it. While he was trying to find an accomplice and a murder weapon before the hit, he bragged about being recruited for it. Afterward, he had flatly admitted it. "I did this lady," he had blurted out to Carl Swanson. "It was her or me, and I wasn't going back to prison," he had told his trusted brother, Doug Meyer. Basile had been seen with more money than he had ever had before, and he had been caught red-handed with the chopped-up Blazer. So much for the man who pulled the trigger.

What about the brains behind the murder, Rick DeCaro? Braun paced before the jury as he ticked off the evidence that so irrefutably proved that Rick had carefully plotted every detail of his wife's murder. First, the most obvious: Rick had solicited James Torregrossa for both the van theft and the murder. Then Rick passed money through his personal conduit—Craig Wells—to his hired killer—Basile. After the murder, Rick had tried to get Torregrossa to lie. And then Rick had denied even knowing Basile, the man who had hung around the station for months and whose car Rick had inspected for state certification. That denial was Rick's "big lie," Braun said. "He can't know Basile, because he won't walk out of here if he does."

Those facts were overwhelming evidence of Rick's guilt. But there was so much more, Braun said. Rick had isolated Elizabeth at home alone for the first time in her life. And for the first time in his life, he had taken the kids and the dog and left town. Earlier that week, Rick had gone to the stables urgently looking for Basile to schedule the murder for the suddenly perfect day. With the kids out of school early on Friday, Rick could leave Elizabeth all alone—an easy target for Basile and his hundred-dollar pistol. Braun pointed at Rick DeCaro across the courtroom. "This was an execution—paid for by this man."

The prosecutor sorted through all of the evidence from thirteen days of trial. Nothing about this case suggested that Rick was innocent. The theft and arson of the van benefited no one, not even him; it was just the device he had used to set up everything and everyone. His plot to make Elizabeth's death look like the panic of a persistent car thief had been oddly brilliant. Having the van stolen not only set that stage, but it chained Basile helplessly to Rick's murderous intentions. If Basile was reluctant to carry out the second act of the "double job," Rick simply had to explain that a word to the authorities by a vindictive,

340 *Charles Bosworth, Jr.*

soon-to-be-divorced Elizabeth would violate Basile's parole and send him back to the joint. It had indeed been "her or me" for Basile.

Motive. Opportunity. Means. Who had all of the essential elements of a crime? Only Rick DeCaro.

Motive? It wasn't the affair between Elizabeth and Mike Carroll; Rick didn't even know about that. No, it was even simpler. Rick wasn't in love with his wife anymore, but he wanted to keep his house and his boat and his children and his dream—a condo at the lake. Two bullets and $100,000 could make all of that come true—in one deadly instant. If he was acquitted on this day, Braun cautioned the jury, that dream still could come true.

What about the van crash? Rick had hurried into the house to find out if his children had heard him kill their mother. His tears afterward? Weeping because he had failed to pull off his plan. And what about the repairs and the building material in the garage ten days later? Everyone had testified the work was finished in barely a day; Rick had been in a hurry to eliminate the evidence of what he had done—and what he had tried to do.

Opportunity? A unique window of time on Friday, March 6, 1992. Rick had created it so carefully. What proved that better than his conversation with Pam Hanley just days earlier? He told her that he was too busy at work to go to Kansas City with Elizabeth and the kids. But the next Friday, he had miraculously found the time to go out of town with the kids.

Means? Rick had provided Basile with the transportation, picking him up at the stables and driving him to the house. What about money? Braun held up Rick's financial records. What about these debits in the checking account? Could they be ATM withdrawals? Two hundred dollars on February 2, and another $100 just four days later—all right before the theft of the van. A week before the murder, another debit for $100—on February 29. How much did Basile pay for the gun? Coincidentally, a hundred bucks.

The jurors were entitled to consider, Braun prodded, the evidence of Rick's emotionless reactions. Braun specifically cited Rick's lack of response when he saw Basile's photo on TV. Is that how an innocent husband would react to his first look at the creep who had killed his wife?

Braun turned directly to the jurors. All of the evidence they had heard pointed inescapably toward a verdict of premeditated murder.

"You know this is a guilty man."

Never in his career, Don Wolff told the jurors, had he asked so many times for the judge to order jurors to disregard testimony. If that or anything else he had done had offended them, he hoped they wouldn't hold it against Rick DeCaro. And then Wolff moved smoothly to the evidence. Surely, what the prosecutors had shown had left room for reasonable doubt. All the evidence really proved was that Rick and Elizabeth had been high school sweethearts who married early, bonded by the birth of their first child. As they grew up over the next years, one of them grew in a different direction. Elizabeth wanted more space, and her husband felt rejected; he swung to the other extreme and had an affair. "It is not my place to judge," Wolff said. And then he put his finger directly on the heart of this sad matter. "Does anyone believe this short affair had anything to do with this case?"

In the audience sat many who were absolutely convinced it had everything to do with this case. They just wondered if the twelve at the front of the room understood that, or if Wolff had misdirected them.

Cathy Dillon had told the jurors, Wolff recalled, that it had been a short affair that Rick had ended because he wanted to save his marriage. There was absolutely no evidence that Rick had his wife killed so he could be with Cathy Dillon.

What about the life insurance? A policy for Elizabeth had first come up for discussion a year before the murder, and Rick hadn't even wanted it. And, if he was planning to rake in the big bucks after her murder, why hadn't he added a few dollars each month and bought a double-indemnity clause that would have made the payoff a cool $200,000? Rick had never even filed a claim for the benefits.

The DeCaros were not riddled with debt, Wolff insisted.

They paid their bills on time. Finances certainly offered no motive to kill.

Next, a look at Torregrossa. He said all of the dramatic events at the service station happened after his arrival about five-thirty P.M. on January 10. But Rick's time card showed he had clocked out at five-thirty, and his calendar from home showed an appointment for a haircut at six o'clock. This alleged conversation about a van theft and a hit man had happened when Rick wasn't even there.

What about this "insurance scam" that Rick was supposedly setting up to get out from under the heavy payments on the van? All false; Rick wasn't even making the payments and he made practically nothing on the insurance settlement. And who would set up the theft of two of his cars in the same month in an attempt to draw attention *away* from himself? It just made no sense.

The van crash? If that was an attempt to murder Elizabeth, why hadn't the medical records supported that? They didn't even record this supposedly huge bruise on Elizabeth's left leg.

What about Craig Wells? He had repeatedly changed his story about the number of meetings between Rick and Basile. Wells said that he picked up his paycheck that Thursday night of the first meeting between Basile and Rick, but Wells didn't even have access to the checks and everyone else testified they got paid on Fridays. Wells had admitted lying to police, and Wolff detailed each of those lies. Who had really said, "It was her or me, and I wasn't going to prison?" Wolff had his own theory: it was Craig Wells.

What about Elizabeth's lovely card to Rick? Did that sound like a woman about to divorce her husband? "Is this woman angry?" Wolff asked. "It sounds to me like she loved him." It sounded as if she wanted both of them to work on their marriage.

Why, Wolff asked, hadn't the state brought in the two witnesses from the condo complex who had seen Doug Meyer there on Sunday? Why hadn't the state drawn from Jerry Gromer his recollection of Meyer's comment, "I could have used your pickup truck to move a Blazer shell"?

Why had Meyer asked Gromer to lie about their activities that Wednesday?

What had Basile told everyone he talked to? That he was planning a murder? No, that he was going to steal a vehicle, strip it, and make some money. Basile expected this to be an "in and out" job; that hardly sounded like a description of a cold-blooded murder. Obviously, "double job" referred to two vehicles stolen from one owner.

The police had searched Basile's old car. Did they find anything related to Rick? No. Did they find records of any incriminating phone calls between Rick and Basile? No. Where was the evidence to support these theories and opinions offered by the prosecution?

Wolff turned toward what he considered a patently inflammatory statement by Tim Braun. Where was the evidence to show that the killer was in the house when the children came home, that Rick had put his own children in danger? The testimony proved that Rick had even asked them if they wanted to change clothes before leaving for the lake. Wouldn't that have been an unnecessary risk if his hired killer was hiding in the basement?

Wolff's voice turned deeper and even more resonant. The jurors had listened intently to the evidence, he knew. After he sat down in just a few seconds, he would not get another chance to speak to them before they deliberated Rick's fate. So, he reminded them, they must focus on the state's burden of proof beyond a reasonable doubt—beyond the point that left them firmly—*firmly*—convinced.

"If you have a reasonable doubt, you must do the courageous thing," he urged them. "You must decide if the evidence has proven what the accusers set out to prove. I tell you it has not."

Dan Basile had pulled the trigger behind Elizabeth De-Caro's head at 2:50 P.M. March 6. But between December and March 6, Rick DeCaro had shot her a thousand times more in his mind, and then another thousand times as he drove to the Lake of the Ozarks on March 6. Tim Braun offered the jurors that dramatic image as he opened his rebuttal statement. Rick could have called off his murderous plot anytime, even from the highway that day. But he didn't. That wasn't theory; it was fact.

Who chose Dan Basile? Rick DeCaro. Who came in on Dan Basile with the police? His friends; they had all drawn the line at murder. The Major Case Squad had done a great job, solving the case with evidence from people who were either relatives or longtime friends of Basile. Had Braun made deals with Craig Wells, Sue Jenkins, and Doug Meyer? He sure did, to get their testimony about a murder. Had he made a deal with the murderer? Absolutely not. What about these witnesses with questionable backgrounds or criminal records? Simple, Braun said: "You can't expect plots hatched in hell to be witnessed by angels."

What supported Torregrossa's testimony? His recollection of Cathy Dillon's brief appearance in the office. Rick had told Torregrossa that the blonde was the one his wife thought he was romancing. If Rick wasn't even there, how did Torregrossa know that?

Who backed up Craig Wells's testimony? Sue Jenkins, for one; she had seen the map that Basile brought with him to steal the van—the map prepared by Rick and funneled through Wells. Could Wells get his check on Thursday? Cathy Dillon said he could. Wells had no criminal record and had worked steadily for seven years; he had received treatment for alcoholism and had stayed the course. He had told the truth, and so had Sue Jenkins.

What about Doug Meyer? He didn't kill Elizabeth. He had worked that day, and he spent part of the afternoon buying material at an electrical company. Sure, he had been reluctant to come forward—his brother was involved in a terrible crime. But Meyer hadn't held back about Rick De-Caro. He had seen Rick drive up in his Blazer and talk to Basile, and he had seen the money in Basile's fist after Rick drove away.

And what about Roberta Paulus—a witness noticeably omitted from Wolff's criticism? She had seen Rick at the stables urgently looking for the man he told everyone later he didn't even know. And the owner of the stables, Gladys Fingerhut, saw Rick there as well.

Who alone among this cast had reason to lie? Rick De-

Caro. He had been lying from day one. He lied to Elizabeth about the silly "drug deal" scenario he dreamed up to cover his meetings with Basile. Rick lied to manipulate Elizabeth into that fatal position on her last day. He lied to Pam Hanley about being too busy to go to Kansas City. He lied about the VCR, the Nintendo, and the video camera he said were stolen with the van. Why had he lied? Because he was a guilty man trying to protect himself.

Why didn't Rick eat the sack lunch Elizabeth had lovingly packed for him that day? Because he was too busy hurrying to pick up her killer and deliver him to the house. Remember Rick's call from the van at 11:07 A.M. Why was he calling home if not to make sure the coast was clear for his special delivery?

Could it have been just a horrible coincidence that Elizabeth was shot to death on the very first day she had ever been in that home alone? No, it was evidence of premeditated murder. This was not second-degree murder, Braun said firmly. The time had come for the jury to do its job and convict Rick DeCaro of first-degree murder.

"This is the day," Braun said.

SIXTY-NINE

Mary Cordes could not restrain the flood that had been building for several days. As the Van Iseghems ate dinner after the jury had started its deliberations about two o'clock, Mary began to cry uncontrollably. Worries that had been mounting during the trial now loomed so large that she could not escape the fear that Rick DeCaro was about to be acquitted. Don Wolff had delivered a seamless, coherent argument that logically and directly challenged Tim Braun's evidence and theory of the case. Mary thought that Braun's closing had lacked the qualities that distinguished Wolff's. Braun seemed to hopscotch around the evidence without direction or form. Mary was buoyed by the general tone of the testimony; prosecution witnesses had seemed strong to her, while Wolff seemed to fail to make any significant points with his lacerating cross-examinations or even with his own witnesses. But Mary was forced to admit that if she were a juror who knew nothing more than what she had heard in the courtroom, she would be able to find room for doubts about Rick's guilt. And that terrified her beyond belief or endurance. She could not stop the tears as she told her family of her wrenching misgivings.

Melanie could agree with some of Mary's concerns. Melanie thought Braun's summation did not match Wolff's polished demeanor and presentation. To Melanie, Braun just had not tied his evidence together in a package the jurors could handle—and Wolff had done exactly that. Melanie also worried that the trial had dragged on too long, perhaps pushing the jurors' patience beyond its limits. The judge's instructions to the jurors had seemed woefully confusing, too, especially as he explained the requirements for convictions on murder in the first or second degree. The Van Iseghems were not pleased about giving the jury that choice.

Melanie also was haunted by the tip whispered by one of the court bailiffs earlier that day: the word in the jail was that Rick DeCaro would walk. It was over already, the buzz was; this jury would never convict Rick on this evidence. Rick was already making his preparations to walk free.

But for Melanie, none of the negative factors was sufficient to sway her opinion about the outcome. She insisted that, above all else, they had been in an American court of law and, dammit, justice would prevail. Rick would be convicted of the first-degree murder of Elizabeth. Melanie refused to accept any other result. How could anyone— even jurors who had never heard anything else about this case—find enough cause to doubt Rick's guilt, enough reason to acquit? No explanation other than Rick's guilt was possible for this murder and the evidence surrounding it. Nothing else fit the facts, and nothing else would do.

Lieutenant Pat McCarrick had attended the trial and was more than a passive observer. He knew this case as well as anyone, and he feared that Don Wolff had eaten the prosecution alive. Wolff's closing argument left McCarrick worried about the jury's decision. McCarrick greeted Wolff in the hallway later and offered his hand.

"I don't know what you're getting paid," the cop told the lawyer, "but you certainly earned it with that closing argument."

Wolff accepted the compliment with a smile and cracked, "Not enough."

Pat McCarrick liked and respected Tim Braun. He was a hardworking, sincere advocate who always did his best. But McCarrick thought Braun had made several decisions that could have been damaging. First, Braun should have pursued a plea bargain with Wolff instead of going for the death penalty in a trial. McCarrick was disturbed by what struck him as a political decision made behind Braun's tough-on-crime election campaign. McCarrick didn't like seeing that decision made for political or public-relations reasons, and he had told Braun that. The prosecutor had disagreed with McCarrick's assessment of his motives. To Braun, the case and DeCaro deserved a capital sentence, the police and family agreed with that, and he sought it because it was appropriate.

McCarrick also had some problems with Braun's trial strategy, especially the concentration on Ozzie the dog. McCarrick heard observers criticize the recurring references to Ozzie and the repeated use of the blown-up photograph of the pooch. McCarrick and others thought Braun was overdoing it, and perhaps irritating the jurors.

McCarrick also agreed with the Van Iseghems' assessment of the judge's instructions to the jury. McCarrick couldn't imagine how anyone was supposed to understand such confusing language.

There would be no repeat of the quick Basile verdict in Rick DeCaro's trial on this Tuesday. The deliberations stretched uncertainly into the evening—hours and hours of torture for the fifty or so Van Iseghem partisans who awaited this decision. They paced the halls. They made phone calls to the ones who couldn't attend. They checked regularly on the brood of children at home, including Elizabeth's four. They had not wanted to come to court this time, and the adults had been in agreement with that.

At eleven o'clock, Judge Lohmar finally told the jurors to break for the night and dispatched them to their motel for some rest. It was a disappointing way to end this day for the Van Iseghems.

At home later that night, Melanie Enkelmann sat outside for hours and stared at the sky. She begged God for a conviction.

SEVENTY

Melanie Enkelmann awoke Wednesday morning, September 14, 1994—her thirty-sixth birthday—with renewed strength and optimism. She put on her new, bright-red "power" suit and headed for court as the jurors began their second day of deliberations. While the others worried about what these hours of delay meant to the verdict, Melanie reinforced her positive thinking by writing the victim-mpact statement she would deliver in support of the death sentence—after this jury had convicted Rick. That was the path that Dan Basile had followed, and Melanie was sure that Rick was soon to go down the same course to death row. There was no way Rick would be acquitted on her birthday.

"Not guilty" was not in her vocabulary today.

Mary and Phil Cordes had made a difficult decision to stay home with all of the kids. They took them out of school and tried to keep them busy with activities as this second day of deliberations crawled by. When the inevitable conviction came down, Mary and Phil agreed, they had to be with Elizabeth's children to help them deal with the pain it certainly would cause.

As the day inched along at the St. Charles County Courthouse, speculation abounded. Braun told the Van Iseghems he was worried about a verdict of second-degree murder, and he began to second-guess a trial strategy that he had been confident about just twenty-four hours earlier. Pat McCarrick concluded that the judge's instructions had indeed confused the jurors enough for them to reject first-degree murder and to get hung up arguing about a compromise verdict of second-degree.

The only good news was the opinions offered by the departing alternate jurors. Two of them had said they would not hesitate to vote for a verdict of guilty of first-degree murder.

Finally, word that the jurors had their verdict came down just after three o'clock—following some fifteen hours of deliberations. The overflow crowd packed the courtroom, and Melanie felt her stomach reacting to the incredible tension. The Van Iseghems knew the rest of their lives and Elizabeth's memory depended on the next few seconds. They anxiously searched the jurors' faces as they filed into the box, but found these twelve "good and true citizens" unwilling to return the family's gaze. Courtroom observers always interpreted that as a bad sign. Georgianna prayed again for a conviction of first-degree murder. Second-degree would be a travesty, and she could not even allow the thought of the other alternative to form in her mind.

Melanie was shocked when what seemed a small army of deputy sheriffs swept into the courtroom and took up positions at strategic points, even forming a row across the front of the room between the audience and the trial participants. Just who, Melanie wondered, was being protected from whom?

A man in the jury—the foreman—handed a form to the clerk and she began reading to the courtroom that was deathly silent but for that one voice.

"We, the jury, find the defendant . . ."

Silence and tension and prayers.

". . . not guilty."

The words hung over the courtroom as everyone seemed to take a deep breath as one. The Van Iseghems waited for the inevitable correction. Surely the clerk had meant to

say, "Guilty." Or surely the jurors would announce that
there had been some clerical error—that they had signed
the wrong form. They could not have meant "not guilty."

But slowly the verdict—this inconceivable acquittal—
bored its way into the hearts and minds of those still frozen
in their seats.

And then the screams began. Almost in unison, Melanie
and Margie and Theresa began to scream, "No, no, no!"
Jim and Georgianna sat in stunned, furious silence. Jim's
face turned fire-red, and the muscles in his jaw flexed until
they seemed ready to explode. He was unable to make a
sound as he squeezed Georgianna's hand tightly. Margie
worried that he was having a heart attack. She looked at
her motionless mother and saw hatred in Georgianna's face
that had never been there before. Margie had never felt
so helpless.

Jimmy Van Iseghem was still waiting. Wasn't there something else? Wasn't Rick guilty of something else? Fraud or
theft or something? But nothing else was happening; nothing else coming from the jurors. Was that it? he was
wondering.

His brother, Randy, was in shock too. Randy knew Wolff
was one of the best in the business, but he still had expected a conviction. Who could have predicted anything
else? He had wondered why all the deputies were brought
into the courtroom; now he understood. What in the hell
would happen now? Randy wondered.

Pam Hanley and Mary Marchetto were still screaming
and crying in protest of this unbelievable injustice. As the
Van Iseghems and their dear friends began to fall into each
other's arms, looking for some strength or solace, some
answer, Melanie fled the room in sheer panic as she
screamed, "How can they say not guilty?" Her furious husband, John, was right behind her. For a moment Margie
had feared that John would leap over the rail and attack
Rick.

Across the aisle, the acquittal was greeted with shrieks
of shocked delight from the DeCaro family—and with what
many would describe as a look of absolute surprise on the
face of defense attorney Don Wolff. Rick hugged the

stunned Wolff, and then his own family as the Van Iseghems continued to wail and cry. Georgianna stared at the
DeCaros in disbelief; she had been so ready to feel sorry
for them after Rick was convicted, and now she had to
witness their joy and celebration that a murderer would go
free. Georgianna was stricken with the same urge to scream
out denials that she had felt at the hospital when she was
told Elizabeth was dead. Her mind still was shouting, "No,
no, no!"

Through her tears and pain, Margie looked around the
courtroom and saw all of the faces she loved now contorted
and convulsed in anguish and horror. Others sat with their
faces buried in their hands, their shoulders shaking violently as sobs tore through them.

From the box, the jurors watched in shocked silence.
Two of the women jurors had begun to cry. Margie thought
she saw looks of realization washing over them all, as if
they had begun to ask themselves, "My God, what have
we done?" You have freed a murderer, Margie wanted to
scream in answer to their unspoken question. She looked
at the judge and saw absolute shock in his face, too. At
least, she thought, he was not pounding his gavel and trying
to restrain these stricken mourners in his courtroom, this
place of "justice."

Margie felt as if she would be violently ill; she clutched
her abdomen and doubled over in pain. What was she feeling? Horror, anger, hatred, contempt. My God, this was
just like the night Elizabeth died. Margie screamed again,
hoping to purge herself of this illness, of this newest storm
in this new world. Now she was moaning; she couldn't go
through this grief again. She felt her body slipping into
shock. Finally, Margie and Theresa turned and ran screaming from the courtroom. Margie had to find Melanie. The
bathroom, somebody said. Margie found her sister there,
pacing and screaming and beating her fists on the wall.

"It's not fair," Melanie was yelling. "What the hell is
wrong with those people?" Margie ran to her and hugged
her, and the two women stood there, crying as if they never
would stop. Margie realized that Theresa was standing
alone, trembling and crying. Margie and Melanie went to

her and enveloped her in their arms; the three of them clung desperately to each other.

No one could remember witnessing anything like the scene in that courthouse that afternoon.

Never in Pat McCarrick's wildest dreams had he envisioned an acquittal. A straight-up conviction was the proper verdict, and he could have understood compromising on second-degree murder. But he could not believe that twelve reasonably intelligent people had agreed unanimously that there was enough doubt to free Rick DeCaro.

Tom O'Connor felt as if he had been shot in the heart. He had come to hold the Van Iseghems and their murdered daughter in deep affection and respect, and they did not deserve this injustice. He could not remember this feeling of being hurt, of being injured, by anything like this before. "Thunderstruck" was the word that came to mind. When he left later, a TV reporter asked O'Connor how he felt about the verdict. He mouthed the standard line: "The jury has spoken." But he had to struggle hard to keep from revealing just how badly this hurt.

Chief King was dashing toward the courtroom after hearing that the verdict was coming in when he encountered a TV reporter in the hallway. "Acquittal," she told the stunned chief. He walked into another surreal scene—but oh, so different, from his memory of the first night of the investigation. Now there was screaming and yelling by outraged and grief-stricken Van Iseghems in what King would recall as one of the most awful moments of his life.

Tim Braun was crushed. He had presented a strong case the best way he could, and it had not been enough. Never before had he put so much effort into a case, only to lose it. And he ached for the Van Iseghem family; he knew how much they had invested in this verdict, and he regretted not delivering it for them. He was so crestfallen that he would not even return a call later from a TV producer interested in bringing this story to the screen. And it was a long, lonely walk from the courtroom to the front of the building to talk to reporters that afternoon. He tried never to be a sore loser or a whiner, but to live by the axiom "The jury has spoken." This one would test his resolve.

*   *   *

At her home in Florissant, Mary was anxiously awaiting the word on the verdict when one of her girlfriends called. The kids were playing cards at the kitchen table, and all sound and activity stopped at the ringing of the phone. Mary picked up the receiver and was greeted by a hysterical voice she barely recognized, and the unmistakable, heart-wrenching sound of Melanie screaming, "No, no, no!" in the background. "He's not guilty, he's not guilty," the voice on the other end was repeating. They were the most God-awful words Mary had ever heard in her life. With all of the kids' eyes on her, she struggled to restrain her reaction. But she wanted to join in with the sobbing and screaming she still could hear from Melanie. Mary hung up and walked to the table.

"He's not guilty," she said softly, trying to keep her voice from betraying her. Rachel leaped up, stomped her foot, and screamed, "No, no, no. I don't want to leave here and live with him." Patrick looked stricken; "I don't believe it." But Bill was thrilled. Later that night his innocence would break Mary's heart again when he told her, "That must mean my daddy didn't do it." Little Erin was nearly oblivious to it all. She barely acknowledged the verdict and then was ready to play again.

Now Mary was beginning to experience another terror—the one she had tried not to think about in the years since Elizabeth's murder. Rick could now try to reclaim the children that had come to be her own.

At the courthouse, pandemonium still ruled. Braun and the police ushered the Van Iseghems into a conference room to let them compose themselves before facing the media outside. But the family was inconsolable. For Melanie, this was like finding Elizabeth's body all over again; she had just been murdered again. Melanie had sworn to her sister's spirit that justice would be done, and she had failed. How could she live with that? Rick would be free, allowed to walk out of jail as if he really were innocent. She could not reconcile that with her idea of a just God.

The Van Iseghems had done everything right, and this was what they got for it?

The police were almost as devastated as the family. The grief and strain showed in Mike Miller's eyes and face as he repeated, "I can't believe it's over. I can't believe it's over." Hardened detectives could not stop the tears that rolled down their cheeks.

Finally, everyone decided to go to Mary's to grieve together. As the group left the building, they were mobbed by reporters and TV cameras. Melanie offered the most aggressive response, refusing to restrain her outrage. "How can they say he's not guilty?" she screamed into the microphones. "He has to live with this. When he dies, he'll burn in hell for what he did!"

When asked about Elizabeth's children, Melanie's eyes narrowed even more intensely and she delivered what everyone knew was her own death vow: "He'll never get them."

Don Wolff offered reporters a simple analysis of the verdict; the state's witnesses were "all liars" and the jurors had recognized them as such. He had been convinced there was not enough evidence to justify a guilty verdict for first-degree murder but had been concerned that the jurors might convict on second-degree.

What he did not say then and would not disclose until later—although still rather obliquely—was that, ever since jury selection, he had harbored serious hopes of, at the least, a hung jury, and even perhaps an acquittal. Without identifying DeCaro by name—referring only to a recent high-profile, murder-for-hire case that led to a truly shocking verdict—Wolff later would disclose to a reporter for the *Riverfront Times* in St. Louis that he had seated the jury he wanted. His point man on the panel had wanted desperately to be excused from serving, but the prosecutor had refused. The fuming juror was really "ticked off" at the prosecutor, Wolff said. "That angry guy ended up being the foreman." Learning to pick a jury—even reading the body language of potential panelists—is a science that every lawyer should study carefully, Wolff advised from experience.

A few hours after the verdict, the TV cameras followed a gaunt and characteristically emotionless Rick—his mother holding one arm and his sister the other—as he was released from the county jail, a free man for the first time in thirty months. As other family members pushed him through the crowd of reporters toward a waiting car, Rick's sole comment was, "I only want to get my children as soon as possible."

His brother Dan offered this to the *St. Louis Post-Dispatch:* "We've been through so much. We haven't been able to grieve our sister-in-law's death. . . . It was tearing our family apart, not knowing. We want to be a family again."

The jurors told reporters that they had decided during deliberations not to comment about their verdict. They refused to answer questions when they arrived at their motel in St. Charles. But forty-five minutes later, the foreman relented, telling reporters he had decided that the public deserved some sort of explanation. What he offered was pretty basic: the prosecutors just had not proved their case beyond a reasonable doubt. And, being from the Kansas City area, none of the jurors had known that another man had been convicted and sentenced to die as DeCaro's trigger man.

Melanie had to go home to be alone with John for a while before she could join everyone else at Mary's. Within minutes, however, the phone began to ring. A unfamiliar woman offered her sympathy; she remembered how she had felt when the man who killed her brother was acquitted. Even one of the alternate jurors called to apologize; she was in tears, too, as she described confronting the other jurors and telling them how disgusted she was with their verdict. She had even refused to ride back to Kansas City with them on the bus. She was flying home. Two of the male alternates who agreed with her had almost come to blows with some of the jurors, the woman added.

As the night passed, Melanie could not escape the feeling that she had let Mary down, as well as Elizabeth. Mary was taking care of the children; it had been Melanie's mission to get justice for Rick and thereby help Mary keep the children. That was not what had happened in that courtroom today.

While the family was gathered at Mary's that night to cry and discuss this catastrophe, Rick called from a celebration party with his family. He wanted only to speak to the children; he did not know when he would see them.

Back in the quiet, lovely subdivision where the DeCaros had lived—where their old home now belonged to a new family and was painted brown to cover its past, where Liz DeCaro was remembered fondly with love—the people were unhappy. A bedsheet proclaiming their sentiments appeared on a large barricade at some street repairs.

The sign said simply, JUSTICE FAILED FOR LIZ.

It was a quiet protest on this night, but those who remembered were not about to let it rest there. They had loved Elizabeth too much. They didn't know how far they could take this, but they knew they had to speak out. They immediately began making protest signs and rallying the troops. They soon targeted the courthouse. They would make their feelings about this grave injustice known as soon as possible—and very directly.

Georgianna found herself in a darker world than she had imagined possible. Her heart had broken when Elizabeth died, but this new outrage seemed to have pushed Elizabeth and her spirit even farther away. The blow was so crushing that Georgianna had not even been able to cry yet. She would not find tears for three days, until she attended an old friend's funeral, and the dam burst. The flustered cop who would stop this weeping woman for speeding on her way home would send her off with only a warning.

But on the night of this godforsaken verdict, Georgianna tried desperately to find some light in this world that seemed nothing but black. She could not. Somehow she found the strength to write in her journal, describing the disaster that had befallen them and recognizing the new threat: they were now in for a fight to keep Rick from taking his children away from Mary. Georgianna spoke directly to Elizabeth again.

"Give me the strength and the will to make that happen. Show me the way. Guide me and guide those helping us to right this wrong. He is guilty. God knows that. Elizabeth, you know more about this than anyone here on Earth. I know that your spirit is very troubled, but we will fight to make this turn out right. I love you, darling, and we will triumph over this. Help us to do it."

When Georgianna noticed that evening that the grandfather clock in her dining room had wound down and stopped, she decided to turn this favorite clock into a symbol. She would not rewind it, would not bring it back to life, until Rick had been imprisoned or executed. After all, this clock was a gift to Georgianna and Jim from their children—a gift delivered through a plan led by Elizabeth. The clock now would remain a silent, still witness to the injustice that had been done in Elizabeth's name that day, and it would not record another second of time in the Van Iseghems' lives until justice had been served.

PART FOUR

PART FOUR

SEVENTY-ONE

A dark and haggard Rick DeCaro looked uncomfortable and out of place on the elegant white sofa in his lawyer's expensively decorated living room. But as the TV cameras rolled and the reporters scribbled on their notepads on this Thursday, the newly freed man sent a message to those he knew were listening: he had every right to take back his children and reestablish his family now that a jury had confirmed what he had been saying all along. "I'm an innocent man, and it's been proven," he announced in his first comments to the public.

The day after the earthshaking acquittal, Rick sat for a series of interviews at Wolff's house. Wearing a green T-shirt and jeans, he offered monotone answers to a variety of predictable questions.

How did he feel about the Van Iseghems, the former relatives so convinced of his guilt and so outspoken about it?

"I'm not bitter towards them at all. I love them all very much, out of respect for Elizabeth and my children. I can't force anybody to love me back."

Had he talked to his children?

Yes, he said, offering something approximating a slight grin for the first time; he hoped to get them back by next week. "They're all very excited, and I explained to them that it might be a few days yet."

Did he have any thoughts about his late wife, now that the trial was over?

"I miss her very much—very much. I would just tell her that I love her very much, and I'm just going to do everything for all those children like we had planned."

His detached nature had kicked in. "*Those* children"? Why hadn't he said "*My* children"?

A reporter asked why someone had murdered Rick's wife.

"I don't think anybody wanted to kill Elizabeth. I think they were there to get whatever they could get—to rob the house. Everybody thought the family was going to the lake."

Did he know Daniel Basile?

"I never knew that name—Basile. He was a customer and he was Craig Wells's brother. That's all I knew."

What about the life insurance on Elizabeth?

Wolff fielded that one. Rick had never made any claim on those benefits, and it had been his position since the start that he hadn't even known if the brand-new policy was in effect when Elizabeth died.

Rick was not the only one of Elizabeth's survivors being interviewed that day. The media had also shown up at Mary's house; she wanted them to leave, but Margie and Melanie took advantage of the opportunity to vow that they would never forgive Rick and would fight forever to keep those children safe in the Van Iseghems' arms and custody.

At Wolff's house, Rick was asked for a reaction to that.

"I don't think that's right, and I really think it's a shame. They're not thinking about Elizabeth at all. Elizabeth would never want them to act like that." He suggested the Van Iseghems were being motivated by "their greed or something."

That was the cut that outraged the Van Iseghems the most. *Their* greed? Rick's greed had taken Elizabeth's life, and he had the gall now to make such an idiotic remark about "their greed" because they wanted to care properly for his children?

One TV reporter even challenged Rick on that comment. "They might argue that you never thought of Elizabeth."

"That's totally untrue. That's very untrue. I loved Elizabeth very much."

Very convincing indeed.

What would Rick do now?

"Focus on the children, is the main thing. I've got a couple of job offers. I'll just pick out what's the best one, where I can be home with the children as much as possible."

Wolff was asked about the charge of theft by deceit still pending against Rick for the van job. Wolff doubted it would be pursued now. And even if it were, the worst sentence would be less than the thirty months Rick already had served.

Then Wolff himself made some news. Rick DeCaro's case would be the last capital case for this veteran distinguished and respected barrister. He was no longer comfortable carrying the burden of someone else's life in his hands. And he was tired now. He had even sought medical attention during the end of the trial, fearing he was having a heart attack. He never slept much when a life depended on him; he kept asking himself if he had done enough each day to justify going to bed.

Wolff also confirmed the reports that death threats had been made against him and his client. Yes, many people across the St. Louis area were incredibly unhappy with what had happened in that courtroom.

SEVENTY-TWO

Ed Dowd walked down the hallway and went into Tom Dittmeier's office early Thursday morning. Dowd held up a copy of the morning paper and pointed to the headline.

"Did you see this? Is there anything we can do about it? This is a travesty."

Tom Dittmeier was nodding in agreement. He had just finished reading about the jury's acquittal of Rick DeCaro the afternoon before and, if Dowd hadn't come to see him, Dittmeier would have been dropping in on Dowd.

"Yeah, I saw it, and I was thinking about talking to you. If there is life insurance involved, as they say here, I think we should take a look at it."

Dowd nodded enthusiastically. "Good, Tom. See if there's anything we can do."

No one else in the St. Louis area could know what had

just happened in the St. Louis offices of Edward L. Dowd Jr., the U.S. attorney for the Eastern District of Missouri. In a conversation that lasted barely seconds with his chief trial lawyer, assistant U.S. attorney Thomas E. Dittmeier, he had just revved the engines of the federal government and aimed it directly at Rick DeCaro.

Tom Dittmeier had handled some of the most dramatic, headline-grabbing prosecutions in the St. Louis area for the last twenty-five years. At just fifty years old, he had an amazing record of convictions and a reputation as a direct, hardworking, professional prosecutor. A man of few words outside the courtroom, he had the look, build, and style of someone with substantial time in the amateur boxing ring— another telling page of his résumé. Few defense attorneys wanted to go ten rounds with Tom Dittmeier; a knockout was virtually assured, and Dittmeier would inevitably be the one standing when the final bell rang. Missouri's attorney general once compared him to Marshal Matt Dillon on *Gunsmoke*—an apt description.

The Republican had begun his career in 1969 as an assistant prosecutor in St. Louis County, becoming chief trial attorney and staying until 1976. He moved to the City of St. Louis as a special prosecutor and rose to the position of chief trial lawyer for the city's prosecuting attorney. In 1981 he was appointed U.S. attorney for the Eastern District by President Ronald Reagan and built an impressive record before his controversial replacement in 1990. Few people bought the claim by Republican U.S. Senator John Danforth that he was merely going along with President George Bush's desire to field a new team of prosecutors across the country. Many concluded that Dittmeier was terminated for offending Big Business with his prosecution of the Emerson Electric Company. The company pleaded guilty to submitting phony, inflated cost estimates to the Defense Department for four military contracts; Emerson paid the government $14 million in civil claims and a $40,000 criminal fine. Danforth denied that the company had lobbied for Dittmeier's replacement, but the rumor persisted.

Dittmeier was succeeded by Edward Higgins and then

spent some time in private practice—shunning criminal defense work and serving as a special prosecutor across the St. Louis area, including St. Charles County. That lasted until November 1993, when President Bill Clinton named a new U.S. attorney—Ed Dowd, the son of a former St. Louis circuit attorney who had run for governor. The night Dowd got the appointment, one of the first calls he made was to Tom Dittmeier. Ever a classy guy, Dittmeier happily returned to the job that fit him so well; he became Dowd's chief trial prosecutor.

So, in September 1994 when a misguided jury set Rick DeCaro free, Ed Dowd and Tom Dittmeier were ready to move. They were no strangers to tough cases and the legal twists involved in flexing the jurisdictional muscles of the federal government. Dittmeier had seen just about every kind of case imaginable. He had won mail-fraud convictions against a serial, murder-for-profit killer—Dr. Glennon Englemann, a seemingly goodhearted dentist who got his girlfriends to marry men that the good doctor would then kill for their life insurance, and for the sport of it.

One of Dittmeier's biggest cases was his prosecution of the members of the Leisure gang, who waged a bloody three-year war on their organized-crime enemies. And while serving as a special prosecutor for Tim Braun, Dittmeier delivered justice in the murder of pop singer Walter Scott. Scott's widow pleaded guilty of hindering the prosecution of her boyfriend and eventual husband, James Williamson Sr., who was convicted of killing his own wife and then Scott.

And now Dittmeier had set his sights on Rick DeCaro.

Some miles away on this horrible Thursday morning, the Van Iseghem family had gathered again—but this time to work. It was moving day for the kitchen at Georgianna's catering business. Everyone showed up to help her relocate to a new building and to display their faith that God had a plan and that life went on, no matter how heavy the burdens became.

SEVENTY-THREE

The crowd that began the protest outside the St. Charles County Courthouse at noon Friday soon grew to at least fourscore. Their numbers seemed even greater as they lined the sidewalks outside the modern red-brick-and-white-stone building. The focal point was the family of Elizabeth De-Caro, led by Georgianna, who carried a large portrait of her daughter.

JUSTICE MUST PREVAIL IN HELL—IT SURE HASN'T HAPPENED HERE, one of the dozens of hand-lettered signs read. Another proclaimed, WOMEN HAVE NO RIGHTS—DEAD OR ALIVE. The best sign referred to the strangely similar case that was awaiting trial in Los Angeles. In an eerily appropriate prediction, the sign read, "O.J. HAVE WE GOT A JURY FOR YOU!" He wouldn't need it. He would have a very similar jury of his own.

The protest signs were carried by Elizabeth's friends, neighbors, and relatives, who could find no better word than "outrage" to describe this acquittal. Melanie, Mary, Jimmy, Margie, Theresa, Randy—they all were there with Jim and Georgianna to honor Elizabeth and decry the system that had spawned this verdict. As they took their turns in front of the TV cameras, they called for changes in laws that banned the use of evidence that could assist jurors in reaching just verdicts while giving advantages to defendants. Jimmy Van Iseghem's anger erupted as he demanded that the system provide prosecutors the tools they needed to deliver justice.

Forty-five minutes into the protest, everyone was surprised to see Tim Braun come outside to the plaza at the curved front of the building—carrying his own posters. One was a chart of evidence he had prepared for the trials of Rick DeCaro and Dan Basile and the other listed the most-asked questions about the verdict. He focused on the chart, which showed several incriminating statements by witnesses that had been used against Basile but had been banned by Judge Lohmar in Rick's trial—on motions to suppress by Wolff. Braun found sympathetic ears as he told the crowd that he had done everything he could, only to be frustrated by an imported jury that could not be told about Basile's conviction; the law prohibited that too.

Braun admitted that the credibility of some witnesses was a problem; they were associated with Basile or had criminal records of their own. Trying a murder case was always hard, he explained, because the state's best witness is, by definition, already dead. He explained that the Van Iseghems and Chief King had opposed a plea bargain for Rick. Going to trial was always a roll of the dice, and this time the state had lost.

Wolff would respond later that probing the possibility of a plea bargain did not admit guilt; it was standard in all cases, especially in a capital case. He emphasized that he had spoken to Braun before he had even broached the subject with Rick; therefore, no guilt could be inferred by Wolff's overture.

During the protest, the Van Iseghems sent a message to Judge Lohmar in the courthouse and were surprised when he agreed to see them. While Braun addressed the crowd outside, the relatives of the victim crowded into Lohmar's chambers. He explained graciously that his rulings had been based on the laws of Missouri. Each time someone asked why a piece of evidence had been excluded, Lohmar offered the same answer: it's the law. Evidence that was proper against Basile was sometimes improper against Rick. Different cases, different circumstances, different applications of the law.

As they prepared to leave, someone asked the judge's opinion of the verdict. He smiled wanly and answered, "I can't say. But if I did, we all would not be here right now."

The Van Iseghems accepted that as a sign that he agreed with them about the performance of the jury in his court. It was at least some comfort on this painful day.

The march around the courthouse was not the only protest. The radio waves and coffee shops were filled with complaints about the jurors. How incompetent and mindless could they be? How could they ignore what had seemed to everyone outside the courtroom to be an overwhelming, doubt-destroying mountain of evidence?

Some of the protests were more personal. In addition to the death threats against Rick DeCaro and Don Wolff, people angrily called for boycotts of Wolff's radio jazz show to denounce his role in what so many saw as an inexcusable injustice.

Reporters were tapping their sources to learn what they could about the jurors' deliberations. Nine-to-three for acquittal on the first ballot was the report. Two women had held out for conviction as long as they could. Calls to jurors' homes failed to draw any comments, but the word in St. Charles was that jurors had told court bailiffs the verdict would have been the same even if Basile had testified against Rick.

One report that had never surfaced until now described an unfortunate pretrial coincidence. On the Sunday before the trial—with the jurors already in St. Charles and sequestered—they went en masse to a morning service at Judge Lohmar's church. The minister delivered a sermon on mercy, using as an example a murder case from Florida— a woman whose four children were murdered had forgiven the killer. Not exactly the message some sources would have hoped for on that day for that special part of the congregation.

Braun would meet with some of the jurors a month after the verdict when he went to Kansas City on business. After several hours with them, he concluded that the jurors had missed the big picture; they had allowed Wolff to bog them down in the details—picking apart the case, looking for tiny contradictions. A criminal case has to be seen as a whole; jurors who focus too much on detail may blind themselves to an overview of the entire, completed project. The "forest and the trees" cliché applied here.

Not far from the demonstration at the courthouse on Friday, a quite different event was under way—a gathering at a cafe for the DeCaros and their supporters to discuss the acquittal. Reporters found Don Wolff there to seek his response to the protest and Braun's comments. The prosecutor should not be using a judge's rulings or a jury's performance to justify a verdict, Wolff said, and he was offended that Braun would do that. Wolff insisted that Lohmar's rulings had been absolutely correct under the law. Statements about, or by, coconspirators were inadmissible if they were not made in furtherance of the conspiracy, he explained.

The gathering for the DeCaros did not have a complete cast that day. Rick was absent; he had stayed away, on Wolff's advice.

SEVENTY-FOUR

Two or three days after the verdict, Chief David King realized he had to do something in response to this injustice. He had been unable to sleep; knowing that Rick DeCaro was free chased away all hope of rest. From that first night, he had spent a lot of time talking to his wife, looking for a way to make sense out of it all. He had dedicated his life to upholding justice, and now he wondered how something so patently unjust could happen? What was wrong with the system? How could something so clear to everyone else be shrouded in such fog for the twelve people in the jury box?

Tom O'Connor was suffering much the same anguish over only the second loss of his career. But his pain was intensified by some spiteful telephone calls. "O'Connor, you screwed it up," was the kindest of the anonymous comments. He knew they were coming from other cops, his colleagues who for years had been rubbed the wrong way by his approach and perhaps by his success. But he found it hard to believe that any cop could take perverse pleasure in this verdict and use it to batter O'Connor out of personal spite.

Finally, King decided that even futile efforts were better

than none. He called U.S. attorney Edward Dowd Jr. "Ed, I'm begging you," King said, "please take a look at this and see if there is something you can do." The cautious Dowd held his cards close; he said only that he would talk to Tom Dittmeier about it. Even that vague offer was enough to send spirits soaring. Detective Mike Miller could not resist the urge to call Melanie Enkelmann and tell her the news—under an oath of secrecy. She was almost speechless; for the first time in days she felt a tug of hope. The word spread quickly among the Van Iseghems, and they were thrilled. Georgianna found it difficult to get too excited, worrying that the same system that acquitted Rick once could blow the case again.

Dittmeier called King and arranged to spend a couple of days in St. Charles quietly going through the file. When he finished, he told King only, "I think we might have something." Within a week, however, Dittmeier had concluded that there was sufficient evidence to establish federal jurisdiction and justify an investigation. Rick DeCaro had mailed applications for insurance benefits from the theft of the van and the loss of its contents; that got federal authorities into the game—with a bid of mail fraud.

King was thrilled by even this thread of hope. He called O'Connor and told him of Dittmeier's interest. O'Connor wanted to shout for joy. Among prosecutors, Dittmeier was O'Connor's hero. The Toms had known each other for years, had worked together on the Englemann serial killer case, and still worked out together at the gym. If this case could be won, O'Connor knew, Dittmeier was the man who could do it.

SEVENTY-FIVE

By the end of September 1994, Rick DeCaro had tipped his hand. He had hired one of the best and most aggressive family-law attorneys in the region—Margo Green—and she had filed a petition seeking restoration of full custody of his kids. The order granting temporary custody of the children to Mary and Phil Cordes should be dissolved, Green argued. Judge Sandra Farragut-Hemphill of the St. Louis County Juvenile Court set the first hearing for December 15.

The kids began formal visits with their father a week after the verdict: one-hour sessions in a public park, supervised by a social worker from the Department of Family Services. Patrick had refused to go to the first one—favoring his soccer game instead. Their grandmother thought all four of the children seemed less excited about their hour with Rick than might have been expected; Patrick and Rachel were noticeably uninterested in the gifts he had brought for each of them. Later that night Erin was unable to sleep, crying to Mary and Phil for what seemed hours about her fear that someone was going to break into the house and take her away. The Cordeses did not need doctorates in psychology to interpret that.

Rick, now working at a different automotive garage, rented a home in Florissant, not far from Mary and Phil. That brought him what was probably a surprising and bitter taste of public sentiment. He was greeted in his new neighborhood with direct and blunt signs protesting the intrusion of a murderer into what had been a safe, secure community. The Van Iseghems found it difficult not to take satisfaction in that. "He can't fool the public," Georgianna said.

His new proximity bothered Mary. She began to fear that he might even drive up in front of her home someday and simply demand the immediate return of his children—his own flesh and blood. A new and terrifying nightmare had begun to visit the Van Iseghems, especially Mary and Phil. This wasn't simply about the devastating loss of Elizabeth's children to someone they all felt was purely evil. This was about the loss of four children who had become the Cordeses' own; Patrick and Rachel and Bill and Erin were part of the family now. And they would not be lost without one hell of a fight.

By October, the friends and loving residents of the community who had come forward after Elizabeth's death stepped up again. Jackie Balunek—Elizabeth's neighbor who was so outraged by the verdict—began a tireless effort to protect the children and seek justice for Elizabeth. Jackie led two lines of attack. She organized a fund-raiser that brought in about $2,000 to help finance the court fight to keep the kids where they belonged—under Van Iseghem wings; another event a few months later would raise twice that much. On the advice of Frank Vatterott, the trusted Van Iseghem attorney, the family turned to expert lawyer Bill Grant to protect them against Rick's court assault. The cost of this war would be at least $10,000.

Frank Vatterott also urged the Van Iseghems to file a wrongful-death lawsuit against Rick. Not for the money, the outraged Vatterott said, but just to force Rick to face another jury that might have enough sense to find him liable for his actions. All of the evidence from the criminal case, and even some that wasn't allowed there, could be used against him. That would have created another amazing similarity to the case against O.J. Simpson, who was acquitted a year after Rick. The Van Iseghems liked the idea of another chance at a court ruling in their favor and putting the evidence in front of the public again; they would give it serious thought. Only the events of the next few months would prevent them from proceeding.

Meanwhile, Jackie Balunek began printing and circulating petitions calling for U.S. attorney Edward Dowd Jr. to open an investigation. "All possible rights were bestowed on Rick DeCaro, while the system raped Elizabeth DeCaro of her rights," the petition charged. It respectfully asked Dowd to file charges alleging that Rick had violated Elizabeth's civil rights by plotting and carrying out her murder.

Dowd was not yet ready to disclose that he already was investigating; his spokeswoman said only that a civil rights case was unlikely. That kind of prosecution required circumstances similar to the recent federal prosecutions of the police in Los Angeles who had beaten motorist Rodney King in 1991, she explained.

By the time the petitions and hundreds of letters calling for the prosecution of Rick began arriving at Dowd's office, the federal investigation was well under way. With assistance from Detective Mike Miller, the FBI, and others, Dittmeier was assembling what he needed to pursue Rick—transcripts of earlier hearings and trials, a two-foot stack of police reports, and records of insurance claims already filed by Rick.

And Tom O'Connor was working behind the scenes, in his own way. He was not a witness to anything that would help Dittmeier, so he was looking for other avenues. Chatting with friendly investigative TV reporter Jamie Allman, O'Connor suggested that condemned killer Dan Basile might be receptive to an interview. Allman jumped at the suggestion, and the cop even offered some insightful questions to ask Basile. On October 20, KMOV-TV, Channel 4 taped an interview with Basile on death row at the Potosi Correctional Center. The condemned man looked into the camera and refused to point the finger of guilt directly at Rick DeCaro. But he did the next best thing; he admitted that Rick had hired him to steal both of the DeCaro vehicles.

"Somebody set me up," Basile told Allman. "I was doing an insurance job on the vehicles and basically, from there, everything fell my way."

That might not put Rick behind bars, O'Connor thought, but it could help the Van Iseghems retain custody of the kids in family court.

In late October, the Van Iseghems briefly had hope for even more help from Basile. He had called Doug Meyer and Iva Hanson from prison to tell them "everything," but then he stuck to his story that he had done nothing but steal the vehicles for Rick. Rick hired him to kill Elizabeth, Basile admitted, but he still denied pulling the trigger. Could that be enough to torpedo Rick's hopes of getting his kids back? Georgianna hoped to turn the custody battle into a retrial of the criminal case, perhaps proving—at least in that forum—that Rick's murder conspiracy made him undeserving of the children he had made motherless. The Van Iseghems even heard that Basile's lawyer would allow him to testify about the murder plot with Rick in the custody hearing.

The Van Iseghems learned about Basile's comments through Melanie's latest detective work. She not only had arranged for people to watch Rick's new house in Florissant for any suspicious signs, but she was digging for information about the bank accounts he was opening. When she picked the kids up at Rick's before he was home one afternoon, Melanie even took a quick tour of the house. She could find only one photograph of Rick and Elizabeth—a family shot that the Van Iseghems also had in their album, except they had cut Rick out of it. His refusal to provide even a photographic symbol that Elizabeth had once been part of his life angered Melanie enough that she anonymously mailed him a nice picture of his late wife. She carefully wiped off any fingerprints, and typed a little note that explained to Rick that the sender knew he didn't have a photo in the house because he couldn't stand to see what he had done. "When you die and go to Heaven," the letter added, "what big-time lawyer will you get to defend you then?"

But perhaps Melanie's most devious effort was to convince Iva Hanson to tape a couple of telephone calls between Basile and Doug Meyer. The tapes yielded little that was really exciting, but it was interesting to hear that Basile was angry about rotting on death row while Rick was free and fighting for custody of the kids. Despite hopes that Basile might be angry enough to turn on Rick—at least to help the family with the custody case—it didn't work out. Before long, Basile's lawyer decided there would be no testimony anywhere about anything while the appeal was pending.

Meanwhile, Braun's loss of the DeCaro case was haunting him as election day drew near. Republican William Hannah, trying to avenge his loss to Braun four years earlier, said DeCaro was Braun's albatross. The tactic didn't work; on November 8, Braun drew 53 percent of the votes to win reelection.

SEVENTY-SIX

The Van Iseghems should prepare, lawyer Bill Grant began warning them in December, for the likelihood that Judge Farragut-Hemphill would award Rick DeCaro full custody of his children. In the eyes of the law, he was an innocent man, presumed the best caretaker of his own children. The Van Iseghems' certain knowledge that he was guilty of the premeditated murder of the children's mother, and even the community's outrage at the jury's disgraceful miscarriage of justice, would play no role in the custody decision. A judge's order sending those four kids back to their father's house could come as soon as the first hearing—December 15.

Mary and Phil were almost frantic with worry. Mary became so paranoid that she was convinced Rick would arrange surveillance on her and her family; she became afraid to sip an occasional beer, worrying that Rick would use it against them in court.

Georgianna could not imagine what kind of lives the children would have with this man. She found herself confused almost beyond coping. She and the others had been praying that Rick would face federal charges soon; but even that caused concern. How would another round of charges and jail for their father affect the children? Which was the lesser evil? The greater good? She could find no comforting answer. She even wondered if they should all just do what Rick arrogantly expected—pretend nothing had ever happened and just go on with life as it had been before March 6, 1992. Every time that thought slipped into Georgianna's mind, she chased it out. My God, she would think, the man killed my daughter!

After nine months of worry, the hearing in December brought unexpected good news. Under law, no one but the Cordeses and Rick could attend the private sessions in juvenile court; the welfare of the children demanded confidentiality. Georgianna stewed all day, anxious to hear the results. Finally, word came that the judge had extended temporary custody of the children to Mary and Phil for another ninety days. Rick had to undergo psychological evaluation, but he would get the kids for visitation every Thursday night and every third weekend until the next hearing, on March 9. "A glorious surprise," Georgianna pronounced the decision. There was no way to know what the judge was thinking, but someone suggested that officials from the Department of Family Services had expressed displeasure with the interview that Rick had granted a television station the night before. The Van Iseghems heard that the judge was furious, despite the fact that Rick's interview was a response to Basile's appearance on TV earlier. Regardless of the cause, the judge was in no mood to have the custody of these children become the media cause célèbre that the murder case had been. She imposed a gag order on everyone—all relatives on both sides—forbidding them from talking to anyone about what happened behind the courtroom doors.

The winter months passed slowly. The Van Iseghems were getting fairly regular updates on the feds' progress, but the pace seemed so slow that Georgianna's faith began to waver. "Please, God," she prayed every day, "let something happen soon." Tom Dittmeier assured her that an FBI agent was working on it full-time and that Dittmeier was dealing directly with the Justice Department in Washington to get the approval he needed to prosecute this complicated case.

Meanwhile, Georgianna worried that Rick's appearances with the rest of the family at his children's events were sending the wrong message to the community—that the Van Iseghems believed Rick was innocent and had accepted him back into the fold. Nothing could be further from the truth; they simply tolerated his presence for the good of the children. But even that did not mean they had to be too civil. When Rick called the Cordeses' house one night to demand an unscheduled visit with the kids, the easygoing Phil finally popped his cork. After an angry exchange, Phil told Rick to "go to hell" and slammed down the phone. At Erin's first communion some time later, Rick would approach the family pew at the church and ask glibly if there was room for him. Georgianna was shocked; he actually expected everyone to slide down and let him sit right in the middle of them. Phil came to the rescue again. "Yeah," he drawled as he motioned toward the other end of the pew, "if you want to walk around and sit on that end." Rick was furious at the public slight; everyone else was proud of Phil.

When the second custody hearing rolled around on March 9—three years and three days after Elizabeth's murder—the judge was upset to see the media camped in full force outside the St. Louis County Courthouse. How could they have known about this supposedly secret hearing? The judge tried ordering them to leave, only to be informed that their lawyers had advised them that they had every right to watch from the public streets. But because of the gag order, they got no interviews; they had to settle for a few feet of videotape of Rick getting out of his car.

In the courtroom, the judge received a psychological report that was less than flattering to Rick. The Van Iseghems would learn later that Rick's responses to testing had been so defensive that the results were significantly weakened. He seemed to perceive any admission of psychological problems as a sign of weakness or inadequacy. He had even insisted that his relationship with his children had not changed over the last three years. The Van Iseghems learned that the psychologist concluded that Rick was not sensitive to the children's emotions or concerns about what had happened, and that he saw things very differently from the way they did. The family was told that the report did conclude, however, that Rick was committed to being a good parent.

Georgianna was fascinated to hear that the report cited an incident between Patrick and Bill that had concerned the rest of the family. Patrick had accidentally shot Bill in the hand with the BB gun that Rick had given Patrick for Christmas. Patrick was terribly upset, crying and fretting that he might have hurt Bill more seriously. Rick failed to see why the boy should be so upset, and Rick reportedly wasn't receptive to the psychologist's suggestion that Patrick's extreme reaction was related to the fact that his mother had been shot to death. Georgianna was pleased to learn that the psychologist agreed with the Van Iseghems that the incident was another indication that Rick wasn't sensitive to the way the children felt about their mother's death, or their father's alleged role in it.

Continued therapy for all five DeCaros was recommended by the psychologist.

But the bottom line was the question. And, for the second time, the judge issued a ninety-day extension of temporary custody to Mary and Phil; a third hearing was set for June 9, 1995. The judge's order banned the Cordeses and the children from fund-raising efforts using the DeCaro name, and contained a stern warning about any leaks about this hearing or any other related matter from this case. Any violation would lead to an intense investigation, and the judge would haul everyone onto the witness stand to determine the source of the leak.

The Van Iseghems were grateful for another temporary victory, but they all knew they were running out of time. Unless the federal investigation bore fruit soon, Rick would win his claim to the children. As did all of the Van Iseghems, Georgianna found that thought unbearable, so unjust as to defy description. She still could not understand a court system that could free a murderer everyone knew was guilty and then try so mightily to reunite him with the children that everyone knew would be better off with Mary and Phil.

In early May, the Van Iseghems learned a couple of other interesting pieces of information about Rick's return to the outside world. He had begun bringing Cathy Dillon along on his visits with the children. They went out for pizza together, and Patrick had even watched Cathy's two kids along with his own brother and sisters when Rick and Cathy went out together. Erin had offered a typically innocent remark to Mary: "I'm going to have a new mommy." It seemed, she explained, that Daddy's friend, Cathy, was always with them lately. That would have been surprising enough, but there was more. Cathy was pregnant.

SEVENTY-SEVEN

Federal agents began serving subpoenas for the federal grand jury investigating Rick DeCaro and Daniel Basile the week of April 27, and Georgianna would have paid very good money to see the surprised faces of those who received these greetings.

Melanie Enkelmann and Mary Cordes had met with Tom Dittmeier in March for a long session to go over each and every detail of Elizabeth's life in the year before her death. The prosecutor listened carefully, and the questions he asked seemed to the sisters to be the right ones. He never promised them anything, but he offered his immediate analysis of how to prosecute this case and what he saw at the heart of the plot to murder Elizabeth.

"This is the story," Dittmeier mused, "of a man who met another woman and wanted out of his marriage. It happens all the time."

That was the kernel, the basic truth, that had been glossed over the last time this story was told in court. The sisters were shocked by the simplicity and the honest truth of it. This wasn't a complicated case about high finances and deep debt. It was a rudimentary case about a man obsessed with his mistress, finished with his wife, and determined to keep his children, home, and everything else he had worked for. The only thing in Rick DeCaro's life that had been expendable was Elizabeth.

The grand jury summoned the witnesses for testimony in the U.S. district court in downtown St. Louis on May 8. The investigation remained a secret until then, then word began to slip out and the media picked it up. Stories hit the TV and the newspaper. By then publicity was no problem for Dittmeier; his investigation was too far along to be damaged. And he had already talked with Cathy Dillon's husband, Jeff. He told the prosecutor he would do anything he could to get Rick DeCaro out of his life.

The day after a *Post-Dispatch* story on the new investigation, Mary had a state social worker come to the house to tell the kids what was happening. Georgianna was there for support, but she was surprised again by how little the children reacted to the news. She still didn't know what to make of it. She knew Rachel had been having a very hard time dealing with the renewed and intensified contact with her father and the possibility of returning permanently to his house. Patrick was angry about that too. But Georgianna still thought the kids were handling the awful situation with amazing calm.

Mary had been a rock, but Georgianna knew her daughter was suffering terribly from the strain; she was even breaking out in hives from dealing with Rick. She was the one who spent the most time with him, at all of the sports and other events. When Rick arrived, the rest of the crowd often moved away and stared at Mary as she sat alone with this pariah; Melanie even ribbed Mary about her "new best friend." But the real problem was that he was becoming more demanding about unscheduled visits and weekends with the kids, often interrupting the Cordeses' plans. When Mary once refused his demand, Rick released his anger in that cold, cold voice, warning that she would be sorry; he wouldn't forget, and he would get even. Mary took him at his word.

The big news for the investigation arrived on May 17, when the Justice Department notified Tom Dittmeier that he had approval to prosecute Rick DeCaro and Dan Basile. The fact that Basile was already on death row would not be used as an excuse to prevent his prosecution in the federal case, according to the department officials who reviewed the request. To Dittmeier's surprise, he didn't even have to go to Washington to plead his case—though he had been more than ready to do exactly that.

The first issue—concern over double jeopardy—was resolved easily. Although some might see federal charges as trying Rick for the same crime for which he had already been acquitted, this new prosecution involved different jurisdictions—federal versus state—and different crimes. They grew out of the same events, of course, but they involved different acts, which violated different laws in different jurisdictions. The case law was clear—all the way to the U.S. Supreme Court: this was not double jeopardy.

And just as clear was the feds' jurisdiction. Not only did Rick's use of the federal mails to file his insurance claims for the van theft in 1992 establish jurisdiction, but he had been busy since then. In December 1994, three months after his acquittal, Rick had mailed applications for insurance benefits from his homeowner's policy for quite a number of items he said were stolen on the day Elizabeth was murdered.

And he also claimed the $100,000 benefit on her life.

This new activity would improve Dittmeier's position significantly in court later. He now could argue that Rick was involved in an ongoing federal violation. That was an important factor for federal authorities, and Rick's decision in December to try to collect the final proceeds from his plan had played into their hands perfectly. Now his greed would cost him.

When Detective Mike Miller told Chief King that Rick had applied for the life insurance benefits, King was unable to restrain an uncharacteristic "Whoop!" in excitement. He now had real hope that the final piece of the puzzle was in place and the system could try to right itself.

SEVENTY-EIGHT

"Our D-Day," Georgianna wrote in her journal on Wednesday, May 31, 1995.

That afternoon, a federal grand jury in St. Louis indicted Rick DeCaro and Daniel Basile on seven counts—and two of them were whoppers. The big ones were murder for hire and murder conspiracy. Those charges linked Rick and Basile inextricably in the federal system, practically guaranteeing they would be tried together, side by side, facing the same jury at the same time for the same crime. This time, the hit man Rick had hired would be flesh and blood for the jurors, not just a wisp of dark smoke left in the air by a witness's testimony, as in the last trial.

And just as appropriate, as far as the Van Iseghems were concerned, was the possible penalty—life in prison without parole.

The frosting on the cake—insult to Rick's injury—was the grand jury's additional charges. In five counts of mail fraud, the grand jury accused Rick and accomplice Basile of using the mail to file false claims for the benefits from Elizabeth's life insurance, the loss of the Blazer and the van, and the loss of some items that Rick reported missing from the house.

Georgianna got the good news as she and Theresa were visiting Jim at the hospital just three days after angioplasty heart surgery—and three days after Elizabeth's thirty-second birthday. Mary called to fill them in and to add that she was again having the social worker come to the house to talk to the kids.

Dittmeier had called Mary with word of the indictment just five minutes before the kids were to arrive home from school. But Mary still had time to celebrate—jumping up and down in joy after she hung up the phone. The revelry was short-lived. Patrick came home in a few minutes and

Mary broke the news; despite his significant problems with his father, Patrick was devastated. "Why can't they just leave us alone?" he demanded. All of the kids were upset at this newest assault on their battered family. That took some of the joy out of it for Mary and the others, but they still were excited. Finally, Georgianna let herself hope, the family had taken a big step toward justice. But she kept that thought under careful control; the events of the past prevented her from becoming too hopeful.

Detective Mike Miller joined the FBI agent sent to arrest Rick DeCaro about 3:30 P.M. that day. It was a very satisfying moment for the St. Charles officer who had been so wounded by the acquittal. The team drove to Rick's new job and informed him there that he was under arrest. Rick hadn't had a clue this was coming, and he offered a somewhat more noticeable reaction than he had in that motel hallway just over three years earlier. Miller could only describe Rick as "stunned into silence," though still arrogant. After Miller read the sobering and potent charges, the formerly cool character seemed shaken.

He was then swept to the federal courthouse in St. Louis for an appearance before a magistrate judge. Rick—dressed in the uniform of white, short-sleeved shirt and blue work pants—said in that soft voice that he did not have an attorney but would hire one. He was confident there were others—family and friends—who would once again try to help him raise bond to secure his release. The magistrate set the bond at $250,000, and Rick was then whisked away to spend the night in a suburban jail that housed federal prisoners under contract with the government—his first night back in the pokey after an all-too-short eight months of freedom.

U.S. attorney Edward Dowd Jr. and Tom Dittmeier told reporters that the feds had an absolute right to prosecute DeCaro and Basile. "We feel like there is a tremendous amount of evidence that Richard DeCaro and Daniel Basile conspired to murder Elizabeth DeCaro," Dowd announced. "We don't want someone to get away with murder."

The media promptly compared the new indictments to

the famous Rodney King beating case in Los Angeles. When the local courts acquitted the cops in the brutal, videotaped battering of King, the feds had indicted the officers on civil rights violations. Same incident; different offenses. The same principle applied in the DeCaro case.

Georgianna wrote that night: "Thank God for Ed Dowd and Tom Dittmeier. They are my heroes."

Rick's new incarceration was brief. With property posted by his new boss, he made bond and was released by three-thirty the next afternoon. He never missed a beat; by four o'clock, he had picked up the kids at Mary's for his scheduled visitation. But somehow, he just didn't seem as cocky as before.

With Don Wolff declining to take Rick's new case, he turned to one of the rising young Turks of the St. Louis criminal defense bar, Scott N. Rosenblum. Handsome, dark-haired and mustached, flashy, flamboyant, worthy of a *GQ* cover. But Rosenblum was also an experienced, resourceful trial attorney, and this case would be unique and challenging, even for a talented lawyer like him. He faced the daunting task of trying a case that had already been won in spectacular fashion by someone else. With the increased odds against an acquittal in federal court—where the cards seem stacked in the government's favor—the very best Rosenblum could hope for was to equal the accomplishment of his older colleague. But he was a scrapper, and by Thursday afternoon he was fighting back as Rick's new champion. He blasted the charges as perverted examples of the double jeopardy so clearly prohibited by the Fifth Amendment. "We will be attacking this case every step of the way," he vowed.

The Van Iseghems talked back—a little. Georgianna was interviewed by all four local television stations and did her best to keep it low-key. With the children, the DeCaros, and the judge in juvenile court watching, she didn't want to say anything that would damage the family's efforts to keep the kids. Even the Van Iseghems' "victory party" that night was more reserved than might have been expected under the circumstances.

*   *   *

The most important response to Rick's indictment—from the kids—came immediately. They began to show resentment toward the Van Iseghems—especially Mary and Phil. The children obviously were being brainwashed to believe that this federal indictment was the result of the Van Iseghems' vindictiveness. Jimmy Van Iseghem found that particularly ridiculous. How absurd for the DeCaros to believe that Elizabeth's family had the clout to force a federal indictment of an innocent man. Jimmy wondered how the DeCaros could fail to see that Rick alone had put himself back in court.

But nevertheless, the civil war was on.

On Friday, June 16, Judge Farragut-Hemphill awarded custody of the children—for the entire summer—to Rick DeCaro, the man just indicted in their mother's contract killing. From that day until August 17—the week before school would start—the children would live with him. Mary and Phil retained temporary custody, but for the summer they would have to settle for limited visitation—the third Sunday and Monday of the month. Mary actually was not too upset. Some prolonged exposure to their father might be good for the kids. They could use a good dose of reality and revelation about just who this man really was.

Rick had opposed this order; he wanted full, permanent custody right then.

Georgianna learned of the judge's decision while she was visiting Margie in California. As soon as she returned home, she arranged to pick up Erin and take her for ice cream. On the phone, Georgianna had to ask Rick for directions to his house, and she realized that this conversation had been the most "normal" between them for three years and three months. Rick sounded like she remembered him from so long ago—a lifetime ago. And she realized again how very much they had all lost, even this man she detested.

The conversation emphasized something else that worried her. Rick seemed to be the only person in the world who didn't realize how much trouble he was in because of this federal indictment. To Georgianna's sensitive eye and instincts, he seemed to be cruising along with the same casual savoir-faire that had accompanied his dramatic victory nine months ago. She had thought he was crazy before that trial, too. "Well, he was acquitted and we were the fools," she wrote in her journal that night. Did he know something again? Did he have powerful connections somewhere? Did he have, literally, a deal with the Devil?

She also feared the most extreme possibility—that Rick would be so incapable of dealing with a conviction and prison sentence that he might do something harmful to the kids and himself; the potential for a tragic murder/suicide loomed in the back of her mind. Writing directly to her daughter again, she called for help. "Elizabeth, you know how dangerous he is. If there is something to fear, let me know. I won't stand by this time, like I did when you died."

Over the summer, Georgianna was filled with a sense of horror every time she spoke to Rick about picking up the kids. Just the fact that he had custody of them left her deeply depressed. His decision to move into his mother's place in St. Charles—now that she had remarried Rick's father—didn't ease the Van Iseghems' worries. He even enrolled Erin in the third grade for the summer session of the year-round public school there, and that set off the worst series of battles in the entire long, hot summer. Rick and Mary bickered constantly over her refusal to force Erin to go to school on the Mondays that fell during the Cordeses' visitation. By early August Rick was responding by drastically restricting all visits by the Van Iseghems and was even engineering ways to keep the kids, especially Bill, from seeing Mary and Phil on their weekends. When Georgianna complained that the kids were being hurt, Rick explained that he was calling the shots now and that was the way it would be. Mary once enlisted the help of the Department of Family Services, which demanded that Rick deliver Bill to Mary's by no later than Monday morning, even though he supposedly was helping his father paint the house.

Rick had once more reverted to the manipulative, punitive man who had killed Elizabeth.

The last week of Rick's summer custody proved the most

worrisome. On August 21, the kids' counselor called Mary with a concern that Rick was planning to take the kids out of town, keep them past the date he was supposed to return them to Mary, and perhaps never return them. That set off a chain reaction of rapid developments. The counselor called Family Services, which learned that the court's custody order did not bar out-of-town trips. Mary called Dittmeier and he prodded the federal court into action. Under the conditions of Rick's bond, he was required to stay in the St. Louis area; the court ordered him to forgo any trip. Only later did they learn that he had planned to take the kids back to the Lake of the Ozarks—back, in fact, to the same motel where they were when they had learned of their mother's murder. What a sensitive father, everyone marveled. The man didn't have a clue, Melanie cracked.

When Rick's custody ended and he returned the kids to the Cordes home at the end of August, Mary and Phil were surprised by how unaffected they all seemed after the summer of turmoil.

The fall of 1995 started poorly, with the date of Rick's trial delayed until January. Pretrial battles had gone uniformly to the prosecution, however. Rosenblum, joined by Basile's silver-haired federal public defender, Thomas Flynn, had been unsuccessful in their efforts to get the charges dismissed on the double-jeopardy argument. U.S. district judge George F. Gunn Jr. had ruled consistently for Dittmeier—the charges were not double jeopardy. The attorneys couldn't get separate trials for their clients, either, despite their claims of antagonistic defenses. The conspiracy charge, the judge ruled, linked the men properly in a joint trial on their conduct.

Although the Van Iseghems were eager to get the trial under way, Georgianna really didn't mind the delay. She liked the idea of getting through the holidays before facing this new challenge. The family turned down an invitation to appear on the Maury Povich TV show in December to discuss the acquittal of O.J. Simpson. The Van Iseghems wanted to do the show but feared it would be used against them in family court, perhaps even in the coming trial, and certainly by Rick as he bad-mouthed them to the kids.

At the October custody hearing, Rick got even more visitation rights, claiming three of the four weekends a month and every Thursday evening. The order even provided specifically that Rick be allowed to participate in Halloween activities for the children—with the Cordeses. Georgianna was furious and was developing an intense dislike for the judge. Rick's public-relations campaign was incensing her as well. He was telling everyone who would listen that he was doing everything Elizabeth would have wanted to do for the kids. What lies, Georgianna fumed. "God, You should strike him dead," she wrote angrily. "That he could even utter her name is horrific."

SEVENTY-NINE

This third trial in the murder of her daughter filled Georgianna with dread beyond what she had felt before. She knew Rick would be free to roam the courthouse halls, presenting an ever constant discomfort and insult to the family. She found herself fretting about every possible outcome. How could the family survive another acquittal? But what if he were convicted? Could he stay free on bond for months while awaiting sentencing? Or for years, pending an appeal? Would this judge still grant a convicted murderer custody of his kids?

Another slight delay had set the trial for Wednesday, February 7, 1996. Just days before that, the Van Iseghems were shocked again by what they considered a new low, even for Rick: he subpoenaed his own children as witnesses. "Isn't that the most awful thing (besides, of course, murdering their mother) for a father to do?" Georgianna wondered in her journal. And the subpoenas complicated the arrangements for the kids during the trial. Pam Hanley had intended to keep them with her in Ohio, well away from the stress and pain of the courtroom. But now their own father was dragging them back. Rick even announced that he was canceling the trip, forcing Mary to call Family Services again. This time a court order was issued to authorize the kids' time with Pam; Rick was furious that Mary had gone over his head.

The day before the trial was to begin proved Georgianna's belief that the natural order of things—the cosmos, the alignment of the stars, whatever controlled the universe—did not allow anything to be simple for the Van Iseghems. On Tuesday night, hours before efforts to pick a third jury for this case were to start, television stations began running stories about the DeCaro trial. That was bad enough, but Tom Dittmeier learned that the *St. Louis Post-Dispatch* planned a lengthy front-page story about the case on Wednesday morning, just as the jurors would be reporting to court. The article would discuss in detail Rick's acquittal in state court, the controversy over the double-jeopardy issue, his desire to testify in his own defense, and his ongoing battle to win custody of his children. The story quoted Rosenblum as saying, "The kids want to be with him. They are completely supportive of their father and believe in his innocence." Dittmeier's pleas to the editors to avoid contaminating the jury pool by holding the story for a day—until after jury selection—fell on deaf ears. That story was no story the next day; such were the laws of daily journalism.

Georgianna and some of her family waited until Thursday to attend jury selection, and they didn't get a warm welcome. Dittmeier asked them not to come back because of the stir their presence created among the media. But on Friday the news was worse. Dittmeier and Detective Miller called a meeting at Georgianna's house for six o'clock. With Melanie and Mary there too, the officials reluctantly explained that the massive publicity had made selecting a fair and impartial jury in St. Louis impossible. After three days of unsuccessful and frustrating efforts with jurors who knew all about the case, Dittmeier was obligated to seek a change of venue to avoid handing the defense an appeal point if Rick should be convicted. This change also would mean a slight delay and, in turn, that meant that Judge Gunn would run into a scheduling conflict.

So, Dittmeier explained, the situation mandated a new date, a new location, and a new judge. The date would be Monday, February 26, 1995. The location would be Cape Girardeau, the southeastern Missouri town not far from the place where Basile had burned Rick's van—another interesting twist. And the judge would be district judge Stephen N. Limbaugh, the distinguished jurist who also happened to be the uncle of conservative talk-show host Rush Limbaugh—both of them natives of Cape Girardeau. They seemed to have little else in common; the judge was a trim, bright, thoughtful, considerate, impartial, good-humored, and witty man.

But once again the Van Iseghems had to withstand a painful delay. And Mary would have another three weeks of face-to-face meetings with Rick. "My God," she moaned, "will it ever be over?"

EIGHTY

The banner unfurled along the shoulder of Interstate 70 in St. Charles on Monday, February 26, told the story of what was happening some 120 miles to the southeast that morning.

LIZ GETS A SECOND CHANCE, the banner proclaimed proudly and defiantly. Elizabeth DeCaro's friends in the town where she died wanted to be sure everyone remembered what this day was all about.

Sitting in a room in the U.S. district courthouse Georgianna wrote her own sentiment and her own prayer.

"Let the verdict ring out loud and clear! Guilty!"

Jury selection took only a day. Although a burst of early spring warmth sent the temperature in Judge Limbaugh's court soaring above eighty degrees, it didn't seem to affect the jurors' enthusiasm; a lot of the folks around Cape actually wanted to serve on this jury. A marshal at the courthouse told Georgianna that Rick and Scott Rosenblum had been interviewed by the TV station the night before, and it was hard to decide which one was more arrogant. The officer warned that the defense team had better be careful around these country folks; they didn't much go for "city slickers."

That sounded good to the Van Iseghems. But Georgianna and Melanie soon learned that they still would be plagued by a court rule that had haunted them now for years. As prosecution witnesses, they could not sit through the opening statements or the testimony that would begin the next morning—Tuesday, February 27. They wondered why American society seemed unable to resolve this basic, painful clash between a defendant's right to a fair trial and a mother's right to witness justice for her murdered daughter. Melanie told Dittmeier that she desperately wanted to be in that courtroom—a right that she demanded—and he promised to see what he could do. He would come through later, getting special permission for them to attend the rest of the trial.

Throughout that first day, the Van Iseghems thought Rick made a conscious and obvious effort to avoid even a glance toward Basile. Rick looked better than he had for some time; he had regained enough weight that he no longer appeared emaciated, and his dark suit gave him the air of a young businessman. But he still was sitting at the table with Basile. The death-row resident wore a dark jacket and no tie over a white shirt; his long black hair was parted in the middle and pulled back in a ponytail—just as Sue Jenkins had described. The Van Iseghems thought it a glorious sight: Rick paired with a man who could not hide what he was—a crude, low-rent, ex-con hit man.

By Monday evening, seven men and five women had been seated as the jury that would hear the story of these two schemers and would give the Van Iseghems one last hope for justice.

* * *

When Georgianna confronted her wayward son-in-law about his affair in December 1991, Tom Dittmeier explained to the jurors, she could never have known that her daughter had only about twelve weeks to live. Georgianna could never have guessed the plan Rick would devise to solve the emotional and financial dilemma he so bluntly appraised for his mother-in-law that day: "I'm trapped."

In his opening statement on Tuesday morning, the prosecutor took the jurors through the final countdown in the life of Elizabeth DeCaro. He described the events between December and March 6, sweeping the jurors toward what would happen in the kitchen at 12 Hidden Meadow Court. The story had been told in court before—more times that most murder stories are ever told anywhere. But this time Dittmeier had some insights of his own—some twists of his own—to share with the jurors.

He took them to December 31, 1991, a day that he thought offered amazing insight into the heart, mind, and intentions of Rick DeCaro. That afternoon Rick applied for $100,000 of life insurance for his wife. That evening he and that same wife went to a New Year's Eve party at their church, where Rick abandoned Elizabeth, forcing her to beg a ride home. What did Rick do after he left her? He drove to the home of the woman Dittmeier politely called Rick's "paramour," Cathy Dillon, to attend the party she and her husband were hosting. After a while there, Rick and Cathy drove with another couple to a nightclub across the Mississippi River in Illinois. Jeff Dillon—now stranded in a slightly different way from what Elizabeth had been earlier—had to drive to the club and insist that his wife return home.

Happy New Year, indeed.

As the calendar turned to 1992, Rick mailed the life insurance application to the company in Chicago, along with a check paying the premiums for the first two months on his own, more valuable policy and his wife's new one, which went into effect January 9.

What did all of that mean? A man having an affair with a new woman, trapped in a marriage by emotional and financial concerns, and applying for life insurance on his wife for the first time. How did all of that fit? To explain that, Tom Dittmeier took the jurors down the list of amazing events and witnesses that shaped the case against Rick DeCaro and Dan Basile, that had put them in jail the first time.

But some things that happened after that shed new light on what drove Rick DeCaro. From the county jail, Dittmeier said, Rick began a series of collect calls to Cathy Dillon—so many, in fact, that her husband found out and put a stop to it. Jump ahead thirty months, to Rick's release from jail in September 1994. Without Jeff Dillon's knowledge, Rick and Cathy resumed their relationship, going out together with their kids and having dinners out for just the two of them. They also resumed their sexual activities, Dittmeier charged, and Cathy even helped Rick move into his new house with an incredibly domestic touch—she unpacked his dishes.

But the fly landed in Rick's ointment on January 12, 1995, when he mailed claims for the $100,000 from his wife's timely life insurance policy and another $1,900 worth of items he said were stolen the day she was killed. The big money never showed up, but Rick got the check for $1,900—and a federal indictment.

The evidence would prove, Dittmeier finished bluntly, that Rick DeCaro and Danny Basile were guilty as charged.

No, Scott Rosenblum told the jurors, the evidence would show that this was a story of two families—and what the extended family of Craig Wells did to the Van Iseghems. The defender had revealed his trial strategy: Craig Wells would be the bogeyman in this tale.

But first Rosenblum had to prevent Dittmeier's righteous indignation about Rick's extramarital activities from spreading to the jurors. Amid the DeCaros' sad marital problems, Rosenblum said, Rick and Cathy Dillon developed a friendship at work—a "big-brother-type relationship." Nothing had happened until November 1991, when tickets to a hockey game while Elizabeth was out of town became passports to a sexual affair. The liaison lasted about a month, and they had sex four or fives times. But Rick ended it—that was fine with Cathy—and confessed his indiscretion to Elizabeth. In this version, Rick told Elizabeth how he loved her and wanted their marriage to work. He even talked about trust and rebuilding. And thereafter, Rosenblum insisted, there was no sexual relationship between Rick and Cathy—none ever again to this very day. And Cathy would tell this jury exactly that.

In the audience, the Van Iseghems were thinking this was beginning to sound more like a fairy tale than an opening statement.

Rosenblum offered an intriguing explanation for the testimony from James Torregrossa. The only secret request Rick made of Torregrossa had nothing to do with a hit man; it had to do with Rick's affair with Cathy. Rick had asked Torregrossa to alibi for him if anyone ever called the gym. He had been seeing his secretary, so if anybody ever inquired, Torregrossa was to say he and Rick had gone out for drinks a few times. That's all that was ever said between these two men.

The revisionist history didn't stop there. The December trip to the Ozarks for Rick and Elizabeth had been wonderful, Rosenblum swore. "They had a great time; they started to rediscover each other." They looked at more condos. The Van Iseghems shook their heads again; that wasn't the description Elizabeth had given of the trip.

Rosenblum admitted that things had not gone so well on New Year's Eve—but it had been Elizabeth's fault. According to Rick, when he got home from work a few minutes later than promised, Elizabeth angrily confronted him, throwing his affair with Cathy at him again. Rick didn't want to go to the party after arguing, but they went anyway. After being harassed there by nosy, gossipy neighbors, Rick wanted Elizabeth to go to a different party. She refused, so he went alone—to the Dillons'. Rick only drove Cathy and her friends to the nightclub across the river because they were too drunk.

Good ol' Rick. He wasn't a philandering spouse, just the designated driver.

What about slamming Elizabeth into the wall with the van? Just an accident. In this version, Rick had checked Elizabeth to make sure she was okay and then had run inside to keep the kids from walking on broken glass from pictures knocked off the damaged wall. Before he could even call 911, she freed herself and came into the house. "Liz was fine. She was bruised, but fine."

Rosenblum turned his attention back to Craig Wells by focusing on the Old Orchard Amoco Station, where he and Rick worked. Wells often brought in his "brother," the guy known only as Danny. Rick never had spoken to this Danny or had any direct contact with him. Rick had been involved slightly with the inspection of Danny's battered old car. But that was it, folks; that was the entire extent of the contact between the two men who now sat at the defense table together. There were no meetings in the parking lot at Gold's Gym to discuss van thefts or anything else. Never happened.

And then Rosenblum really zeroed in on Craig Wells. He had a reputation for being untruthful. He was looking for money to start his own business. And he had access to a special commodity—information. He knew where Rick kept the keys to the van and Blazer. He knew Rick's address from the employee roster. He knew the DeCaro van would be backed into the driveway to unload supplies the night of February 7. "And lastly, he had access to Dan Basile, a willing thief."

Who was the first person Basile visited after his arsonous van drive to that field not so far away from the courthouse where they all sat at that moment? Whom did he tell the job was done? Craig Wells. Rick didn't even know about the theft until the next morning. And, after all, Rosenblum insisted, Rick made no money on the van, which was leased by the station.

Among the items in the van when it was stolen was something that could be very useful for someone planning a crime, someone planning to return to the scene to steal yet another nice vehicle. Whoever stole the van also got the DeCaros' remote garage-door opener. That device gave its new owner access to the DeCaro home—and was never recovered, Rosenblum noted.

What abut the fateful "Daddy's weekend" at the lake? Had Rick spitefully canceled Elizabeth's plans to go to Pam

Hanley's in Kansas City? Not at all. Rick had left it up to the kids, and "the kids overwhelmingly said, 'We want to go to the Ozarks.'"

The Van Iseghems wanted to groan again. How could Rick and his lawyer get away with these lies?

Rick made his weekend motel reservations on Wednesday, March 4, from the Amoco station, Rosenblum said. And who knew about those out-of-town plans? "Craig Wells—that name again," Rosenblum said. Wells thought the entire family was going; he thought the house would be empty all weekend.

What else happened March 4? Rick asked his mother-in-law to talk to Elizabeth about opening up to him again, about getting past some of these issues. Georgianna had done just that. "And Elizabeth came home that night, and they had a great night. They made love. They held each other, and they talked about their plans for the future, and talked about their plans for the weekend."

The Van Iseghems were furious now. As a witness, Georgianna could not be in the courtroom. But when her family told her later about Rosenblum's account of that night, Georgianna was shocked by the boldness of this lie. She had, indeed, spoken to her daughter at Rick's request that night. But Elizabeth's response had been to bury her face in her hands, cry deeply and pitifully, and say, "Mom, I can't stand to look at him anymore." That was the woman who then went home to make love to her husband and talk about their beautiful future together? My God, Georgianna demanded, how could such lies be told in a court of law?

Rosenblum moved to Friday, March 6. Rick left earlier than usual, but not before he kissed his sleeping wife. Later, when Rick was ready to drive the car pool to pick up Patrick and his friends, Ozzie the dog jumped into the van; Erin asked if Ozzie could ride with them, and Rick reluctantly agreed. After picking up everyone at school, they drove home to pack. Bill had even gone to the basement to get his fishing pole—to the very basement where authorities claimed Basile was hiding. During the drive to the Ozarks, an angry Elizabeth called Rick and chewed him out because he hadn't seen the sentimental greeting card she had packed for him—a card Rosenblum that promised the jurors they would see.

What about Craig Wells on that Friday afternoon? He was missing from work for hours, Rosenblum said.

Very early the next morning, Rick's world caved in on him: the police arrived to tell him that Elizabeth had been murdered. Rosenblum had a significantly different version of that scene than Detective Miller remembered. "Rick looked at him and said, 'What happened?' Let out a breath, and fell into the wall." Rosenblum had his own spin on the events at the police station as well. "As he was interrogated, he put his hands to his face and cried."

What about those collect calls to Cathy Dillon from the jailed Rick? Hardly sordid. Not only was he trying to deal with his grief by talking to a friend, but he was trying unsuccessfully to arrange bond to get out of jail. Only when Rick got out of jail more than two years later did he and Cathy resume their relationship. "They were there for each other—nothing more," Rosenblum insisted again.

The government would fail to offer any direct evidence, Rosenblum promised the jurors, of a murderous link between Rick and Basile. And then, the defender said, he would ask the jurors to acquit them on all charges.

What happened next was a disaster for Rick's defense. Basile's attorney, Tom Flynn, briefly described his client as a down-on-his-luck young man with a sad family history, a man trying hard to get his life on track by taking trade classes and living with his half brother, Doug Meyer. During this difficult time for Basile, he made a fateful mistake after Craig Wells introduced him to Rick.

"Rick DeCaro did, in fact, ask Dan Basile to steal the 1989 van," Flynn said. They did, in fact, have several meetings at Gold's Gym to discuss it. And Flynn announced, "Dan Basile foolishly agreed to become involved in this scheme."

There it was, the tactical move by Flynn that Tom Dittmeier had known would come. Although Flynn would go on to deny that Basile had killed Elizabeth, the defense attorney's words had immeasurably strengthened the criminal bond between the two defendants. Rick's attorney had just denied the "insurance scam" allegation, and his codefendant's attorney had just admitted it, actually labeling it "an insurance scam concocted by Mr. DeCaro."

And then Flynn ratcheted up the damage with an even more devastating broadside at Rick. "In fact, the evidence is going to show, ladies and gentlemen, that Mr. DeCaro did ask Dan to kill his wife, and that Dan refused to do that, and was shocked by that."

What a torpedo! Rick DeCaro now found himself under attack on both flanks, and Dittmeier hoped the jury could appreciate the gravity of what had just happened.

Flynn told the jurors they would hear several witnesses say that Basile had repeatedly denied involvement in the murder—before and after the deed was done. And then Flynn closed by suggesting that the jurors might find enough evidence to convict Basile of mail fraud, but they would soon be convinced that he fit the description others had offered: he was a car thief, yes, but not a murderer.

EIGHTY-ONE

As James Torregrossa laid out his amazing story for Tom Dittmeier and this new jury, it sounded very much the same as it always had before—an absolutely shocking solicitation for a hit man. But defense attorney Scott Rosenblum wanted to know if there was some special bond of trust between these two men, that they could share such a dangerous secret. No, not at all. Had he made any notes after this remarkable conversation? No. What had Torregrossa said when Rick first asked about finding someone to take the van off his hands? Maybe. Was that a lie? No, it was just a "maybe." Rosenblum looked intensely at Torregrossa and asked, "And you said it because you didn't want to look like a bigger fool than you were at the time?" Dittmeier's objection was sustained, but Rosenblum was undeterred. "So when you said, 'maybe,' it was a lie?"

Torregrossa was wearying of the word games. "Maybe is maybe. If you want to look at it that way, you can."

Tom Flynn wanted to know if Torregrossa knew Danny Basile. No, he didn't. Did Rick ask him if he knew anyone who wanted to "buy" the van? No, Rick had asked if he knew anyone who would "take it off his hands." There was a difference in the terminology, Flynn wanted the jury to understand, just as there was when Rick asked if Torregrossa knew anyone who could "take care of someone." Torregrossa was less certain about that surprising term; he had to ask about it, and Rick had offered that bone-chilling definition—"kill someone."

When Rosenblum got the opportunity, he wasted no time zeroing in on Craig Wells during cross-examination. Did Rick and Basile know each other before that first meeting in Gold's parking lot? Yes. But hadn't Wells testified before that he "introduced" them to each other at that first meeting? Yes, he had said that. Had they ever talked to each other before that night? Wells wasn't sure.

Rosenblum's face showed his puzzlement about this situation. If the men didn't know each other before that night, then Rick had asked a virtual stranger to commit a murder for him.

"Is that what you are saying?"

"Yes, sir."

Rosenblum went through the standard business about Wells's initial lies to the police. And then the defender moved on to that long, overnight interview when Wells began telling what he now said was the truth. Hadn't the police talked about their theory of how this murder had happened? Yes. Rosenblum's voice telegraphed the accusation he was about to make.

"That's when you came up with this story about the meeting. Right?"

"That's when I told them about the meetings, yes."

Then Wells got a lawyer, Rosenblum recounted, and got his immunity. "And after you got on board with the police, you said, 'Okay, I'll go with that theory.' Is that how that went down?"

"No, sir."

Didn't Wells get immunity as long as he told "the truth according to Tim Braun"?

"No, the truth according to what I knew."

Rosenblum dug for evidence to back up his implication that the real killer was now on the witness stand. Wasn't Wells looking for money to start his own business? Yes. Didn't Wells have access to the van key when he gassed it up for Rick? Sometimes. Did Wells have access to the home addresses of station employees? Yes. Could Wells have drawn a map to Rick and Elizabeth's house? Probably. Didn't Basile give Wells a speaker from the stolen van? Yes. Didn't Wells know that a key to the Blazer was kept in a pocket in the driver's door? Yes. Hadn't Wells driven the Blazer to the store the week of the murder? Yes. Hadn't he gone to a store not far from the stables where Basile worked? Yes. Wasn't Wells surprised when Rick showed up work for a few hours the morning of the murder? Yes. Wasn't Wells's time card filled out by hand that day, instead of being stamped by the clock? Yes. Weren't he and his car missing from the station for hours on the afternoon of the murder? No, he hadn't left that day at all. When Wells called Rick so the police could tape the conversation, hadn't Rick said to cooperate and answer the cops' questions? Yes.

When Wells talked to the police, hadn't he lied to protect himself? "Myself, and Danny and Rick."

As Dan Basile continued his angry glare at the man he had once called "brother," Tom Flynn moved in for cross-examination without giving Wells a chance to catch his breath. Wells believed that Basile stole the van, didn't he? Yes. When Wells took Basile to the first meeting, didn't he already know that Rick DeCaro wanted someone to kill his wife? No. After that first meeting, didn't Basile say he was not going to kill Rick's wife? Yes. Had Wells seen Basile with $15,000 or any other significant amount of money around the time of the murder? No. After the murder, hadn't Basile denied having anything to do with it? Yes. And hadn't he said he had been set up? He might have.

Dittmeier had a little damage control to do. On the afternoon of the killing, had Wells been working at his regular post at the front of the station? No, he had been doing the vacationing Rick's job in the back. Where did he go after work? To a hospital to see a friend, a place where he had signed a form to get in. What time did he get home on March 6? About nine o'clock.

To Dittmeier, it was more than obvious that Wells had no motive, no opportunity, and simply no time to kill anyone.

EIGHTY-TWO

And so it would go with this third trial. Familiar testimony and attacks by the defense. Even Rick would crack to a reporter that it all had a distinct feeling of "déjà vu." Bill McClellan, the *Post-Dispatch*'s wisecracking columnist with razor-sharp insights on criminal cases, dubbed the trial "DeCaro—The Sequel" and called the defendants "a Mutt and Jeff pair."

On Wednesday morning, the second day of testimony, Sue Jenkins told her riveting story about the night Dan Basile stole the DeCaro van. Scott Rosenblum wanted to know what Basile had said about the planning of this elaborate crime. "It was arranged through Craig Wells and the owner of the van," she explained.

Rosenblum had to massage that answer. Did Basile ever mention the name DeCaro? No. Did he ever say he had any direct contact with this van owner? No. Where did Basile get the keys? From Wells. Why had she gone along for this long, dangerous drive? "Bad judgment." Who was the first person Basile looked for when they got back to St. Louis? Craig Wells.

Rosenblum posed his last question. "And at some point, did you refer to yourself and Basile as Bonnie and Clyde?"

"Yes."

Tom Flynn returned immediately to his theme. When Basile told his brother-in-law that night that someone had offered him $15,000 to kill his wife, hadn't Basile said he wouldn't kill anybody? Yes. What was the tone of that conversation? "They were laughing; it was a joke." When Sue made her taped call for the police, hadn't Basile denied any involvement in the murder? Yes.

The prosecutor wanted just a bit more definition of Basile's reference to the murder offer. Basile hadn't said whom he was asked to kill or who made the offer? No.

"But his words were, 'I was offered $15,000 to kill someone's wife'?"

Sue Jenkins nodded. "Wife."

Since five of the counts against Rick were mail fraud, after all, Dittmeier's second chair for the trial, assistant U.S. attorney Howard Marcus, turned the jury's attention to that evidence. Two claims reps from Allstate Insurance testified about Rick's applications for benefits from the personal items stolen with the van. In a "statement of loss" notarized by Cathy Dillon, signed by Rick, and mailed to the company's office, Rick claimed $2,000 for a VCR, a television set, a Nintendo, a video camera, a leather jacket, a remote control for the garage-door opener, and a few other items. The company paid Rick $652.45 for his personal losses and $405 for the difference between the cash value of the van and the amount still owed the bank for the lease—$17,497.92.

If those claims and statements were false, Rick had committed mail fraud by posting them to the company; there would be more about that later. Dittmeier wanted to keep the trial moving with a witness who would remind the jurors what this was really all about. Georgianna took the stand once again to talk about Elizabeth and her life and her marriage and her children. The testimony that later would become a major point of contention, and a turning point in her life, arrived as she described that astonishing conversation with Rick about his affair.

What did he say about Cathy Dillon? That he loved her.

"Did he tell you how he felt about Elizabeth?"

"He said that he didn't think he'd ever loved Elizabeth."

What was Rick's response when Georgianna reminded him that a divorce could cost him his family and his home? "He just looked at me, and he said, 'I know; I'm trapped.' "

Georgianna drew the most audible reaction from the crowd so far when she recounted her call to Rick at the lake in the early-morning hours after the murder. The spectators there to support the Van Iseghems, and even some of the family, gasped when she said Rick had suggested that he and the kids might stay another day and have some "fun."

Rosenblum's cross-examination had to be delicate. Had Rick been an attentive, caring husband who regularly gave his wife gifts and flowers? Yes. Had it been difficult for Rick when Elizabeth asked him to stop smothering her? He said it was. When they discussed his affair, hadn't Rick told her that he wasn't sure what "true love" was anymore? No.

EIGHTY-THREE

When Cathy Dillon told the jury her name and where she worked, her voice was so soft that Tom Dittmeier asked her to speak louder so everyone could hear. The attractive blonde said she had worked at the Old Orchard Amoco Station since September 1989—employed by Dan DeCaro, who was married to her husband's sister. Cathy had been married to Jeff Dillon since March 5, 1988.

Did she know Basile? She had seen him at the station; she knew him only as Dan, Craig Wells's brother. The day Dan's car was inspected, she had seen him talking to Rick in his office. That same day, she had heard Dan asking Rick if he had an unused fifty-five-gallon drum that the rock band Dan helped as a roadie could use for a smoke machine.

Then it was time for Dittmeier to take Cathy's story to

November 1991 and her affair with Rick. What had Rick
told her during that romance? "He said he loved me."
Cathy supported Rosenblum's contention that Rick had arrived at the Dillons' New Year's Eve party just as Cathy
and another couple were headed out the door to the East
Side nightclub; Rick had, indeed offered to drive because
they were too drunk. Her husband had shown up later to
demand that she come home, but she rode home with Rick
and the other couple.

During their affair, where did she and Rick meet? In the
parking lots of grocery and discount stores, as well as
Gold's Gym; she remembered meeting there twice. What
had happened on March 5, 1992, the Dillons' fourth anniversary and the night before the murder? Cathy had told
Jeff she thought they needed to separate for a while, and
she was going to stay with her mother. She didn't know
until the morning after the murder what had happened.
There was another disclosure that morning, too. After
Cathy was interviewed by the Major Case Squad, she went
home and told her husband about her affair with Rick.

What about all those collect calls to her from the jailed
Rick? Dittmeier asked. Rick was calling about posting everyone's property to satisfy his bond. Eighteen or nineteen
calls about his bond? Yes. Had he sent her a birthday card?
Yes. Over Rosenblum's objection, Dittmeier asked Cathy
if Rick had written anything in the card. Yes. Did she still
have it? No. Had Jeff found it? Yes. What did she do with
it after that? Burned it.

What happened after Rick was released from jail in September 1994? They began seeing each other again—dinners, lunches, joint outings with their kids to Chuck E
Cheese's pizza place. Dittmeier moved in for what he
thought would be some devastating information.

"Now, during that period of time, were you pregnant?"
"Yes."

Her third child had been born on June 13, 1995. Dittmeier did not ask more about that, letting it hang in the
air before dropping his next question. "Now, during that
period, at any time did you and Rick DeCaro have sex
again?"

"Yes, we did."

Kaboom! The sound of Rosenblum's exploding promise about Cathy's chastity rumbled across the courtroom.

Had Rick brought his children to see her new baby? Yes. Was her husband there at the time? No. Did he know about Rick's visit? No. Did Jeff know she was seeing Rick again? No. Did she help Rick move into his new house during the summer of 1995? Yes, she had unpacked his "kitchen stuff." Did her husband know about that? No. Has Rick ever talked about Basile or Wells? No, not once.

"Thank you, ma'am."

The Van Iseghems wanted to cheer from the gallery. The whole truth about this unholy affair finally had been exposed. Surely this jury could grasp the reality behind Rick's piety and see the real motivation for what had happened between November 1991 and March 6, 1992.

Rosenblum began his cross-examination with a subtle, artfully crafted question, the kind that lawyers are paid big money to know how to ask in exactly the right way and at exactly the right time.

"Mrs. Dillon, you have three children with your husband, Jeff?"

"Yes, I do."

Rosenblum hoped that would counteract the unspoken implication so cleverly left behind by Tom Dittmeier.

Rosenblum moved to Craig Wells. Did Cathy have an opinion about his reputation for truthfulness? "He's not very truthful; he's a liar."

The defender tried to put a different face on the relationship between Rick and Cathy. Hadn't they become good friends at work? Yes, they had talked about everything. How was her relationship with Jeff then? "Very rocky; very bad." What troubled her marriage? Jeff had never grown up; he put his friends, his fun, everything else, before his family. Didn't Rick say he was confused about his marriage after Elizabeth told him to stop smothering her? Yes. During their affair, why did they meet in parking lots? Because they couldn't talk seriously at the office about their problems. When Rick ended the affair on December 23, didn't he say he loved his wife? Yes. Loved his family? Yes.

Wanted his marriage to work? Yes. What did she say?
"Fine, I agree." Did they remain friends? Yes. Was she
romantically involved with Rick in January 1992? No. February? No. March? No. April? No.

How many people were at her New Year's Eve party?
Twenty, twenty-five; people from her work, people from
Jeff's; she couldn't remember exactly who. Were they too
drunk to drive? Yes. Did Jeff drive to the nightclub to get
her? No, he was too drunk; a friend drove for him. Why
didn't she ride back with Jeff? His friend was driving a
pickup truck that didn't have room for everyone, and she
didn't feel right leaving her friends with Rick.

Did her request for a separation on March 5, 1992, have
anything to do with Rick? No. What did he write on this
mysterious birthday card he sent her? "He told me how
horrible it was in jail, told me how his life was destroyed,
how much he missed Liz. He didn't know what he was
going to do without her. . . . It said something about him
losing his one and only love." Did he send letters and cards
to other people from Old Orchard? Yes.

Rosenblum had to address the resumption of sexual activity he had denied earlier. Were times still difficult in her
marriage? Yes. Were she and Jeff in counseling? Yes. How
many times did she have sex with Rick after he got out of
jail? Two or three. Why? Just loneliness. Did she tell Jeff?
Yes. Are things better in the Dillon marriage now? Yes.
What about Rick now? "He's my friend."

Tom Flynn needed to put some distance between Rick
and Basile. Was Rick at work the morning of March 6?
Yes. Was Basile there that day? No. Had she seen them
together only twice, briefly? Yes.

And then Dittmeier pulled out another weapon—Cathy's
husband, Jeff Dillon.

How many people were at the New Year's Eve party?
According to his memory, just fifteen. How many from Cathy's work? Just one—Rick DeCaro. What did Jeff do
when he followed Cathy, Rick, and the others to the nightclub? "Confronted her" and asked her to come home.
What happened on the Dillons' fourth anniversary, the day
before the murder? Cathy asked for a separation. What

happened the day after the murder? She told him for the first time about her affair with Rick. What did Jeff do after he saw all the collect calls to his home from Rick in jail? Told Cathy they had to stop. Did he do anything else? Yes, he told Dan DeCaro to tell Rick to stop calling.

Did Jeff find a birthday card to his wife from Rick in April 1992? Yes. How was it signed? Jeff remembered the sentiment as "You are my one and only love, Rick." Did Jeff learn that Cathy had seen Rick after he was released from jail in 1994? Yes. Did Jeff know they had resumed their sexual affair? Yes. Did he know Rick had brought his kids to see Cathy's new baby? No. Did Jeff know Cathy had unpacked Rick's dishes at his new house? No.

Rosenblum wanted to give the jury a clear picture of the Dillon marriage. Were there other times, besides March 1992, when they separated briefly? Yes. Were they still married? Yes.

The defender rolled out another perfectly worded question. "And you recently had your third child?"

"Yes."

Another pointed and perfectly aimed question closed Rosenblum's cross.

"Is it fair to say that you don't like Rick very much?"

Jeff Dillon's voice was cool and restrained, and just as direct as the question.

"Yeah."

EIGHTY-FOUR

Double job. Throwaway. Double digits.

To Eddie Bonds, the slang used by Dan Basile was the clear and unmistakable vernacular of the business they both knew—until Bonds "retired." Basile's "double job" reference in his first phone call to Bonds meant there were two parts to the assignment, although he didn't explain that beyond the reference to stealing the van. When he called back later looking for a "throwaway," he obviously wanted a cheap handgun that could be disposed of when it was no longer needed. "Double digits" meant the take was at least $10,000.

Tom Dittmeier asked Bonds to clue the jury in.

"Is that a lot of money to steal a car?"

"Awfully lot," the retired expert said.

Scott Rosenblum wondered if "double job" could mean stealing two vehicles—the van and the Blazer. Basile hadn't really said.

There were some other terms that Rosenblum wanted Bonds to tell the jury about. Hadn't Basile said the second job was supposed to "a simple job, in and out"? Yes. And then on March 6, hadn't Basile said, "Something went wrong. Things went down. Shit happened. I did what I had to do"? Yes. Wasn't Basile always a big talker, trying to be a big man? Somewhat.

Tom Flynn's attempt to defend Basile demanded a tougher cross-examination. Hadn't Bonds at first agreed to help Basile with this job and then pulled out later? No. Didn't Basile ask Bonds about a "throwaway" because he was the kind of person who might have a gun? Apparently so. Was that an unusual request? "At that point in my life, yes."

When Basile called it a double job, what did he say about his involvement in the second part? "He said he didn't want to do the second job."

Rosenblum had to challenge the next witness's testimony. After Pam Hanley recounted how Rick had told Elizabeth she was not to go to Kansas City that Friday under any circumstances, the defense attorney had to look for an upside. Hadn't Rick been an attentive husband, regularly giving her gifts and flowers? Yes. Had Pam been told that Rick left the decision on the weekend up to the kids and they chose the lake over Kansas City?

Pam's anger flashed as she shot back, "No—to the contrary. The kids said different."

Hadn't Elizabeth said she wouldn't make the trip alone?

Pam wouldn't allow that well-worded, but improperly slanted, question to pass unchallenged either. "She said that Rick told her that under no circumstances could she come, because the Blazer wouldn't make it."

EIGHTY-FIVE

Melanie Enkelmann was confident that her story about Elizabeth's death was getting to the jury this time as she presented her testimony on Thursday, the third day of trial. Tom Dittmeier was doing an outstanding job of drawing out the details that the jurors needed to hear. When she finally recounted her taped conversation with Rick at the police station, Dittmeier asked about Rick's interest in buying a condo at the lake. She explained that she asked how he could do that when he had been talking about trying to get out of debt. She quoted him as responding, "A lake house is something that I've always wanted, and when I want something, I always get it." A revealing sentiment.

Scott Rosenblum wasted no time. Hadn't Rick said he had no idea what happened to Elizabeth? Yes. Hadn't he said he offered to go to Kansas City, but Elizabeth told him to go to the lake? Yes. Didn't he deny being involved in the van theft? Yes. Didn't he say that Erin wanted to take Ozzie on the trip? Yes. Hadn't he agreed to see a marriage counselor? Yes. Hadn't he ended that conversation by saying that he was only thinking then about his four kids? Yes.

Rosenblum then called for a sidebar conference and asked the judge's approval to question Melanie about Elizabeth's affair with Mike Carroll. Melanie's approval of that fling would demonstrate her bias against Rick. Flynn joined the motion, noting that Melanie had originally denied to the police that she knew about the affair; this line of questioning should be allowed so the defense could impeach her testimony. Dittmeier objected; those events had no rel-

evance to the charges, and the character of the victim was
not at issue. Judge Limbaugh agreed. He denied Rosenblum's request; there was no evidence that Rick DeCaro
was aware of his wife's "infidelity," and that made it
irrelevant.

The trial so far from home turf was drawing remarkably
few spectators. The crowd really consisted of just the partisans—the Van Iseghems, grouped behind the prosecution
table, and the DeCaros, lined up on the defense side. The
tension between the camps was much worse than before.
For the Van Iseghems, having to deal with Rick's going in
and out of the courtroom and passing them in the hallways
during recesses was excruciating.

Rick focused intently—but without any emotion in his
face—on everything that happened in the courtroom and
on the witness stand. Basile, however, seemed fairly unconcerned, if not totally uninterested. He often spent his time
perusing the crowd and twiddling with his mustache. Perhaps the threat of a life sentence failed to hold the attention of a guy on death row.

Bonnie Dike had testified before about seeing the blinds
closed for the first time on Elizabeth's patio doors the day
of the murder. But no one had asked her the next logical
question until Scott Rosenblum cross-examined her today.
Did she know when they were closed and who closed
them? Yes, she saw Rick arrive home between 11:15 and
11:30 A.M., park the van on the street, go into the house,
and close the blinds within seconds. A surprised Rosenblum
produced the police report of her interview and asked her
if she hadn't told the police she was unable to say when
the blinds closed. Yes, but she had not meant that; when
she talked to the police, she was trying to say she didn't
know what time Rick had arrived home. She tried to explain that she remembered the time later, but Rosenblum
cut her off and ended his cross.

Tom Flynn wanted to know if it was odd for Rick to be
home at that time of day. Yes, it was the first time Bonnie
had ever seen him there then. Flynn pointed to his client.

Bonnie hadn't seen Basile there that day with Rick, had she? No.

Dittmeier called the prosecutors' special witness, Elizabeth Burrows. Flynn tried to rattle her by showing that despite her recollection of sunny skies when she saw Basile driving the Blazer, the weather service recorded rain at that time. She didn't care what the service said; it was sunny at that place at that time.

Flynn then challenged her claim that she had looked directly at Basile for "a few seconds" while driving her Ford Escort station wagon fifty-five miles per hour in heavy traffic. He offered his own testimony: "I've tried this a hundred times and, I'm going to tell you, you can't look for more than a second." Dittmeier objected to Flynn's comment on the evidence, and the judge agreed that it was improper. Flynn used another approach. Had she tried to reproduce that situation again to see how long she could look at another driver? No. Could it have been only one second? "I don't think so."

John Carman was a mechanic at Old Orchard and had an interesting memory to share with the jury. Rick had asked him to inspect Basile's car in February 1992. But the car was a piece of junk, and Carman had told Rick it wouldn't pass. "He asked me to go ahead and pass it." Carman refused; he wasn't putting his name on a falsified state certificate. Rick then had Carman enter Rick's name into the computer as the test operator, and Rick signed the inspection certificate later.

Basile's car had passed the emissions test, hadn't it? Rosenblum asked. Evidently. Were there judgment calls to be made when inspecting a car? Yes. Did Rick require Basile to install an air cleaner and new tires? Carman didn't know. Had Carman denied remembering anything about this inspection when Rosenblum's associate called him earlier? He may have. "I was terrified for my job; it was my livelihood."

Flynn had just one point to make. Was Basile's car the kind anyone with any money would be seen driving? No.

EIGHTY-SIX

Doug Meyer drew the same barrage of defense flak that had exploded around Craig Wells. Before that, Meyer described seeing Rick DeCaro meet Dan Basile at the stables to give him money four days before the murder, seeing Basile with the pistol two days before the murder, and arranging for Basile to borrow the garage the night of the murder.

Scott Rosenblum attacked Meyer on every possible front. Hadn't Meyer heard all about the missing Blazer and the man named Rick DeCaro before he talked to the police? Yes. Hadn't Meyer lied to the police about which day he found the Blazer in that garage? Yes, but he had finally admitted discovering it on Monday. Didn't Basile offer to sell him the Blazer doors on Sunday? Meyer wasn't sure; it was Sunday or Monday, but he never saw the doors, anyway. Hadn't he been at the garage on Saturday or Sunday? No. In light of Meyer's lies to the police, was the jury getting half-truths or the whole truth today? "You are getting the truth to the best of my knowledge."

Tom Flynn wanted to know if Basile's gun hadn't been so worn as to seem unreliable and unsafe to Meyer. Yes, that was true. Hadn't Basile said he needed to gun to protect himself from the guy who gave him the black eye the week before? Yes. Hadn't Basile consistently denied shooting Elizabeth, despite badgering by Meyer? Yes. Wasn't that line "It was her or me" really just a joke, a way for Basile to laugh off Meyer's suspicions. That's the way Meyer had taken it.

Prosecutor Howard Marcus gave Dittmeier a breather and returned to his special role in this case—evidence of insurance fraud. Marcus's witness was Allstate claims analyst Linda Hines, who testified about a call from Rick on

December 20, 1994. He wanted to know how long he had to submit a claim; she opened a file for him that day. He later mailed in a three-page list of items he said were stolen when Elizabeth was killed, including some Sears Craftsman tools from his basement workroom, Seiko watches for a man and a woman, his wedding band, a necklace, Elizabeth's tenth-anniversary diamond ring, other jewelry, a television set, a clock radio, the phone answering machine, a video camera, and a Nintendo game. Marcus had Hines identify a series of family photos that Rick attached to his claim after drawing arrows to mark the stolen watches and jewelry. The photos offered various combinations of the happy DeCaro couple and their children, and seemed particularly poignant—or disturbingly crass, depending on one's point of view.

Rosenblum had Hines explain, however, that Rick had called back later and said he needed to strike some items from his list. He had learned that the police had recovered the two stereos he had listed and that Elizabeth's family had somehow retrieved some of her jewelry; he also had remembered that he had given Elizabeth's Seiko watch to his mother.

Marcus followed that witness with Robert Frame, the former police detective who testified that police had found no forced entry at the DeCaro house but had found a video camera stashed behind the basement workbench and a Nintendo game on an upper shelf in a closet near the master bedroom. The video camera was identical to the model that Rick reported stolen, and the Nintendo—as Frame demonstrated by holding up the unit—had Velcro on the bottom, the trick used to hold a game in place in a van. A copy of the new life insurance policy on Elizabeth also was found in the master bedroom, along with a letter from Allstate confirming that the policy went into effect on January 9, 1992.

Rosenblum pounced again. Did Frame know that a remote control for the garage-door opener was stolen with the van in February? No. Would that have given a burglar a way to get into the house without leaving signs of forced entry? Yes. He didn't find Elizabeth's keys to the Blazer, did he? No. Weren't there signs of rummaging and ransacking in the house? Rummaging, perhaps; Frame wouldn't call it ransacking. Had he checked to see if the video camera or the Nintendo worked? No. Did he know whether the DeCaros had replaced those broken items with new ones that worked—new ones stolen with the van? No. Among all the items taken from Dan Basile's car, was there a phone number, address, or anything else referring to Rick DeCaro? No. Were Basile's fingerprints found in Rick DeCaro's van after the murder? No.

Flynn added a couple more items to the fingerprint list. Were Basile's prints found in the DeCaro house or on the Blazer? No—just on a toolbox and a can of Busch beer in the garage where the Blazer's dismembered carcass was discovered. Not on the stereo boom box seized from Carl Swanson—supposedly his birthday present from Basile? No.

Marcus had one more insurance-fraud witness—James Armstrong of the Allstate office near Chicago. He had handled Rick's still-unpaid claim of December 29, 1994, for the proceeds from the life insurance policy on Elizabeth. Armstrong and Rick had sent documents back and forth through the mail between Missouri and Illinois and had made several interstate phone calls to discuss it. Marcus had just proved the use of the mails to seek what the prosecutors thought clearly was fraudulent profit from an illegal conspiracy and murder.

Ray Nichols recalled Basile's saying that he was going to steal a van for a friend and that the owner wanted the van and his wife to disappear at the same time. The owner wanted his wife "offed" (obviously a professional term) because he couldn't afford to go through a divorce. The guy owned some kind of service station or transmission place, Nichols said, remembering that Basile had said something about Amoco or Aamco. Basile also had called Nichols later to ask about getting a pistol; when Nichols couldn't help, Basile said he might buy his father's old .22-caliber handgun. A message from Basile on Nichols's answering machine later closed the book—he had said, "This is me, and I found what I wanted. Never mind." And then Nichols recalled Basile's middle-of-the-night, frightened visit—looking for someplace to crash in what would turn out to be his last hours of freedom before he was arrested.

Wasn't Basile the biggest "bull-thrower" Nichols ever met? Rosenblum wondered. Not really. Didn't Basile like to talk tough to impress people? Yes.

Flynn asked what Basile had said about his response to the guy looking for someone to "off" his wife. Nichols had urged Basile to tell the guy to go to hell, and Basile had said he would do exactly that. Wasn't Basile sporting a black eye from a fight when he said he was looking for a gun? Yes. Hadn't Nichols assumed that was the reason for Basile's interest in a weapon? Yes.

Dittmeier needed only one line from his last witness on this Friday. He wanted to know from Richard Harris, the former detective who had arrested Basile, what his prisoner had said. "He asked, 'How did you get on to me'?"

EIGHTY-SEVEN

Moments after he arrived in St. Louis from an abbreviated vacation in Las Vegas, Lieutenant Patrick McCarrick made a sound-barrier-busting drive down Interstate 55 to Cape Girardeau. Tom Dittmeier needed to confer with him on this late Sunday night, March 3. First thing Monday morning, McCarrick was on the witness stand as Dittmeier's thirty-sixth witness in the DeCaro–Basile trial.

McCarrick described an amateurishly staged scene that was supposed to resemble a burglary. There were signs—practically in neon—that an experienced detective could read as proof that the criminal had been taking his own sweet time. This "burglary" lacked the residue of a real burglar's frantic rampage through the house that he desperately wants to escape before someone discovers him. Cables to TVs and VCRs were carefully unscrewed—not ripped apart—and a curtain was neatly tucked behind the bed for easy access to unplugging the answering machine on a nightstand. Using photos of the house from the night of the murder, McCarrick pointed out that a VCR had been removed from atop the big-screen TV without knocking over an adjacent greeting card.

On cross-examination, Rosenblum tried the same approach that Don Wolff had used—that burglars working in a pair might have been less hurried and might have taken the Blazer to haul off the loot. McCarrick resisted that suggestion again—in his substantial experience, such events were extremely rare. Hadn't he seen burglaries with no sign of forced entry? Again, that was extremely rare. Wouldn't an inexperienced burglar do some of the things McCarrick had noted? No, rookie burglars usually made a bigger mess than pros did. Would a burglar take more time if he knew the family was away for the weekend? McCarrick hoped the jury would appreciate his implication when he answered with careful emphasis and a sly grin, "Oh, I think that's what we're talking about, yes, sir." Basile had known exactly where the family was.

Tom Flynn had several points he hoped McCarrick could make. Did this supposed "hit man" have any money on him when he was arrested, or was there any money found in his belongings? No. Did Rick DeCaro's financial records show the movement of any large and unexplained amounts of money? Not that McCarrick knew about. Why had McCarrick asked Doug Meyer for an alibi for the time of the murder if he wasn't a suspect? That was easy; McCarrick was always looking ahead to a defense lawyer's strategy at trial.

Dittmeier brought in two witnesses who would testify only briefly but would make points he thought devastating to Rick DeCaro. Christina Byrd Bishop, Georgianna's recently married niece, described Rick's emotionless response to the televised face of the man just arrested for killing Elizabeth. Rick said he didn't know the suspect shown in the top story for that night's ten o'clock news. Christina asked if this alleged murderer could be a customer at the station or the gym. No, Rick said again.

Jackie Balunek told a similar story. Rick had called Jackie—his neighbor and his wife's friend—from jail on March 29. She asked about Basile, and Rick said he never knew him or even heard of him before he was arrested.

Rosenblum sought an important detail from Rick's call. Hadn't he insisted, "You know I had nothing to do with any of this"? Yes.

Detective Mike Miller—more than anyone else—could tie up a lot of loose ends in the DeCaro investigation. When Miller informed Rick that his wife had been found dead, did he ask who found her? No. Did he ask any other details about his wife's murder? No. When Rick gave Miller a tour of the house the next day, did they go into the basement workroom? No, Rick just peered in and said nothing seemed to be missing. Did he say anything about his wife's jewelry boxes being disturbed? No. When did Rick call Miller to add stolen items to the list? January 18, 1995. What did Miller do before he took that report? He informed Rick of his Miranda right to remain silent. Did Iva Hanson solve the mystery of the "key under the rock" that Basile mentioned when he was arrested? Yes; in October 1994 she and Doug Meyer were cleaning his aquariums when they found what turned out to be a set of keys to the Blazer wrapped in plastic and hidden under the gravel in one of the aquariums.

And then Dittmeier turned to what he considered to be devastating evidence that literally documented Rick's motivation for this whole sordid crime. Using oversized charts displayed to the jury, the prosecutor had Miller list all of the collect calls Rick had made from jail to Cathy Dillon's home between March 30 and April 18, 1992—twenty of them, lasting anywhere from sixty seconds to the jail's maximum, eighteen minutes. In addition, Miller explained, Rick had made three calls to Cathy's mother's house—where she stayed while separated from Jeff. One of those was on April 11—Cathy's birthday.

Miller also tracked calls from Cathy's house to Rick the

week before the murder. She had placed a one-minute call to his house at 11:38 A.M. on February 29, and three minutes later she had called the cell phone in the Blazer for eight minutes. Weren't all of these calls, Dittmeier asked, after Rick claimed their affair had ended? Yes.

In the heat of the affair, Miller explained, Rick had started making calls from the Blazer to the Dillon house—fifteen between November 27, 1991, and February 19, 1992, including the one at 11:26 P.M. on New Year's Eve. There were seven more from the van's phone to Cathy's house between December 4 and February 3.

Dittmeier asked about perhaps the most incriminating call from the van. It went to the DeCaro house—at 11:07 A.M. on Friday, March 6, 1992. The implication was overpowering that Rick was making sure it was safe to deliver Basile to the house.

Four more calls were worth noting. Two calls from the van to the DeCaro house were made later that night—at 10:02 and 10:03 P.M. And two calls from the van on Thursday, March 12, went to defense attorney Ron Jenkins's home—at 9:58 and 10:15 P.M.—just as the news about Basile's arrest was breaking.

Miller continued his telephone analysis by showing how a series of calls between the DeCaro house and Pam Hanley's house in Kansas City documented the events of that last week. Six calls back and forth on Wednesday, as Elizabeth broke the unhappy news to Pam about the canceled weekend.

Dittmeier now turned the tables to ask about a call that was never made. After Craig Wells had told Rick on Thursday about Basile's arrest and the discovery of the Blazer—in that secretly taped call—had Rick called Miller to ask about these startling developments in the investigation into his wife's murder? No.

Rosenblum had a laundry list of issues for Miller. Was there only one proper way to react to tragic news? No. Hadn't Rick's reaction been to fall back into the wall? No, he "leaned" back. Hadn't Rick asked what happened, and hadn't Miller said they didn't know yet? Yes. So Rick had asked for details, only to be told there weren't any? Yes.

Hadn't Rick cried during the interview with the police? "I can't say that," Miller responded; all the detective saw was that Rick's eyes were red after he rubbed them. Did Miller have any evidence that Rick and Cathy were continuing their sexual affair while making calls after the end of December? No. Did the end of those calls about April 18 coincide with the end of the unsuccessful effort to win Rick's release on bond? Yes. Had Rick specifically looked in his wife's jewelry boxes when he toured the house that day? No. Did Miller know how the Van Iseghems came to have some of Elizabeth's jewelry? No. Had Miller checked the video camera and Nintendo from the house to see if they worked? Yes; they were broken. When Rick was interviewed, was he nervous and fidgety? No. Did he make direct eye contact with Miller? Yes. Didn't interviewing classes teach officers that a suspect who is nervous and fidgety may be hiding something? Yes. Was Craig Wells nervous and fidgety when he was interviewed? Yes. The week of the murder, hadn't Craig Wells driven Rick's Blazer to a store close to the stables where Basile worked? Yes.

And finally, hadn't Miller checked every telephone number he could find that might have anything to do with this case? Yes. Had he found any calls between Rick and Basile? No.

Tom Flynn picked up that line of questioning. Were there any phone calls to Rick's motel room the night of the murder from any of the phones Basile could have used, including the phone in the Blazer? No. Any calls from Rick's room to any number associated with Basile? No. Any large amounts of money disappearing from Rick's accounts? No. Any evidence of money getting to Basile's hands, other than the $200 Sue Jenkins said Basile got and the second $200 Wells claimed to have carried from to Basile from Rick? No.

"Now, would you say, officer, that it's unusual for a supposed hit man to do a contract murder on the credit plan?"

Miller had to admit that that was one hell of a clever question. "That would be unusual," he conceded.

Flynn closed with a reference to something Braun had

engineered for the first trials. Hadn't Miller traveled a route similar to what Rick would have driven if he had left the Old Orchard station in Webster Groves, driven to the stables in south St. Louis County to pick up Basile, and then driven home to St. Charles to slip the killer into the basement? Yes. Wasn't that a thirty-nine-mile drive that took fifty-two minutes? Yes.

Dittmeier gave Miller a chance to explain. Miller had opposed Braun's order to re-create the route because Miller wasn't that familiar with the territory and didn't know the best and fastest route. They ended up with what Miller feared were seriously inaccurate results.

And the jewelry. The Van Iseghems didn't have all of the items Rick reported stolen, did they? No. Hadn't the Van Iseghems retrieved some items that Elizabeth had taken to a jeweler's to be cleaned? Yes.

Had Rick DeCaro remained perfectly calm the whole time Miller talked to him that night, in the moments just after he had learned of his wife's murder? Yes. And hadn't Rick even remarked that he and the kids might stay another day at the lake? Yes.

Dr. Mary Case took the stand as Dittmeier's forty-first witness and described the devastating damage done by the two bullets fired point-blank into the back of Elizabeth's neck.

And then Tom Dittmeier rested the government's case against Richard DeCaro and Daniel Basile.

EIGHTY-EIGHT

Rick and Elizabeth DeCaro had seemed happy when condo agent Virgil "Eddie" Gibson showed them some properties at the Lake of the Ozarks in December 1991. That visit, between Christmas and New Year's, was the second time they had shopped with him for a weekend getaway in the

$59,900 range. Rick had made an appointment for yet a third tour on Saturday, March 7, and had showed up with his kids on Friday to confirm the date.

Gibson's accounts of trying to help Rick realize his dream of a condo on the lake opened the defense case on Monday afternoon.

"Did anything unusual strike you about either Mr. De-Caro or Mrs. DeCaro's demeanor?" Rosenblum asked about the December visit.

"No."

"Did they appear happy?"

"Yes."

Tom Dittmeier decided to show the jury how deceiving appearances could be. "Were you aware, during that period of time, that Mr. DeCaro had been having an affair with another woman?"

"No," Gibson shook his head. "No, I wasn't."

Rosenblum's second witness was John Stuber, now the manager at the Old Orchard Station. He recounted making a call in early 1991 to help get a job at a nearby car wash for a guy he knew only as Craig Wells's half brother, Dan. Had Stuber ever seen Rick talking to Dan Basile at the station? No.

"Did you form an opinion during that time as to whether or not Craig Wells was a truthful person?"

"He didn't tell the truth a lot. He lied quite often."

Dittmeier wanted to pursue that in his cross-examination. If Wells lied a lot, why did the DeCaro brothers keep him working at the station for seven years? He was a good worker, showed up most of the time, and did what he was supposed to, Stuber said. But why would Rick take an untruthful person over to help work at Rick's in-laws' home and business? Rick was trying to help Craig, and Craig was eager to learn about building from Rick.

Dittmeier turned his attention to Basile's time at the service station. Hadn't he drawn attention to himself because of his language? Yes, he had a foul mouth; Stuber had even complained to Rick and Dan DeCaro; they told him they would take care of it.

Stuber also remembered the night Basile was arrested.

Stuber recognized him from the photograph on TV and
even called Dan DeCaro. Dan DeCaro had seen the photograph too, but he hadn't realized he was the man they all
knew as Wells's brother. But Stuber didn't call Rick and,
in fact, had never spoken to Rick about any of this.

Rosenblum's next weapon against Craig Wells was the
former cashier from the station. Vickie Hauser recounted
her unsuccessful efforts to locate Wells and his car between
noon and two-thirty on the afternoon of the murder. And
she provided a memorably mixed cliché when Rosenblum
asked if Wells was an honest person.

"I wouldn't trust him with a ten-foot pole," she cracked.

She couldn't offer Dittmeier any reason why someone so
untrustworthy would be retained on the job for so long.
And she admitted that she didn't know if Wells had been
in the back of the shop that afternoon, in Rick's office
performing Rick's duties while Rick was in the Ozarks.
When was the first time she had told anyone that Wells
was missing that afternoon? "The last trial," she said;
everyone let that pass to avoid drawing any improper attention to an event that this jury was not supposed to know
about. So, she didn't remember Wells was missing until two
years after the murder? Ditrtmeier asked. Yes. What time
did she leave work that day? Between 2:15 and 2:30. Would
she be surprised if her time card was punched at 1:27?
Not really.

Scott Rosenblum would apply Dan DeCaro's testimony
in much the same way as Don Wolff had in the first trial.
Rick's brother remained a big gun for the defense, and
Rosenblum had him lobbing shells all over the battlefield.
Didn't everyone at the station use Rick's Blazer to run
errands and didn't they all know the keys were kept in the
door pocket. Yes. Hadn't there been an ongoing mechanical problem with the Blazer's steering and brakes? Yes.
What time did Rick clock out on the night that Torregrossa
claimed to have had this "hit man" conversation about
6:30? Rick's time card showed 5:30. What did his time card
show on the day of the murder? 7:00 A.M. to 11:00 A.M.
What about Craig Wells's hours that day? A twelve-hour

shift, 6:30 to 6:30—but the times were handwritten, not clock-stamped.

Had Dan DeCaro seen Craig Wells's brother, Dan, hanging around the station? Only twice, and then he had been waiting by the street for a ride; never talked to him. Had Dan DeCaro recognized Basile's photograph on TV? No, not until Stuber called.

What time did Rick leave the station for the Ozarks? Probably between 10:45 and 11:00 A.M. When Dan took over Rick's finances after his arrest—still generously paying his incarcerated brother's salary—had it been difficult to meet Rick's financial obligations? No. Had Dan even paid for Elizabeth's funeral? Yes, the full $12,000 to $13,000.

Describe Rick's emotional demeanor. "Very, very reserved; holds his feelings to himself." That was a family trait noticeable in all DeCaros, Dan said. "It's probably in the genes."

He also described how Rick's first attorney, Ron Jenkins, had called a week after the murder and asked Dan to look for a lunch bag Elizabeth had packed for Rick that day; it contained a card, and Jenkins wanted it sent to his office. Dan had found the bag, never looked inside, and had an employee take it to Jenkins.

Dittmeier began a lengthy cross-examination by producing several workers' time cards, including Stuber's and Cathy Dillon's. Didn't many of them contained handwritten times? Yes.

Hadn't Dan told the police that Rick had financial problems? He didn't remember saying that. Dittmeier handed him the police report. Yes, it did say that Dan "conceded" that his brother had financial problems, but he didn't remember saying that. Hadn't Dan loaned Rick $7,500 in late 1991 to pay down his credit card balance before he tried to refinance his house? Yes. Didn't he still fail to qualify for the refinancing? Yes. When Dan was paying Rick's bills, wasn't there a Visa balance in March of $4,538.97 on a credit line of only $4,500? Yes.

Would Dan expect Rick to remain perfectly calm after Detective Miller informed him of Elizabeth's murder? Dan shook his head. "I can't say that. I don't know what I would have expected under those conditions."

Had Rick called Dan after learning about the murder? No. Had they ever talked about the stolen van? No. Had Rick mentioned he was going on a "Daddy's weekend" with just the kids? No, Dan had thought Elizabeth was going too. Had Rick disclosed his affair with Cathy? No. Had Rick confessed in 1994 that he was having sex with Cathy again? No. Had Rick called his brother the night Basile was arrested? No, they had never discussed that at all.

Had Dan asked why the lunch bag with the card in it might be important to Rick's defense? No. Hadn't Dan testified before that he didn't remember who found the bag? Yes, but he now remembered that he had found it. Had he ever asked what was in the bag? No. Had Dan ever talked to Rick about Basile or Craig Wells? No. Had Rick ever broken that silence to say he didn't know Basile? No.

Ron Jenkins remembered the lunch-bag-with-the-card incident differently when he testified next. He had been in the airport in Chicago for a business flight on Thursday, March 12, when he got a message to call Dan DeCaro. Dan had just found a lunch bag and card in Rick's work area; Jenkins told him to have someone besides a family member bring it to his office. Jenkins put the bag and the sealed card in his safe, although he later threw away the sandwich and cookies. The card was not opened until two and a half years later—in court. Jenkins read it now for the jury. The cover sentiment was, "Who knows what tomorrow will bring," and inside it read, "Let's just enjoy each other, one today at a time." Elizabeth had underlined the word "today" and then had written her own message: "Have a nice weekend, Rick. Looking forward to really starting over and loving again, one day at a time. Love to you always, Liz." She had underlined "really" and "loving."

The Van Iseghem heart—that huge heart that beat as one for that entire family—broke again as those who loved Elizabeth heard her last words to Rick one more time.

At Rosenblum's request, Jenkins recounted what had happened when the news of Dan Basile's arrest broke. Rick had heard something about an arrest and had called Jenkins at his home just minutes before the ten o'clock news; Jenkins ran to a TV to watch. Rick called again about ten-fifteen, and Jenkins told him to go to a pay phone; Jenkins never talked to clients about their cases on unsecured cell phones. When Rick called back, Jenkins suggested they meet. They sat in Rick's van in a parking lot, and Jenkins asked if Rick knew the suspect.

"He said, 'I don't *know* him.' It was rather slow and somewhat quizzical. I said, 'What do you mean by that?' He said, 'I know I've seen him. I can't place it. I know I've *seen* him. I don't *know* him.'"

Cross-examination would be something of a duel, with former federal prosecutor Jenkins facing federal prosecutor Dittmeier. Both men knew how the game was played.

How did Jenkins know this card was important? Dan DeCaro had said there were hearts on the envelope and Rick's name appeared to have been written by Elizabeth; the implications to the defense were significant. What if Dan DeCaro remembered the sequence of events differently? Jenkins couldn't explain that, but he knew they had spoken that day about the card.

Dittmeier got in a subtle dig when he asked Jenkins about his late-night conference with Rick. "So, you met on a parking lot with him, too?"

That kind of line did not get by Jenkins. "I don't know what you mean by 'too.' I met him on a parking lot in Maryland Heights at a strip mall, at my request."

Had Rick mentioned that he had ordered a mechanic to pass Basile's car through the state inspection or that Rick had talked to Basile about giving him a fifty-five-gallon drum? No; Rick didn't tell and Jenkins didn't ask. Had Rick ever asked, even demanded, to see that card, to read the last words his murdered wife had written to him? No, Jenkins had explained that he wanted the card to remain unopened to preserve the chain of custody of the evidence until they got to court. What if something in that card would have proved Rick innocent? Rosenblum's objection for speculation was sustained. Dittmeier got tougher: "The simple fact of the matter is, you didn't care what was in that card and he didn't care. Isn't that correct?"

Rosenblum's objection as argumentative was overruled, and Jenkins shot back in kind. Dittmeier knew as well as Jenkins the importance of preserving the chain of custody.

Dittmeier rocketed right back. "What I know as well as you know is that somebody should have been allowed to read the last words of Elizabeth DeCaro prior to two years later."

Judge Limbaugh sustained Rosenblum's objection and instructed the jury to disregard Dittmeier's comment.

Back to the parking lot. Had Rick told Jenkins about the afternoon call from Craig Wells that same day, a call telling Rick that Wells's brother had been arrested? No. Had Rick said that Wells told him the Blazer had been found? No.

Dittmeier offered a last question to put Elizabeth's sweet, loving, forgiving card in perspective. "It doesn't indicate Richard DeCaro's feelings on March the sixth?"

"No, this doesn't."

Rick's sister, Patty Fiehler, and her husband, Richard, described Rick as a grief-stricken, confused, and worried husband and father in the moments after he arrived at their home early on Saturday morning, March 7. He was trying to hold back his tears, and hold it all together, for the sake of his children. But their whole family was wracked by grief that morning, and they all cried.

The Fiehlers also knew that half of Rick's garage was filled with building materials at the time the van was stolen. Patty Fiehler had seen the lumber and other supplies that filled one side of the garage and forced Rick to park in the driveway.

And then Rosenblum presented a series of witnesses in a tactic that made the Van Iseghems' blood boil. One by one, he called Elizabeth's children to the stand to defend their father. The Van Iseghems were convinced that Rick had coached the children to say what he needed—another example of his cruel manipulation; if they didn't do what he wanted, they were being disloyal to poor Daddy. This approached child abuse, they fumed. The only saving grace was that their time on the stand would be mercifully brief.

Eight-year-old Erin testified sweetly about taking Ozzie on the trip. "Whose idea was it?" Rosenblum asked. "Mine." Dittmeier had only one point to make. "How old were you back then?" he asked. "Three or four." Surely the jury knew this child couldn't have any independent recollection of who wanted the dog to go. Whose testimony was she delivering?

Patrick, now sixteen, was next, and he said his mom and dad had allowed the kids to decide whether they would all go to Kansas City or the kids would go to the lake with Dad. "Me and my brother and sisters decided that we wanted to go to the lake," he said. Who wanted Ozzie to go? Erin. Did they get a lot of phone calls in the motel room that night? No.

After Detective Miller left, how was Dad?

"He was very upset, shocked. He wasn't, like, crying, but he was trying to be strong for us, and I could tell he was upset."

Dittmeier wondered what Rick said to the kids then.

"He asked us if we wanted to stick around for a little while, let things cool down a little bit before we went home, or if we just wanted to pick up and leave right then."

Hadn't Patrick told Dittmeier earlier that Rick had asked the kids if they wanted to stay another day and have some fun? Yes. Was that what his Dad had said? "Right."

Rachel, now thirteen, echoed Patrick's explanation of the decision to go to the lake. But Dittmeier approached this witness from a slightly different and subtler angle. Did she remember when she and he had talked a month ago? Yes. Did she remember telling him that Erin was supposed to testify about the dog? Yes. What did she say Bill was going to testify about? How he jiggled open the sliding door. Did she tell Dittmeier that "they" were going to tell her later what she was going to testify to? Yes.

Rosenblum had to rebuff some innuendo. Wasn't Rachel just telling Dittmeier about the questions the kids had been asked? Yes. No one had ever told them how to answer the questions or what to say, had they? No.

Eleven-year-old Bill took the stand last and explained how he had jiggled open the sliding door to get into the house when he and Rachel got home from school on March 6. In the audience, the Van Iseghems had to smile through their pain. Dittmeier had primed the pump for that one just right, like the expert he was.

Rosenblum also had Bill explain that he had gone into the basement to hang up some artwork from school and then down to the workroom to look for his fishing pole. The room was open, and no one was there.

Later, Mary Cordes could only shake her head. Bill had never gone fishing until he came to live with her and Phil, and they had never heard him mention a fishing pole before. So who had put that notion into his young head?

Rosenblum asked about Bill's dad on the day of the funeral. "He was real sad, and he was crying real hard."

Dittmeier had just that one question. How old was Bill that day? Seven.

Mary was glad that ordeal was over. She had stayed with the nervous children from the moment she slipped them in the back door of the courthouse to avoid the media. They spent part of the morning in the hallway, where the DeCaro family talked to the children a lot; being there was awkward for Mary. But later, she accompanied them into the witness room to play cards, and within five minutes, the DeCaros had all disappeared from the room. Apparently having the kids there was more than awkward for the DeCaros. The children didn't testify until after lunch, so Mary spent most of her day with them. She could feel their tension all day; as much as they did not want to testify, they felt it was their duty to their father.

EIGHTY-NINE

"I believe I was a very good husband. I dedicated my life to Elizabeth and the kids," Rick DeCaro told the jury as he took the witness stand for the very first time. He bought Elizabeth flowers and gifts regularly "for no reason whatsoever." They went shopping and they went out together. They did everything together. They raised their children together, went to sporting and church events together. They shared the housework. Thursday night was special; they put the kids to bed early and then sat together to watch *Knot's Landing.*

Yes, ladies and gentlemen, Rick DeCaro was pretty much the perfect husband in America's heartland. But even his own description of his good deeds seemed to falter as he delivered it in that soft, flat, soulless voice, devoid of anything approaching honest emotion. The odd posture and movement of his head, and the slow, sullen blinking of his eyes surely were designed to convey sincerity. But the Van Iseghems wondered how anyone could think he was doing anything but offering self-serving lies.

After Rosenblum led Rick gently through an account of the DeCaros' teenage years and early marriage, they turned to what should have been the couple's happiest years. They went to Lake of the Ozarks five or six times a year, all year around, and were shopping for condos there with his sister and her neighbors, the Brennans. "And we also saw a boat that we liked and purchased." As hard to tolerate as this testimony was for the Van Iseghems, they almost gagged on that one. A boat "they" liked? Rick had practically rammed the damned boat down Elizabeth's throat.

Were they having any financial difficulties on his salary of more than $70,000 in 1991? No; they paid their bills on time and Rick saved money every week. Had he borrowed $7,500 from his brother to pay off his credit cards and refinance his house? Yes, but property values fell and he couldn't refinance; he paid his brother back immediately.

Did everyone at Old Orchard Amoco know he kept a key to his van hidden in the door to the gas tank? Yes. Did everyone know there was a key to the Blazer in the door pocket? Yes. Who filled the van with gas every Friday for him? Usually Craig Wells. Did Rick get free toilet paper and detergent from the station as a benefit? Yes. Who loaded those into his van on Fridays? Usually Craig Wells.

What happened to the DeCaros' relationship in 1991? Elizabeth had complained that he was smothering her, that she wanted him to stop giving her gifts and flowers—"to stop doing the things that I loved to do. . . . It made me very confused. I didn't know what she expected from me at that point."

What about Cathy Dillon? She and Rick were friends and became closer when she began to work for him; they talked a lot about their marital problems. In November 1991, when a salesman gave Rick free tickets to a Blues hockey game, Cathy asked Rick to take her. Elizabeth was visiting Pam Hanley in Kansas City, so Rick agreed to go with Cathy. After the game, Rick and Cathy had sex.

"Do you know why you did that?"

A seemingly confused Rick answered, "I have no idea. It was just something that happened." They had sex "three, maybe four times" over the next few weeks. On Monday, December 23, 1991, he terminated the illicit relationship, explaining to Cathy that he loved his wife and family, and wanted his marriage to work. Four days before that, he had confessed his infidelity to Elizabeth. "I told Elizabeth that I made a mistake, that I loved her very much, that I knew our love could pull us through the mistake that I made." She was rightfully upset and he was ashamed, but they were working through it.

And then came a series of questions that would change Georgiana Van Iseghem's world forever.

Had Rick told Georgianna that he was trapped?

"I told my mother-in-law that *she* trapped me that night." Georgianna had come to the house on the pretense of taking everyone for ice cream, and they even coerced a resistant Patrick into going along. And then Georgianna stayed behind and confronted Rick about the affair. "That's where she trapped me," he said indignantly.

"Did you ever tell her, 'I know I'm trapped in the relationship with Elizabeth'?"

"No, sir, I did not."

"Did you ever tell your mother-in-law in that conversation that you never loved Elizabeth?"

"No, I did not. I told my mother-in-law that I didn't know if I knew what true love was, because we got married at such a young age."

In the audience, Georgianna was suddenly freed of her emotional link to this man she had once loved as a son. In those seconds, he had arrogantly lied to her face about a conversation she could never forget, and he had called her a liar. Could anyone believe that she would have misconstrued or invented the startling things he had said to her about her own daughter? Georgianna was now free of all of those doubts that had plagued her for four years. She was now convinced beyond any doubt that he was absolutely capable of the horrible things he had done to bring them all to this courtroom on this day. With her very own eyes she had just seen the proof—Rick's unblinking, unhesitating ability to lie to her face.

Had Rick met Cathy outside of work after the affair ended? Rosenblum asked. Yes, twice. Once when her van wouldn't start, he drove her home, jump-started her van, and drove it back to the station to fix it. The second time was in February 1992, when he was walking into the gym to work out and she pulled up in the Camaro she had just bought. They went for a ride; she talked about her continuing problems with her husband.

Had Rick found out later that he had been followed that night? Yes, Elizabeth said a private detective—she did not disclose that it was John Enkelmann—had seen him meet Cathy in the parking lot. Rick was upset; he had thought Elizabeth was finally trusting him again, even though he knew she still had up days and down days over his affair. To find out how many times she had him followed, Rick admitted, he had made up a "stupid gimmick" about meeting drug dealers. It was untrue; he had never met any drug dealers or had anything to do with drugs.

Was Rick having a sexual relationship with Cathy during that time? No. What about all those calls to her from jail? He needed someone to talk to about this "tragic event"— losing Elizabeth, the devastation of his family, his confinement in that "horrible place," and his concerns about his children. And Cathy was leading the efforts to get enough property posted to meet his bond. He showed some resentment as he added, "I came within $30,000 of making a million-dollar bond, and they took it away from me."

What did he write in that birthday card to Cathy? "I told her that Elizabeth was my one and only true love, and how hard it was for me to cope with that."

How was the DeCaros' after-Christmas trip to the Ozarks? Terrific. Elizabeth was feeling better, they looked at condos, and went out to dinner. "We made love many times that weekend."

Georgianna was fuming over another round of bold lies. Elizabeth had described the weekend as terrible, and there was no way to reconcile that with Rick's account, except to conclude he was lying.

For the next hour or so, Rosenblum escorted Rick on a tour of all of the major events that prosecution witnesses had described from their viewpoints; Rick contradicted each and every bit of testimony that came close to incriminating him.

New Year's Eve. He was embarrassed to be at the church party where so many people knew about his affair. In a burst of "poor judgment," he left Elizabeth there; he had not "stormed out." But he did go to Cathy's party and he did drive her and another couple to an East Side nightclub because they were too drunk to get behind the wheel. He didn't know Jeff had come after her until later.

Had Rick asked Torregrossa about finding someone to "take care" of his van and his wife? "I absolutely did not." He and Torregrossa had talked briefly about a tire that afternoon, and Rick had filled out a check Torregrossa gave him to pay for it. Rick left work at five-thirty to get a haircut at six, and heard that Torregrossa had come back to the station sometime after that. The only suspicious conversation the two men ever had was when Rick asked Torregrossa in December to cover for him if anyone called at the gym. Explaining that he had taken his secretary out a couple of times and didn't want his wife to know, Rick asked Torregrossa to say the men had gone out for beers together.

What about the van crash? An accident, pure and simple. After the van hit Elizabeth, Rick checked to make sure she was okay, ran into the house to call 911, and warned the children not to come downstairs because of broken glass from the pictures knocked off the wall. Before he could call 911, Elizabeth appeared in the house and told him not to bother, that she was fine. He held her all night, and she wouldn't even go to the hospital until the next morning. He began fixing the wall that day.

Did Craig Wells know about the repair job? Yes, he had hauled off some of the trash, and Rick had given him the damaged bicycle and lawnmower. Rick had to park his van in the driveway because of the sheets of drywall and other construction material. He was still parking it there when it was stolen after Boo's birthday party on February 7, just eleven days after the crash. And, he testified, he hadn't even known about the party until the day before. He was eager to go because Boo was a childhood friend.

Did Rick have two video cameras? Yes, the kids had broken the viewfinder on one, so he had replaced it. He put the broken one in his workshop to fix it and hid the new one in the van. He also had three Nintendo games, one of which was broken. He put that one in a closet and planned to scavenge parts off it.

Had Rick asked Georgianna to talk to Elizabeth for him? Yes, he wanted his mother-in-law to reassure his wife that he loved her and to encourage her to "open her heart" to him again. While Elizabeth and Georgianna were having coffee that night, Rick installed the new vertical blinds on the patio doors. He closed them then and never touched them again. And when Elizabeth came home, she was changed for the better. "Elizabeth had a spark in her eye that I hadn't seen for weeks—that I'd seen many years prior to that—and it was like a new beginning. We made love that night, and it was like a new beginning."

What about that fatal weekend? When Rick suggested his "Daddy's weekend," he was unaware that Elizabeth had planned a Kansas City trip. He left the decision to her and the kids, and the kids wanted to go to the lake with him. Elizabeth planned a weekend of activities with her sister and mother, perhaps even spending the night at Georgianna's. As far as Rick knew, she wasn't even going to be home on Friday, March 6.

His account of that day sounded like nothing so much as

a hectic day for a dad trying to get out of town early with his kids. It began with a kiss for his sleeping wife. He left work early, ventured into the unfamiliar territory of the car pool, and then made a hasty departure for the lake with the kids. He had taken Ozzie only at Erin's request. His 11:07 A.M. call from the van to the house had been an attempt to check on Bill and Rachel, whom he knew would be arriving before he got home.

Had he eaten the surprise lunch Elizabeth packed for him? No, he had left it at the office and hadn't even known about the card until Elizabeth called him on the way to the lake. She was disappointed that he hadn't read it. Jenkins had kept it, and Rick never got a chance to see it.

Rosenblum handed Rick the card and asked him to read it to himself. In the first demonstration of drama or emotion by witness Rick DeCaro, he clutched the card to his chest and began to cry.

"And was that the card she left you on the day she was killed?"

"Yes, sir," he said softly as his voice broke.

Phony, phony, phony, the Van Iseghems insisted. They looked at the jurors, but could not read their faces. What were they seeing? Could they interpret this as genuine emotion? Could this creature on the stand strike them as a grieving, wounded, innocent husband? Could Rick's tears help him pull off another miracle? They looked at Dittmeier, who continued to scribble furiously on his legal pad, as he had all during Rick's testimony.

Judge Limbaugh soon recessed for the day—and thereby unintentionally set up an unbelievably ironic and dramatic twist. Rick DeCaro would complete his direct testimony and face cross-examination by Dittmeier on Wednesday, March 6, 1996—the fourth anniversary of Elizabeth's murder.

The Van Iseghems wondered what to read into that sign.

NINETY

Rick DeCaro's account of how he learned of his wife's death was characteristically lacking in drama or emotion as he returned to the stand Wednesday morning. Detective Miller had told him in that motel hallway only that Elizabeth had been found dead. Rick had responded softly, "Oh, my God. What happened?" Miller didn't know; the details hadn't begun filtering through until Rick was being questioned by the police later. That was when he learned Elizabeth had been shot. Oddly, Scott Rosenblum didn't ask Rick to describe his feelings when he had heard how death had come to the woman he had dedicated his life to. That moment was given less time than concerns about who had wanted to take the dog along.

Had Rick answered truthfully every question the police asked? Yes. Had he signed every form they asked him to sign? Yes. Did he wake up Patrick, tell him the horrible news, and let the police interview him? Yes. How was Rick feeling then? "Very upset, shocked, confused, concerned about the children."

Why did Rick add to the list of stolen items in 1994 and file for Elizabeth's life insurance? After he was released from jail, he had the opportunity to go through his belongings and try to "pick up the pieces of my life." Did he change his insurance claim when he learned where some of those missing items had gone? Yes.

Why did Cathy Dillon notarize his insurance applications? She was the only notary he knew. Did they have sex in 1995. Yes, "two, maybe three times." What was their relationship now? Strictly friends.

And then Rosenblum turned his attention toward the other man at the defense table. "How have you felt the last week and a half, sitting next to Dan Basile?"

"Makes me absolutely sick to my stomach," Rick said

softly, without any deep conviction, "and it disgusts me to be in the same courtroom with him."

Did he knew Basile before March 6, 1992? He may have passed him once at the station and may have seen his face a couple of times while reviewing the station's surveillance tapes after the complaints about Basile's mouth. Rick never knew his name was Basile—only that he was Craig Wells's brother.

What about the car inspection? John Carman wouldn't complete it because he was concerned about a cracked windshield. Rick knew the car belonged to Craig Wells's brother, so he was willing to pass it as it was. Rick told Carman to use Rick's Social Security number if he was reluctant to sign off on it.

What about the fifty-five-gallon drum? Wells asked if his brother could have it, and Rick said yes.

Why didn't Rick say he knew Basile when Christina Byrd Bishop asked him? Rick hadn't been sure about the photo on TV, and he didn't recognize the Basile name at all. Besides, Jenkins had told him not to talk about the case to anyone, and he was following his lawyer's advice. Same with Jackie Balunek? Yes.

"Did you hire Dan Basile to steal your van or your Blazer?"

"Absolutely not."

"Did you hire Dan Basile to kill your wife?"

"Most certainly not."

"Thank you."

Tom Dittmeier recalled Rick's claim that Basile disgusted him. "And it's been four years since your wife's been murdered, and that's the first time you've ever told anybody that he disgusts you, isn't it?"

"That's the first time I've been asked."

Dittmeier went down the list. Rick never said that to his own brother? "The name disgusts me; we didn't talk about it." Never said that to Cathy Dillon? No. Never told anyone that Craig Wells was lying about the meetings with Basile? No, but many people said to Rick that Wells was lying. When did anyone say that? "It was after the last trial, sir."

That slip caught Judge Limbaugh's attention, and he recessed court for an off-the-record session with the attorneys at the bench. Limbaugh warned that Rick was perilously close to revocation of his bond and immediate jailing for violating the judge's direct prohibition against any mention of the first trial. Rosenblum assured the judge that it wouldn't happen again.

As testimony resumed, Dittmeier wanted to know why Rick failed to tell Christina Byrd Bishop that the man on the TV screen looked familiar. Jenkins had said not to discuss it. Hadn't Craig Wells called Rick at noon that day and said his brother, Dan, had been arrested for the murder? "He was rattling on and on. I didn't know what he meant, sir." As Dittmeier doggedly dissected the conversation, a frustrated Rick insisted he had forgotten about Wells's call by the time the news came on that evening.

Hadn't Rick talked to Basile face-to-face about his car inspection? No, Rick had talked to Wells; Basile had been standing behind him. Dittmeier pounced sarcastically; "Oh, he was standing behind Wells, so you couldn't see him real good. Is that what the deal was?"

"I was directing my attention to Craig."

What about Cathy's testimony that Rick talked to Basile about the drum for the rock band? Rick thought he talked to Wells about that. What about Jackie Balunek's testimony that on March 29, Rick denied knowing Basile? She had misunderstood; he said he hadn't heard Basile's name before. Did he tell Carman to pass Basile's car on the inspection? No.

Hadn't Rick told Detective Miller that the van crash was "no big deal"? Yes, and that was accurate. How far into the garage was the van when Rick's foot slipped? Just barely inside. About even with the door? Real close. How far away was Elizabeth? Probably twenty feet. Dittmeier paced across the courtroom, marking twenty feet from the witness stand. About this far? That's about right. And his foot slipped, he drove this far, and hit her? Maybe a little farther. Dittmeier backed up. Here? Possibly. Dittmeier stepped back again. Here? Possibly that far.

In the audience, the Van Iseghems almost gasped at how dense, how stupid, Rick was. How could he miss what Dittmeier was doing to him? The farther away the van had been from Elizabeth, the more time Rick had had to stop. The farther away, the more likely the quick trip across the garage was intentional. The farther away, the less accidental and the more homicidal.

What happened after the van struck Elizabeth? Rick checked her; the van had pinned her among the bicycles and pushed the bikes into the wall. Did Rick pull her out? No, he told her not to move while he ran to call 911. If Rick fixed the damaged wall that day and the next, why did he still have building materials in the garage eleven days later? He had bought too much.

Had Rick changed his mind about going to Boo's party that day? No. Hadn't Melanie testified that Elizabeth said he changed his mind that day? Yes, but that wasn't true. What time did they get home? About 1:00 A.M. Why did he back the van into the driveway? To unload the toilet paper and other supplies. He waited until 1:00 A.M. to do that? He hadn't had time earlier.

Where did he buy his second video camera? Used, for $200 from someone at the station. What kind was it? It was an unmarked brand, just like Rick's broken camera that was in evidence. But didn't Rick claim a $900 loss for the camera from the insurance company, and wasn't that fraud? Rick hadn't been sure which camera was in the van when he filed the claim. Did Rick tell the insurance company that the cameras were the same brand? He couldn't remember. Dittmeier produced the transcript from Rick's deposition with the insurance company. Hadn't Rick testified that one of the cameras was from Sears, and he didn't know what kind the other was? Yes.

How well did Rick know Torregrossa? Not that well. Well enough to ask him to cover for Rick if someone called the gym? Yes. Why did Rick tell Torregrossa to say they had gone for beers together? Because that was what Rick had told Elizabeth. If Torregrossa arrived at the station about dark on January 10—say about five o'clock—wouldn't Rick still have been there? No, he did not see Torregrossa that evening. Did Rick have any problems with Torregreossa? No. Any animosity? No. Then why did Torregrossa say that Rick asked him to find someone to steal his van and kill his wife? "I don't know what provoked him to say something like that."

Did Rick tell Georgianna that he was in love with Cathy? "No, I did not tell my mother-in-law that." Had Rick heard Georgianna testify that he said, "I love Cathy and I'm not sure if I've ever loved Elizabeth?" Rick stiffened. "Yes, sir. She is lying."

Georgianna couldn't suppress a wry smile as she stared at him across the courtroom. The two of them knew the truth, and he knew he was lying. She was convinced that Rick DeCaro was burying himself with his cheap, perverse perjury.

Did Elizabeth know Rick was going to Cathy's on New Year's Eve? No, he decided to go at the last minute because he thought his friends from work would be there. Did Elizabeth know Rick was meeting Cathy in the evenings in February? There was only once, when Cathy wanted to talk to him and he told her he would be at the gym that evening. Dittmeier was surprised; wasn't that a little more planned than the chance meeting Rick had described on direct examination? Rick had still been surprised to see her. Wasn't it unfortunate that John Enkelmann happened to be following Rick on the one night he met Cathy? Yes.

Why did Rick make up the drug dealer gimmick? He wanted to know if she had him followed when he took Cathy to her house to start her van. Was it because he was also meeting Dan Basile in that same parking lot during that same time period? Rick had never met with Basile at all.

Had Rick told Pam Hanley on Sunday that he was too busy to go to her house the next weekend? No, she was mistaken; that conversation was the previous November. Had Rick told Elizabeth she couldn't go to Kansas City because of the Blazer's mechanical condition? "I did not say that to Elizabeth, and there was never a conversation about Elizabeth going to Kansas City by herself." Did Pam make that up? He didn't know what Pam was doing.

Was Rick "calm" after Detective Miller told him about Elizabeth's murder? "I was in shock." So, based on his tears when he read that card in front of the jury yesterday, did it have more impact on him than hearing of his wife's murder? No, that was just the first time he had held that card in his hands; he had cried often in the hours after he talked to Miller. Had Rick told the police that he and the kids might stay at the lake another day—after his wife had been murdered, funeral arrangements were pending, and relatives were waiting for him? No, he had just been asking Miller for advice about how to handle the children. Wasn't that lack of urgency because the murder was not a surprise? No, it was very much a surprise. Had Rick said they might stay and have "fun"? No, he never used that word. Well, Rick had put his own son on the witness stand, and Patrick used the word "fun." But Patrick didn't say Rick used it. When Dittmeier asked if Patrick was making that up, Rick launched a salvo toward the Van Iseghems that they still found shocking, even after all that had happened.

"My in-laws have been trying to turn my children against me for a long time, sir, and that was the same thing his grandma said, so he could very well have heard it many times. They have been trying to turn them against me for four years."

For Georgianna, this new outburst proved her belief that Rick was a true sociopath. He didn't care how many lies he told or whom he hurt or used.

The night of the funeral, did Rick leave his children with the Brennans and go to Dan DeCaro's house to talk to a lawyer? Yes. The day after the funeral, did Rick take the kids on a tour of the public school he was transferring them to? Yes. On the day after that, did Rick spend $1,300 on new stereos and VCRs? Yes, at the counselor's urging.

Dittmeier shook his head. "So, basically, your wife was buried, and you didn't miss a beat."

"I did what the therapist recommended," Rick said calmly. Did he sign Cathy's birthday card, "You are my only love, Rick?" No, just "Love, Rick." Did Rick ever ask Jen-

kins to read the card that Elizabeth had put in the lunch
sack? No. He never wanted to read his wife's last words?
Rick had asked his other attorney, but he said no; the card
was to remain sealed. So Rick was willing to follow his attorney's advice "even to the point of not reading your wife's last
words to you for almost two years. Is that correct?"

"That's correct."

Tom Dittmeier had made his point and completed his
cross.

Tom Flynn went right to the heart of it all. Was it Rick's
testimony that he had made no agreement with Dan Basile
to steal the vehicles for insurance proceeds? Yes. And Rick
never met Basile anywhere other than at the service station? Correct.

Suddenly Rick DeCaro's time on the hot seat was over.
As Rick left the stand, the judge called a recess. Rick's
family greeted him as if he had just won the Nobel peace
prize. They hugged him and congratulated him on what a
great job he had done in his four hours and forty-five minutes of testimony.

Across the courtroom, the Van Iseghems wondered if they
had seen the same performance. They thought Tom Dittmeier
had utterly and totally and mercilessly destroyed any shred
of credibility Rick had carried with him to the stand. Dittmeier had restored Georgianna's shaken faith in the justice
system. He had laid bare all of Rick's lies and deceits, forcing
him to contradict every prosecution witness and to brand the
mother of his murdered wife a liar. Margie was overwhelmed
by Dittmeier's ability to dig down into Rick's psyche and use
his own pathology against him, to make him show his true
nature to this jury. For Melanie, that cross-examination delivered the most satisfaction of the entire trial. Jimmy and
Randy had thought Rick was "toast" from the moment Dittmeier started on him; it had been no contest.

And Tom Dittmeier had done it on March 6. Now, that
was as close to real justice as they could come at that
moment.

With Rick's performance on the stand complete, Scott
Rosenblum rested his case.

The only time Dan Basile ever took the stand was to confirm that he understood and agreed with Tom Flynn's advice that he should not testify in his own defense. It was standard practice in capital cases to verify that on the record. The jury was not in the room when Basile told the judge that he had some hesitation about remaining silent but had to go with his lawyer's advice.

There wasn't much of a defense case to follow for Dan Basile. With little to work with and even less to accomplish, Tom Flynn called only two of the EMTs who had tried to resuscitate Elizabeth. There was little surprising or enlightening in their testimony that she had been shot and they could not revive her.

And then the defense rested.

NINETY-ONE

Rick DeCaro was a man obsessed with a new love. And that had led to the murder of his wife—for one very simple, heinously twisted reason.

"She was an obstacle to his obsession with Cathy Dillon," assistant U.S. attorney Tom Dittmeier told the jury bluntly in closing arguments on Thursday, March 7, 1996.

Rick had once been obsessed with Elizabeth that way. He had bought her flowers and gifts, smothering her with his affection. But when she couldn't take it anymore, when she pushed him away, he found a new target for his obsessive personality. Cathy Dillon became his obsession.

The prosecutor's simple, direct words rolled across the packed courtroom and dropped on Mary Cordes like a ton of bricks. Dittmeier's modest, unadorned eloquence left her dumbfounded. Everything she and the others had been feeling for four years, Dittmeier had just summed up in a very few, perfectly chosen words.

But he had much more to say to these jurors before they

retired to begin their deliberations. Did any of them believe that the affair—an undisputed fact in this case—ever ended? Could they believe that Rick told his lover that it was over on December 23—and then called her twice at her home the next day from the phone in his Blazer? Was this affair over when Rick left his wife on New Year's Eve and brazenly went to Cathy's party? No—he was obsessed.

Dittmeier began showing the jurors how—once this murderous deal was sealed—Rick and Basile had begun moving on parallel paths toward March 6. On December 31, Rick filled out the application for life insurance on Elizabeth— and dumped her at the party that night. He mailed the insurance application January 3, and both of them took the physical on January 9. On January 10 Rick began his search for a killer in the conversation with James Torregrossa, a man who had no motive to lie about Rick.

Once Craig Wells made the connection between Rick and Basile—a package deal for $15,000, Basile said—their dual efforts began. On February 6, Rick gave Wells the map, keys, and money for Basile. On February 7, Rick suddenly decided to go to Boo's party after all, and that night the van was stolen. On February 11, Rick arranged and signed off on the inspection for Basile's car; the man Rick would claim he had never seen before had stood right in his office with him in front of several witnesses.

On February 18, Rick mailed the proof of loss to the insurance company for the van and its contents. That night John Enkelmann followed Rick to his parking lot rendezvous with Cathy (Cathy Camaro, as the cops remembered her). When Elizabeth told Rick he had been followed, she unknowingly hastened her death, Dittmeier believed. Rick made up the ridiculous "drug dealer" story in case his wife's PI had seen him meeting with the unsavory-looking Basile. "Those are the words of a guilty man," Dittmeier insisted.

On Monday, March 2, Rick met Basile at the stables, and the deal was sealed before Doug Meyer's eyes. On Tuesday, March 3, Rick announced the change in plans for the weekend, and made absolutely certain Elizabeth would be home alone. That same day Basile called Ray Nichols, looking for a gun.

Wednesday, March 4, was a big day. While Elizabeth and Pam traded disappointed calls about the canceled weekend, Basile was showing his gun to Doug Meyer and calling Nichols to say, "I got what I needed." Rick made his reservations at the Holiday Inn. "They're moving together," Dittmeier explained.

On Thursday, March 5, Rick worked on his van to get it ready for the trip, and Basile asked Sue Jenkins about latex gloves for the job he had to do the next day. Cathy Dillon chose that same day—her wedding anniversary—to ask her husband for a separation.

Everyone knew what happened on Friday, March 6. And by six-thirty that evening, Basile was giving Carl Swanson a boom box with Rick's fingerprint on it and was admitting, "I did this lady." Later that night, a nervous Basile called Eddie Bonds looking for a ride. And that alone proved that no one else—not Craig Wells or Doug Meyer—was involved in this murder; if they had been, Basile wouldn't have needed a lift.

What happened after the murder? Sue Jenkins, Craig Wells, and Doug Meyer told the police what they knew about Basile and the myriad guilty statements he had made. "It was her or me," he said to Meyer. Had Meyer and Wells and Swanson and Bonds lied to police at first? Yes, but the jurors could judge for themselves whether those witnesses told the truth on the stand.

When Detective Miller informed Rick of his wife's murder, Rick was eerily calm. "He didn't have a jury down there to cry in front of," Dittmeier suggested. What about Elizabeth's sweet card to Rick? It proved that their marriage still was troubled, and it offered absolutely no insight into Rick's feelings. "He had murder in his heart." After he was arrested, his obsession with Cathy kept him on the phone to her from jail; he even called her at her mother's to wish her a happy birthday. Could the jurors possibly believe that all of those calls were made to discuss his bond? "That was love talk, ladies and gentlemen." When he got out of jail in September 1994, they took up where they'd left off. Nine months later, Cathy had a baby—a baby that Rick took his children to visit while Jeff Dillon was gone. And in January 1995, Rick moved to close the deal he had started thirty months earlier; he applied for the $100,000 value he had put on Elizabeth's life.

This had been a "paid-for execution," the prosecutor said. And he was confident that the jurors would convict Rick and Basile on all counts.

Scott Rosenblum stood before the jury to offer his own appraisal of the evidence. What had happened to Elizabeth was a "senseless, vile tragedy" that sickened everyone. But the jurors could not convict her husband on the unsupported theories of prosecutors using witnesses "comprised of liars, of opportunists, of con men like Craig Wells, like Doug Meyer, like James Torregrossa, and Swanson and Bonds and Nichols." The entire case built on those witnesses had been "orchestrated by an out-of-control state prosecutor by the name of Tim Braun," and it was unworthy of belief. Rosenblum motioned toward Dittmeier and cracked, "This man was left to pick up Tim Braun's garbage."

The prosecution's case failed on the first test, the defender insisted. Everyone involved supposedly called this an "insurance scam." But Rick didn't even own the van and only recovered the cost of the items he lost in it. And could there be any surer way to draw attention to yourself amid a horrible murder than to have two vehicles stolen out of your house in thirty days? Rick was not a dumb man. And everyone knew Rick had two video cameras—including Elizabeth, who filled out the loss claim from the van.

The government's case was built on the words of Dan Basile—as repeated by admitted liars. Did the jurors want to make any decision beyond a reasonable doubt based on Dan Basile's word? "Who's zooming who? Whose lies are being repeated? Who's making up the lies? We don't know." Rosenblum plunged into his theory that the real killer was Craig Wells—the man who knew about the keys to Rick's vehicles, who knew the DeCaros were leaving town for the weekend, who Basile told others had set up the van theft, who needed money to start his own business, who knew he could get his brother to do the job, who was missing from work that Friday afternoon. The van theft had worked, and that made the next step easy. "He came back for the Blazer."

Had Rick been obsessed with Elizabeth? No, he had loved her. Was his affair with Cathy a mistake? That was for the judgment of a higher authority, not Scott Rosenblum. "But I'm telling you that relationship had absolutely nothing to do with the death of Elizabeth DeCaro." Rick had ended the affair, confessed it to Elizabeth, and then tried to repair his marriage. Was it poor judgment and naive to think Rick and Cathy could continue to work together? Yes, but that was not a crime, no matter how hard Dittmeier tried to make it one. Rick's calls to Cathy in jail? He needed help to make his bond, and he needed someone to talk to about the tragedy that had befallen his life. He called lots of people and sent them lots of letters and cards.

What about the testimony of Georgianna and Pam Hanley? They weren't intentionally lying, Rosenblum was sure; but they had wanted something to be true for so long that they now believed it.

How could Rick have planned this murder so carefully when Elizabeth wasn't even supposed to be home that day? She was supposed to be out with her sister and mother. Rosenblum had not enjoyed calling Rick's kids to the witness stand, but their father was on trial and they knew the truth. They had backed Rick on every important point, including Bill's search for his fishing pole in the basement that lacked any hint of a lurking murderer. And the kids had testified without the telltale mannerisms that the prosecutor's witnesses had displayed—stumbling and stuttering to remember their lies or concoct new ones right in front of the jury.

What about Basile's defense strategy that Rick had hired him to steal the vehicles and set him up as the murder suspect? What else could Basile say? He had been caught red-handed. But that didn't prove any link to Rick.

Finally, what about Rick's failure to react in the way that

would have pleased the prosecutors and police? "Where is the manual that tells a person how they're supposed to act, the proper way to act when your world's been turned upside down?" Rosenblum wondered. In his eyes, Rick had done what normal people do. They don't cry in front of the police. They cry with their family.

As Rosenblum ended his argument, he reminded the jurors that Rick had lived for four years with all of this hanging over his head. "He has faced the last few weeks with the further insult and the further indignity of having to sit next to the man that has killed his wife." Rosenblum called on the twelve in the jury box to decide that it all stopped now. "Find Rick DeCaro not guilty."

The prosecutor had called Elizabeth's death "a paid-for execution," Tom Flynn reminded the jurors. So, his question for them was, "Where's the money?" The testimony suggested that Basile collected $200 to steal the van and $250 to steal the Blazer, just as Flynn had admitted in his opening statement ten days earlier. But if Basile also committed a murder-for-hire, where was the big money for that? Did the jury believe that Basile had risked his life and liberty for a man he hardly knew and the faint promise of $15,000 later, if the insurance paid off? A "hit" on credit?

Did Craig Wells set all of this up to make money to start a business? Where was the money? The van was burned, and Wells certainly didn't get a penny of the insurance money.

Who had lied? Rick had obviously lied when he said he didn't know Basile. The proof was abundant that they knew each other. Rick sent the keys, map, and money to Basile, and Basile stole the van. Case closed. Why did Rick have Basile steal the van? To frame him up as the killer. If Basile really had been planning Elizabeth's murder, would he have been running around telling everyone that some guy had asked him to kill his wife? "He's not an honest man, but he's not stupid."

Rick—the man who had everything anyone could want—had also had the perfect guy for such a scheme—a man who had nothing. "Heaven-sent, you might say."

Flynn looked intently at the jury as he appraised the life

of Dan Basile. "He doesn't have any family, to speak of. He's got people that are half brothers. He's got people that are 'play' brothers. He's got people he calls 'mom' that really aren't 'mom.' He's got no money. He's got a $200 car. And now he's got me. And that's all he has. He doesn't have $15,000, ladies and gentlemen, and he didn't have money to hire a high-powered lawyer."

Flynn launched into a lengthy challenge to the testimony by Elizabeth Burrows, whose seemingly rock-solid identification put Basile in the Blazer. Flynn was buying none of it, especially her ability to see from a short little Ford Escort into a big high Chevy Blazer and get a good look at a man she didn't notice had a dark mustache, a goatee, and scraggly sideburns. And all of this happened while she was doing fifty-five in some of the worst Friday-afternoon rush-hour traffic in the St. Louis metropolitan area.

Flynn also tied in the seemingly pointless testimony offered by his witnesses. Hadn't the EMTs said Elizabeth was still warm to the touch and was still bleeding when they arrived after eight o'clock? Hadn't they called her body supple, not rigid? Didn't that all suggest that she was killed later than three o'clock, and much closer to eight o'clock, long after Basile was gone? Didn't that suggest that the real killer had put the Blazer somewhere else for Dan Basile to pick up and drive away? Rick DeCaro had indeed planned his wife's murder, but his trigger man wasn't Dan Basile. No, Basile was Rick's "sucker." To Flynn, Basile was facing a murder charge for stealing a Blazer. The jurors could convict him of the mail fraud charges on the van and the Blazer thefts, but they should acquit him of murder.

Tom Dittmeier had one chance left to convince this jury and get justice for Elizabeth.

So, Rick expected Elizabeth to be away from home that Friday night, shopping with her family? Then why did he make two calls to their house from his van phone just after ten o'clock? Could he have been checking to see if the police were there, if they had found his wife's body yet?

Why didn't Rick talk to anyone about his wife's horrible murder? Why didn't he ask anyone about the investigation?

Why didn't he tell the police or Georgianna after Craig Wells called Thursday and said the police had arrested Dan and had found the Blazer? Wouldn't the confused, grieving husband of a murdered woman be insistent on constant updates from the police, driving them crazy with questions? "Not this guy. He didn't care."

Why hadn't Rick insisted on seeing that card from Elizabeth, the one he cried over for the jury? The answer to that question was the answer to this case.

"He didn't care what she said in that card. He was through with her."

NINETY-TWO

As the jurors filed out of one end of the courtroom to begin their deliberations about four o'clock, the families of Elizabeth and Rick DeCaro filed out of the other end to begin their vigils. They all had so much riding on that group of twelve.

Mary Cordes felt that no matter the verdict, at least the Van Iseghems had been heard, had been given a fair trial in a case presented the way they wanted it presented. Tom Dittmeier had found a way to put into words everything the Van Iseghems had been feeling about Elizabeth and about Rick; Mary felt almost as if that were enough to keep her going even if the jurors acquitted him again. Somehow, she found herself at peace, her heart lightened about the final outcome this time.

Melanie Enkelmann could agree with part of that. They had received a fair trial, and that was all they had ever wanted. But she had added something even deeper now. Watching Rick DeCaro testify had breathed new fire into her will for the ultimate justice for her sister; after his shameless, hateful, arrogant lies, she wanted the bastard convicted.

But after Mary and Melanie talked about it, they decided

that—this time—they could live with an acquittal. They couldn't accept that verdict in the first trial because they did not believe they had been heard. They had been heard this time, and they would accept this jury's decision.

Margie felt differently. She could not begin to imagine what an acquittal would wreak on this family. A loss now meant a lost cause forever; this was their last chance. As the waiting began, she couldn't hold back the surge of memories from that verdict almost eighteen months ago— the fifteen hours of waiting that ended in shock, horror, and outrage. She did not think she could go through that again.

Georgianna agreed. This had to be the end now, and there was only one way for it to end. That killer, that liar, had to be convicted for what he had done to Elizabeth, what he had done to their children, and what he had done to the family and friends who loved Elizabeth. She wondered if she had ever prayed harder than she did at that moment.

Mary left the courthouse and drove back to the motel where all ten of the children—Mary's three, Melanie's three, and Elizabeth's four—were waiting. Mary's place was with them on this night. The last four years had been all about being there when the kids needed her, and that could never be truer than now.

Despite the intensity of the last ten days, the family still had managed to turn the motel stay into a party for the kids. When Mary arrived, they wired a VCR to one of the TVs, began watching movies, and brought in fast food. Mary had no idea how long the deliberations would take this time, but she was ready to wait it out with the people who mattered most in this whole affair.

At the courthouse, the waiting was under way. The last four years of Theresa's life—growing from a child into a young woman—had been consumed by the loss of her sister, the one who had understood her so well. Now, she prayed, was the moment for those years of pain to mean something, to stand for something, to make Elizabeth's memory come alive—the way Theresa did so beautifully in her poetry.

When the word came about seven o'clock that the jury

had reached its verdict, everyone looked at each other in confusion. Was this good? Was this bad? Basile's first jury had taken less than two hours to convict. Rick's first jury had taken fifteen hours to acquit. What did three hours mean?

For the third time the tension built in a courtroom about to resonate with a verdict in the murder of Elizabeth De-Caro. The Van Iseghem partisans numbered more than two dozen again, with half that many for the DeCaro family. Melanie refused to look at the jurors, to search their faces for a sign; remembering St. Charles County, she decided not to risk jinxing the verdict with the bad vibes she had felt when that other jury filed in.

Judge Limbaugh accepted the thick stack of verdict forms from the foreman, inspected them briefly, and then handed them to his clerk. She would make the announcement that so many lives depended upon. The murder conspiracy count would be the first verdict, followed by murder-for-hire and then the five mail-fraud charges.

"On count one," the clerk read, "we find the defendant, Richard DeCaro, guilty as charged in the indictment."

That glorious word—"guilty"—filled the air in the silent courtroom, only to be overpowered by the Van Iseghems' mildly successful efforts to muffle their gasps and moans and tears of joy. They could barely remain in their seats as the clerk read the next six verdicts and delivered that same glorious word on each of them. Guilty, guilty, guilty, guilty, guilty, guilty. Seven times the clerk had read that word—a verdict that seemed to almost reach the biblical proportions of seven times seven.

Stone-faced at the defense table, Rick shook his head slowly.

In this courtroom, the roles on the different sides of the aisle seemed a reversed déjà vu from the first trial. As the Van Iseghems now cried in relief and joy at this victory over evil, the DeCaros on the other side of the room were left to weep and sob in pain. Angelo and Grace held each other, and Richard Fiehler put his arms around his crying wife, Rick's sister, Patty.

At the front of the room the clerk was reading through

the same seven counts—and the same seven guilty verdicts—for Daniel Basile. He was unfazed, sitting there with
what appeared to be a knowing half-smile on his face. He
even cast a contemptuous glance toward his somber
codefendant.

In this courtroom, for the first time, the trigger and the
bullet—together forming the deadly weapon that had killed
Elizabeth—were equally guilty.

At the defense table, Scott Rosenblum was pragmatic.
He knew the die had been cast when Rick and Basile were
tried together. Rosenblum had found himself battling not
only the awesome power of the United States government,
but the dreadful evil of the man sitting just a few feet away
from Rick.

After Judge Limbaugh excused the jurors with his
thanks, he called Rick, Basile, and their lawyers forward.
He did not need a motion by prosecutors to order Rick
taken into custody and jailed immediately; two murder-
related counts certainly justified that. With no small amount
of satisfaction, the Van Iseghems watched the federal marshals escort Rick from the courtroom to begin another period of incarceration—a period they hoped would never
end. Melanie's only disappointment was that the marshals
didn't handcuff Rick right there in front of everyone.

But in an incredibly sardonic moment, Basile almost
laughed out loud as Rick walked by under federal guard.
Basile pursed his lips and began to whistle the immediately
familiar tune of the operatic "Death March."

Randy Van Iseghem wondered if the little-noticed transaction he saw before the jury filed in had, indeed, been an
omen. He had seen Rick slip his wallet to his lawyer in a
move that few others had caught. Thinking back to the Van
Iseghem brothers' analysis of Dittmeier's cross-examination
of Rick, Randy wondered if his brother-in-law had realized
then, that he was "toast." One report later would suggest
that Rick still expected to be acquitted but thought he
would be sent to jail briefly for contempt of court because
of his remark on the witness stand about the first trial.

The Van Iseghems were sure that Rick had fully expected to be acquitted again and had been shocked to his

dark soul by the verdict. He always thought he was too smart to be caught.

Later that night, Detective Mike Miller would call a man he considered to be another of Rick DeCaro's victims. Miller's phone message for Jeff Dillon was a simple, "This one's for you, too."

As the marshals escorted the now-handcuffed Rick De-Caro and Dan Basile to the van behind the courthouse to take them to the Cape Girardeau County Jail, reporters yelled their questions to Rick. He never glanced in the direction of the media and never offered an answer to any of the queries. But when the reporters asked Basile what he thought of DeCaro, he had a ready answer. "He is sick and disturbed," Basile yelled back.

In front of the courthouse, the Van Iseghems were offering reporters their reactions. Jim—often content to stand behind the women in this family—stepped forward to praise the verdict as "a victory that takes forty tons off my chest. I feel the hole in my heart is going to be healed. I have a new life." And then he added another thought that all the Van Iseghems shared: "We can move forward now."

Georgianna also spoke from her heart. "I know that justice has been served." And then she reminded everyone what the real point of all of this had been all along: the children. The victory on this night was the end of Rick's power to hurt his children anymore.

But before that healing could begin, the children had to suffer one more horribly painful assault.

At the motel, Mary had received the news that sent her almost into orbit with celebration in the hallway. She found a way to scream without making any noise as she cried and pumped her fist into the air in a victory dance with the relatives who had delivered the word—"We got him." But then she realized that she had to walk back into the room where Patrick was watching a movie and break the news to him. She rubbed her hand across her mouth, wiping off the wide smile she had been wearing, and told Patrick that the jury had convicted his father. The teenager's face fell, and his eyes betrayed the devastation that he felt. He slumped back onto the sofa and Mary sat next to him. She looked into his face and said, "Patrick, you've known all along that your dad was guilty." He looked at her again, and this time his eyes asked the unspoken question, "How did you know that?" And then he cried. Mary put her arms around him and whispered, "I know you love your dad, and that's okay."

Phil Cordes broke the news to Rachel, who sobbed, "It's not fair." Mary told Erin; she was upset, but her still-tender years kept her from being as destroyed as the others. Bill took the news the hardest when Phil told him. He had been the most willing to accept his father back into the world, hoping to reconstruct a normal relationship. And now, with that hope joining so many others that had been dashed, Bill curled up in a fetal position in the bathtub and wailed so pitifully that Mary actually thought her heart would break. Poor Rachel stood above him, crying as she watched his anguish. Georgianna and Melanie arrived and wondered if they had ever seen anything more horrible than the misery inflicted on these kids. The women all tried to comfort them, but it seemed as if they would never stop crying. Bill sobbed from deep inside for at least thirty minutes.

Mary thought there surely had never been such a heart-wrenching scene as what happened in those rooms that night. There had been no winners there. Despite the joy she felt over Rick's conviction, she realized that the children she loved so much had been hurt terribly again. And she felt another, new flash of anger; if Rick had been convicted in 1994, as he should have been, the kids would not have had to go through all of this again.

Later that night, the kids went to spend the night with the DeCaros at their motel. Rick's family was already predicting that the conviction would be overturned and he would be free by the end of 1996.

But the day after the verdict, Tom Dittmeier and Mike Miller met with the kids to explain to them why their father had been convicted and what he had done to deserve it. What had happened in court was not the Van Iseghems' fault, he added. Despite the concern and sensitivity in his voice, Dittmeier told them the truth: "Your dad did this, and he's never getting out of jail again."

NINETY-THREE

One June 20, 1996, Daniel Basile stood before Judge Stephen Limbaugh again. Basile's black hair now hung to the center of his back and he wore a scruffy beard. He seemed amazingly calm as the judge reviewed the presentence report from the probation department. Was it true, the judge asked, that Basile had participated in a riot in prison since the verdict? No, all he had done was cuss out a guard. Well, the judge said, swearing at a guard could cause a disturbance and could be part of a riot. Basile shrugged; yeah, you could look at it that way and, besides, the outcome of this hearing would be the same either way. The judge knew Basile was absolutely correct.

As the small crowd—mostly members of the Van Iseghem family—listened, public defender Tom Flynn told Limbaugh there was little that could be said, or that needed to be said. The judge had no discretion in the sentence. Prosecutor Tom Dittmeier—a firm believer that the less said, the better—said nothing. When offered a chance to make a statement on his own behalf, Basile said softly that he had several complaints about the way his trial had been conducted and the way he had been represented by counsel. But, he added, he would just save them for his appeal.

There was little for the judge to say, either. He affirmed that there was ample evidence to support the jury's verdicts of guilty, and then he imposed the mandatory sentence on a conviction for murder-for-hire—life in prison without parole. That was hardly a shock, or a threat, for a man already on death row.

The crowd in Judge Limbaugh's courtroom was bigger the next day, when Rick DeCaro appeared for his sentencing. And Scott Rosenblum had more to say than the lawyer that preceded him by a day. Rosenblum asked Limbaugh to reconsider his rulings on the issues of double jeopardy and a joint trial. Rosenblum couldn't imagine more conflicting defenses than those for a man like Rick DeCaro and a man like Dan Basile—someone "on holiday from death row." The judge disagreed with the "holiday" comment and then affirmed his earlier rulings against Rick. There would be no consideration of a new trial today.

Did the defendant wish to make a statement in his own behalf? the judge asked.

"Just that I'm innocent, Your Honor." Rick's soft, flat voice was difficult to hear in the large courtroom. "I did not do this. I loved Elizabeth. There is no way on God's green earth that I would do this crime."

Once again, Tom Dittmeier stood mute.

The judge's face turned grim—perhaps disgusted—as he looked down at the tall man in the gray suit. "Well, Mr. DeCaro, the jury didn't believe you, and I don't believe you. It was not only a despicable act, it was a cowardly act."

And when Judge Limbaugh sentenced him to life in prison without parole, Rick DeCaro had no reaction.

In the audience, Georgianna Van Iseghem closed her eyes and took a deep breath. Judge Limbaugh had said it powerfully and eloquently. Now everyone knew exactly what Rick DeCaro was—cowardly and despicable.

And then Melanie Enkelmann got her wish; she watched as the marshals snapped the handcuffs on Rick—right there in the courtroom—and led him away in disgrace, never to breathe another free breath.

Angelo and Grace DeCaro waited until most of the reporters and cameras had disappeared from the front of the courthouse before they left. But one camera crew had persisted. As the DeCaros walked briskly away, Angelo offered only one comment. You don't see them trying O.J. Simpson in federal court, do you?

Once again, the comparison between Rick and O.J.—the one Georgianna had found so remarkable—had been invoked.

Elizabeth's children were visiting the Hanley family on these two days, the days that the Van Iseghems hoped would write the final chapter in their four years of grief. Those years had, indeed, been all about them. But they did not need to be there on these days.

Georgianna and Jim and their children and grandchildren gathered at the house on St. Francis Lane that evening to do what they did best—share their love. And when the evening had ended, Georgianna quietly walked to the majestic grandfather clock in the foyer. The clock had been Elizabeth's gift to her parents, and now they had done all they could to return their special gift to her. Her children would be raised and protected and cherished in the Van Iseghem hearts, where Elizabeth would always remain alive.

And then Georgianna wound the clock for the first time in almost two years. It was, indeed, time for all of the Van Iseghems to get on with life.

EPILOGUE

The Missouri Supreme Court affirmed the murder conviction and death sentence for Dan Basile on March 25, 1997, rejecting every point he raised on appeal. His appeals continue and no date for execution by lethal injection has been set.

On April 1, just seven days after the state high court's decision, a panel of the U.S. Eighth Circuit Court of Appeals in St. Louis affirmed the federal convictions of Rick DeCaro and Daniel Basile, rejecting all of their appeal points. Their trial was not double jeopardy, and they had no right to separate trials, the appellate court concluded. A few weeks later, the court refused their request for hearing before all of the appellate judges. In October 1997, the U.S. Supreme Court refused to hear their appeal in a decision handed down without comment by the justices.

". . . but there's something about him I *don't* like."
In the summer of 1997, the Van Iseghems were surprised

when a childhood friend of Elizabeth's sent them an unso-
licited package—some letters Elizabeth had sent her when
they were just teenagers. The surprise was even more profound when one of the letters discussed Elizabeth's new
boyfriend, Rick DeCaro, and included a startling picture
of the teen lovers—Rick at fourteen and Elizabeth at just
thirteen. Amid typical gossip between girlfriends, Elizabeth
included a description of Rick—tall, six-foot-three, dark-
complected, 166 pounds, all-muscle, great athlete. And then
she revealed her concerns abut their troubled relationship.

"We have been going together for a month and a half,
and now I don't think I like him. It's just something about
him I don't know how to explain to anybody. I just hope
I can find the right words to tell him." Elizabeth added,
"A really great guy, but there's something about him I
don't like."

In a amazingly profound observation, she recounted how
angry Rick had become a few days earlier when he accused
her of ignoring him. "He was so mad. And I can just imagine how mad he's gonna be when I tell him I want to
break up."

Sixteen years later, that scene would be repeated in an
eerie, fatal way. When Elizabeth "ignored" Rick by asking
for some space, he had an affair with Cathy Dillon. When
Elizabeth told him she wanted to break up, he was so mad
he orchestrated her murder.

The Van Iseghems were stunned at the maturity and ac-
curacy of Elizabeth's thirteen-year-old instincts. If only she
had listened to her own heart then.

". . . but there's something about him I *don't* like."

Patrick, Rachel, Bill, and Erin continue to live with Mary
and Phil Cordes, and their three children. The Missouri
Department of Family Services has legal custody of the
DeCaro children, and the Cordeses retain physical custody
under court order. The children still have contact with
Rick, who is serving his sentence in the maximum-security
prison in Florence, Colorado. He calls once a week and
writes them often. He promises that he will be free soon.

THE CAST

Cathy Dillon*—Rick DeCaro's lover and coworker at the Old Orchard Amoco Station. She was married to Jeff Dillon,* whose sister was married to Dan DeCaro, Rick's brother.

Michael Carroll*—A friend of Elizabeth's who drifted into a brief sexual relationship with her as her marriage deteriorated. Carroll was driving the night Melanie Enkelmann found Elizabeth's body.

Craig Wells—The link between Rick and Dan Basile. Wells worked for DeCaro at the Old Orchard Amoco Station and considered himself a "brother" to Basile because of an unusual foster-family connection. Wells arranged for Rick to meet Basile, and he knew that they had discussed vehicle thefts—and Elizabeth's murder.

Doug Meyer—Basile's half brother, who worked at a condo complex and arranged for Basile to use a garage there— only to learn that Basile was chopping up the Blazer. Four days before the murder, Meyer saw Rick drive his Blazer to the stables and talk to Basile; after the meeting, Basile had cash he said he got from the man in the Blazer for a job. When Meyer asked Basile if he had killed Elizabeth, he responded, "It was her or me, and I wasn't going back to prison."

James Torregrossa—Worked out at Gold's Gym with Rick. Rick asked Torregrossa if he knew someone who could "get rid of cars" and then if he knew someone who could "hit someone—who could kill someone for me."

Susan Jenkins—A close friend of Basile's who went along when he stole and burned the DeCaro van. The night before the murder, Basile asked her about getting him some latex gloves because he had "a job" to do the next day.

Eddie Bonds*—A friend whom Basile called to tell about a plan to steal a van in an "insurance scam" that would bring him "double digits" in profits. Basile later asked Bonds about a "throwaway" gun. The night of the murder, a frightened Basile called to ask about getting a ride and said, "I was doing this job and something really went wrong. . . . I did what I had to do."

Carl Swanson*—The evening of the murder, Basile arrived at Swanson's in the Blazer and gave him a birthday present—the boom box stolen from the DeCaros. Basile said, "I did this lady."

Lloyd Nichols*—Basile called Nichols several times to discuss the van and Blazer thefts and said that the owner also wanted his wife killed to avoid the costs of a divorce.

Ray Nichols*—Lloyd Nichols's brother. Basile told Ray Nichols that a man wanted his van stolen and his wife "offed." Basile also asked Ray Nichols about a "throwaway." A nervous Basile came to Ray Nichols's home, saying the police were looking for him because they thought he "did the van and the lady."

Iva Hanson—Doug Meyer's fiancée, who went with Basile to rent the tools she learned later were used to chop up the Blazer.

Gaylor Dorman—Craig Wells's girlfriend, who said Basile reeked of gasoline the morning after the van was torched. She also saw a suspicious amount of cash in Basile's wallet that day.